AF899497

Cities Network Along the Silk Road

Pengfei Ni · Marco Kamiya
Ruxi Ding

Cities Network Along the Silk Road

The Global Urban Competitiveness Report 2017

中国社会科学出版社
CHINA SOCIAL SCIENCES PRESS

Springer

Pengfei Ni
Center for City and Competitiveness
Chinese Academy of Social Sciences
Beijing
China

Marco Kamiya
Urban Economy and Finance Branch
UN Habitat
Nairobi
Kenya

Ruxi Ding
School of Economics, Southwestern University of Finance and Economics
National Academy of Economic Strategy, CASS
Beijing
China

ISBN 978-981-10-4833-3 ISBN 978-981-10-4834-0 (eBook)
DOI 10.1007/978-981-10-4834-0

Jointly published with China Social Sciences Press

The print edition is not for sale in China Mainland. Customers from China Mainland please order the print book from: China Social Sciences Press.

Library of Congress Control Number: 2017942974

© China Social Sciences Press and Springer Nature Singapore Pte Ltd. 2017
This work is subject to copyright. All rights are reserved by the Publishers, whether the whole or part of the material is concerned, specifically the rights of translation, reprinting, reuse of illustrations, recitation, broadcasting, reproduction on microfilms or in any other physical way, and transmission or information storage and retrieval, electronic adaptation, computer software, or by similar or dissimilar methodology now known or hereafter developed.
The use of general descriptive names, registered names, trademarks, service marks, etc. in this publication does not imply, even in the absence of a specific statement, that such names are exempt from the relevant protective laws and regulations and therefore free for general use.
The publishers, the authors and the editors are safe to assume that the advice and information in this book are believed to be true and accurate at the date of publication. Neither the publishers nor the authors or the editors give a warranty, express or implied, with respect to the material contained herein or for any errors or omissions that may have been made. The publishers remains neutral with regard to jurisdictional claims in published maps and institutional affiliations.

Printed on acid-free paper

This Springer imprint is published by Springer Nature
The registered company is Springer Nature Singapore Pte Ltd.
The registered company address is: 152 Beach Road, #21-01/04 Gateway East, Singapore 189721, Singapore

Group Members

Advisory Committee
Wang Weiguang (President, CASS)
Joan Clos (Executive Director, UN-HABITAT)
Gao Peiyong (Director of Institute of Economic, CASS)
He Dexu (Director of National Academy of Economic Strategy, CASS)
Fan Gang (Vice President of China Society of Economic Reform, Director of Institute of the Chinese Economy)
Saskia Sassen (Professor of Columbia University, USA)
Peter Taylor (Academician of UK Royal Academy of Social Science, Director of Globalization and World Cities Research Network)

Authors
Pengfei Ni (Professor and Director of the Center for City and Competitiveness, CASS)
Marco Kamiya (Coordinator of Urban Economy and Finance Branch, UN-HABITAT)
Ding Ruxi (School of Economics, Southwestern University of Finance and Economics; National Academy of Economic Strategy, CASS)
Peter Karl Kresl (Bucknell University, USA)
Kathy Pain (Professor at Center for Real Estate & Planning Research University of Reading)
Ronald Wall (Institute for Housing and Urban Development Studies, Erasmus University Rotterdam, Netherlands)
Pedro B. Ortiz (Milano Politecnico University, Italy, and Senior World Bank Consultant)
Shuai Shi (Real Estate & Planning, Henley Business School, University of Reading, UK)
Wang Yufei (School of Economics, Beijing University of Posts and Telecommunications; National Academy of Economic Strategy, CASS)
Zhang Anquan (School of Economics, Southwestern University of Finance and Economics)

Wei Jie (School of Economics and Management, Northwest University)
Guo Han (School of Economics and Management, Northwest University)
Zhou Xiaobo (Postdoctoral Research Station of Agricultural Bank of China & University of International Business and Economics)
Tang Yu'e (School of Economics, Southwestern University of Finance and Economics)
Yang Jie (Center for City and Competitiveness, CASS)

Members of Editorial Board (Research Group for Global Urban Competitiveness)
Richard Legates (Professor at San Francisco State University)
David Maurrasse (Professor at Columbia University)
Dong-Sung Cho (Professor at Seoul National University)
Jaime Sobrino (Professor at El Colegio de Mexico)
Guido Ferrari (Professor at Università degli Studi di Firenze)
Kathy Pain (Professor at Center for Real Estate & Planning Research University of Reading)
Peter J. Brain (Director of the Commonwealth Scientific and Industrial Research Organization, Australia)
Francois Gipouloux (Director of Centre National de la Recherche Scientifique)
Harold Wolman (Professor at George Washington University)
Stefano Mollica (President of Associazione Italiana Incontri e Studi sullo Sviluppo Locale)
Berg Van den Leo (Professor at Erasmus University Rotterdam)
Shen Jianfa (Professor at the Chinese University of Hong Kong)
Zhang Ming (Lead urban economist at the World Bank)
Shen Wei (Associate professor at ESSCA Ecole de Management)
Pengfei Ni (Professor, and Director of the Center for City and Competitiveness, CASS)
Banji Oyelaran Oyeyinka (Director of Regional Office for Africa, ROAf, UN-HABITAT)

Global Urban Competitiveness Assessment Team

Team leaders, Chief Urban Economist
Pengfei Ni (Director of the Center for City and Competitiveness, CASS)
Marco Kamiya (Coordinator of Urban Economy and Finance Branch, UN-HABITAT)

Team members
Ding Ruxi (School of Economics, Southwestern University of Finance and Economics; National Academy of Economic Strategy, CASS)

Tang Yu'e (School of Economics, Southwestern University of Finance and Economics)
Wang Yufei (School of Economics and Management, Beijing University of Posts and Telecommunications; National Academy of Economic Strategy, CASS)
Zhou Xiaobo (Postdoctoral Research Station of Agricultural Bank of China & University of International Business and Economics)
Zhang Anquan (School of Economics, Southwestern University of Finance and Economics)
Wei Jie (School of Economics and Management, Northwest University)
Guo Han (School of Economics and Management, Northwest University)
Yang Jie (Center for City and Competitiveness, CASS)
Yiyang Chenzi (Natural Resources Defense Council)
Huang Jin (Research Center for Urban Competitiveness, CASS)
Li Chao (National Academy of Economic Strategy, CASS)
Liu Shangchao (Graduate School of Chinese Academy of Social Sciences)
Cai Shaopeng (School of Economics, Southwestern University of Finance and Economics)
Yang Xiaolan (School of Economics, Central University of Finance and Economics)
Zhang Yangzi (Graduate School, CASS)
Liu Xiaonan (Graduate School, CASS)
Shen Li (Graduate School, CASS)

Data collection (in random order)

Wang Huan (Center for City and Competitiveness, CASS), Huang Qiwen (Central University of Finance and Economics), Hu Yang (Central University of Finance and Economics), Wang Yan (Central University of Finance and Economics), Han Xiaohong (Central University of Finance and Economics), Yan Junwei (Central University of Finance and Economics), Zhou Linan (Central University of Finance and Economics), Guo Ke (China University of Geosciences), Xu Wenying (Peking University Health Science Center), Zou Tao (Ocean University of China), Zhao Yun (Beijing Foreign Studies University), Zhang Hai (Nanjing Normal University), Liu Zheng (Henan University), Hua Fengyi (Tianjin Normal University), Li Xiaojiang (Southwestern University of Finance and Economics), Yang Xu (Nankai University), Wu Zefang (Nankai University), Zhu Yaping (University of Science and Technology of China), Zang Angang (University of Science and Technology of China), Wang Menghan (University of Science and Technology of China), Wang Ying (University of Science and Technology of China), Xu Wenxin (Graduate School of Chinese Academy of Social Sciences), Huang Jing (Graduate School of Chinese Academy of Social Sciences), Li Xian (Nanjing Normal University), Kuang Chenhui (University of Science and Technology of China), Gao Meng (Nanjing Normal University), Fan Chunli (University of Science and Technology of China), Qin Rui (Southwest Nuclear and Radiation Safety Surveillance Station, Ministry of Environmental Protection), Su Chao (Nanjing Normal University), Hu Jiawei (Jiangxi University of Finance and Economics), Cui Yilun (Renmin

University of China), Cheng Xia (Renmin University of China), Guo Xinwei (Beijing Foreign Studies University), Peng Jie (Beijing Foreign Studies University), Mi Lan (Beijing Foreign Studies University), Zhang Yu (Beijing Foreign Studies University), Wang Di (Beijing Foreign Studies University), Li Lingshuang (Beijing Foreign Studies University), Song Chanjing (Beijing Foreign Studies University), Wei Wei (Beijing Foreign Studies University), Yuan Fei (Beijing Foreign Studies University), Lu Yuanye (Beijing Foreign Studies University), Deng Jialai (Beijing Foreign Studies University), Zhu Yanyan (Beijing Foreign Studies University), Tu Chang (Beijing Foreign Studies University), Liu Huizhen (Beijing Foreign Studies University), Bi Wenhui (Beijing Foreign Studies University), Mei Bin (Beijing Foreign Studies University), Zhu Shangwen (University of International Business and Economics), Zhu Sunan (University of International Business and Economics), Zhou Bowen (Beijing Language and Culture University), Wang Yiran (Beijing Language and Culture University), Li Hengguang (Beijing Language and Culture University), Li Zheng (Beijing Foreign Studies University), Jiang Wei (Beijing Language and Culture University), Zhang Zijiao (Beijing Language and Culture University), Zhang Qi (Beijing Language and Culture University), Li Chen (Graduate School of Chinese Academy of Social Sciences), Wu Qian (Graduate School of Chinese Academy of Social Sciences), Meng Ruiqia (Graduate School of Chinese Academy of Social Sciences), Li Yuan (Graduate School of Chinese Academy of Social Sciences), Cui Jing (Graduate School of Chinese Academy of Social Sciences), Mei Xiaomeng (Graduate School of Chinese Academy of Social Sciences), Yang Luojun (Graduate School of Chinese Academy of Social Sciences), Wang Haicheng (Graduate School of Chinese Academy of Social Sciences), Wu Hao (Graduate School of Chinese Academy of Social Sciences), Shi Junnan (Graduate School of Chinese Academy of Social Sciences), Cao Longbiao (Graduate School of Chinese Academy of Social Sciences), Si Yanan (Graduate School of Chinese Academy of Social Sciences), Yu Ze (Graduate School of Chinese Academy of Social Sciences), Shi Xiaofei (Graduate School of Chinese Academy of Social Sciences), Li Yilan (Graduate School of Chinese Academy of Social Sciences), Shi Yi (Graduate School of Chinese Academy of Social Sciences)

Contents

Contributors

Global Urban Competitiveness Assessment Team (Chapter 1)

Ni Pengfei and Marco Kamiya (Chapter 2)

Ni Pengfei, Yang Jie and Ding Ruxi (Chapter 3)

Zhou Xiaobo and Tang Yu'e (Chapter 4)

Wang Yufei and Tang Yu'e (Chapter 5)

Ni Pengfei, Ding Ruxi and Zhou Xiaobo (Chapter 6–9)

Zhang Anquan (Chapter 10)

Wei Jie (Chapter 11)

Guo Han (Chapter 12)

Peter Karl Kresl (Chapter 13)

Shuai Shi, Ronald Wall and Kathy Pain (Chapter 14)

Pedro B. Ortiz and Marco Kamiya (Chapter 15)

Introduction

Today, more than half of the world population live in cities, and globalization and informatization progress rapidly. Cities are playing a growingly important role in the development of our world today, and competitions between cities grow fiercer as time goes by. Urban competitiveness is attracting more and more attention from decision-makers, and a growing number of research institutes and scholars are now working on this topic. The Global Urban Competitiveness Project (GUCP), launched in 2005, gathers experts from all over the world, under the support of the Chinese Academy of Social Sciences and the National Academy of Economic Strategy under it, to write academic papers and publish the Global Urban Competitiveness Report (biannually, five up to now). GUCP aims at building itself into a world-renowned brand of city-related academic research. Comparing of previous versions, this Report is vastly different in content, structure, and quality.

This report is comprised of a General Analysis, Topic Report, and Specialized Analysis. It first gives a summary of the competitiveness of global cities. With the latest data of 505 sample cities around the world, covering the period of 2001–2011 and occasionally extending to 2013 or 2015, it analyzes the overall situation of global urban competitiveness and outlines the changes from various perspectives and dimensions.

For the first time ever, we composed topic report to form the second part of the Report. Titled “Cities Network Along the Silk Road,” this report depicts with ample data the new developments in the urban development and inter-city connections among cities along the Silk Road. Generally, the peripheral areas are development centers while the middle section is somewhat marginalized; city networks have taken shape on the two ends of the Silk Road while in the middle, the route cities are distributed in belts; and the outline of a vast city network has emerged with irregular distribution of cities. Commercial services, production factors, and industrial systems constitute the core content of the Silk Road Cities Network; profound changes in the hardware and software environments have their impacts on the structure of the Silk Road Cities Network and its evolution.

Part III of this Report is articles on special subjects. Like what we have been doing for previous versions, we invited experts from international organizations to join the GUCP and UN-HABITAT team in compiling the Global Urban Competitiveness

Report. In Part III, Dr. Zhang Anquan, Dr. Wei Jie, and Dr. Guo Han elaborate on subjects related to the global connection of cities; Prof. Peter Karl Kresl of Bucknell University, USA, analyzes the reasons behind the selection of location by large companies from North America, and Kathy Pain and Shuai Shi from the Center for Real Estate & Planning Research, Henley Business School, University of Reading, UK, together with Ronald Wall from Erasmus University Rotterdam, examine the networking and clustering effects of Chinese cities in a systematic and well-grounded way by focusing on foreign direct investment and domestic investment and present the findings in a visual manner. Pedro B. Ortiz, Senior Urban Consultant for international governments and multilaterals, together with Marco Kamiya from UN-HABITAT, analyzes competitiveness of the metropolis in the Global North and South in some important aspects including economics, planning, financing and governance.

We are glad to see that after years of strenuous efforts, we have created a complete yet concise indicator system and evaluation methods and found various reliable channels and methods to obtain data. Making available key data that are authentic, reliable, and stable lays solid foundation for the GUCP to become a world-renowned brand in city-related academic research.

This Report, especially the part on global urban competitiveness, is a challenging and onerous task. The research group worked for two years under the leadership of Dr. Pengfei Ni and the coordination of Dr. Tang Yu'e to collect, verify, and compare data, make adjustment to the indicator system and evaluation methods, and do the calculations and tests. Dr. Pengfei Ni is the leading figure who proposed the basic theories, indicator system, research framework, and major conclusions. Dr. Hou Qinghu gives instructions on statistical techniques. Dr. Tang Yu'e and Dr. Wang Yufei are responsible for specific work on data collection and index compilation. Dr. Ruxi Ding draws charts to visualize the research findings, authors the topic reports, and coordinates the compilation of the other parts of the Report.

Our research project has been supported by a great number of scholars and city authorities from all over the world during the process preliminary data collection, and the analysis, research, and compilation processes that come later. Kind help and assistance have come from many international experts, and we would like to express our heartfelt thanks to everyone who has offered help to us.

All our advisors have been selfless in helping us out. Many colleagues at the Chinese Academy of Social Sciences and the National Academy of Economic Strategy under it have offered kind assistance, and the Chinese version of this Report is published thanks to the great efforts of Mr. Zhao Jianying and his peers at China Social Sciences Press. We would like to thank them all.

January 2017

Pengfei Ni
Director of Center for City and Competitiveness, CASS

Marco Kamiya
Coordinator of Urban Economy and Finance Branch
UN-HABITAT

Prologue 1

With over half of the world population living in urban areas, the worldwide urbanization is accelerating. Today, cities are becoming more and more important—as the economic, political, and cultural center of human society, cities have become drivers of technological innovations, engines of economic growth, platforms for cultural development, and centers of decision-making. Meanwhile, the rapid progress of globalization and informatization and the free flow of production factors, commodities, and services across the world are also contributing to the cooperation and competition among global cities. Moreover, shortage of resources, environment pollution and climate change as well as divergences in society, conflicts between different cultures and frequent outbursts of violent crimes and wars are posing a challenge to the sustainability of cities as major human habitats. Under such circumstances, it's necessary for global authorities to join hands and improve studies on urban subjects, especially on how to strengthen the sustainable competitiveness and development of cities. We must give analyses, draw experiences, reach conclusions, and develop strategies in response to the challenge of global development. By giving directions to the world's future development, we will bring prosperity to our cities and benefit all our citizens.

As the highest institution of Chinese philosophy and social sciences and a world-famous think tank, the Chinese Academy of Social Sciences has been devoting itself to more productive international cooperation and exchange so that it can contribute to the development of social sciences and bring prosperity to the rest of the world while furthering the development of China's philosophy and social sciences and serving the decision-making of its government.

It has been 30 years since the country's reform and opening up. In the past 30 years, China has worked world-known wonders and at the same time, gained a lot of experience, which is of great interest to the international community and the academic world. Of China's many achievements, urban development is undoubtedly the most important one. The successful development of Chinese cities can act as valuable examples for cities around the world, especially those in developing countries.

As a United Nations agency for human settlements, the United Nations Human Settlements Programme (UN-HABITAT) aims at promoting socially and environmentally sustainable human settlements development to achieve adequate shelter for all. Since its foundation, the Programme has been committing itself to theoretical studies, knowledge communication, and experience sharing through international cooperation, with the goal of eliminating urban poverty, meeting urban challenge, and facilitating urban development and prosperity around the world. With more than one authoritative institutions on urban issues and a large pool of senior researchers, especially in urban competitiveness, Chinese Academy of Social Sciences has published a lot of research findings, gaining great academic influence at home and beyond. The annual Global Urban Competitiveness Report co-published by CASS (National Academy of Economic Strategy) and experts from UN-HABITAT with a series of significant issues as its subjects will definitely be helpful to cities around the world, especially those in developing countries, to develop through comparing with other cities, identifying their own problems and drawing on international experience. In the meantime, it can also provide theoretical inspirations, cases to share, and data support for worldwide theoretical and empirical studies on urban issues.

Connections are the basic features of things. The development of human society is also the product of connections and exchanges within and between peoples and regions. For example, the ancient Silk Road is known as a witness to the history of inter-regional connections and exchanges as well as a major driving force of the development of countries and regions along the Silk Road. Today, countries and regions are closely connected by information and internet technologies. This has created unprecedented convenience for the connection, exchange, and even integration of goods, personnel, funds, technologies, and information. However, to achieve real cooperation and exchange and to pursue common development, we should abandon the old practice of exclusion and discrimination and promote inclusive and non-discriminate cooperation. In this sense, the ancient Silk Road is also a perfect example of such cooperation, as regions along the Road used to follow the principles of inclusion and non-discrimination. In the future, we will carry on such principles and aim our efforts at revitalizing traditional Silk Road regions and expand the mutual beneficial cooperation among them. This is significant both to regional development and to multilateral and bilateral cooperation among countries and regions around the world. Since cities serve as the major carrier and pivot of the cooperation of all regions including the Silk Road itself, studies on the development of and connections between cities on the Silk Road Network will be of great significance to a deep understanding of the current situation, problems, impetuses, trends, and patterns of regional cooperation within the Silk Road area. Therefore, this 2017 report will focus on "Network Along the Silk Road" through analyzing and predicting the future development and evolution of the Network and its influence on the world economic-geographic landscape based on investigations into some new changes happening to the development of and connections between cities within Silk Road regions, which cover nearly half of the world's land area. This Report enriches and develops theories relevant to global urban competitiveness and offers decision-making references for investment choices of enterprises around the world and urban administration of relevant decision-making government departments.

I hope that the National Academy of Economic Strategy, CASS and the Human Settlements Programme can seize this opportunity of co-writing the report to seek deeper cooperation and produce more research findings in the future.

Wang Weiguang
President of Chinese Academy of Social Sciences

Prologue 2

I am delighted to present the Global Urban Competitiveness Report 2017, a joint project between the Chinese Academy of Sciences and UN-Habitat. The release of this report comes at a strategic moment for urbanization worldwide, immediately following the adoption of the New Urban Agenda in Quito, Ecuador, in October 2016. The New Urban Agenda embraces the crucial role of urbanization as a driver of sustainable development and prosperity. The case of China is quite representative, as its urban transformation over the last three decades has been an essential driver for development, poverty eradication, and prosperity. Today, China continues to push forward the largest urbanization process in the history of mankind. China's urbanization rate rose from 17.9% in 1978 to 56.1% in 2015. Some 770 million people in China live in cities.

Cities competitiveness and its development are clearly interlinked. The way that cities are designed, planned, governed, and financed has a direct impact on the competitiveness of each urban model, which ultimately reflects the quality of services and quality of life for our growing world urban population. The report also analyzes emerging global urban challenges with a particular emphasis on climate change, social exclusion, rising inequality, security concerns, and migration. Cities with a competitive edge attract foreign direct investment and talent, creating a virtuous circle of prosperity. "Good urbanization" generates the values of location and agglomeration.

The Global Urban Competitiveness Report is a valuable tool for analyzing the competitiveness of urban models globally and an important reference for the implementation of the New Urban Agenda.

By examining these complex issues surrounding sustainable urban development, the Urban Global Competitiveness Report 2017 serves as an authoritative study that present main topics developed by senior Chinese researchers with UN-Habitat experts.

Dr. Joan Clos
Executive Director, UN-HABITAT

Part I
General Analysis

Chapter 1
Global Urban Competitiveness Index: Annual Ranking

Global Urban Competitiveness Assessment Team

City	Rank	Global Urban Competitiveness Index
London	1	1.0000
New York	2	0.9436
Tokyo	3	0.8617
Paris	4	0.7990
Singapore	5	0.7695
Hong Kong	6	0.7544
Shanghai	7	0.7395
Beijing	8	0.6833
Sydney	9	0.6687
Frankfurt	10	0.6608
Seoul	11	0.6543
Moscow	12	0.6477
Chicago	13	0.6454

© China Social Sciences Press and Springer Nature Singapore Pte Ltd. 2017
P. Ni et al., *Cities Network Along the Silk Road*,
DOI 10.1007/978-981-10-4834-0_1

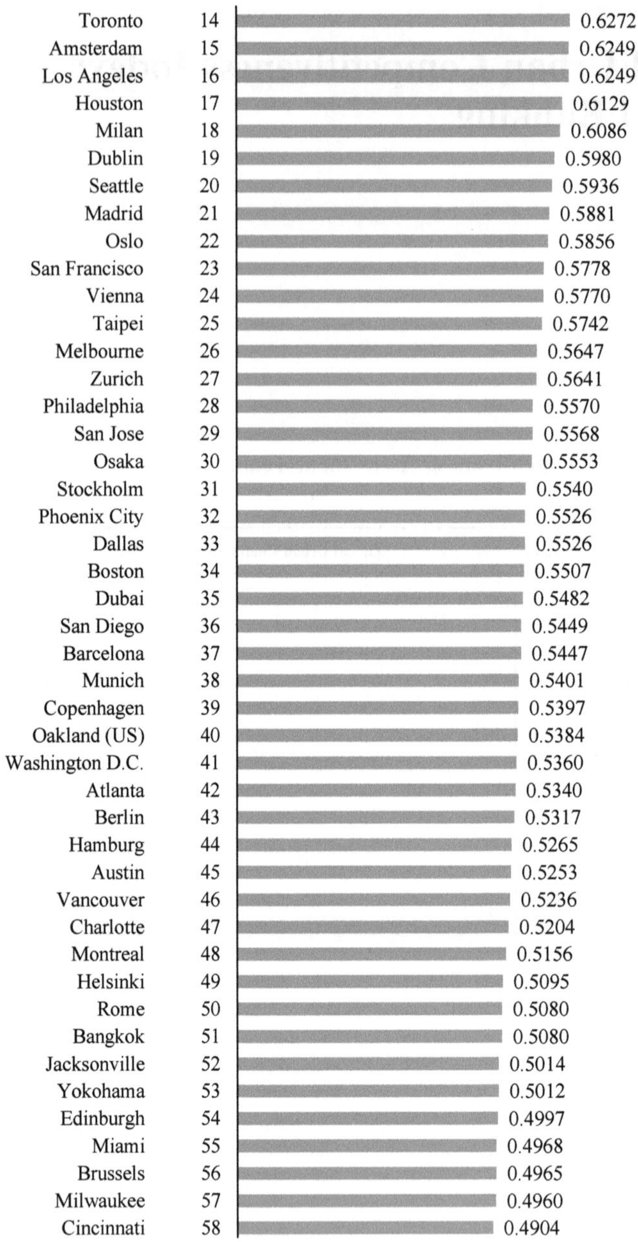
Toronto 14 0.6272
Amsterdam 15 0.6249
Los Angeles 16 0.6249
Houston 17 0.6129
Milan 18 0.6086
Dublin 19 0.5980
Seattle 20 0.5936
Madrid 21 0.5881
Oslo 22 0.5856
San Francisco 23 0.5778
Vienna 24 0.5770
Taipei 25 0.5742
Melbourne 26 0.5647
Zurich 27 0.5641
Philadelphia 28 0.5570
San Jose 29 0.5568
Osaka 30 0.5553
Stockholm 31 0.5540
Phoenix City 32 0.5526
Dallas 33 0.5526
Boston 34 0.5507
Dubai 35 0.5482
San Diego 36 0.5449
Barcelona 37 0.5447
Munich 38 0.5401
Copenhagen 39 0.5397
Oakland (US) 40 0.5384
Washington D.C. 41 0.5360
Atlanta 42 0.5340
Berlin 43 0.5317
Hamburg 44 0.5265
Austin 45 0.5253
Vancouver 46 0.5236
Charlotte 47 0.5204
Montreal 48 0.5156
Helsinki 49 0.5095
Rome 50 0.5080
Bangkok 51 0.5080
Jacksonville 52 0.5014
Yokohama 53 0.5012
Edinburgh 54 0.4997
Miami 55 0.4968
Brussels 56 0.4965
Milwaukee 57 0.4960
Cincinnati 58 0.4904

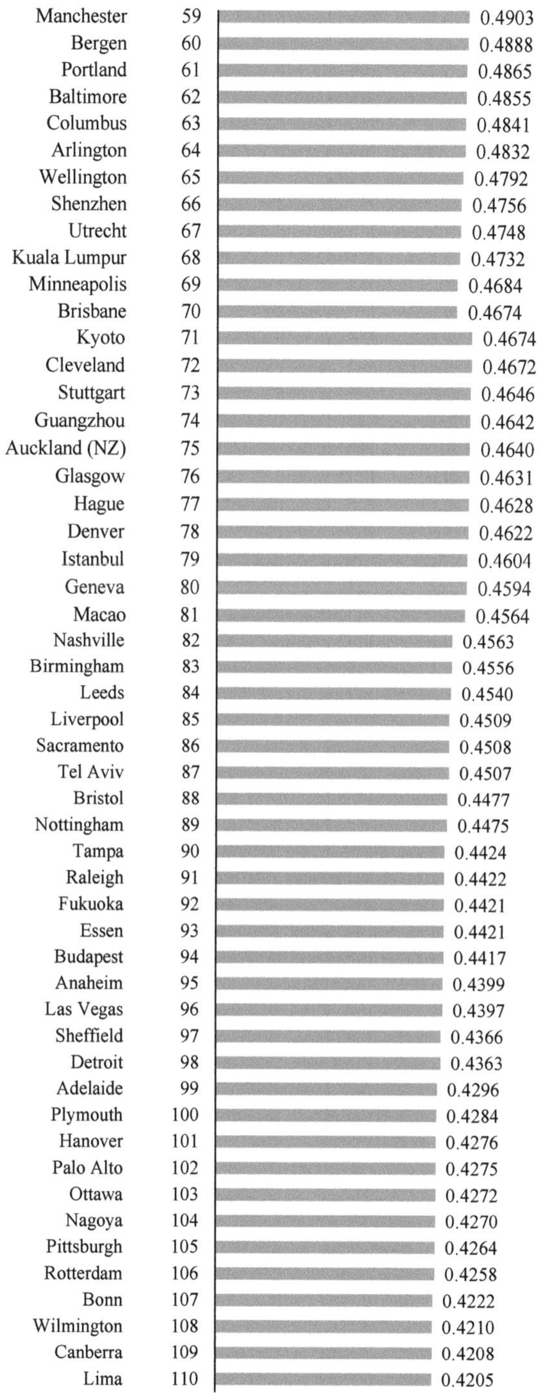
Manchester 59 0.4903
Bergen 60 0.4888
Portland 61 0.4865
Baltimore 62 0.4855
Columbus 63 0.4841
Arlington 64 0.4832
Wellington 65 0.4792
Shenzhen 66 0.4756
Utrecht 67 0.4748
Kuala Lumpur 68 0.4732
Minneapolis 69 0.4684
Brisbane 70 0.4674
Kyoto 71 0.4674
Cleveland 72 0.4672
Stuttgart 73 0.4646
Guangzhou 74 0.4642
Auckland (NZ) 75 0.4640
Glasgow 76 0.4631
Hague 77 0.4628
Denver 78 0.4622
Istanbul 79 0.4604
Geneva 80 0.4594
Macao 81 0.4564
Nashville 82 0.4563
Birmingham 83 0.4556
Leeds 84 0.4540
Liverpool 85 0.4509
Sacramento 86 0.4508
Tel Aviv 87 0.4507
Bristol 88 0.4477
Nottingham 89 0.4475
Tampa 90 0.4424
Raleigh 91 0.4422
Fukuoka 92 0.4421
Essen 93 0.4421
Budapest 94 0.4417
Anaheim 95 0.4399
Las Vegas 96 0.4397
Sheffield 97 0.4366
Detroit 98 0.4363
Adelaide 99 0.4296
Plymouth 100 0.4284
Hanover 101 0.4276
Palo Alto 102 0.4275
Ottawa 103 0.4272
Nagoya 104 0.4270
Pittsburgh 105 0.4264
Rotterdam 106 0.4258
Bonn 107 0.4222
Wilmington 108 0.4210
Canberra 109 0.4208
Lima 110 0.4205

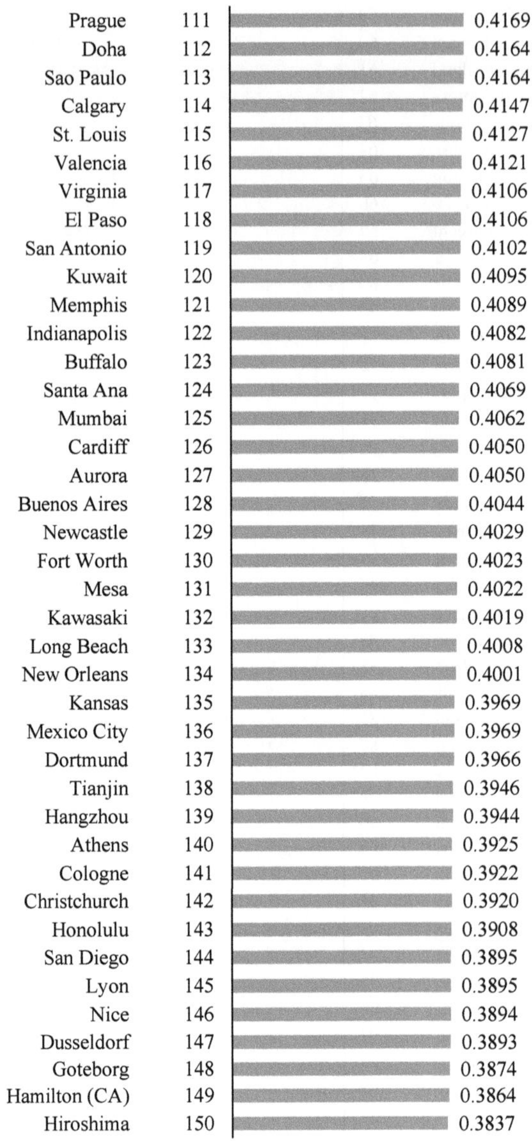
Prague 111 0.4169
Doha 112 0.4164
Sao Paulo 113 0.4164
Calgary 114 0.4147
St. Louis 115 0.4127
Valencia 116 0.4121
Virginia 117 0.4106
El Paso 118 0.4106
San Antonio 119 0.4102
Kuwait 120 0.4095
Memphis 121 0.4089
Indianapolis 122 0.4082
Buffalo 123 0.4081
Santa Ana 124 0.4069
Mumbai 125 0.4062
Cardiff 126 0.4050
Aurora 127 0.4050
Buenos Aires 128 0.4044
Newcastle 129 0.4029
Fort Worth 130 0.4023
Mesa 131 0.4022
Kawasaki 132 0.4019
Long Beach 133 0.4008
New Orleans 134 0.4001
Kansas 135 0.3969
Mexico City 136 0.3969
Dortmund 137 0.3966
Tianjin 138 0.3946
Hangzhou 139 0.3944
Athens 140 0.3925
Cologne 141 0.3922
Christchurch 142 0.3920
Honolulu 143 0.3908
San Diego 144 0.3895
Lyon 145 0.3895
Nice 146 0.3894
Dusseldorf 147 0.3893
Goteborg 148 0.3874
Hamilton (CA) 149 0.3864
Hiroshima 150 0.3837

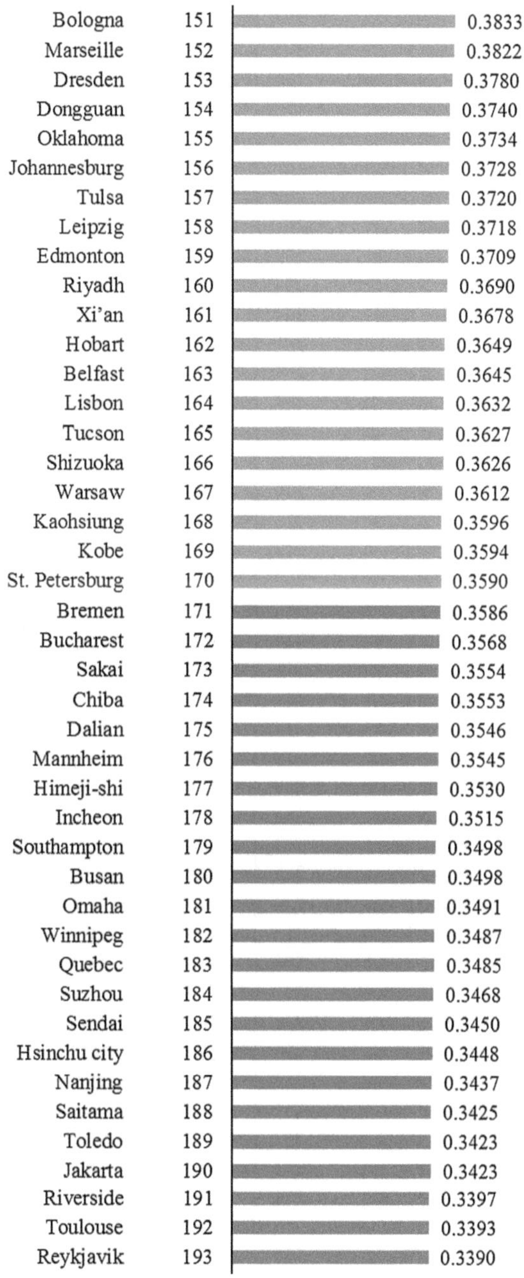
Bologna 151 0.3833
Marseille 152 0.3822
Dresden 153 0.3780
Dongguan 154 0.3740
Oklahoma 155 0.3734
Johannesburg 156 0.3728
Tulsa 157 0.3720
Leipzig 158 0.3718
Edmonton 159 0.3709
Riyadh 160 0.3690
Xi'an 161 0.3678
Hobart 162 0.3649
Belfast 163 0.3645
Lisbon 164 0.3632
Tucson 165 0.3627
Shizuoka 166 0.3626
Warsaw 167 0.3612
Kaohsiung 168 0.3596
Kobe 169 0.3594
St. Petersburg 170 0.3590
Bremen 171 0.3586
Bucharest 172 0.3568
Sakai 173 0.3554
Chiba 174 0.3553
Dalian 175 0.3546
Mannheim 176 0.3545
Himeji-shi 177 0.3530
Incheon 178 0.3515
Southampton 179 0.3498
Busan 180 0.3498
Omaha 181 0.3491
Winnipeg 182 0.3487
Quebec 183 0.3485
Suzhou 184 0.3468
Sendai 185 0.3450
Hsinchu city 186 0.3448
Nanjing 187 0.3437
Saitama 188 0.3425
Toledo 189 0.3423
Jakarta 190 0.3423
Riverside 191 0.3397
Toulouse 192 0.3393
Reykjavik 193 0.3390

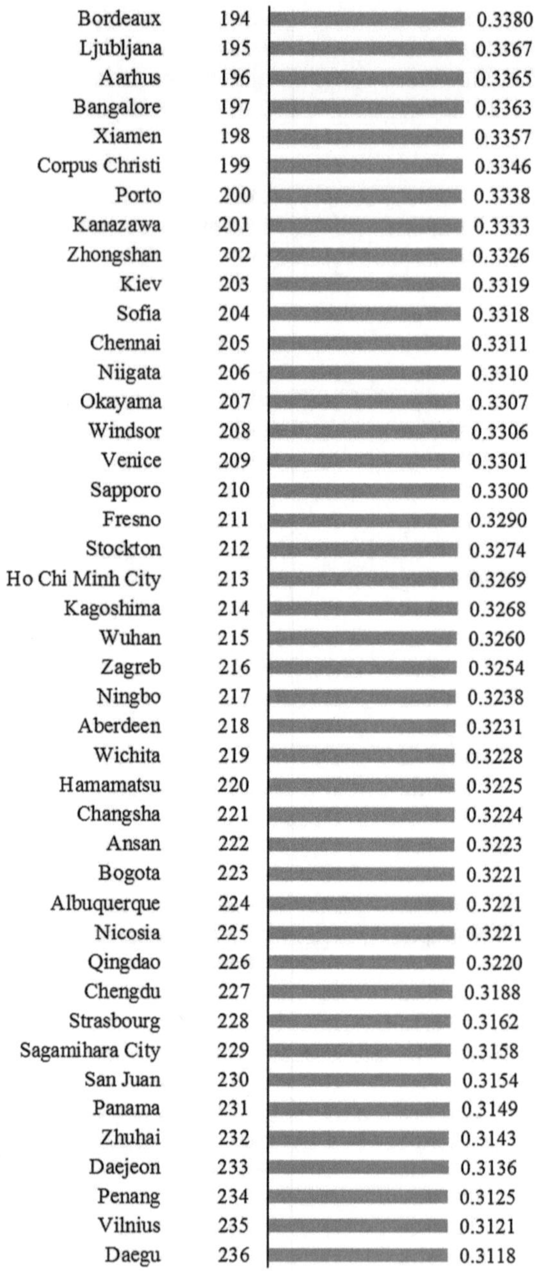
Bordeaux 194 0.3380
Ljubljana 195 0.3367
Aarhus 196 0.3365
Bangalore 197 0.3363
Xiamen 198 0.3357
Corpus Christi 199 0.3346
Porto 200 0.3338
Kanazawa 201 0.3333
Zhongshan 202 0.3326
Kiev 203 0.3319
Sofia 204 0.3318
Chennai 205 0.3311
Niigata 206 0.3310
Okayama 207 0.3307
Windsor 208 0.3306
Venice 209 0.3301
Sapporo 210 0.3300
Fresno 211 0.3290
Stockton 212 0.3274
Ho Chi Minh City 213 0.3269
Kagoshima 214 0.3268
Wuhan 215 0.3260
Zagreb 216 0.3254
Ningbo 217 0.3238
Aberdeen 218 0.3231
Wichita 219 0.3228
Hamamatsu 220 0.3225
Changsha 221 0.3224
Ansan 222 0.3223
Bogota 223 0.3221
Albuquerque 224 0.3221
Nicosia 225 0.3221
Qingdao 226 0.3220
Chengdu 227 0.3188
Strasbourg 228 0.3162
Sagamihara City 229 0.3158
San Juan 230 0.3154
Panama 231 0.3149
Zhuhai 232 0.3143
Daejeon 233 0.3136
Penang 234 0.3125
Vilnius 235 0.3121
Daegu 236 0.3118

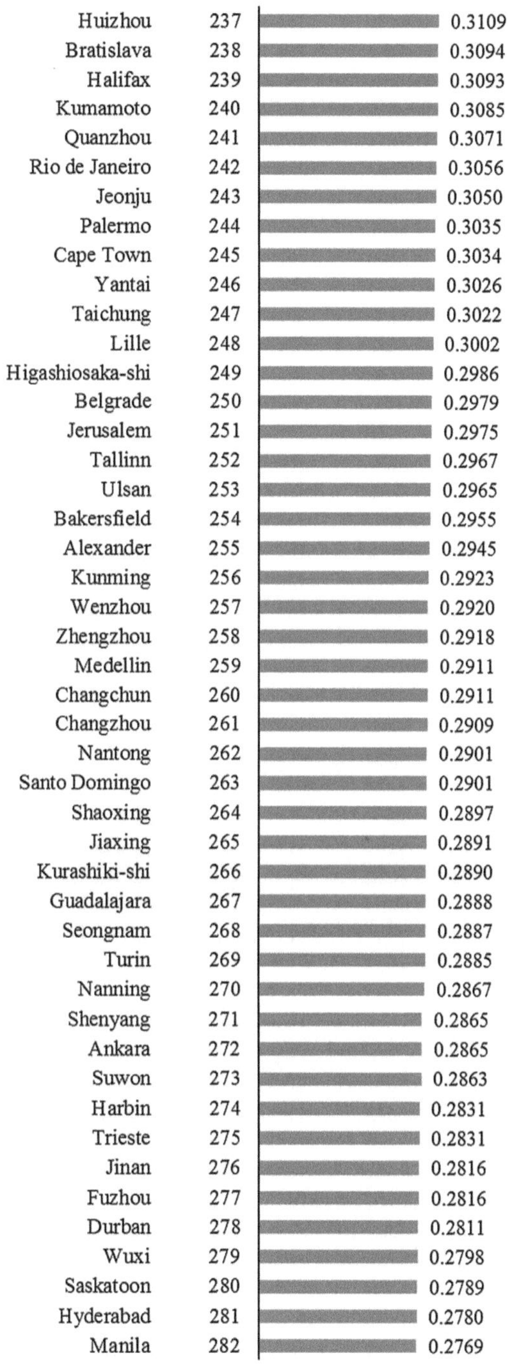
Huizhou 237 0.3109
Bratislava 238 0.3094
Halifax 239 0.3093
Kumamoto 240 0.3085
Quanzhou 241 0.3071
Rio de Janeiro 242 0.3056
Jeonju 243 0.3050
Palermo 244 0.3035
Cape Town 245 0.3034
Yantai 246 0.3026
Taichung 247 0.3022
Lille 248 0.3002
Higashiosaka-shi 249 0.2986
Belgrade 250 0.2979
Jerusalem 251 0.2975
Tallinn 252 0.2967
Ulsan 253 0.2965
Bakersfield 254 0.2955
Alexander 255 0.2945
Kunming 256 0.2923
Wenzhou 257 0.2920
Zhengzhou 258 0.2918
Medellin 259 0.2911
Changchun 260 0.2911
Changzhou 261 0.2909
Nantong 262 0.2901
Santo Domingo 263 0.2901
Shaoxing 264 0.2897
Jiaxing 265 0.2891
Kurashiki-shi 266 0.2890
Guadalajara 267 0.2888
Seongnam 268 0.2887
Turin 269 0.2885
Nanning 270 0.2867
Shenyang 271 0.2865
Ankara 272 0.2865
Suwon 273 0.2863
Harbin 274 0.2831
Trieste 275 0.2831
Jinan 276 0.2816
Fuzhou 277 0.2816
Durban 278 0.2811
Wuxi 279 0.2798
Saskatoon 280 0.2789
Hyderabad 281 0.2780
Manila 282 0.2769

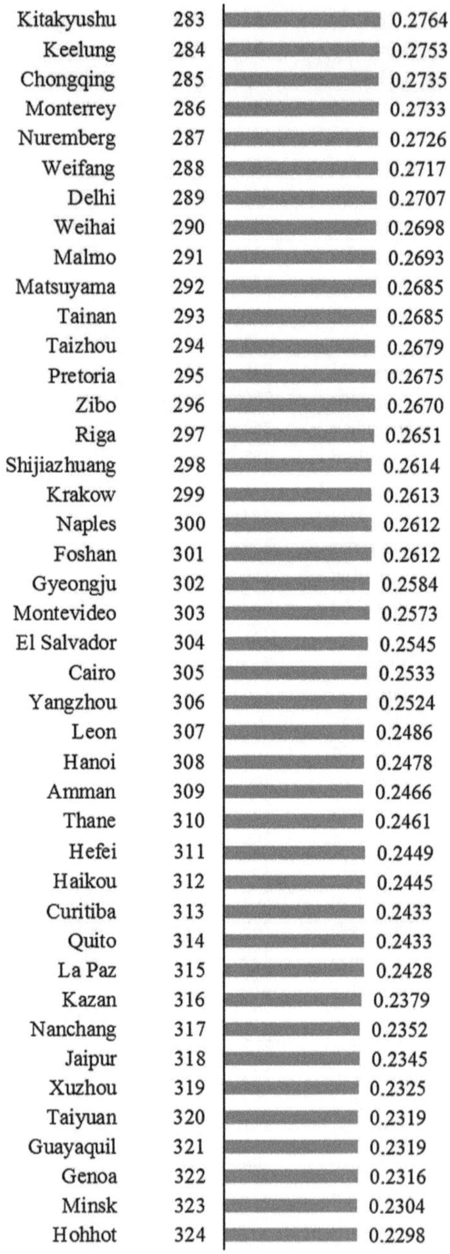

Kitakyushu 283 0.2764
Keelung 284 0.2753
Chongqing 285 0.2735
Monterrey 286 0.2733
Nuremberg 287 0.2726
Weifang 288 0.2717
Delhi 289 0.2707
Weihai 290 0.2698
Malmo 291 0.2693
Matsuyama 292 0.2685
Tainan 293 0.2685
Taizhou 294 0.2679
Pretoria 295 0.2675
Zibo 296 0.2670
Riga 297 0.2651
Shijiazhuang 298 0.2614
Krakow 299 0.2613
Naples 300 0.2612
Foshan 301 0.2612
Gyeongju 302 0.2584
Montevideo 303 0.2573
El Salvador 304 0.2545
Cairo 305 0.2533
Yangzhou 306 0.2524
Leon 307 0.2486
Hanoi 308 0.2478
Amman 309 0.2466
Thane 310 0.2461
Hefei 311 0.2449
Haikou 312 0.2445
Curitiba 313 0.2433
Quito 314 0.2433
La Paz 315 0.2428
Kazan 316 0.2379
Nanchang 317 0.2352
Jaipur 318 0.2345
Xuzhou 319 0.2325
Taiyuan 320 0.2319
Guayaquil 321 0.2319
Genoa 322 0.2316
Minsk 323 0.2304
Hohhot 324 0.2298

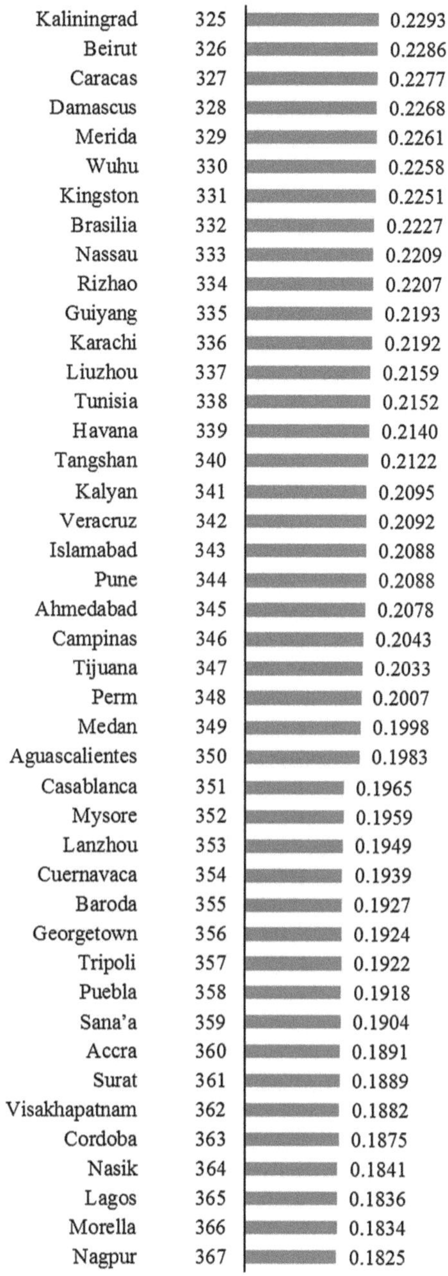
Kaliningrad 325 0.2293
Beirut 326 0.2286
Caracas 327 0.2277
Damascus 328 0.2268
Merida 329 0.2261
Wuhu 330 0.2258
Kingston 331 0.2251
Brasilia 332 0.2227
Nassau 333 0.2209
Rizhao 334 0.2207
Guiyang 335 0.2193
Karachi 336 0.2192
Liuzhou 337 0.2159
Tunisia 338 0.2152
Havana 339 0.2140
Tangshan 340 0.2122
Kalyan 341 0.2095
Veracruz 342 0.2092
Islamabad 343 0.2088
Pune 344 0.2088
Ahmedabad 345 0.2078
Campinas 346 0.2043
Tijuana 347 0.2033
Perm 348 0.2007
Medan 349 0.1998
Aguascalientes 350 0.1983
Casablanca 351 0.1965
Mysore 352 0.1959
Lanzhou 353 0.1949
Cuernavaca 354 0.1939
Baroda 355 0.1927
Georgetown 356 0.1924
Tripoli 357 0.1922
Puebla 358 0.1918
Sana'a 359 0.1904
Accra 360 0.1891
Surat 361 0.1889
Visakhapatnam 362 0.1882
Cordoba 363 0.1875
Nasik 364 0.1841
Lagos 365 0.1836
Morella 366 0.1834
Nagpur 367 0.1825

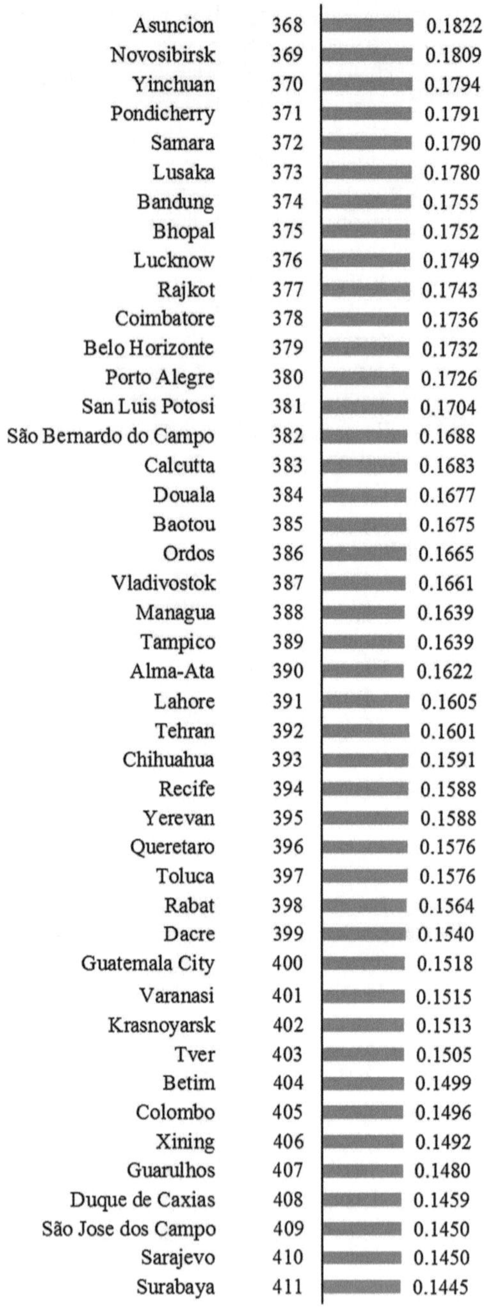
Asuncion 368 0.1822
Novosibirsk 369 0.1809
Yinchuan 370 0.1794
Pondicherry 371 0.1791
Samara 372 0.1790
Lusaka 373 0.1780
Bandung 374 0.1755
Bhopal 375 0.1752
Lucknow 376 0.1749
Rajkot 377 0.1743
Coimbatore 378 0.1736
Belo Horizonte 379 0.1732
Porto Alegre 380 0.1726
San Luis Potosi 381 0.1704
São Bernardo do Campo 382 0.1688
Calcutta 383 0.1683
Douala 384 0.1677
Baotou 385 0.1675
Ordos 386 0.1665
Vladivostok 387 0.1661
Managua 388 0.1639
Tampico 389 0.1639
Alma-Ata 390 0.1622
Lahore 391 0.1605
Tehran 392 0.1601
Chihuahua 393 0.1591
Recife 394 0.1588
Yerevan 395 0.1588
Queretaro 396 0.1576
Toluca 397 0.1576
Rabat 398 0.1564
Dacre 399 0.1540
Guatemala City 400 0.1518
Varanasi 401 0.1515
Krasnoyarsk 402 0.1513
Tver 403 0.1505
Betim 404 0.1499
Colombo 405 0.1496
Xining 406 0.1492
Guarulhos 407 0.1480
Duque de Caxias 408 0.1459
São Jose dos Campo 409 0.1450
Sarajevo 410 0.1450
Surabaya 411 0.1445

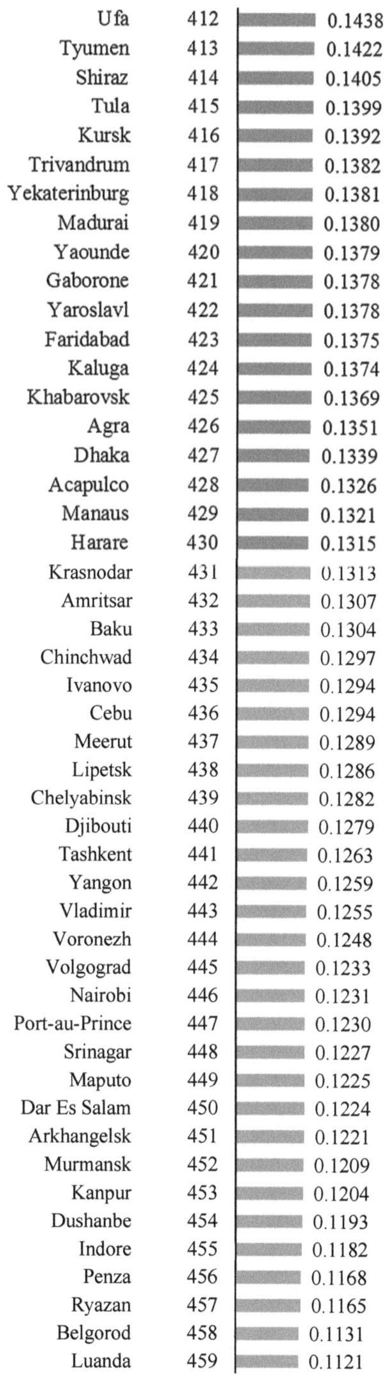
Ufa 412 0.1438
Tyumen 413 0.1422
Shiraz 414 0.1405
Tula 415 0.1399
Kursk 416 0.1392
Trivandrum 417 0.1382
Yekaterinburg 418 0.1381
Madurai 419 0.1380
Yaounde 420 0.1379
Gaborone 421 0.1378
Yaroslavl 422 0.1378
Faridabad 423 0.1375
Kaluga 424 0.1374
Khabarovsk 425 0.1369
Agra 426 0.1351
Dhaka 427 0.1339
Acapulco 428 0.1326
Manaus 429 0.1321
Harare 430 0.1315
Krasnodar 431 0.1313
Amritsar 432 0.1307
Baku 433 0.1304
Chinchwad 434 0.1297
Ivanovo 435 0.1294
Cebu 436 0.1294
Meerut 437 0.1289
Lipetsk 438 0.1286
Chelyabinsk 439 0.1282
Djibouti 440 0.1279
Tashkent 441 0.1263
Yangon 442 0.1259
Vladimir 443 0.1255
Voronezh 444 0.1248
Volgograd 445 0.1233
Nairobi 446 0.1231
Port-au-Prince 447 0.1230
Srinagar 448 0.1227
Maputo 449 0.1225
Dar Es Salam 450 0.1224
Arkhangelsk 451 0.1221
Murmansk 452 0.1209
Kanpur 453 0.1204
Dushanbe 454 0.1193
Indore 455 0.1182
Penza 456 0.1168
Ryazan 457 0.1165
Belgorod 458 0.1131
Luanda 459 0.1121

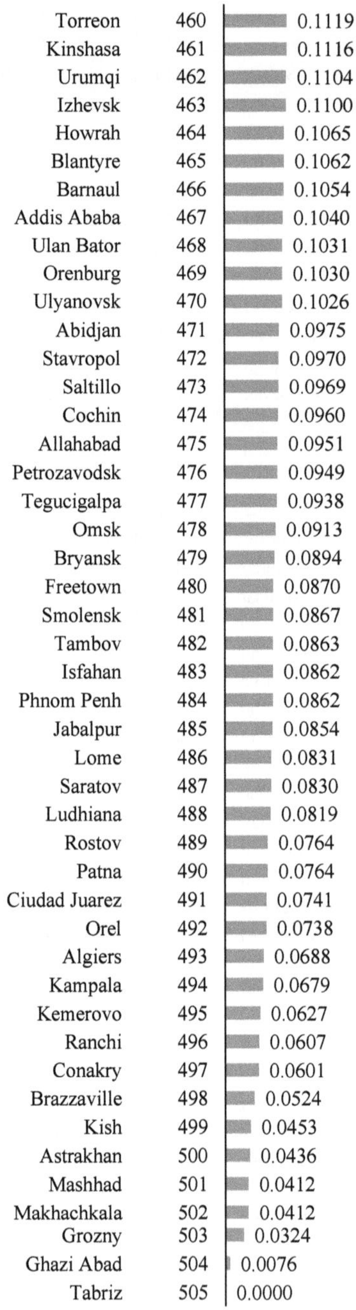
Torreon 460 0.1119
Kinshasa 461 0.1116
Urumqi 462 0.1104
Izhevsk 463 0.1100
Howrah 464 0.1065
Blantyre 465 0.1062
Barnaul 466 0.1054
Addis Ababa 467 0.1040
Ulan Bator 468 0.1031
Orenburg 469 0.1030
Ulyanovsk 470 0.1026
Abidjan 471 0.0975
Stavropol 472 0.0970
Saltillo 473 0.0969
Cochin 474 0.0960
Allahabad 475 0.0951
Petrozavodsk 476 0.0949
Tegucigalpa 477 0.0938
Omsk 478 0.0913
Bryansk 479 0.0894
Freetown 480 0.0870
Smolensk 481 0.0867
Tambov 482 0.0863
Isfahan 483 0.0862
Phnom Penh 484 0.0862
Jabalpur 485 0.0854
Lome 486 0.0831
Saratov 487 0.0830
Ludhiana 488 0.0819
Rostov 489 0.0764
Patna 490 0.0764
Ciudad Juarez 491 0.0741
Orel 492 0.0738
Algiers 493 0.0688
Kampala 494 0.0679
Kemerovo 495 0.0627
Ranchi 496 0.0607
Conakry 497 0.0601
Brazzaville 498 0.0524
Kish 499 0.0453
Astrakhan 500 0.0436
Mashhad 501 0.0412
Makhachkala 502 0.0412
Grozny 503 0.0324
Ghazi Abad 504 0.0076
Tabriz 505 0.0000

Chapter 2
Global Urban Competitiveness: Theoretical Framework

2.1 Introduction

As mankind enters an era of globalization and urbanization, the importance of cities has grown, with competition between cities becoming increasingly intense. The competitiveness of cities is clearly an important topic for theoretical propositions. Cheshire (1986) was the first to investigate and pay attention to the reasons and problems that led to the declining competitiveness of some European cities. Porter (1990) is the most renowned expert on competitiveness research. His study on the competitiveness of nations is also applicable to cities. Kresl and Singh (1995) later conducted an in-depth investigation to study the competitiveness of 24 metropolitan areas in the United States. Not long after that, some academics had a theoretical discussion on the topic of urban competitiveness, and Begg (1999) made his case for an antithetical system based on the issue of urban competitiveness. A growing number of academics have begun to study urban competitiveness since then (Pengfei 2010).

For the study on urban competitiveness, it is very important to measure the extent of urban competitiveness and to analyze the factors contributing to it. As urban competitiveness is a composite concept, no single indicator can be used in its measurement. A few academics have attempted to use single indicators like labor productivity (Porter 1990), GDP per capita or economic growth (Kitson 2005) as alternative measurements of urban competitiveness. Most academics used composite indicators to create an urban competitiveness index. Some academics and organizations tried to combine input and output factors of urban competitiveness to create an index for its measurement. Even more academics and organizations (Rondinelli and Vastag 1996; Kela-oluosi 2005; Tuerck 2002; Sharma 2006; Cho 2006; Diaz 2001; Shen 2002) put together the factors affecting urban competitiveness to build an index for measuring urban competitiveness. Even though the

© China Social Sciences Press and Springer Nature Singapore Pte Ltd. 2017

P. Ni et al., *Cities Network Along the Silk Road*,
DOI 10.1007/978-981-10-4834-0_2

factors affecting urban competitiveness are generally similar, the advantages are different for each city, or at the very least for different types of cities (e.g. differences in development stage, industrial structure, natural resource endowment and city size). Therefore, the factors affecting urban competitiveness are not the same, with different levels of influence. As such, it is obviously impossible to measure and reflect the urban competitiveness of all sample cities accurately using the same type of indicators and giving them the same weight in creating the urban competitiveness index.

The factors affecting urban competitiveness are complex and multi-dimensional. Academics combed through and analyzed different perspectives around factors that affect urban competitiveness respectively, such as controllable and uncontrollable factors, economic and strategic factors structural and dynamic factors (Sotarauta 2001), economic, social and environmental factors (Duffy 1995), internal and external factors, main city and environmental factors, and supply and demand factors (Porter 1990).

The evaluation of urban competitiveness is theoretical and it is a core issue that relevant sectors are interested in. This is because an evaluation of urban competitiveness allows a city to know its own competitive edges, disadvantages, problems and conditions in comparison to other cities. Investors and enterprises can understand situations that affect commercial factors in related cities and residents can have knowledge of their current welfare entitlements and future opportunities. The realistic importance of urban competitiveness evaluation attracted international organizations, national governments, companies and organizations, and academics of different nationalities to embark on the study of this topic and its actual measurement. Currently, a growing number of organizations are involved in such study and measurement. These organizations evaluate relevant cities from different perspectives, using different indicators and methods, providing governments, companies and residents with a lot of valuable information about cities (see Table 2.1).

There are some overall commonalities in the theoretical models and indicator systems of the above authors, which reflect the key areas involved in urban competitiveness: economic performance and standard of living, indicators related to urban environment attractiveness, such as human resources, technological innovation, external economies, economic structure, economic aggregation, etc. However, due to the fact that the authors are studying this from different angles and focus on different things, they come with varying degrees of flaws and biases.

2.2 Determining Mechanism

A city is an unofficial and open organization consisted of people, private sectors, quasi-public sectors and public sectors. In a city, enterprises organize their employees to create and provide private products and services for local and external

Table 2.1 Urban competitiveness evaluation of world cities

Approach	Author/organization	Composites	No. of sample cities	No. of indicators
Output	Organization for Economic Co-operation and Development	1	78	1
	Peter Kresl (USA, 1999)	3	24	3
	Ni Pengfei (China, 2001)	6	200	12
	Cho Dong-Sung (South Korea, 2006)	3	75	5
	William Lever (England, 1999)	3		3
Input	Ni Pengfei (China, 2003)	12	60	199
	Douglas Webb (World Bank, 2000)	4		75
	Augusto (World Economic Forum, 2005)	3	55	40
	David Tuerck (USA, 2002)	8	50	37
	Abhishek Sharma (USA, 2006)	2	21	27
	Cho Dong-Sung (South Korea, 2006)	5	75	90
	Alvin Diaz (Philippines, 2001)	7	65	71
	Shen Jianfa (Hong Kong, China, 2002)	3	286	52
Input–output	Robert Huggins (England, 2003)	3	44	7
	Core Urban City Workgroup (England, 2004)	6	50	21

markets; public sector organizations create and provide localized public products and services. Together, they form a compound structure in the relatively independent space of the city.

2.2.1 Determining the Competitiveness of a Single City

In reality, the business choices of a company are determined based on the environmental conditions of the region it is located in, and these choices in turn determine the value-added created by the companies. As for a city, the element environment and external elements that can be effectively used determine the size, structure and efficiency of the city's industrial system (including industries and its different links); and the condition of the industrial system determines the ability of the city to create value. The combination of various influencing factors determines the choice of industrial system of an urban company cluster and the value-added it creates.

2.2.2 Global Comparison of Urban Competitiveness

In the context of global integration, there are so many urban areas around the world. Different cities are naturally different in their overall merits and elements. There are also differences in costs. It costs differently for a city to reach out to and make use of external elements. In an open economy, there is difference in the competitive advantages of various cities that arise from differences in key elements, resulting in the industrial differences and division of labor between different urban areas. The size, level, structure and efficiency of industrial systems in the corresponding cities thus vary widely, and the value-added they create is also very different. From a company's point of view, a global company may set up its global industry chain based on how key elements are distributed in different cities, and this will form the company's global value chain. From a city's point of view, a system formed on the basis of how key elements are distributed in different cities around the world determines the industrial network of global cities, and the distribution of this industrial network in different cities around the world determines the global value chain.

2.2.3 Changes in Global Competitiveness and Patterns

As population, companies and some important factors of production can move between cities, the differences in element endowments of cities lead to different potential benefits. Therefore, not only are there division of labor, cooperation and trade between cities, there is also complicated and diverse competition going on. Competition leads to the flow and redistribution of resources and elements across different cities, seeking maximal overall interests. Economic systems favor a state of general equilibrium, which includes the equilibrium of urban spaces. However, as elements, environments, as well as the overall merits of cities all keep changing, resources, factors, and industries tend to be redistributed in spatial terms, shifting the overall trend from one state of equilibrium to another.

Figure 2.1 is a simplified illustration: City A's open system of key elements is formed through attracting elements, industries and even wealth from City B and City C, as well as through making use of B and C's element environments and industrial cooperation with B and C, and this fosters an open industrial system that creates City A's value system and forms its urban competitiveness; City A's value system and industrial system also exert influence on its own element system amid global competition. The same is true for City B and City C.

The competitiveness of various cities is determined at the same time in the midst of cooperation and competition of their element environments, industrial systems and value gains and the situation changes constantly.

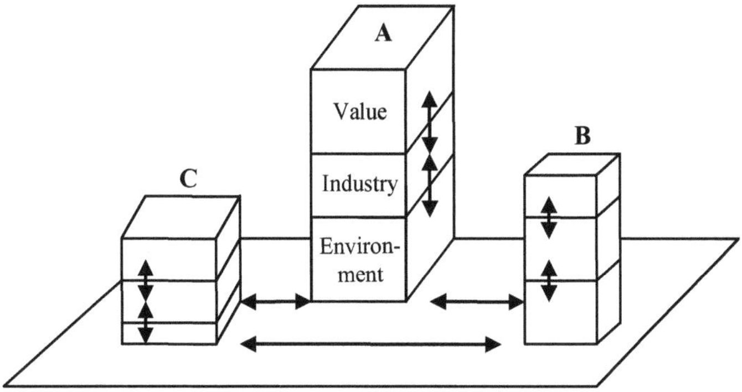

Fig. 2.1 Determination urban competitiveness

2.3 Conceptual Framework

According to mechanisms of urban competitiveness and development, a city's global competitiveness (potential competitiveness) can be seen as its ability to attract, contest, own, control and transform resources, and to contest, seize and control the market, creating greater value faster, more efficiently and more sustainably, in comparison with other cities in the process of cooperation, competition and development.

From the perspective of element environment, with reference to the national economic cycle model and the national competitive advantage model of Michael Porter, We hereby establish an urban competitiveness model encompassing six latent variables:

$$\mathrm{UC} = f(\mathrm{EQ}, \mathrm{LE}, \mathrm{LD}, \mathrm{LC}, \mathrm{GC}, \mathrm{SE}, \mathrm{HE})$$

UC stands for urban competitiveness, EQ for enterprise quality (i.e. the merits of a city); LE for local elements (i.e. the city's local supply of elements); LD for local demand (i.e. the city's local market demand); LC for internal structure (reflecting links and clusters within the city); GC for global connection (the city's communication with external bodies to utilize elements and market of these external bodies, and to face opportunities and threats from these external markets); SE for software environment (institutional arrangements and environment for exchanges); HE stands for hardware environment (the local infrastructure and ecological conditions). These six latent variables contribute in different ways to urban competitiveness but each and every one is indispensable.

This model centers on the overall merits (quality) of a city, its internal and external links, the systems for interactions and exchanges and its supply and demand to take into consideration a variety of factors: the city and its environment,

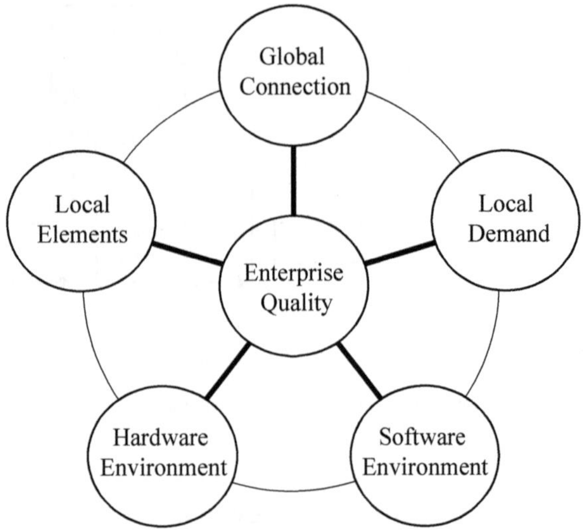

Fig. 2.2 Global urban competitiveness: determining factors

supply and demand, existing stock and increment, short-term and long-term factors, static and dynamic factors, software and hardware, internal and external factors etc. (Fig. 2.2).

2.4 Indicator System

The six latent variables mentioned above point to six areas, all of which contain several specific factors of urban competitiveness. Taking hold of key factors and ensuring data availability, we selected a total of 22 indicators to construct the urban competitiveness indicator system (see Table 2.2).

2.5 Research Methodology

2.5.1 Definition of a City

A city usually means an area of residential neighborhoods with a high degree of urbanization. However, the specific definition and scope of a city are different from country to country. A city is defined in this report as a residential area under one administrative center that includes urbanized areas and may also include suburbs or villages. From this definition, it is obvious that we are looking at cities from the administrative perspective. It needs to be noted that due to issues with data availability during the process of the research, some individual cities have been classified as urbanized districts, while some other cities are classified as metropolitan

Table 2.2 Global urban competitiveness indicator system

Category	Indicator	Data source and index composition
I1 Company strength	I1.1 Multinational company index	The data is taken from Forbes Global 2000, with additional points assigned to ranked companies in the city and multinational companies, 5 points for global headquarters, 4 points for continental headquarters, 3 points for country headquarters, 2 points for regional headquarters, and 1 point for city headquarters
	I1.2 Forbes 2000 total	Company total on the Forbes Global 2000 list (2011)
	I1.3 Industrial structure	According to relevant information and scores given by experts in the relevant disciplines
	I1.4 Industrial standard	According to relevant information and scores given by experts in the relevant disciplines
I2 Local elements	I2.1 No. of patents	The data is taken from the World Intellectual Property Organization (WIPO) website (https://patentscope.wipo.int/search/en/search.jsf)
	I2.2 Unemployment	Relevant statistical data of countries and cities (2011)
	I2.3 Bank index	Number of financial enterprises in Forbes Global 2000 (2011)
	I2.4 University rankings	Ranking of world universities (Webometrics Ranking) (2011)
I3 Local demand	I3.1 Population	Relevant statistical data of countries and cities (2011)
	I3.2 GDP	Relevant statistical data of countries and cities (2011)
	I3.3 National per capita income	World Bank website data (2011)
I4 Software environment	I4.1 Crime rate	United Nations International Centre for the Prevention of Crime statistical data reported by the governments of the respective countries http://www.uncjin.org/Statistics/WCTS/wcts.html
	I4.2 Language diversity index	Measured by on the language diversity of hotels in each city with four stars and above (2011)
	I4.3 Ease of doing business	*Global Business Environment Report* published by World Bank (2011)
	I4.4 Ratio of central versus local taxation	Relevant statistical data of countries and cities (2011)

(continued)

Table 2.2 (continued)

Category	Indicator	Data source and index composition
I5 Hardware environment	I5.1 PM 2.5 emissions	Information on the World Health Organization (WHO) website on the urban air quality figures (2011)
	I5.2 Benchmark hotel prices	The data is obtained from searching on the Holiday Inn site (http://www.holidayinn.com/hotels) and calculating the average value of 4–5 medium prized prices. Newly added website: http://www.booking.com
	I5.3 Ease of road travel	The data is based on Holiday Inn using Google search (the nearest Holiday Inn to the city center is found and its nearest distance, time and cost of travelling to the airport, metro/railway stations and the city's administrative offices are calculated
	I5.4 Distance from sea	The distance of the city from the nearest harbor is calculated according to the coordinates (latitude/longitude) data obtained from Google Maps (2011)
I6 Global connection	I6.1 Multinational company connection	The data is taken from Forbes Global 2000 calculations (2013)
	I6.2 International reputation index	The data is taken from searching, on Google, the English names of cities or English websites on the cities (http://data.worldbank.org.cn/indicator/NY.GDP.MKTP.CD)
	I6.3 No. of air routes	The data is taken from the websites of the various airports in cities, Wikipedia and relevant data on the International Air Transport Association (IATA) website (2015)

areas. We have included special notes regarding this at the relevant sections accordingly. Those without special notations are all cities based on an administrative definition.

2.5.2 *Sample Cities*

Evaluation of global urban competitiveness then proceeded to the selection of the cities. The diversity and typicality of samples contribute to the accuracy and value of research results and 505 cities from around the world were selected as sample cities for the purpose of this report. The sampling process is detailed below:

Firstly, for a preliminary round of screening, a brief study was conducted on cities in various countries and regions across the six continents, with major cities as candidates.

Secondly, with the aim of including a total of 505 sample cities, the number of sample cities in each country or region was determined on the basis of population and per-capita income.

Then, select sample cities from each country or region involved based on the principle of searching from the largest to smallest, best to worst, and highest to lowest.

Lastly, necessary adjustments were made to ensure the availability of accurate and standard statistics for every sample city.

The 505 cities selected according to the above steps spread across the six continents, 130 countries and regions, including 186 Asian cities, 143 European cities, 100 North American cities, 36 African cities, 28 South American cities, and 12 Oceanian cities. Based on the development stage of the cities determined by their GDP per capita, the 505 cities were divided into four groups. There are 91 cities with GDP per capita of more than USD 40,000, 72 cities with GDP per capita between USD 30,000 and 39,999, 74 cities with GDP per capita between USD 10,000 and 29,999, and 268 cities with GDP per capita below USD 10,000. The 505 sample cities are basically representative of cities today in different parts of the world and at different development stages. Please refer to the Consolidated Global Urban Competitiveness (Potential Competitiveness) Index in Chap. 1 for the list of the 505 sample cities.

2.5.3 Data Sources

The global urban competitiveness study requires a large amount of high-quality data. Data collection started in July last year to organize the translation and collection of data in many languages, including English, French, German, Spanish, Portuguese, Italian, Arabian, Russian, Japanese, Korean etc. from various channels, including official statistical publications, official websites and academic research findings. In this process, we also received a lot of help from researchers and research organizations from other countries, as well as students abroad. After nearly half a year of searching and collation, we covered a decent number of indicators. To address the differences in statistical standards in different countries, we first delved into the statistical data and standards of international organizations such as the statistical distributions of the United Nations Statistics Division (UNSD), World Development Indicators of the World Bank and the Organization for Economic Co-operation and Development (OECD) database. Then, the actual situation of the various countries were consolidated to establish a statistical standard that is statistically appropriate, easily comparable and with a most extensive coverage, before applying such standard to the data collection and processing stages to arrive at a unified database of 505 international cities. The measured data of the 22 indicators used here was mainly obtained from three sources. The statistical organizations of various countries, international statistical organizations, international research organizations or thematic reports and research data of companies are also major

of the original variable, Xj(j = 1, 2, …, p) on the principal components Fi (i = 1, 2, …, m).

$$l(Z_i, X_j) = \sqrt{\lambda_i a_{ij}} \quad (i = 1, 2, \cdots m; j = 1, 2, \cdots, p)$$

In the principal components results analyzed by the SPSS software, the "component matrix" reflects the principal component loading matrix.

(5) **Calculation of principal component scores**

Calculation of the scoring of the sample on ***m*** number of principal components:

$$F_i = a_{1i}X_1 + a_{2i}X_2 + \cdots + a_{pi}X_p \quad i = 1, 2, \ldots, m$$

Indicator dimensions are often different during practical application. It is, therefore, necessary to eliminate dimensional influence before the calculation of principal components. There are many ways of eliminating dimensional influence in data. A common method is the standardization of raw data, and to convert the data using the following formula:

$$X_{ij}^{*} = \frac{X_{ij} - \bar{X}_j}{S_j} \quad i = 1, 2, \ldots, n; j = 1, 2, \ldots, p$$

of which: $\bar{X}_j = \frac{1}{n}\sum_{i=1}^{n} X_{ij}, \quad S_j^2 = \frac{1}{n-1}\sum_{i=1}^{n} \left(X_{ij} - \bar{X}_j\right)^2$

2.7 Special Notes

Urban competitiveness is a profound and complex topic and looking at it from different perspectives, using different methodologies or targeting at different population groups can generate different conclusions. The evaluation system for global urban competitiveness is built upon the model created by Dr. Ni Pengfei in *China Urban Competitiveness Report* and improvements were made by taking into consideration the latest development trends in the world's urban areas and the many factors affecting urban competitiveness, as well as research work of other organizations and institutions around the world on national and urban competitiveness, encompassing theories in urbanization, urban economics, spatial economics, etc. The analytical framework and main thoughts on competitiveness in this book is of the same strain as that found in *China Urban Competitiveness Report*, learning much from it in setting up the indicator system. However, due to changes in research subject, research topic and target audience, as well as limitations during the process of data collection, the competitiveness evaluation system and calculation method in this book is slightly different from the one found in *China Urban Competitiveness Report*. In the spirit of academic prudence, the results and main conclusion indicated by the indicator system in this book are not directly comparable to those in *China Urban Competitiveness Report*. We suggest that readers view the two studies as a gauge of urban competitiveness from different angles and levels.

References

Begg, I. 1999. Cities and competitiveness. *Urban Studies* 36 (5): 795–809.

Begg, I. 2000. *Urban competitiveness: Policies for dynamic cities*. Bristol: Policy Press.

Cheshire, P., G. Carbonaro, and D. Hay. 1986. Problems of urban decline and growth in EEC countries: Or measuring degrees of elephantness. *Urban Studies* 2: 131–149.

Duffy, H. 1995. *Competitive cities: Succeeding in the global economy*. London: Routledge.

Boddy, Martin. 1999b. Geographical economics and urban competitiveness: A critique. *Urban Studies* 36: 811–842.

Friedmann J. 1995. *Where we stand: A decade of world city research. Knox P L. and Taylor P J. World cities in a world system*, Cambridge: Cambridge University Press.

Lever, W.F. 1999. Competitive cities in Europe. *Urban Studies* 36 (5): 1029–1044.

Linnamaa. 2001. The role of the city government in the urban economic development network. *Professionals and Public Expectations* 22–25.

Logan, J., and H. Molotch. 1987. *Urban fortunes: The political economy of place*. Berkeley, CA: University of California Press.

Longnan, Liang. 1998. A study on urban planning and development of Korea. *Urban Planning Overseas* 2: 35–41.

Martin, L.E. van Duren, R. Westgren and M. Le Maguer. 1991. *Competitiveness of Ontario's Agri-food sector*, prepared for the Government of Ontario, May.

Mattoo, A., R. Rathindran, and A. Subramanian. 2001. Measuring services trade liberalization and its impact on economic growth: an illustration. *World Bank Working Paper*, No. 2655.

Meadows, D.H., D.L. Meadows, J. Randers, W.W. Behrens, and Rome Club. 1972. *The limits to growth*. New York: Universe Books.

Molotch, H. 1976. The city as a growth machine: Toward a political economy of place. *American Journal of Sociology* 82: 309–330.

Montgomery, C.A., and M.E. Porter. 1991. *Strategy: Seeking and securing competitive advantage*. Boston, Mass: Harvard Business School Press.

Ni, Pengfei, and Peter Karl Kresl. 2006. *Global Urban Competitiveness Report*. Beijing: Social Sciences Academic Press.

OECD. 2006. *OECD territorial reviews, competitive cities in the global economy*. Paris: OECD Publications.

OECD. 2008. *Competitive cities and climate change: OECD conference proceedings*. Paris: OECD Publications.

Parkinson, M., M. Hutchins, J. Simmie, G. Clark, and H. Verdonk. 2004. Competitiveness European cities: Where do the core city stand, Final report to core cities working group, Oct.

Parr, J.B. 1979. Regional economic change and regional spatial structure: Some interrelationships. *Environment and Planning A* 11: 825–837.

Parr, J.B. 2002. Missing elements in the analysis of agglomeration economies. *International Regional Science Review* 25: 151.

Schumpeterian, Joseph. 1961. *The theory of economic development: An inquiry into profits, capital, credit, interest and the business cycle*. NY: Oxford University Press.

Sotarauta, M., R. Linnamaa. 2001. Urban competitiveness and management of urban policy networks: Some reflections from Tampere and Oulu. *Technology, Society and Environment* 2.

Yong, Mao. 2002. On talent strategy of Singapore and its promotion to economy. *Around Southeast Asia* 9: 21–24.
Pengfei Ni. (2001–2015). *China urban competitiveness report*. Beijing: Social Sciences Academic Press.
Heilbroner, Robert. 1970. On the limited relevance of economics. *The Public Interest* 21 (fall): 80–93.
Ni, Pengfei. 2010. *Global urban competitiveness report 2010*. UK: Edward Elgar Cheltenham.
Ni, Pengfei. 2011. *Global urban competitiveness report 2011*. UK: Edward Elgar Cheltenham.
Ni, Pengfei. 2013. *Global urban competitiveness report 2013*. UK: Edward Elgar Cheltenham.
Peter, Karl. 2005. The determinant urban competitiveness: A survey, In: *North American cities and the global economy*, ed P.K. Kresl and G. Gappert, 45–68.
Porter, M.E. 1985. *The competitive advantage: Creating and sustaining superior performance*. New York: Free Press.
Porter, M.E. 1990. *The comparative advantage of nations*. New York: Free Press.
Porter, M.E. 1996. Competitive advantage, agglomeration economies, and regional policy. *International Regional Science Review* 19: 85–90.
Porter, M.E. 1998a. Clusters and the new economics of competition. *Harvard business review* 76: 7–90.
Porter, M.E. 1998b. *The microeconomic foundations of economic development*. The Global Competitiveness Report 1998, World Economic Forum.
Porter, M.E. 2000. Location, competition, and economic development: Local clusters in a global economy. *Economic Development Quarterly* 14: 15.
Porter, M.E. 2001. Innovation: Location matters. *MIT Sloan Management Review* 4: 42.
Porter, M.E. 2003. The economic performance of regions. *Regional Studies* 37: 6–7.
Posner, Michael V. 1961. International trade and technological changes. *Economics and Social Sciences* 13 (3): 323–341.
Prahalad, C.K. and Hamel, G. 1990. The core competence of the corporation. *Harvard Business Review* 79–91.
Robert, E.Lucas. 1988. On the mechanics of economic development. *Journal of Monetary Economic* 22: 3–42.
Roberto, Camagni. 2002. Urban mobility and urban form: The social and environmental costs of different patterns of urban expansion. *Ecological Economics* 40: 199–216.
Romer, Paul. 1986. Increasing returns and long run growth. *Journal of Political Economy* 67–68.
Rondinelli, Dennis A. 1998. The changing forces of urban economic development: Globalization and city competitiveness in the 21st century. *Cityscape* 3 (3): 36.
Solow, Robert. 1970. Science and ideology in economics. *The Public Interest* 21 (Fall): 94–107.
Taylor, P.J. 2004a. *The World City Network*. London: Routledge.
Taylor, P.J. 2004b. Competition and cooperation between cities in globalization. *GaWC Research Bulletin 351 (A)*.
Taylor, P.J., and Pengfei Ni. 2010. *Global urban analysis*. London: Earthscan Press.
Ronald I. McKinnon. 1976. *Money and finance in economic growth and development: Essays in honor of Edward S. Shaw, editor and contributor*. New York: Marcel Dekker.
Gruber, William, Dileep Mehta, and Raymond Vernon. 1967. The R&D factor in international trade and international investment of United States industries. *Journal of Political Economy* 25 (1): 20–37.
Hong, Sha. 2004. The strategy of Singapore's education and talents. *Journal of Tianjin Academy of Educational Science* 12: 6.
Rosenthal, S.S., and W.C. Strange. 2003. Geography, industrial organization, and agglomeration. *Review of Economics and Statistics* 85 (2): 377–393.
Sassen, S. 1994. *Cities in world economy*. London: Pine Forge Press.
Saxenian, AnnaLee. 1994. *Regional advantage: Culture and competition in silicon valley and route*. New York: Harvard University Press.
Scott, A., and E. Soja. 1986. Los Angeles: The capital of the twentieth century. *Environment and Planning, D: Society and Space* 4: 201–216.

Stone, C. 1989. *Regime politics: Governing Atlanta, 1946–1988*. Lawrence KS: University Press of Kansas.

Storper, M. 1997. *The Regional world: Territorial development in a global economy*. New York: Guilford.

Tang, Hua. 2000. *U.S. government management-phoenix as an example*. Beijing: Renmin University Press of China.

Terrence, E.Deal, and A.Kennedy Allan. 1999. *Revitalizing the workplace after downsizing, mergers, and reengineering*. Cambridge, MA: Perseus Publishing.

Terrence, E.Deal, and A.Kennedy Allen. 1982. *Corporate cultures: The rites and rituals of corporate life*. Reading, MA: Addison-Wesley Publishing.

Terrence, E. Deal and Allan, A. Kennedy. 1982. Corporate culture. *The American Economic Review* 56–58.

Theodore, W.Schultz. 1962. *Investment in human beings*. Chicago: University of Chicago Press.

Thompson, G.F. 2003. *Between hierarchies and markets: The logic and limits of network forms of organization*. Oxford: Oxford University Press.

Thünen, J.H.V. 1966. *Isolated state; an English edition of Der isolierte Staat*. New York: Pergamon Press.

Timmer, Marcel P., and Adam Szirmai. 2000. Productivity growth in Asian manufacturing: The structural bonus hypothesis examined. *Structural Change and Economic Dynamics* 11 (4): 371–392.

Van den Berg, Leo and Antonio Paolo Russo. 2007. *The impacts of culture on the economic development of cities*. Rotterdam: EURICUR.

Verikios, G. and X-G Zhang. 2001. *Global gains from liberalizing trade in telecommunications and financial services*. Productivity Commission Staff Research paper, No. 1683.

Weber, A.Y. 1909. *Theory of the location of industries*. Chicago: The University of Chicago.

Webster, D., and L. Muller. 2000. *Urban competitiveness assessment in developing country urban regions: The road forward*. Washington, D.C: Urban Group, INFUD, The World Bank.

World Bank. 2009. *Doing business 2009*. http://www.doingbusiness.org. Accessed 10 Sep 2008.

World Bank. 2010. *Doing business 2010*. http://www.doingbusiness.org. Accessed 9 Sep 2009.

Griliches, Zvi. 1957. Hybrid corn: An exploration in the economics of technological change. *Econometrical* 25 (4): 501.

Guang, Zhao. 1994. Looking at China's urban history from a macroscopic perspective. *Social Science in China* 15 (3): 171–179.

Ye, L. 2004. *Is Shanghai really a global city?*. Chicago: International conference on Globalization and Urban Change.

Zhang, T. 2000. Urban sprawl in China: Land market force and government's role. *Cities: The International Journal of Urban Planning and Studies* 17(1).

Zhang, Tingwei. 2001. Community feature and urban sprawl: The case of the Chicago metropolitan region. *Land Use Policy* 18: 221–231.

Zhang, L., and X.B. Zhao. 2001. The impact of state resource allocation on urbanization in socialist China. *Post-Communist Economies* 13 (4): 505–524.

Zhu, J. 1999. *The transition of China's urban development: From plan-controlled to market-led*. London: Praeger, Publishers.

Chapter 3
Global Urban Competitiveness: General Analysis

3.1 Overall Situation: Rapid Rise of Asian Cities and a Tripod Pattern of Europe, America and Asia

The top 10 of urban competitiveness are: London, New York, Tokyo, Paris, Singapore, Hong Kong, Shanghai, Beijing, Sydney and Frankfurt. Four of them are European or North American cities, one is in Australia and the remaining five are Asian cities. As Asian cities take more positions than European and North American cities, we can say that leading Asian cities are rising rapidly, leveling themselves with leading European and American cities. The global arena is now dominated by three global powerhouses-Europe, America and Asia. However, three out of the top five cities are still in Europe and America, with the top two spots securely in their hold. So, even though Asian cities are rapidly climbing up the ranks and changes occur frequently in the world situation, cities from Europe and America are still holding onto their leading positions. However, with the rapid development of Chinese cities, the leading edges of European and American cities will reduce further in the future. Chinese cities, Shanghai and Beijing, especially, are now placed among the top 10 global cities. As China develops further, the competitiveness of these two cities will definitely grow for them to become serious contenders of even higher positions (see Table 3.1).

As we move down the urban competitiveness global ranking, the gap between the urban competitiveness index scores of two adjacent cities first narrows and then widens, showing a V-shaped trend. Specifically, as we move down the rankings from 1 to 100, the urban competitiveness score decreases by 0.572; from 100 to 200, it decreases by 0.095; from 200 to 300, by 0.073; from 300 to 400, by 0.109; and from 400 to 505, by 0.152. The gap is bigger in the upper and lower ranges, whereas the gap in urban competitiveness between the cities ranked in the middle range is smaller (Table 3.1 and Fig. 3.1).

© China Social Sciences Press and Springer Nature Singapore Pte Ltd. 2017

P. Ni et al., *Cities Network Along the Silk Road*,
DOI 10.1007/978-981-10-4834-0_3

Table 3.1 Top 10 global cities in urban competitiveness

City	London	New York	Tokyo	Paris	Singapore	Hong Kong	Shanghai	Beijing	Sydney	Frankfurt
Continent	Europe	North America	Asia	Europe	Asia	Asia	Asia	Asia	Oceania	Europe
Score	1.000	0.944	0.862	0.799	0.770	0.754	0.740	0.683	0.669	0.661
World ranking	1	2	3	4	5	6	7	8	9	10

Source CASS city and competitiveness index database

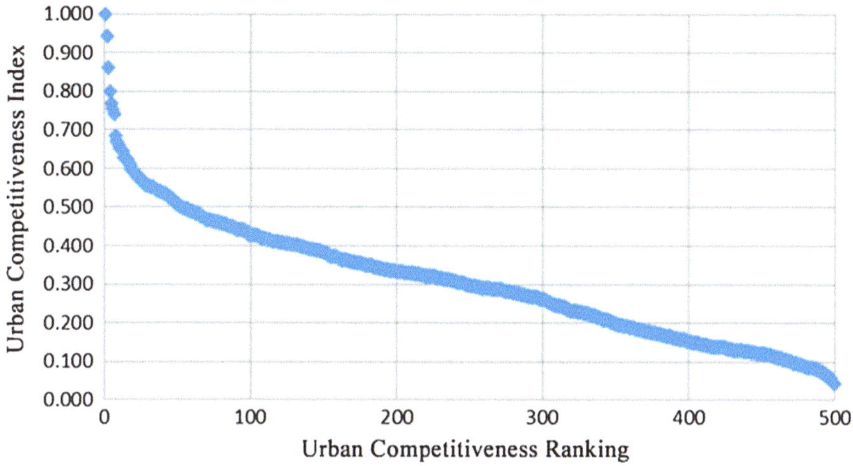

Fig. 3.1 Global urban competitiveness ranking distribution. *Source* CASS city and competitiveness index database

Globally, Europe and North America have respectively 37 and 38 cities in the top 100 by urban competitiveness, a clear numerical lead over the other continents. Oceania has 66.67% of its sample cities in the top 100, the biggest share of all continents, which means that many sample cities in Oceania are among the world's most advanced cities in terms of urban competitiveness. Oceania also has the highest average urban competitiveness score, at 0.472, followed by North America and Europe, which shows that European and American cities still have a clear advantage in terms of average scores. The region with the highest coefficient of variation in the urban competitiveness index is Europe, at 0.551, greater than the overall world value of 0.518. The coefficient of variation of the remaining regions is all lower than the overall world value. This shows that the difference in urban competitiveness between the cities in Europe is the greatest. The average urban competitiveness scores of Asia, Europe and North America are lower than their median values; while the average of South America, Oceania and Africa are greater than their medians. This shows that for the former three regions, more cities have an urban competitiveness score higher than the regional average and the opposite is true for the latter three regions. Oceania has 66.67% of its sample cities scoring lower than its regional total, which is the highest proportion while North America has the lowest proportion at 43.93%. The most competitive cities in Asia, Europe and North America have similar scores and the highest-ranking city of Oceania is also in the top 10, whereas the performance of the most competitive cities in South America and Africa are weaker in comparison. The most competitive city in South America is Lima, 110th in the world ranking; the most competitive city in Africa is Johannesburg, 156th. There is indeed quite a wide gap between the advanced cities of these two continents and those of the other continents (see Table 3.2 and Fig. 3.2).

Table 3.2 Global urban competitiveness by continents

Region	Sample size	Number (percentage) of cities in top 100	Mean	Coefficient of variation	Number (percentage) of cities below the mean	Median	Maximum		
							City	Score	World ranking
Asia	192	19 (9.90%)	0.277	0.498	95 (49.48%)	0.277	Tokyo	0.862	3
Europe	136	37 (27.21%)	0.321	0.551	62 (45.59%)	0.335	London	1.000	1
North America	107	38 (35.51%)	0.380	0.391	47 (43.93%)	0.402	New York	0.944	2
South America	28	0 (0.00%)	0.237	0.367	16 (57.14%)	0.225	Lima	0.421	110
Oceania	9	6 (66.67%)	0.472	0.198	6 (66.67%)	0.464	Sydney	0.669	9
Africa	33	0 (0.00%)	0.159	0.493	20 (60.61%)	0.138	Johannesburg	0.373	156
World average	505	100 (19.80%)	0.304	0.518	262 (51.88%)	0.297	London	1.000	1

Source CASS city and competitiveness index database

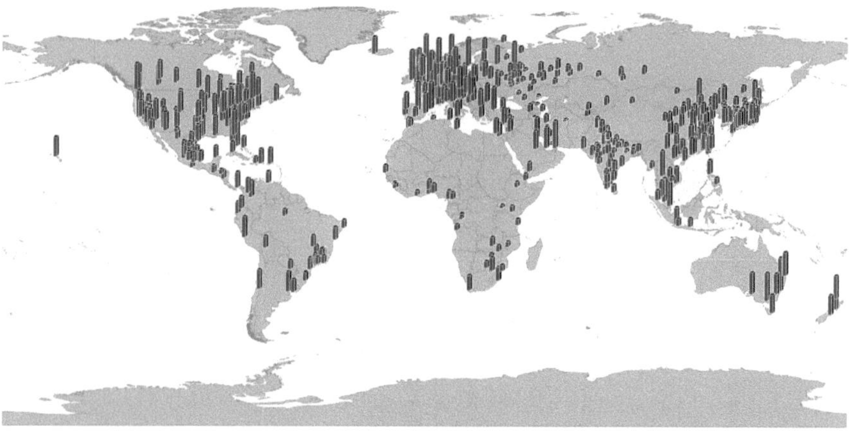

Fig. 3.2 Global urban competitiveness distribution. *Source* CASS city and competitiveness index database

3.1.1 Asia: Most Cities are Low in Ranking, with a Small Number Among the Top in the World

Among the 192 sample cities of Asia, the top 10 in urban competitiveness (in order of ranking) are Tokyo, Singapore, Hong Kong, Shanghai, Beijing, Seoul, Taipei, Osaka, Dubai and Bangkok. Four of them are Chinese cities, two Japanese, and the remaining four are from four different countries. Two cities from Mainland China are among the top 10 in the global ranking, both of which are among the top 5 of Asia. This shows that as the cities of Mainland China develop, the urban competitiveness of advanced ones are now on par with the advanced cities of Japan, all along the top rankings in the world (see Table 3.3). However, looking at Asia as a whole, the competitiveness of the majority of its cities is still below the world average.

As we move down the urban competitiveness ranking for Asia, the decrease in the urban competitiveness score first reduce and then grow. This shows that the gap between the urban competitiveness of two adjacent cities on the list narrows first and then widen as the urban competitiveness ranking falls. Specifically, in the first 100 cities on the list, the 19 Asian cities show a gap of 0.420 between the highest- and the lowest-ranking ones; from 100 to 200, the 28 Asian cities have a score gap of 0.091; from 200 to 300, the 61 Asian cities have a score gap of 0.072; from 300 to 400, the 48 Asian cities see a gap of 0.102; and from 400 to 505, the 36 Asian cities have a gap of 0.152. This shows that in Asia, the greatest number of cities, or 31.77% of the total, fall within the range of 200 to 300 and the gap in competitiveness scores within this range is the smallest. The least number of cities are in the 1 to 100 range, accounting for 9.90% of the total, and the gap in competitiveness score is the greatest (see Fig. 3.3).

Table 3.3 Top 10 Asian cities in urban competitiveness

City	Tokyo	Singapore	Hong Kong	Shanghai	Beijing	Seoul	Taipei	Osaka	Dubai	Bangkok
Country	Japan	Singapore	China	China	China	South Korea	China	Japan	UAE	Thailand
Score	0.862	0.770	0.754	0.740	0.683	0.654	0.574	0.555	0.548	0.508
World ranking	3	5	6	7	8	11	25	30	35	51

Source CASS city and competitiveness index database

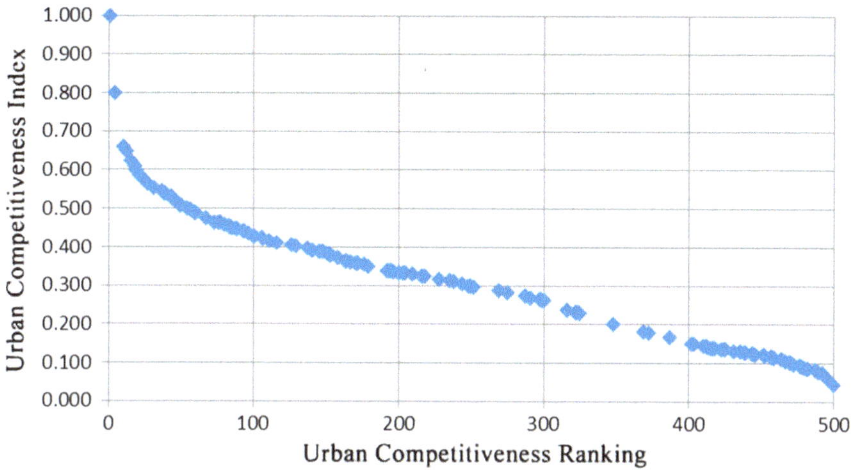

Fig. 3.3 Urban competitiveness ranking distribution in Asia. *Source* CASS city and competitiveness index database

In terms of the distribution of samples cities in different Asian countries, four cities of Mainland China and five from Japan are among the top 100; Korea, in comparison, has only one city in the top rankings, and India has none. Japan has 18.52% of its sample cities ranking in the top 100, the most of all and the highest average score of 0.379, followed by South Korea and Mainland China. This shows that the average competitiveness of Japanese and South Korean cities is higher than that of Mainland Chinese cities. India sees the highest coefficient of variation, which is 0.458, not much higher than the coefficient of Mainland China, Japan or South Korea, meaning that the variation in urban competitiveness is not significant between cities within each of these countries. Japan's most competitive city ranks much higher than the leading cities of the other three countries. The leading cities in Mainland China and South Korea are close in ranking, while the most competitive city in India is 125th in the world rankings. It is clear that the advanced cities in India still has a long way to go before catching up with the leading cities in Asia (see Table 3.4).

3.1.2 Europe: Small Gap Between Advanced Cities, with Russian Cities Lagging far Behind

Among the 136 European sample cities, the top 10 in urban competitiveness (in order of ranking) are London, Paris, Frankfurt, Moscow, Amsterdam, Milan, Dublin, Madrid, Oslo and Vienna. Great Britain, France, Germany and Russia each has one city in the top 10, holding the top four positions. This shows that the urban competitiveness of these countries' advanced cities are in the lead in Europe (see Table 3.5).

Table 3.4 Urban competitiveness distribution of key Asian countries

Country	Sample size	Number (percentage) of cities in top 100	Mean	Coefficient of variation	Maximum		
					City	Score	World ranking
China	61	4 (6.56%)	0.297	0.345	Shanghai	0.740	7
Japan	27	5 (18.52%)	0.379	0.310	Tokyo	0.862	3
South Korea	11	1 (9.09%)	0.340	0.317	Seoul	0.654	11
India	41	0 (0.00%)	0.170	0.458	Mumbai	0.406	125
Regional average	140	10 (7.14%)	0.279	0.448	Tokyo	0.862	3

Source CASS city and competitiveness index database

As we move down the urban competitiveness rankings of Europe, the gap between the competitiveness scores of two adjacent cities first reduces and than grows. This shows that the score gap first narrows and than widens as the urban competitiveness ranking falls. Specifically, as we move down the rankings from 1 to 100, 37 European cities show a score gap of 0.572; from 100 to 200, 32 European cities show a score gap of 0.095; from 200 to 300, 19 European cities show a score gap of 0.073; from 300 to 400, eight European cities show a score gap of 0.095; and from 400 to 505, 40 European cities show a score gap of 0.119. This shows that European cities form a dumbbell-shaped pattern in the world rankings with the greatest number of cities in the first 100 and last 105 cities, 27.21% and 29.41% of all European sample cities respectively, and a lower number of cities in the middle ranges (see Fig. 3.4).

Examining the situation of major countries in Europe, Great Britain has 11 and Germany has six among the top 100, while France and Russia each has one. The country with the highest number of their sample cities in the global urban competitiveness top 100 cities is England, at 68.75%, which means that about two thirds of all British sample cities are at the advanced level of global urban competitiveness. The country with the highest mean urban competitiveness score is also Great Britain, at 0.464, followed by Germany and France. The mean urban competitiveness score of Russia is at a much lower 0.138, far below that of the other three countries. The country with the highest coefficient of variation in the urban competitiveness index is Russia, at 0.678; the country with the lowest coefficient of variation is Germany, at 0.217. This shows that Germany's development is the most balanced among the four countries. The urban competitiveness scores of leading British and French cities are close; so are the sores of the most competitive cities in Germany and Russia. However, the first pair has a large leading edge over the second pair (see Table 3.6).

Table 3.5 Top 10 European cities in urban competitiveness

City	London	Paris	Frankfurt	Moscow	Amsterdam	Milan	Dublin	Madrid	Oslo	Vienna
Country	England	France	Germany	Russia	Netherlands	Italy	Ireland	Spain	Norway	Austria
Score	1.000	0.799	0.661	0.648	0.625	0.609	0.598	0.588	0.586	0.577
World ranking	1	4	10	12	15	18	19	21	22	24

Source CASS city and competitiveness index database

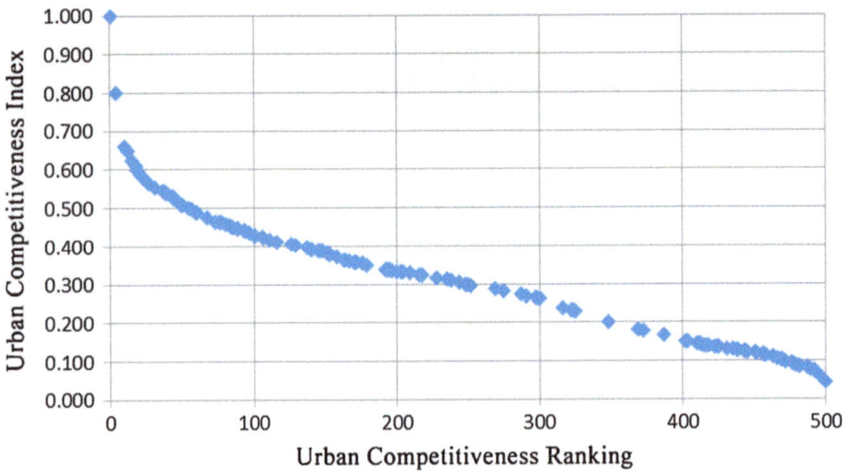

Fig. 3.4 Urban competitiveness ranking distribution in Europe. *Source* CASS city and competitiveness index database

Table 3.6 Urban competitiveness distribution of key European countries

Country	Sample size	Number (percentage) of cities in top 100	Mean	Coefficient of variation	Maximum		
					City	Score	World ranking
Britain	16	11 (68.75%)	0.464	0.326	London	1.000	1
France	8	1 (12.50%)	0.407	0.399	Paris	0.799	4
Germany	16	6 (37.50%)	0.433	0.217	Frankfurt	0.661	10
Russia	47	1 (2.13%)	0.138	0.678	Moscow	0.648	12
Regional average	87	19 (21.84%)	0.277	0.681	London	1.000	1

Source CASS city and competitiveness index database

3.1.3 North America: US Cities Clearly in the Lead, with Small Gaps Within the Region

Among the 107 sample cities of North America, the top 10 cities in urban competitiveness (in order of ranking) are New York, Chicago, Toronto, Los Angeles, Houston, Seattle, San Francisco, Philadelphia, San Jose and Phoenix. Nine of the top 10 cities are in the United States, and the remaining one is from Canada. This shows that the advanced cities in the US have the absolute lead in urban competitiveness in North America (see Table 3.7).

As we move down the urban competitiveness ranking for North America, the decrease in the urban competitiveness index reduced at the beginning before increasing. This shows that the gap between the urban competitiveness of cities has the pattern of reducing at first before increasing as the urban competitiveness ranking falls. Specifically, as we move down the rankings from 1 to 100, 38 North

Table 3.7 Top 10 North American cities in urban competitiveness

City	New York	Chicago	Toronto	Los Angeles	Houston	Seattle	San Francisco	Philadelphia	San Jose	Phoenix
Country	USA	USA	Canada	USA	USA	USA	USA	USA	USA	USA
Index	0.944	0.645	0.627	0.625	0.613	0.594	0.578	0.557	0.557	0.553
World ranking	2	13	14	16	17	20	23	28	29	32

Source CASS city and competitiveness index database

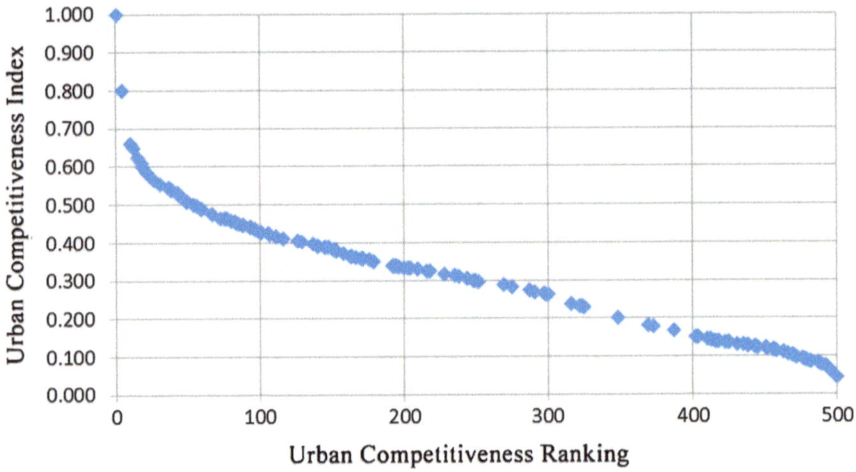

Fig. 3.5 Urban competitiveness ranking distribution in North America. *Source* CASS city and competitiveness index database

American cities show a score gap of 0.507; from 100 to 200, 32 North American cities show a score gap of 0.093; from 200 to 300, 13 North American cities show a score gap of 0.057; from 300 to 400, 18 North American cities show a score gap of 0.097; and from 400 to 505, six North American cities show a score gap of 0.078. This shows that in North America, the greatest number of cities (35.51%) fall within the first 100 in the ranking. The gap in competitiveness within this range is also the greatest. It has the least number of entries among the last 105 cities, accounting for only 5.61% of the total. However, the gap in urban competitiveness between the cities within this range is relatively large (see Fig. 3.5).

Looking at the situation with the major countries in North America, the United States has 35 cities among the top 100 cities in the global urban competitiveness ranking, the most number of cities in the top 100 from any one country; Canada has 3 cities while none of the Mexican cities are in the top 100. The country with the highest number of their sample cities in the global urban competitiveness top 100 cities is the United States, at 53.85%, which means that more than half of the US's sample cities are at the advanced level of global urban competitiveness. The country with the highest mean in the urban competitiveness index is also the US, at 0.459, followed by Canada, at 0.407. The mean of the urban competitiveness index of Mexico is only 0.192 and there exists a wide gap between Mexico and the first 2 countries ahead of it. The country with the highest coefficient of variation in the urban competitiveness index is Mexico, at 0.379; the country with the lowest coefficient of variation is the US, at 0.223. This shows that the US's development is the most balanced among them. The urban competitiveness of the most competitive city in the US is clearly well ahead that of the most competitive city in Canada; the most competitive city in Mexico is only 136th in the global urban competitiveness ranking, far behind the first two countries (see Table 3.8).

Table 3.8 Urban competitiveness distribution of key North American countries

Country	Sample size	Number (percentage) of cities in top 100	Mean	Coefficient of variation	Maximum		
					City	Score	World ranking
USA	65	35 (53.85%)	0.459	0.223	New York	0.944	2
Canada	12	3 (25.00%)	0.407	0.251	Toronto	0.627	14
Mexico	20	0 (0.00%)	0.192	0.379	Mexico City	0.397	136
Regional average	97	38 (39.18%)	0.397	0.361	New York	0.944	2

Source CASS city and competitiveness index database

3.1.4 *Oceania, South America and Africa: Oceania Ahead of the Pack in Southern Hemisphere and South American Cities Fare Slightly Better than African Cities*

Among the 70 sample cities in the Southern Hemisphere of Oceania, South America and Africa, the top 10 cities in urban competitiveness (in order of ranking) are Sydney, Melbourne, Wellington, Brisbane, Auckland (New Zealand), Adelaide, Canberra, Lima, Sao Paulo and Buenos Aires. Five of them are Australian cities and two are from New Zealand. Peru, Brazil and Argentina eave have one city in the top 10. This shows the lead Australian cities have in urban competitiveness among Southern Hemisphere cities (see Table 3.9).

As we move down the urban competitiveness ranking for Southern Hemisphere, the gap in the urban competitiveness scores of different cities first reduce and then grow. This shows that the gap between the urban competitiveness of cities narrows first and then widens as the urban competitiveness ranking falls. Specifically, as we move down the rankings from 1 to 100, six Southern Hemisphere cities show a gap of 0.239; from 100 to 200, eight Southern Hemisphere cities show a gap of 0.056; from 200 to 300, seven Southern Hemisphere cities show a gap of 0.055; from 300 to 400, 26 Southern Hemisphere cities show a gap of 0.103; and from 400 to 505, 23 Southern Hemisphere cities show a gap of 0.097. This shows that in Southern Hemisphere, the least number of cities fall within the first 100 in the ranking, accounting for 8.57% of the total, but the gap in competitiveness within this range is the greatest. The most cities, 37.14% of the total, fall within the 300–400 range, and the gap is also great in this range (see Fig. 3.6).

Looking at the situation with the major countries in Southern Hemisphere, Australia has four cities among the top 100 cities in the global urban competitiveness ranking, while Brazil and South Africa have none. The proportion of Australian sample cities that made it into the top 100 is 66.67%. The country with the highest mean urban competitiveness score is also Australia, at 0.486, followed

Table 3.9 Top 10 Southern Hemisphere cities in urban competitiveness

City	Sydney	Melbourne	Wellington	Brisbane	Auckland	Adelaide	Canberra	Lima	Sao Paulo	Buenos Aires
Country	Australia	Australia	New Zealand	Australia	New Zealand	Australia	Australia	Peru	Brazil	Argentina
Index	0.669	0.565	0.479	0.467	0.464	0.430	0.421	0.421	0.416	0.404
World ranking	9	26	65	70	75	99	109	110	113	128

Source CASS city and competitiveness index database

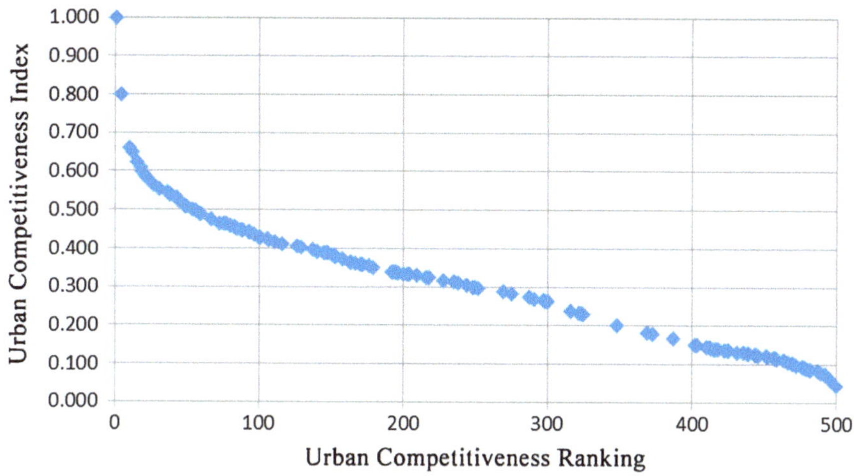

Fig. 3.6 Urban competitiveness ranking distribution in Southern Hemisphere. *Source* CASS city and competitiveness index database

by South Africa, at 0.306; there is a relatively wide gap between Brazil's mean score and the averages of Australia and South Africa. The country with the highest coefficient of variation in the urban competitiveness index is Brazil, at 0.380. This shows that the urban competitiveness of Brazilian cities is relatively low and the gap between them relatively big. The urban competitiveness of the leading city in Australia is way ahead of those of the other two countries, taking the 9th place in the world ranking. The most competitive city in Brazil is 113th in the global urban competitiveness ranking; South Africa's leading city is only 156th (see Table 3.10).

3.2 Relationship Between Economic Development and Urban Competitiveness

Economic development and urban competitiveness are positively correlated and the impact of economic development is greater on the urban competitiveness of larger cities. A city's level of economic development can be measured by its GDP per capita. When we divide the 505 sample cities into groups by GDP per capita[1] and

[1]Separate the 505 sample cities into 5 groups according to GDP per capita from the highest to the lowest. Cities with GDP per capita of more than USD 40,000 shall be Highest Income cities, cities with GDP per capita of more than USD 20,000 and less than USD 40,000 shall be Higher Income cities, cities with GDP per capita of more than USD 7,000 and less than USD 20,000 shall be Mid Income cities, cities with GDP per capita of more than USD 3,000 and less than USD 7,000 shall be Lower Income cities, and cities with GDP per capita of less than USD 3,000 shall be lowest income cities.

Table 3.10 Urban competitiveness distribution of key Southern Hemisphere countries

Country	Sample size	Number (percentage) of cities in top 100	Mean	Coefficient of variation	Maximum		
					City	Score	World ranking
Australia	6	4 (66.67%)	0.486	0.229	Sydney	0.669	9
Brazil	15	0 (0.00%)	0.203	0.380	Sao Paulo	0.416	113
South Africa	4	0 (0.00%)	0.306	0.153	Johannesburg	0.373	156
Regional average	25	4 (16.00%)	0.287	0.501	Sydney	0.669	9

Source CASS city and competitiveness index database

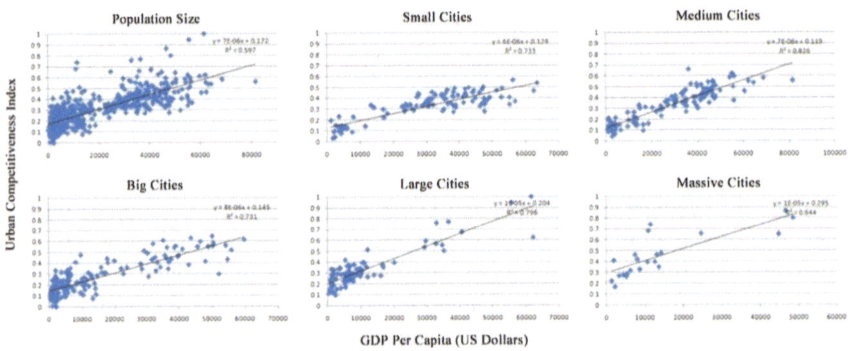

Fig. 3.7 GDP per capita and urban competitiveness index distribution of the population size sub-groups. *Source* CASS city and competitiveness index database

by population size,[2] we find that the GDP per capita of a city is significantly positively correlated to its urban competitiveness, while the population size of a city does not show clear correlation with its competitiveness.

Specifically, as shown in Fig. 3.7, inclusive of all the 505 sample cities, urban competitiveness is continuously growing as GDP per capita increases and the same is true when these cities are divided into groups based on their population size. However, there are obvious differences in the impact on urban competitiveness from the same degree of GDP per capita increase for the different population size sub-groups. It can be seen that as the population size increases, the same increment

[2] Separate the 505 sample cities into 5 groups according to population size from the largest to the smallest. Cities with population size of more than 10 million people shall be Massive cities, cities with population size of more than 3 million and less than 10 million people shall be Large cities, cities with population size of more than 1 million and less than 3 million people shall be Big cities, cities with population size of more than 500,000 and less than 1 million people shall be Medium cities, and cities with population size of less than 500,000 people shall be Small cities.

in GDP per capita brings about greater and greater increase in urban competitiveness, i.e. the effect on urban competitiveness from increasing GDP per capita is continuously increasing.

At the same time, as shown in Fig. 3.8 in groups of different GDP per capita, there are differences in the correlation between the cities' urban competitiveness and GDP per capita. In the low-income and middle-income groups, no significant positive correlation is found between the cities' urban competitiveness and GDP per capita. In lower-income, higher-income, and high-income groups, the positive correlation is more significant.

As shown in Fig. 3.9 for all 505 sample cities, urban competitiveness and population size do not show significant positive correlation. No positive correlation has been found between urban competitiveness and population size in the different groups.

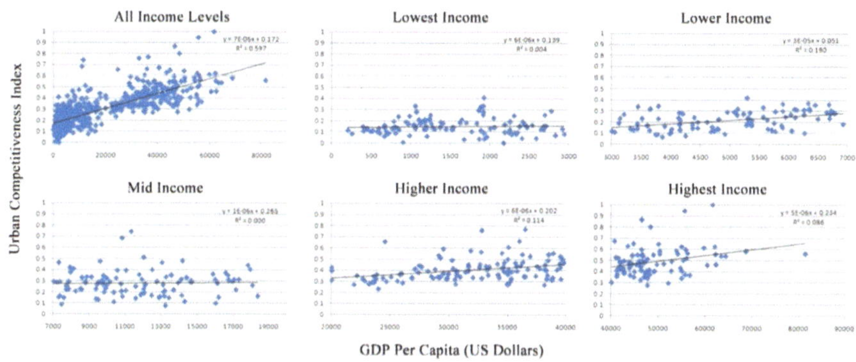

Fig. 3.8 GDP per capita and urban competitiveness index by income groups. *Source* CASS city and competitiveness index database

Fig. 3.9 Population size and urban competitiveness index by population groups. *Source* CASS city and competitiveness index database

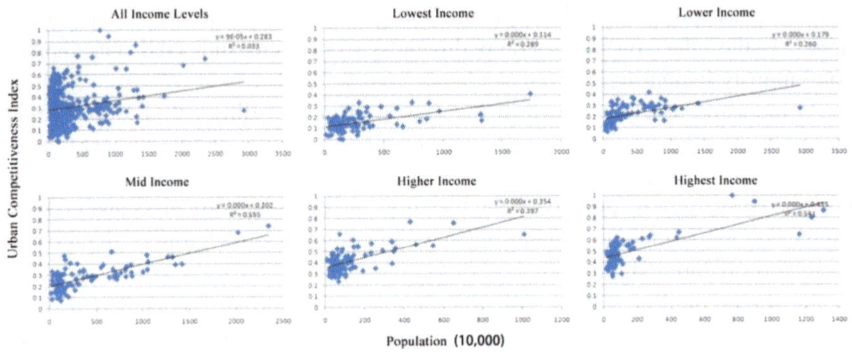

Fig. 3.10 Population size and urban competitiveness index by income groups. *Source* CASS city and competitiveness index database

At the same time, as shown in Fig. 3.10 in different GDP per capita sub-groups, there are some signs of positive correlation between urban competitiveness and GDP per capita. This shows that the cities' population size and urban competitiveness are positively correlated only when the cities' income levels are close.

3.3 Urban Competitiveness is a Composite of Economic Scale and Density

Urban competitiveness reflects trade competition between cities and more importantly, competition of economic scale between cities. A city's GDP shows how much resources the city attracts and uses and how much value it creates in the market. The former reflects the economies of scale and economies of scope of a city's production, while the latter reflects more of the city's economies of scale and economies of scope in consumption. As the city continues to expand in these two areas, the residents of the cities are able to obtain greater benefits from the economies of scale and economies of scope in the areas of production and consumption, thus enhancing the welfare of city residents. Urban competitiveness is the ability of a city to provide welfare for its residents. Therefore, a city's GDP is an important part of its urban competitiveness.

A city's GDP reflects the size of its economies of scale and economies of scope, while GDP per capita embodies the density of the city's economies of scale and economies of scope. Competitive between cities occurs in unmovable land areas and spaces. The unmovable location is where the city truly exists. The density of a location's economies of scale and economies of scope is the best reflection of the location's competitiveness, and it is also where there are differences in competition for spaces between locations (city, region) and between companies and people. The GDP per unit of land area of a city reflects the economic rent and returns, as

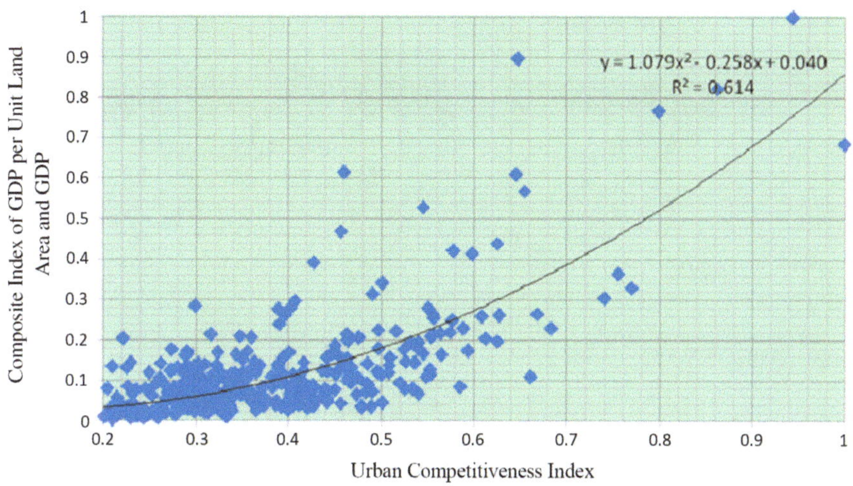

Fig. 3.11 Correlation between urban competitiveness index and the composite index of GDP per unit land area and GDP of 505 sample cities. *Source* CASS city and competitiveness index database

well as the city's efficiency of land use, which also reflects the city's density and efficiency of wealth creation and accumulation. As such, a city's GDP per unit land area reflects the relative size of the city's economies of scale and economies of scope in spatial terms, and therefore, it also shows the relative efficiency of the city in the provision of welfare for its residents. Therefore, a city's GDP per unit land area is also an important part of its urban competitiveness (Pengfei 2013).

The composite index of GDP and GDP per unit land area is derived by standardizing GDP and GDP per unit land area and adding the two after giving them equal weights. The method of standardization is the same as that used in the calculation of the urban competitiveness index.

Figure 3.11 shows significant positive correlation between the urban competitiveness index of the 505 sample cities and the composite index of GDP and GDP per unit land area during 2013–2014. The consistency between the two is also seen in Fig. 3.12.

Night lights reflect the economic prosperity of a place to a great extent, and therefore, can be used as a frame of reference for urban competitiveness. Figure 3.13 is an image of the world distribution of night lights (2012) released by the National Aeronautics and Space Administration (NASA) of the United States. By comparing the image with the above figures, we can see that the world distribution of urban competitiveness and the world distribution of the composite index of GDP and GDP per unit land area during 2013 to 2014 are pretty much consistent with the world distribution of night lights. This confirms that the urban competitiveness index and the composite index of GDP and GDP per unit land area during 2013 to 2014 are relatively accurate depictions of global urban competitiveness.

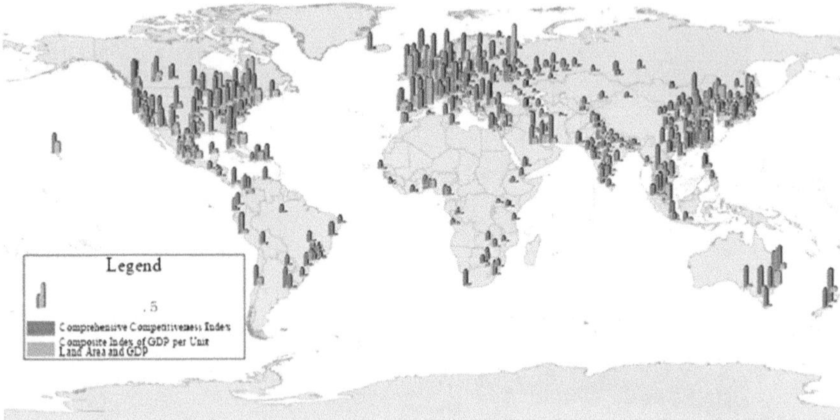

Fig. 3.12 Distribution of urban competitiveness index and composite index of GDP per unit land area and GDP of 505 sample cities. *Source* CASS city and competitiveness index database

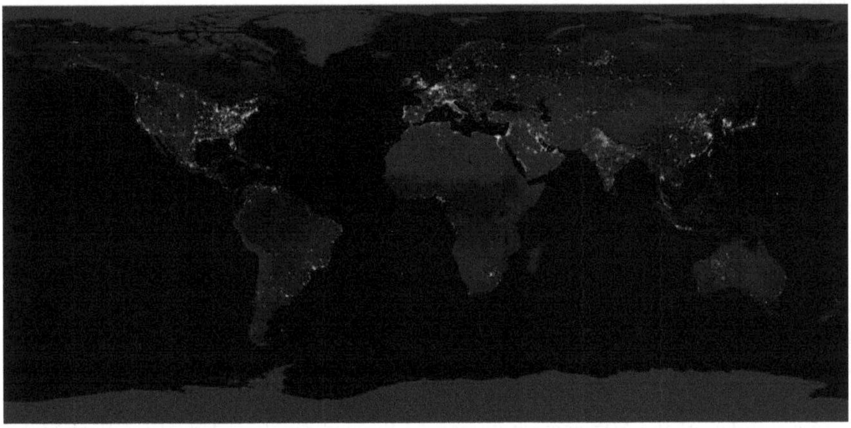

Fig. 3.13 World Distribution of Night Lights (2012). *Source* NASA (http://visibleearth.nasa.gov)

In summary, after theoretical analysis on the correlation between urban competitiveness, GDP and GDP per unit land area, as well as analysis on the correlation between urban competitiveness index and the composite index of GDP and GDP per unit land area, a comparison was made between the world distribution of these two indicators and the world distribution of night lights. Based on all these, we come to the conclusion that urban competitiveness index is reflective of the actual competitiveness of cities around the world and that urban competitiveness is a composite of a city's GDP and GDP per unit land area.

Chapter 4
Global Urban Competitiveness: Comparative Analysis from Different Perspectives

4.1 Comparison of the Top 100

In general, London is the strongest in terms of overall competitiveness and on all lower-level indicators. Cities from Asia constitute half of the global top 10, but there are fewer of them in the global top 50 and they are missing from the middle to high rankings. Looking at the population size and GDP, the variations among the first 100 cities is greater and the dispersion more scattered than the cities ranked lower than 100. Mega cities concentrate in the Asia Pacific. Aside from Singapore in Southeast Asia, all the other five mega cities are in East Asia.

The top 10 cities in the global rankings include five cities from Asia, two from Europe, two from North America, and one from Oceania. The first three cities in the global ranking (in order of ranking) are from Britain (London), the United States (New York) and Japan (Tokyo). There are three Chinese cities in the top 10 and they are Hong Kong, Shanghai and Beijing, ranked 6th, 7th and 8th respectively. The United States, Germany, Britain, France, Japan, Australia and Singapore have one city each in the top 10. London is the strongest performer in the overall competitiveness rankings as well as by all lower-level indicators. Among the six competitiveness level-2 indicators, London tops the cities globally in the areas of company strength, local elements, institutional environment and global connection. It is also among the top cities for the other two indicators, i.e. local demand and material environment. Specifically, London is No. 1 in terms of the number of multinational corporations, industry structure, financial services, multiculturalism, natural geographic location and economic ties, and is among the top cities in the world in environmental quality, reputation, ease of doing business, per capita income, GDP, population and higher education.

Among the cities ranked 11th to 20th, there are four cities from Europe, i.e. Milan in Italy, Moscow in Russia, Dublin in Ireland, and Amsterdam in Netherlands; there is only one city from Asia, i.e. Seoul from South Korea; there are five cities from North America, i.e. Chicago, Los Angeles, Houston and Seattle

© China Social Sciences Press and Springer Nature Singapore Pte Ltd. 2017

P. Ni et al., *Cities Network Along the Silk Road*,
DOI 10.1007/978-981-10-4834-0_4

Table 4.1 Competitiveness of top 100 cities versus remaining sample cities

Indicator	Ranking	Mean	Standard deviation	Coefficient of variation
Urban competitiveness	1–100	0.5379	0.1060	0.1971
	101–500	0.2462	0.1062	0.4315
GDP	1–100	85,586	120,447	1.4073
	101–500	19,228	23,685	1.2318
GDP per capita	0–100	419	132	0.315
	101–500	141	145	1.0284
Population	1–100	2,644,266	4,190,689	1.5848
	101–500	2,393,835	3,146,162	1.3143

Source CASS city and competitiveness index database

from the United States, and Toronto from Canada. Overall, with the exception of the four cities from the US, other countries only have one city each in the 11–20 range. China does not have any city in this range. In the 21–50 range of the global rankings, there are three cities from Asia and one from Oceania, losing out in terms of numbers compared to the 12 cities from Europe and 14 from North America. The three Asian cities are Taipei, Dubai and Osaka; the city from Oceania is Melbourne; the 13 European cities include three from Germany (Berlin, Munich and Hamburg) and only one city each from the other countries; among the 14 cities in North America, 10 are US cities and the other two are from Canada (Vancouver and Montreal).

Looking at the urban competitiveness of the top 500 global cities (see Table 4.1), the urban competitiveness mean and coefficient of variation of the top 100 cities are 0.5379 and 0.1971 respectively; the urban competitiveness mean and coefficient of variation of cities ranking 101st to 500th are 0.2462 and 0.4315 respectively. This shows that the urban competitiveness gap and dispersion between the cities ranked lower than 100 are relatively large. In addition, looking at the GDP of the 500 cities in the global urban competitiveness rankings, the GDP mean and coefficient of variation of the top 100 cities are 85,586 and 1.4073; the GDP mean and coefficient of variation of cities ranking 101st to 500th are 19,228 and 1.2318. This shows that the gap and dispersion in GDP between the cities in the top 100 cities are relatively large. Looking at the GDP per capita of cities ranking 101st to 500th in the global urban competitiveness rankings, the GDP per capita mean and coefficient of variation of the top 100 cities are 419 and 0.315; the GDP per capita mean and coefficient of variation of cities ranking 101st to 500th are 141 and 1.0284. This shows that the GDP per capita gap and dispersion are relatively large between the cities ranked below the top 100. Looking at the overall population of the first 500 cities in the global urban competitiveness rankings, the overall population mean and coefficient of variation of the top 100 cities are 2,644,266 and 1.5848; the overall population mean and coefficient of variation of cities ranking 101st to 500th are 2,393,835 and 1.3143. This shows that the overall population gap and dispersion are relatively large between the top 100 cities.

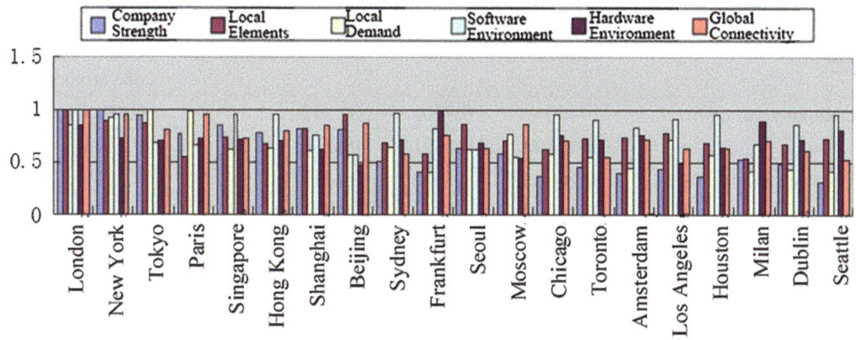

Fig. 4.1 Top 20 most competitive global cities. Source CASS city and competitiveness index database

Among the top 100 cities in the global rankings, the number of entries from Asia and Oceania is far lower than that from Europe and North America; and South America does not have a single city in the top 100. There are 19 cities from Asia, among which seven are from China, five are from Japan and the remaining seven are from seven different countries. There are 38 North American cities, predominantly from the United States, 37 European cities and six Oceanian cities. Out of the six Oceanian cities, four are from Australia, namely Sydney, Melbourne, Brisbane and Adelaide, and the two of Auckland and Wellington are from New Zealand.

Looking at the lower-level indicators of urban competitiveness of the 20 most competitive cities globally (see Fig. 4.1), the top performers in company strength are London, New York and Tokyo, and the worst performers are Chicago, Houston and Seattle; the top performers in local elements are London and Beijing, and the worst performers are Paris and Milan; the top performers in local demand are Tokyo and Paris, and the worst performers are Milan and Frankfurt; the top performers in institutional environment are London and Sydney, and the worst performers are Beijing and Moscow; the top performers in hardware environment are Frankfurt and Milan, and the worst performers are Los Angeles and Beijing; the top performers in global connection are London and Paris, and the worst performers are Toronto and Seattle. London has the best overall performance on these indicators, followed by Tokyo and New York. In addition, among the top 100 cities globally (see Table 4.2), the mean values of institutional environment and hardware environment are the highest, while the mean values of company strength and local demand are the lowest; the coefficients of variation of global connection and company strength are the highest, while the coefficients of variation of institutional environment and hardware environment are the lowest. Among cities ranked below 100, the mean values of institutional environment and hardware environment are the highest, while the mean values of company strength and global connection are the lowest; the coefficients of variation of global connection and company strength are the highest, while the coefficients of variation of local demand and hardware environment are the lowest. Overall, the coefficients of variation of the six

Table 4.2 Top 100 cities by level-2 indicators

Indicator	Ranking	Mean	Standard deviation	Coefficient of variation
Company strength	1–100	0.3701	0.1812	0.4896
	101–500	0.1491	0.0860	0.5768
Local elements	1–100	0.5960	0.1317	0.221
	101–500	0.3254	0.1471	0.4521
Local demand	1–100	0.4656	0.1369	0.2940
	101–500	0.2913	0.087	0.2987
Software environment	1–100	0.8076	0.1146	0.1419
	101–500	0.5085	0.1870	0.3677
Hardware environment	1–100	0.7012	0.0983	0.1402
	101–500	0.5833	0.1401	0.2402
Global connection	1–100	0.5240	0.1618	0.3088
	101–500	0.2091	0.1244	0.595

Source CASS city and competitiveness index database

lower-level indicators of the top 100 cities are all lower than those of the cities ranked below 100. This shows that the gap and dispersion of the urban competitiveness sub-items between the cities below 100 are relatively large.

4.2 Regional Perspective: Top 20 Cities in Asia

The countries with the most number of competitive cities in Asia are China and Japan; the distribution of top cities within Asia is quite balanced in that every country has its own first class city.

Among the top 20 cities in Asia, seven are from China, the most number from any Asian country. Japan has six cities and comes second among all the countries in Asia. This is consistent with the Asian rankings of economic aggregate. The other seven cities (in order of ranking) are Singapore, South Korea, UAE, Thailand, Malaysia, Turkey and Israel. Each of these countries has one city among the top 20 in Asia. The economic aggregate of India is the 3rd largest in Asia, but none of its cities has made it into the top 20 of Asia. This is somewhat inconsistent with its economic strength. Overall, a large proportion of the world's most competitive cities are in Asia. The distribution of the top Asian cities within the region is relatively balanced; every country has its own first class city. These two aspects reflect the changes in the world situation, i.e. first class cities no longer cluster in a few mature economies.

In terms of geographical distribution, the top 20 Asian cities are mainly located in East Asia, Southeast Asia and West Asia (see Table 4.3). There are no cities from South Asia in the Asian top 20, and the greatest contributor of cities in this ranking is East Asia, with a total of 14 cities. Southeast Asia has three entries namely,

Table 4.3 Geographical distribution of top 20 cities of Asia

Ranking	City	Region	Ranking	City	Region
1	Tokyo	East Asia	11	Yokohama	East Asia
2	Singapore	Southeast Asia	12	Shenzhen	East Asia
3	Hong Kong	East Asia	13	Kuala Lumpur	Southeast Asia
4	Shanghai	East Asia	14	Kyoto	East Asia
5	Beijing	East Asia	15	Guangzhou	East Asia
6	Seoul	East Asia	16	Istanbul	West Asia
7	Taipei	East Asia	17	Macao	East Asia
8	Osaka	East Asia	18	Tel Aviv	West Asia
9	Dubai	West Asia	19	Fukuoka	East Asia
10	Bangkok	Southeast Asia	20	Nagoya	East Asia

Source CASS city and competitiveness index database

Table 4.4 Comparative analysis of top 20 cities of Asia

	Southeast Asia	West Asia	East Asia	China	Japan
Mean	0.5836	0.4864	0.5755	0.5925	0.5425
Standard deviation	0.1323	0.0438	0.1343	0.1225	0.1488
Minimum	0.4732	0.4507	0.4270	0.4564	0.4270
Maximum	0.7695	0.5482	0.8617	0.7544	0.8617
Coefficient of variation	0.2267	0.0901	0.2334	0.2068	0.2743

Source CASS city and competitiveness index database

Singapore, Bangkok and Kuala Lumpur. West Asia also has three, namely, Dubai, Istanbul and Tel Aviv.

With reference to Table 4.4, the highest urban competitiveness mean is seen in Southeast Asia, followed by East Asia, and then West Asia. This means that the urban competitiveness of cities in Southeast Asia is generally higher and competitiveness of West Asian cities is lower in comparison. The rankings by the coefficient of variation from the largest to smallest are South East Asia, East Asia and West Asia. This shows that the disparity between the cities in Southeast Asia is larger, whereas that between West Asian cities are smaller. In addition, the urban competitiveness mean of Japanese cities is lower compared to that of Chinese cities; the urban competitiveness coefficient of variation of Japanese cities is greater than that of Chinese cities. This shows that the urban competitiveness of Japanese cities are comparatively lower than that of Chinese cities, and the gap between them is also greater, meaning that the urban competitiveness dispersion of Japanese cities is greater than that of Chinese cities.

The top 20 most competitive cities in Asia are ranked among the top 104 cities in the global rankings, the last of them being Nagoya of Japan, ranked 104th on the list. The other 19 cities at the top of the Asian competitiveness rankings are all within the top 100 of the world. The top city in Asia, Tokyo, has a high position on the global rankings, coming in 3rd. There are six Asian cities that are ranked alongside the top cities of Europe and North America within the top 11 positions in the global rankings, and they are Tokyo, Singapore, Shanghai, Hong Kong, Beijing and Seoul. It can be seen that mega cities in the world now tend to concentrate in the Asia Pacific. Aside from Singapore in Southeast Asia, the other five cities are all in East Asia, which is further evidence of the changes in the world situation, i.e. first class cities are no longer clustered in a few mature economies.

Among the six level-2 indicators of urban competitiveness, the top 20 Asian cities show good performance on three: company strength, institutional environment and hardware environment. Their performance on the other three indicators, local elements, local demand and global connection, is not as good. Specifically (see Fig. 4.2), the Asian city with the strongest performance in company strength is Tokyo, followed by Singapore and Shanghai, and the worst performers are Macao, Nagoya and Kyoto. The Asian cities with the strongest performance in local elements are Beijing and Tokyo; the Asian city with the best performance in local demand is Tokyo. The performance of the other cities on these two indicators is not as good. The Asian cities with the strongest performance in institutional environment are Singapore and Hong Kong, and the worst performers are Guangzhou and Istanbul. The Asian cities with the strongest performance in hardware environment are Macao, Dubai and Kyoto, and the worst performers are Istanbul and Beijing. The Asian cities with the strongest performance in global connection are Beijing, Shanghai and Tokyo, and the worst performers are Fukuoka and Nagoya. In addition, looking at GDP of the top 20 Asian cities, the top spot is taken by Tokyo, followed by Shanghai and Seoul; the cities on the lower end are Tel Aviv, Macao and Kuala Lumpur. Looking at GDP per capita, the top spots are taken by Nagoya, Tokyo and Dubai; the cities on the lower end are Beijing, Kuala Lumpur and Istanbul. In general, there is only one Asian city that is performing well across all the six indicators, GDP per capita and GDP, that is, Tokyo.

4.3 China versus the United States: Top 10 Cities

The development of cities is batter balanced in the United States than in China. China is similar to the US in its distribution of cities across three main regions, i.e. the Yangtze River Delta, the Pearl River Delta and the Beijing-Tianjin-Hebei region.

What we have found, from looking at the characteristics of the top 10 cities in China and the United States, is that the top 10 US cities are all among the top 40 of the global urban competitiveness rankings, whereas the top 10 Chinese cities are more dispersed across the rankings-three of them are in the top 10, seven in the top 100, and the other three are ranked below 100 in global urban competitiveness. In comparison, the top city of the US has greater urban competitiveness than the top city of China, while the second and third cities of China rank higher than the second and third cities of the US. Other than that, the other cities in the US top 10 have

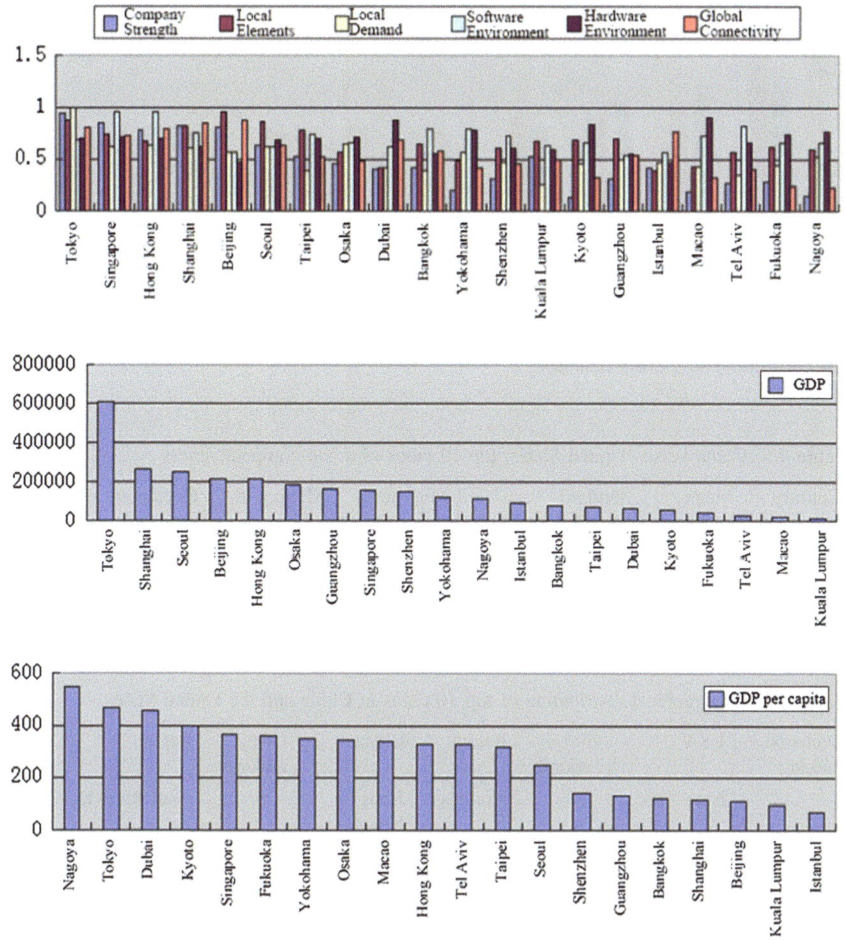

Fig. 4.2 Level-2 indicators, GDP and GDP per capita of the top 20 cities of Asia. Source: CASS city and competitiveness index database

greater urban competitiveness than the corresponding cities in China (see Fig. 4.3). In general (see Table 4.5), the average competitiveness of the top 10 US cities is 0.6217, which is evidently greater than the 0.5311 average competitiveness of the top 10 Chinese cities. In addition, the competitiveness coefficient of variation of the top 10 US cities is 0.1798, which is lower than China's 0.2619. This means that the gap between the competitiveness of these 10 Chinese cities is larger than that among the top 10 US cities.

As can be seen from the spatial distribution of the top 10 cities in China and the United States (see Table 4.6), the top 10 cities of the US are mainly located in the three main industrial regions of the country-Northeast, West and South. Out of the 10 cities, three are in the Northeast, and they are (in order of ranking) New York,

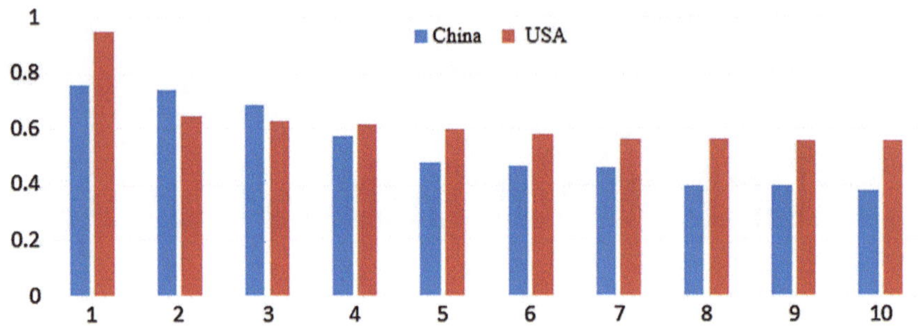

Fig. 4.3 China versus the United States: top 10 cities in urban competitiveness. *Source* CASS city and competitiveness index database

Table 4.5 China versus United States: top 10 cities in urban competitiveness

Country	Mean	Standard deviation	Minimum	Maximum	Coefficient of variation
USA	0.6217	0.1118	0.5526	0.9436	0.1798
China	0.5311	0.1391	0.3740	0.7544	0.2619

Source Chinese Academy of Social Sciences and the competitiveness index database

Table 4.6 Geographical distribution of top 10 cities in China and the United States

Domestic ranking	USA	Global ranking	Region	China	Global ranking	Region
1	New York	2	Northeast	Hong Kong	6	Pearl River Delta
2	Chicago	13	Northeast	Shanghai	7	Yangtze River Delta
3	Los Angeles	16	West	Beijing	8	Beijing-Tianjin-Hebei
4	Houston	17	South	Taipei	25	Other
5	Seattle	20	West	Shenzhen	66	Pearl River Delta
6	San Francisco	23	West	Guangzhou	74	Pearl River Delta
7	Philadelphia	28	Northeast	Macao	81	Pearl River Delta
8	San Jose	29	Other	Tianjin	138	Beijing-Tianjin-Hebei
9	Phoenix	32	Other	Hangzhou	139	Yangtze River Delta
10	Dallas	33	South	Dongguan	154	Pearl River Delta

Source Chinese Academy of Social Sciences and the competitiveness index database

Chicago and Philadelphia; three are in the West, and they are (in order of ranking) Los Angeles, Seattle and San Francisco; and two are in the South, and they are (in order of ranking) Houston and Dallas. The top 10 cities of China are located mainly in the three regions of the Pearl River Delta, the Beijing-Tianjin-Hebei region and the Yangtze River Delta. The largest number of top 10 Chinese cities can be found

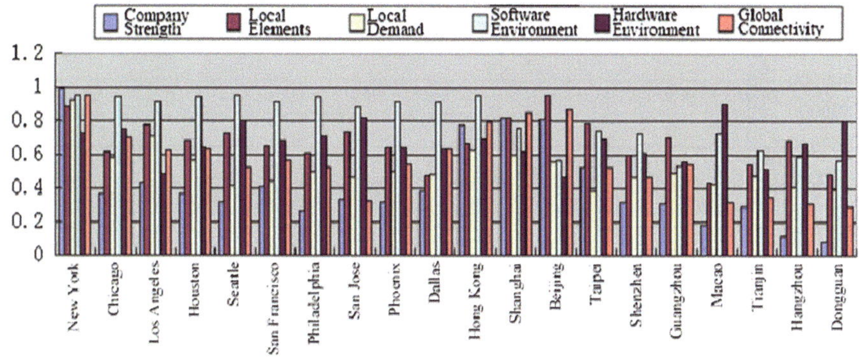

Fig. 4.4 China versus the United States top 10 cities sub-indicators. *Source* CASS city and competitiveness index database

in the Pearl River Delta. There are five in this region and they are (in order of ranking) Hong Kong, Shenzhen, Guangzhou, Macao and Dongguan. Two cities are in the Beijing-Tianjin-Hebei region and they are (in order of ranking) Beijing and Tianjin. The other two cities are in the Yangtze River Delta and they are Shanghai and Hangzhou. In general, among the three regions with the top 10 US cities in urban competitiveness, the Northeast has the strongest performance, followed by the West, and the South coming in 3rd; among the four regions with the top 10 Chinese cities in urban competitiveness, the Pearl River Delta has the strongest performance, followed by the Yangtze River Delta, and the Beijing-Tianjin-Hebei region coming in 3rd.

As shown in Fig. 4.4, New York is the top performer among the top 10 cities of China and the US in urban competitiveness. Among the six level-2 indicators it is top in company strength, local demand and global connection. Specifically, the three strongest performers in company strength are New York, Shanghai and Beijing, and the three worst performers are Macao, Hangzhou and Dongguan; the three strongest performers in local elements are Beijing, New York and Shanghai, and the three worst performers are Dongguan, Dallas, and Macao; the three strongest performers in local demand are New York, Los Angeles and Hong Kong, and the three worst performers are Hangzhou, Dongguan and Taipei; the three strongest performers in institutional environment are Hong Kong, Seattle and New York, and the three worst performers are Beijing, Dongguan and Guangzhou; the three strongest performers in Hardware Environment are Macao, San Jose and Dongguan, and the three worst performers are Tianjin, Los Angeles and Beijing; the three strongest performers in global connection are New York, Beijing and Shanghai, and the three worst performers are Macao, Hangzhou and Dongguan. In general, China lags behind in the area of institutional environment while having an advantage in the areas of company strength and local elements. With the exception of New York, US cities lag behind in local elements, and in contrast to China, US cities are relatively strong in institutional environment.

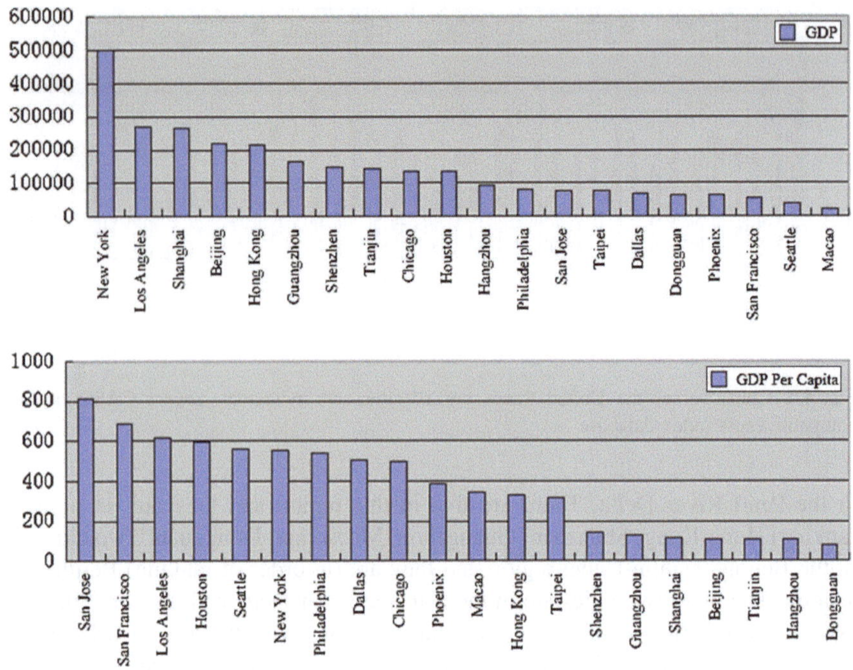

Fig. 4.5 China versus United States top 10 Cities in GDP and GDP per capita. *Source* CASS city and competitiveness index database

As shown in Fig. 4.5, the GDP per capita of US cities is generally higher than that of Chinese cities among the top 10 in urban competitiveness. The US city with the highest GDP per capita is San Jose, followed by San Francisco and Los Angeles, and the city with the lowest GDP per capita is Phoenix; the Chinese city with the highest GDP per capita is Macao, followed by Hong Kong and Taipei, and the cities with the lowest GDP per capita are Tianjin, Hangzhou and Dongguan. In addition, the GDP of Chinese cities are generally higher than that of US cities when comparing the top 10 of the two countries. In the rankings of cities based on GDP, US cities, New York and Los Angeles, head the list, followed by six Chinese cities close behind, namely Shanghai, Beijing, Hong Kong, Guangzhou, Shenzhen and Tianjin. A city with good overall performance in both GDP per capita and GDP is Los Angeles.

4.4 Political Centers: Competitiveness of Capital Cities

Generally, countries with larger land areas tend to have separate political and economic centers and history shows that when the functions of a capital city move away from what is required of a capital city, is usually cease being the capital city.

Table 4.7 Urban competitiveness of global capital cities

Capital	Global ranking	Domestic ranking	Capital	Global ranking	Domestic ranking
London	1	1	Riyadh	35	1
Tokyo	2	1	Lisbon	36	1
Paris	3	1	Warsaw	37	1
Singapore	4	1	Reykjavik	38	1
Beijing	5	3	Kiev	39	1
Seoul	6	1	Bogota	40	1
Moscow	7	1	Panama City	41	1
Amsterdam	8	1	Ankara	42	2
Dublin	9	1	Manila	43	1
Madrid	10	2	Delhi	44	3
Oslo	11	1	Pretoria	45	4
Vienna	12	1	Cairo	46	1
Stockholm	13	1	Hanoi	47	2
Copenhagen	14	1	La Paz	48	1
Washington	15	14	Minsk	49	1
Berlin	16	2	Beirut	50	1
Helsinki	17	1	Caracas	51	1
Rome	18	2	Damascus	52	1
Bangkok	19	1	Kingston	53	1
Brussels	20	1	Brasilia	54	3
Wellington	21	1	Tunis	55	1
Kuala Lumpur	22	1	Havana	56	1
Tel Aviv	23	1	Islamabad	57	2
Budapest	24	1	Tripoli	58	1
Ottawa	25	4	Tehran	59	1
Canberra	26	5	Rabat	60	2
Lima	27	1	Djibouti City	61	1
Prague	28	1	Tashkent	62	1
Doha	29	1	Nairobi	63	1
Kuwait	30	1	Port-au-Prince	64	1
Buenos Aires	31	1	Dushanbe	65	1
Mexico City	32	1	Ulaanbaatar	66	1
Athens	33	1	Phnom Penh	67	1
Santiago	34	1			

Source CASS city and competitiveness index database

There are some characteristics in the urban competitiveness of capital cities highlighted in Table 4.7. Capital cities top the domestic urban competitiveness rankings for the majority of countries. Among the 68 capital cities listed, only 13 are not the highest-ranking city of their respective country. Among these 13 capital cities, six are 2nd namely, Berlin, Rome, Ankara, Hanoi, Rabat and Islamabad; three rank 3rd, namely Beijing, New Delhi and Brasilia; two rank 4th namely Pretoria and Ottawa; and the urban competitiveness of the remaining two capital cities are ranked 5th and 14th respectively in their own countries, and they are Canberra and Washington.

In summary, the urban competitiveness of capital cities in Europe tends to place them higher up in rankings, followed by capital cities in Asia. The top capital city in Asia is Tokyo; the top capital city in Europe is London; the top capital city in North America is Washington; the top capital city in South America is Lima; the top capital city in Oceania is Wellington; the top capital city in Africa is Pretoria. Among the top 10 capital cities in urban competitiveness, Europe has the greatest number of capital cities, with as many as six cities; Asia comes second in terms of the number of cities, with four cities in the top 10; the other continents have no city in the top 10. Among the capital cities ranked 11–20 in urban competitiveness, Europe has the greatest number of capital cities too, with a total of eight cities; Asia and North America have one city each in this range. Among the capital cities ranked 21–30 in urban competitiveness, Asia has the greatest number of capital cities, with a total of four cities; Europe and Oceania have two cities each in this range; South America and North America have one city each in this range.

In most countries, the political center is also the economic center; however, a political center may not always be an economic center. Examples include China, United States, Canada, India, Brazil and Australia. China's political center is Beijing while its economic centers are Shanghai, Hong Kong and Shenzhen; the United States' economic centers are New York, Los Angeles and Chicago, while its political center is Washington; Canada's economic centers are Toronto and Vancouver, while its political center is Ottawa; India's economic centers are Mumbai and Kolkata, while its political center is New Delhi; Brazil's economic centers are Sao Paulo and Rio de Janeiro, while its political center is Brasilia; Australia's economic centers are Melbourne and Sydney, while its political center is Canberra, located between these two cities. In addition, there are also countries like Switzerland, which has its capital at Bern, while its economic center is Zurich, Switzerland's largest city, and Geneva, a city renowned for hosting international conferences, is Switzerland's 3rd largest city; Germany's political center is Berlin, while its economic center is Frankfurt; Italy's political center is Rome, while its economic center is Milan; Pakistan's administrative capital is Islamabad, while its economic center is Karachi; Turkey's capital is Ankara while its economic center is Istanbul; Nigeria's capital is Abuja, while its economic center is Lagos; Kazakhstan's capital is Astana, while its economic center is Almaty; Vietnam's capital is Hanoi, while its economic center is Ho Chi Minh City; Myanmar's capital is Naypyidaw, while its economic center is Yangon; New Zealand's capital is Wellington, while its economic center is Auckland; Cameroon's capital is Yaounde, while its economic center is Douala; South Africa's administrative capital is Pretoria, its judicial capital is Bloemfontein, the legislative capital is Cape Town, and its economic center is Johannesburg; UAE's capital is Abu Dhabi, while its economic center is Dubai; Morocco's capital is Rabat, while its economic center is Casablanca. In general, with the exception of Russia, countries with larger land areas typically do not have capitals that also function as economic centers, i.e. the economic centers and political centers of countries with larger land areas are usually separate, and examples include China, United States, Canada, Brazil, India, Nigeria, South Africa, Australia, Pakistan and Kazakhstan. There does not seem to be any such rules for the economic and political centers of countries with smaller land areas. Some have one center, e.g. Britain, France, Japan and South Korea; whereas others have separate centers, e.g. Myanmar, Vietnam, Switzerland, Germany, Italy and New Zealand.

Judging from the history of world cities, capitals are usually relocated whenever there are conflicts between what is required of a capital city and the functions of the city serving as capital. In the more than 200 years since the 18th century, a third of the countries in the world have seen the relocation of their capital cities. For example, India relocated its capital from Kolkata to New Delhi, Kazakhstan from Almaty to Astana, Turkey from Istanbul to Ankara, Myanmar from Yangon to Naypyidaw, and Nigeria from Lagos to Abuja. Other prominent examples of capital relocation can be found in Brazil's Brasilia and Pakistan's Islamabad. Another way of resolving the conflict between capital functions and city development is to put all political functions in a dedicated capital city, such as Washington of the United States, Ottawa of Canada, and Canberra of Australia. Beijing is also currently facing such conflicts but its resolution is to relocate the city rather than the capital, i.e. relocating non-capital functions away from the city center and freeing up more space for capital functions. This is done by relocating the municipal administrative organizations of Beijing to the eastern fringes of the city, in the hope of moving non-capital functions out and ultimately reducing the population, economic activities and transportation pressures of the city center.

As shown in Fig. 4.6, it has been found in the comparative analysis of the top 20 global capital cities in urban competitiveness that the strongest performer in company strength is London, followed by Tokyo and Singapore, and the worst

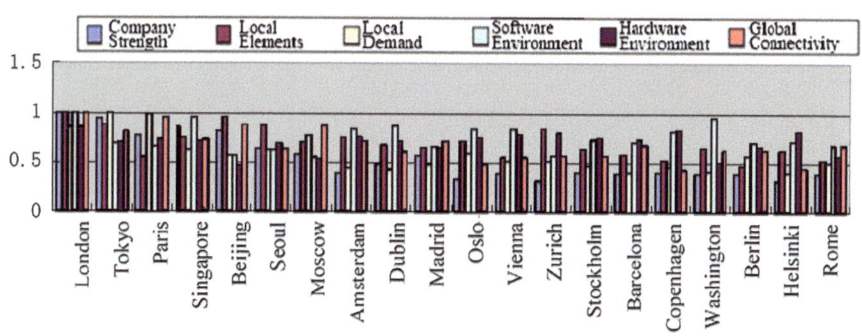

Fig. 4.6 Performance of capital cities on level-2 indicators. Source CASS city and competitiveness index database

performer is Zurich; the strongest performer in local elements is Tokyo, and the worst performer is Dublin; the strongest performers in local demand are Tokyo and Paris, and the worst performer is Washington; the strongest performer in institutional environment is London, followed by Singapore and Dublin, and the worst performer is Moscow; the strongest performer in hardware environment is London, and the worst performers are Mexico City and Beijing; the strongest performer in global connection is London, followed by Paris and Singapore, and the worst performer is Mexico City. In general, the capital city with the strongest performance across the six indicators is London.

Chapter 5
Global Urban Competitiveness: Comparative Analysis of Level-2 Indicators

5.1 Company Strength

Companies are the performers of urban activities on the microscopic level. When companies of the same kind or on the same value chain gather at specific locations, industrial clusters take shape. The business performance of companies is the most direct reflection of a city's industrial and commercial conditions, and the nature of the groups of industries formed is reflective of the economic characteristics and quality of the cities in that region. The economic value created by companies and industries is what makes urban development possible. Therefore, companies and industries play an important part in urban competitiveness. The company strength index is constructed from four lower-level indicators: Total number of multinational corporations (measurement of company scale), Forbes Global 2000 Index (measurement of company quantity), industrial structure and industrial quality. These indicators are used in the examination of the overall standard of a city's companies and industrial development.

5.1.1 Summary of Company Strength Index

5.1.1.1 Overall Pattern: Low Company Strength Index and Significant Gaps Between Cities; Major Cities Clearly in the Lead With Most Cities Below World Average

According to the company strength rankings, the top 3 cities are London, New York and Tokyo. Among the top 10 cities, six are Asian cities, three are European cities and one is a North American city. There are no cities from South America, Oceania or Africa in the global top 10. From a national point of view, China is the country with the most number of cities in the top 10, with Shanghai, Beijing and Hong

© China Social Sciences Press and Springer Nature Singapore Pte Ltd. 2017

P. Ni et al., *Cities Network Along the Silk Road*,
DOI 10.1007/978-981-10-4834-0_5

Table 5.1 Global company strength index top 10 cities

City	London	New York	Tokyo	Singapore	Shanghai	Beijing	Hong Kong	Paris	Seoul	Moscow
Continent	Europe	North America	Asia	Asia	Asia	Asia	Asia	Europe	Asia	Europe
Score	1	0.990	0.947	0.840	0.816	0.813	0.776	0.773	0.635	0.577
Ranking	1	2	3	4	5	6	7	8	9	10

Source CASS city and competitiveness index database

Table 5.2 Company strength index of global urban competitiveness

Indicator	Sample size	Mean	Standard deviation	Coefficient of variation	No. of cities below mean	Median
Company strength	505	0.192	0.142	0.739	320	0.153

Source CASS city and competitiveness index database

Kong respectively coming in 5th, 6th and 7th (see Table 5.1). The top 10 cities in company strength are all located in the most active global economies. Good economic foundation provides cities with sound infrastructure. Convenient traffic and locality, as well as the status of world financial centers, allow cities to have an excellent environment for doing business. These are all important conditions for attracting global companies to settle down in a city.

The company strength index mean of the 505 sample cities is 0.192. There are as many as 320 cities (63% of all) with a score that is below the mean. This shows that company strength scores globally are on the low side. Multinational corporations and a large number of strong companies are to be found concentrated in a small number of cities. The rationality of the industrial structure and the sophistication of industries have left many cities far behind. The coefficient of variation is a statistical measurement of the extent of variation in the observed values of the sample data. The company strength coefficient of variation is 0.739, which shows that the gap between the company strength scores of various sample cities is relatively large and the dispersion is high (see Table 5.2).

The mean is higher than the median and the distribution is right-skewed

The company strength index mean is 0.192, which is higher than the median, 0.153. It can be seen in the left chart of Fig. 5.1 that the overall world mean is boosted by a small number of cities at the top of the rankings with high company strength. There are 17 cities (or 3.4%) in the 1 to above 0.5 segment; there are 67 cities (or 13.3%) in the 0.5–0.3 segment; there are 301 cities (or 59.6%) in the 0.3–0.1 segment; there are 120 cities (or 23.8%) below 0.1. It can be seen that more than 80% of the cities are closer to the lower end. As can be seen from the company

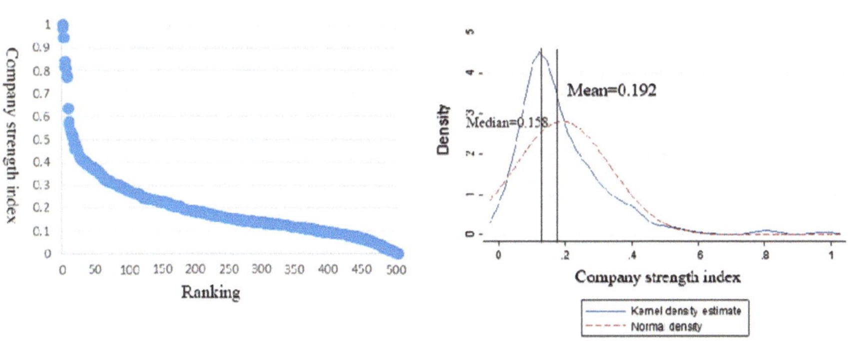

Fig. 5.1 Company strength index by segments and kernel density distribution. *Source* CASS city and competitiveness index database

strength index kernel density distribution (see Fig. 5.1, right), the distribution pattern of the global company strength scores can be found like this: The peak of the frequency distribution is flushed to the left with a long tail that extends towards the right. In contrast to normal distribution, the peak is higher for the overall left-skewed distribution of the company strength scores, once again ascertaining the mediocre performance of world cities in the company strength and that the gap in the performance of cities is large.

5.1.1.2 Regional Pattern: Continental Imbalance with Europe and America in the Lead and Africa Lagging Behind; Cities in Europe, North America and Asia Pacific Taking Over 90% of the World Top 100

We marked out the company strength scores of various cities on a world map (see Fig. 5.2) and it is quite obvious that cities with higher company strength scores concentrate in Europe, North America and the Asia Pacific. The company strength scores of European cities are comparatively high and there is balanced distribution between cities. North American cities with high company strength scores are mainly to be found in the United States and Mexico. In Asia, they concentrate in the Asia Pacific region, especially in countries and regions like Japan, southeast China, as well as the four Asian dragons and the four Asian tigers. In South Asia, Indian cities with high company strength indexes are aplenty, although scores are lower in comparison. The company strength scores are relatively low in cities in central South America, western Oceania, northern and central Africa, as well as in the expansive central and northern Asia.

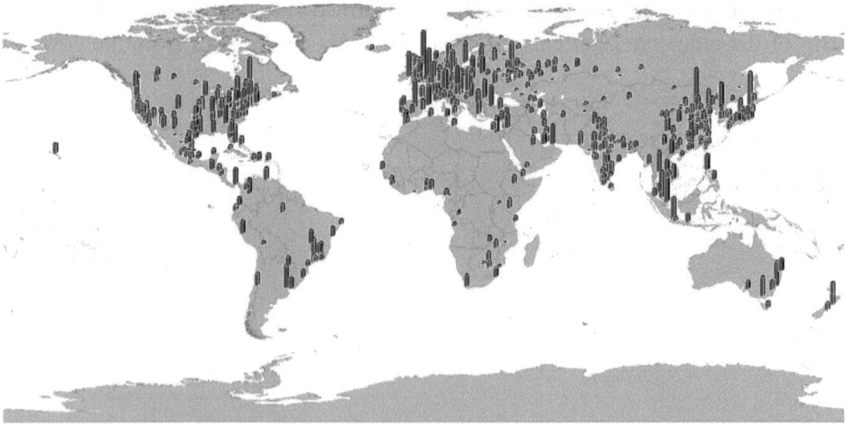

Fig. 5.2 Company strength score distribution of 505 cities. *Source* CASS city and competitiveness index database

Table 5.3 Company strength index: continental analysis and proportion in the top 100

Region	Sample size	Number (percentage) of cities in top 100	Mean	Coefficient of variation	Maximum		
					City	Score	World ranking
Asia	192	25 (13.02%)	0.177	0.837	Tokyo	0.947	3
Europe	136	39 (28.68%)	0.212	0.714	London	1	1
North America	107	27 (25.23%)	0.209	0.636	New York	0.990	2
South America	28	4 (14.29%)	0.188	0.632	Buenos Aires	0.511	16
Oceania	9	3 (33.33%)	0.255	0.498	Sydney	0.511	17
Africa	33	2 (6.06%)	0.130	0.615	Johannesburg	0.337	61
World Average	505	100 (100%)	0.192	0.739	London	1	1

Source CASS city and competitiveness index database

Looking at the distribution of the company strength scores of the top 100 cities by continents (see Table 5.3), Oceania has the highest proportion of cities in the global top 100 as well as the highest mean score. There are only nine sample cities from Oceania in this research, one third of which are in the top 100, albeit in a lower range. The best performing regions are Europe and North America, with respectively 28.68 and 25.23% of all their sample cities making it into the top 100. Asia has the most sample cities in this range, close to two fifths of the total. However, the proportion of its cities that made it into the top 100 is far from satisfactory, which goes to show that with the exception of the developed cities in the Asia Pacific, the overall company strength of other Asian cities is rather disappointing.

Table 5.3 shows the company strength mean and coefficient of variation of the various continents. Oceania, Europe and North America are the top 3 regions of company strength. The company strength score mean for Asia is lower than the world average and there is no equilibrium in the company strength of Asian countries and cities. Asia Pacific tops the world rankings by region but the expansive central Asia is relatively underdeveloped. The relatively high coefficient of variation for Asia highlights this point very clearly. Oceania has the highest mean and the lowest coefficient of variation. Although it has the lowest number of sample cities in this study, the development of its cities in terms of company strength is more balanced.

5.1.2 *Forbes Global 2000*

The Forbes Global 2000 Index is published by US economic magazine Forbes, with equal weighting given to four indicators—turnover, profits, assets and market value—in the creation of a ranking for the largest and most powerful listed companies in the world. The Global 2000 is a reflection of the dynamic changes in global

Table 5.4 Forbes global 2000 index

Indicator	Sample size	Mean	Standard deviation	Coefficient of variation	No. of cities below mean	Median
Forbes global 2000	505	0.137	0.129	0.943	338	0.096

Source CASS city and competitiveness index database

business, which can be obtained from historical data. US companies have always been leading the pack in this area. Chinese companies are climbing upwards in terms of rankings and the number of companies in the list. However, the number of companies that made it into the rankings from Mainland China and Hong Kong combined is still less than half that of US companies, although the number of its new entries is greater than that of all other countries. The performance of Japanese companies is falling year after year and the ranked Chinese companies are generally now performing on par with them. The performance of European companies has also declined somewhat. Looking at the industries affecting the overall global business outlook, banks and diversified finance have a significant presence in the rankings, followed by the petroleum and natural gas industries. Here, we will explore the distribution patterns of Forbes Global 2000 companies.

5.1.2.1 Overall Pattern: Quality Enterprises are Concentrated in Mega Cities and Most Cities Score Below World Average

The Forbes Global 2000 index mean of the global cities is 0.137, with more than 60% of the cities having a score lower than the world average (see Table 5.4). This shows that global companies that are stronger and larger in size choose to establish themselves in mega cities around the world and are less likely to consider most of the other cities. A high coefficient of variation is also further evidence of an unequal distribution of Forbes Global 2000 companies and the large gap in the performances of cities.

Ranking cities by their scores of the Forbes Global 2000 companies, we can see that Chinese cities occupy four coveted positions in the top 10 cities, and they are Hong Kong, Beijing, Shanghai and Taipei. Hong Kong has excellent conditions in institutional and transportation systems, as well as an edge in talents, making it the preferred location of strong companies. The four Asian Dragons, with the exception of South Korea, all have cities in the global top 10. The largest city in the United States, New York, is in the 2nd place, and the British capital, London, is in the 3rd place (see Table 5.5).

Table 5.5 Top 10 cities by forbes global 2000 index

City	Hong Kong	New York	London	Tokyo	Beijing	Singapore	Shanghai	Moscow	Paris	Taipei
Continent	Asia	N. America	Europe	Asia	Asia	Asia	Asia	Europe	Europe	Asia
Score	1	0.855	0.834	0.810	0.806	0.773	0.769	0.581	0.569	0.526
Ranking	1	2	3	4	5	6	7	8	9	10

Source CASS city and competitiveness index database

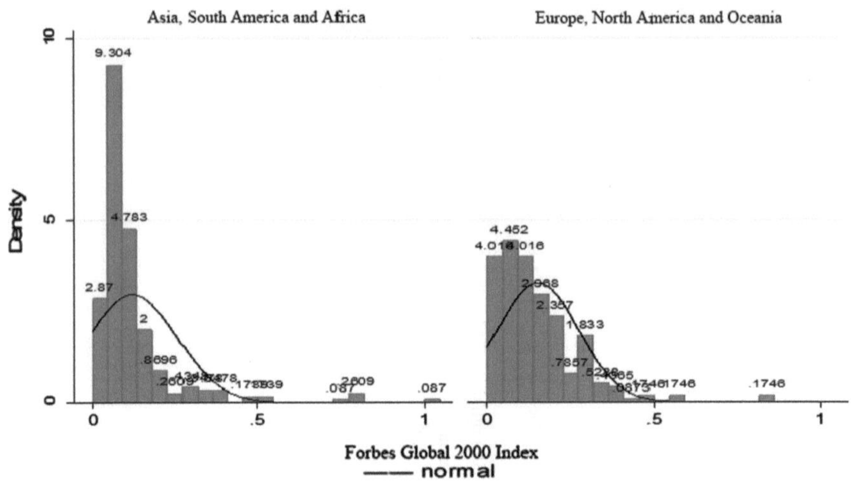

Fig. 5.3 Forbes global 2000 index kernel density estimation and classification. *Source* CASS city and competitiveness index database

5.1.2.2 Regional Pattern: Europe, America and Oceania have a Close-to-Normal Distribution, While Asia, Africa and Latin America have a Distribution that is Extremely Unbalanced

We split the sample cities into continental groups to look at their kernel density estimation and normal distribution (see Fig. 5.3). The continents with high means, namely, Europe, North America and Oceania, are in one group, and those with lower means, namely, Asia, South America and Africa are in another. A pattern can be found from the graphs: The kurtosis and skewness for Europe, North America and Oceania are close to that of a normal distribution, which goes to show that the distribution of strong companies in various cities is relatively even. Whereas, the overall distribution of the Forbes Global 2000 in Asia, Africa and Latin America is skewed towards the left with higher peaks, showing a mediocre performance in the three continents and an extremely large gap in the performances of the cities in this group.

5.1.2.3 Local Demand Index and Global Connection Index are Positively Correlated to Forbes Global 2000 Index

Among the various indicators of global urban competitiveness, the distribution of Forbes Global 2000 shows positive correlation with the cities' local demand (inclusive of population and GDP). As local demand score increases, Forbes Global 2000 index increases at a rising rate (see Fig. 5.4, left). This shows that among the many factors affecting company location, the economy and population of the host countries are more important. This is why there is a trend of companies congregating in big cities. There is also positive correlation between global connection index and Forbes Global 2000 index (see Fig. 5.4, right). However, the rate of the

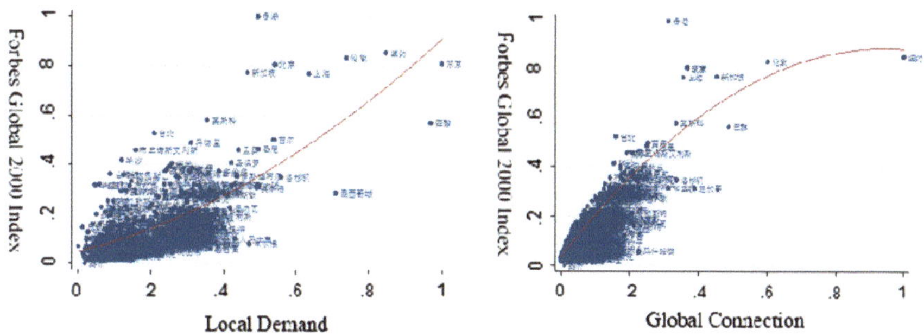

Fig. 5.4 Local demand and global connection versus forbes global 2000. *Source* CASS city and competitiveness index database

increase slows down. Factors such as the connection of economies and infrastructure are also factors of consideration in the selection of company location, but none of these have a greater effect than demand.

5.2 Local Demand

Local demand is the demand on a city's local market; the scale of a city's demand affects the scale of the city's industries, the level of the city's demand affects the level of the city's industries, and the growth potential of a city's demand affects the growth of the city's industries. Therefore, local demand is critical to the trade and sustainable economic growth of a city. Local demand includes three lower-level indicators: population size (reflecting growth in local demand), GDP and per capita income. These indicators yield a comprehensive study on a city's demand.

5.2.1 Summary of Local Demand Index

5.2.1.1 Overall Pattern: Local Demand Index has a Close-to-Normal Distribution, with Little Variation Between Cities

The mean is close to the median and the curve has two peaks

The local demand index mean of the 505 sample cities is 0.325. The number of cities with a score lower than the mean is 258, or 51% of the total. The local demand scores of the majority of the cities fall below 0.5. The local demand index median is 0.319, and the mean is close to the median. The local demand index coefficient of variation is 0.373, which goes to show that the gap in local demand is not significant. The dispersion of the cities is not high in comparison to other indexes (see Table 5.6).

The local demand index kernel density estimation of world cities (see Fig. 5.5, right) shows the overall pattern of the index's distribution: The scores are

Table 5.6 Local demand index of global urban competitiveness

Indicator	Sample size	Mean	Standard deviation	Coefficient of variation	No. of cities below mean	Median
Local demand	505	0.325	0.121	0.373	258	0.319

Source CASS city and competitiveness index database

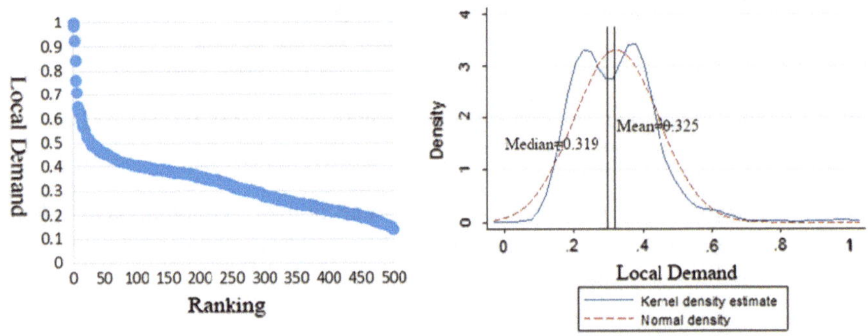

Fig. 5.5 Local demand index by segments and kernel density distribution. *Source* CASS city and competitiveness index database

concentrated on the left side (below 0.5). There are, however, two peaks. In comparison with the distribution of other indexes, the local demand index is doing reasonably well, with a considerable portion of the cities falling within the 0.2–0.4 range. Even so, the overall picture for the global local demand index is not too rosy. Less than 6% of the cities have a score higher than 0.5. This shows that the local demand of most cities is at a lower-middle level.

The top 10 cities are from Europe, Asia, North America and Oceania; Africa and South America do not have representation in the top 10

The top 10 cities by the local demand index (see Table 5.7) are mainly concentrated in Europe, Asia, North America and Oceania. These are powerful regions with enormous potential in terms of both economic development and natural resource endowment. There are the two top economies in the world, United States and China; there are also the four Asian Dragons, countries and regions that have been in active development since the 1980s; Japan, South Korea and the West Coast of the US are all areas from where the world's most important technologies originate; the Russian Far East and Australia are rich in natural resources; China and Southeast Asian countries have an abundance in human resources. These advantages have made these regions the world's most dynamic economies and the local markets are massive.

Table 5.7 Global local demand index top 10 cities

City	Tokyo	Paris	New York	London	Moscow	Los Angeles	Sydney	Osaka	Melbourne	Hong Kong
Continent	Asia	Europe	North America	Europe	Europe	North America	Oceania	Asia	Oceania	Asia
Score	1	0.984	0.923	0.841	0.763	0.709	0.649	0.643	0.629	0.628
Ranking	1	2	3	4	5	6	7	8	9	10

Source CASS City and Competitiveness Index database

5.2.1.2 Regional Pattern: Europe and America are Well-Matched Rivals While Asia has Enormous Potential

Developed countries are strong while the developing countries are right behind in hot pursuit

As can be seen in the local demand index distribution of the 505 sample cities in Fig. 5.6, the local demand scores of developed countries and regions are very high. High-scored cities concentrate in developed countries like the United States and European Union, as well as Australia, Japan and the four Asian Dragons. With the development of economic globalization, developing countries have also accelerated their pace of growth through foreign trade, capital flows and the transfer of technologies. Countries such as China, India and Brazil also have important cities and city clusters that are comparable with those of developed countries. The gap between cities with good economic foundation is gradually narrowing, but there are still quite a number of cities in developing countries that are relatively backward, with slow growth. The gap that these cities have with the developed cities is continuously widening.

A high proportion of the top 100 cities are from North America and Oceania while the performance of cities in Asia and Europe are mediocre

Looking at the distribution of the top 100 cities by local demand (see Table 5.8), the strongest performer is Oceania, with close to 45% of its cities in the top 100. It is followed by North America, with more than one third of its cities in the top 100. The United States is the largest economy in the world. Development of its cities is relatively balanced and it is the biggest contributor to the performance of North America. The performance of Asian and European cities in local demand is not spectacular. The economic development of Asian countries is unbalanced and the gap between cities is large, with many cities still relatively backward. Although the

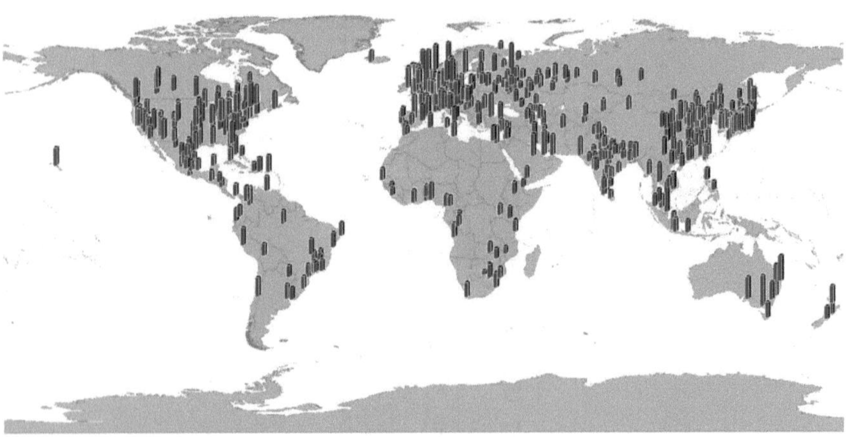

Fig. 5.6 Local demand index distribution of 505 global cities. *Source* CASS city and competitiveness index database

Table 5.8 Global local demand index: continental analysis and proportion in the top 100

Region	Sample size	Number (percentage) of cities in top 100	Mean	Coefficient of variation	Maximum		
					City	Score	World ranking
Asia	192	36 (18.75%)	0.330	0.352	Tokyo	1	1
Europe	136	26 (19.12%)	0.311	0.433	Paris	0.984	2
North America	107	33 (30.84%)	0.364	0.311	New York	0.923	3
South America	28	1 (3.57%)	0.120	0.257	Sao Paulo	0.449	56
Oceania	9	4 (44.44%)	0.424	0.356	Sydney	0.649	7
Africa	33	0 (0)	0.241	0.260	Cairo	0.358	198
World Average	505	100 (100%)	0.325	0.373	Tokyo	1	1

Source CASS city and competitiveness index database

economies in Europe are pretty strong, there are population limitations and many of the countries and cities are seeing a decline in population. This limits the scale of urban development in these cities, which affects their local demand scores.

5.2.2 *Economic Scale*

5.2.2.1 Overall Pattern: More than 70% of the Cities are Below World Average, and Economic Development is Unbalanced

GDP is the most common and most direct indicator used in the measurement of a city's economy and level of economic development. Looking at the data of GDP (see Table 5.9), the overall mean of global cities' level of economic development is relatively low and extremely unbalanced in distribution, with about three quarters of the cities below the mean and a coefficient of variation of 1.973. The economic levels of cities are highly dispersed. In addition, the mean is higher than the 0.025 median, which goes to show that a few cities with well-performing economies are pushing up the overall score. The mean is low enough even without this unrealistic component factored in, which makes this imbalance in global economy even more worrying.

Table 5.9 GDP in global urban competitiveness

Indicator	sample size	Mean	Standard deviation	Coefficient of variation	No. of cities below mean	Median
GDP index	505	0.053	0.104	1.973	376	0.025

Source CASS city and competitiveness index database

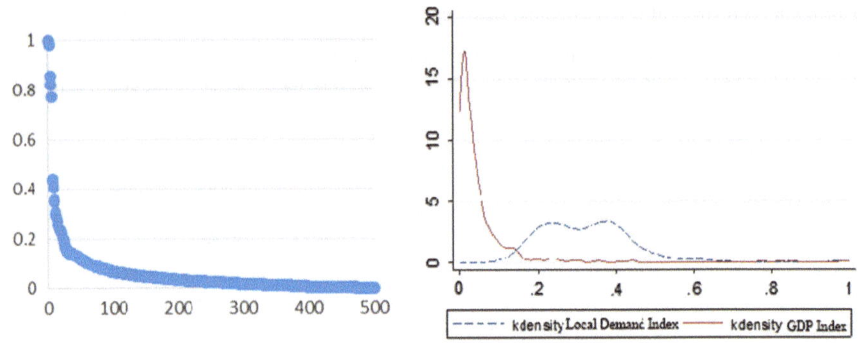

Fig. 5.7 GDP index by segments and kernel density distribution. *Source* CASS city and competitiveness index database

The left-hand graph of Fig. 5.7 is the GDP rankings by segments. The X-axis represents the rankings and the Y-axis represents the GDP index. A small number of cities at the top of the rankings are pushing up the world average. Looking at the index in segments, there are only 11 cities (or less than 2.2% in proportion) within the range of 1–0.3; there are 50 cities (or less than 10% in proportion) in the range of 0.3–0.1; there are 444 cities (or close to 88% in proportion) below 0.1. This shows that nearly nine tenths of the cities are at a disadvantageous position. The GDP kernel density distribution (Fig. 5.7, right) shows that the GDP index distribution has a left-skewed frequency distribution peak, with a long tail extending towards the right. In comparison to normal distribution, the distribution here is left-skewed with a higher peak. This once again proves that the overall economic level of world cities is low and the gap between cities large. In comparison as well with the kernel density distribution of the local demand index, the kernel density of the GDP index is heavily skewed towards the right. The GDP mean of the 505 cities is USD 32.19 billion and the city with the highest GDP globally, Tokyo, has a high value of USD 608.3 billion. There is a very large gap between cities for this particular indicator.

5.2.2.2 Regional Pattern: Developed Countries of Europe, America and Oceania are in the Lead while Asian Countries have the Highest Dispersion

Looking at the GDP top 10 cities (see Table 5.10), Asian cities fare rather well, with five cities in the list. Tokyo, with the largest economic output, takes the 1st place. Chinese cities, Shanghai, Beijing and Hong Kong, are in the second half of the top 10. Paris of France is 2nd in the rankings. Moscow of Russia is 3rd. New York and Los Angeles of the US are also in the top 10. It is worth noting that, with the exception of China being the country with the most number of cities in the top

Table 5.10 GDP index top 10 cities

City	Tokyo	Paris	Moscow	New York	London	Los Angeles	Shanghai	Seoul	Beijing	Hong Kong
Continent	Asia	Europe	Europe	North America	Europe	North America	Asia	Asia	Asia	Asia
Score	1	0.983	0.855	0.821	0.774	0.440	0.437	0.408	0.359	0.350
Ranking	1	2	3	4	5	6	7	8	9	10

Source CASS city and competitiveness index database

Table 5.11 Global GDP: continental analysis and proportion in the top 100

Region	Sample size	Number (percentage) of cities in top 100	Mean	Coefficient of variation	Maximum		
					City	Score	World ranking
Asia	192	58 (30.21%)	0.064	1.589	Tokyo	1	1
Europe	136	17 (12.50%)	0.046	2.814	Paris	0.983	2
North America	107	17 (15.89%)	0.056	1.713	New York	0.822	4
South America	28	4 (14.29%)	0.031	1.058	Sao Paulo	0.137	39
Oceania	9	4 (44.44%)	0.097	1.080	Sydney	0.298	12
Africa	33	0 (0%)	0.010	1.178	Johannesburg	0.044	160
World Average	505	100 (100%)	0.053	1.973	Tokyo	1	1

Source CASS city and competitiveness index database

10, the other cities in the top 10 are all from developed countries. The economic position of China in the world has improved.

Among the top 100 cities in GDP (see Table 5.11), Asia has the most number of cities as well as a high proportion of its cities in this range; its mean is significantly higher than that of Europe and America. North America has 17 cities in this range, which is 15.89% of the total of the continent. Its mean comes in second. The proportion of cities from Europe is on the low side. Although Europe also has 17 cities in the top 100, the proportion out of all its cities is only 12.5% and the mean is low. An important point is that the GDP coefficient of variation of European cities is the largest, which shows a large economic gap between its cities. Even though the number of sample cities from Oceania is small, nearly half of its cities are in the top 100. It has a high proportion of cities in this range and the highest mean.

5.2.2.3 The Overall Competitiveness of Economically Developed Regions is Stronger and Economic Development is Affected by Location

With GDP index as the weight, we map out the correlation between geographical location and overall global urban competitiveness index in a bubble chart. The larger a bubble in the chart, the higher the GDP index it represents, and the stronger its economy. Figure 5.8 shows the close relation between the overall competitiveness of cities and the level of their economic development. Generally, the more developed an economy, the stronger its overall competitiveness, and the more underdeveloped a region is, the lower the comprehensive competitiveness it has. This is represented by the small bubbles at the bottom of the chart. The bigger the

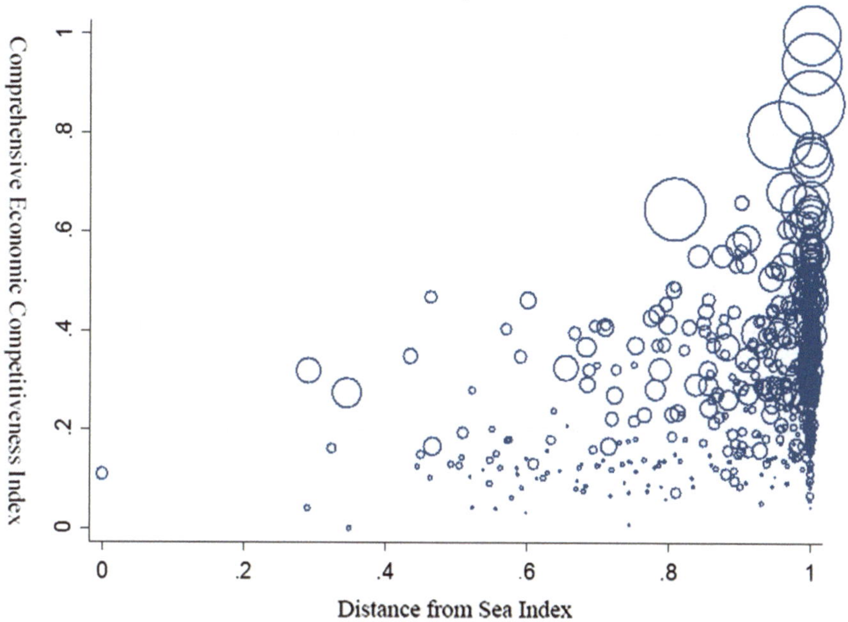

Fig. 5.8 Correlation between location and competitiveness based on GDP index

bubble, the higher its corresponding overall competitiveness; the two are positively correlated. In addition, factors affecting city location and the GDP have a joint effect on the urban competitiveness. The higher the distance from sea index on the X-axis in Fig. 5.8, the nearer a city is to the ocean. Cities with high competitiveness indexes are almost all located on or near the coast.

5.3 Local Elements

Different cities are endowed with different local elements. In an open economy, differences in key elements lead to differences in comparative advantages between cities, differences in industries and division of labor between the urban regions, which in turn, affects the distribution of resources, elements and environment between the cities. Local elements involve four lower-level indicators: patent index (measurement of scientific output), unemployment rate, bank index (measurement of financial industry development) and university index (measurement of higher education and high-end talents). These indicators provide a consolidated picture of the development of various elements in a city.

5.3.1 *Summary of Local Elements Index*

5.3.1.1 Overall Pattern: The Index has a Close-to-Normal Distribution and the Overall Mean is on the Low Side

We charted the rankings of cities by segments according to the local element scores (see Fig. 5.9, left) and the kernel density distribution (see Fig. 5.9, right) of the 505 sample cities. More than a quarter of the cities have a local element score higher than 0.5; the local element global mean is 0.377 and the median is 0.371. The two values are very close. However, from a numerical point of view, the local element index mean is still on the low side. From the kernel density estimation, the local element index is observed to have a close-to-normal distribution. However, in comparison to normal distribution, the number of cities with a score of 0.4–0.5 is quite low.

5.3.1.2 Regional Pattern: Asia is in the Lead, While the Performance of North America is Poor

It can be seen from the global distribution of the local element index (see Fig. 5.10) that cities in Europe have relatively high scores, and cities in South America, Africa and the central and western regions of Asia have relatively low scores. The cities with high scores in Europe are mainly from the north and south of the continent. The performance of East Europe is generally poor. The strong performers in Asia are mainly concentrated in the Asia Pacific region. India in South Asia is also doing well. However, the local elements performance of the two major developed countries of North America, the United States and Canada, is unsatisfactory. This is especially so in the central and western regions of the US, as North American cities generally have high unemployment rates and low bank scores, which results in a low local element score.

Asia takes half the positions in the top 10 by local element index, making up half of the cities (see Table 5.12). China is the country with the greatest number of cities

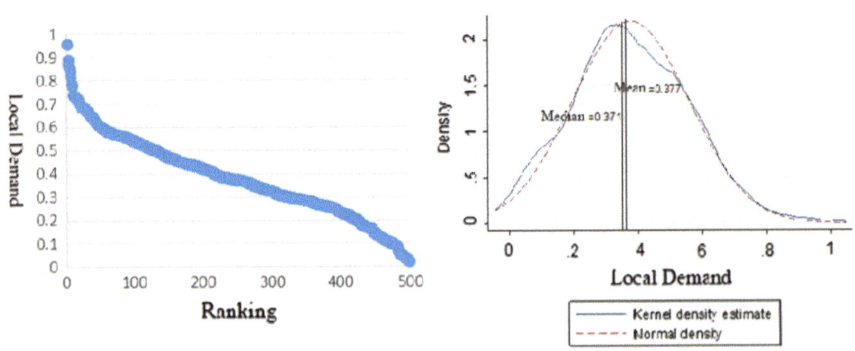

Fig. 5.9 Local element index by segments and kernel density distribution. *Source* CASS city and competitiveness index database

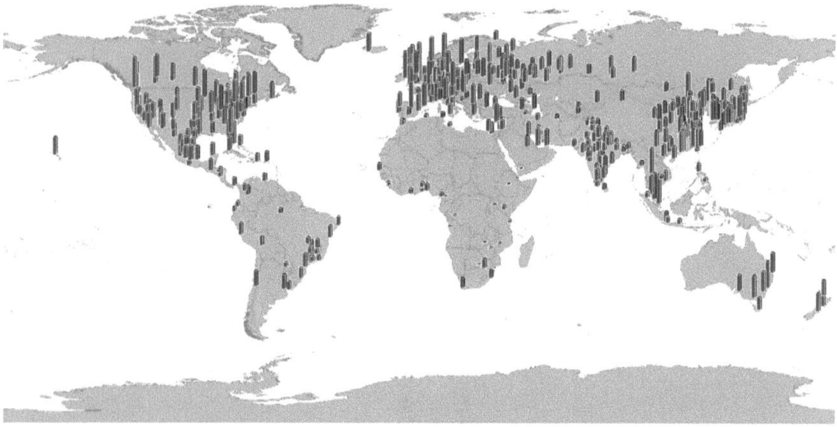

Fig. 5.10 Local element index distribution of the 505 cities. *Source* CASS city and competitiveness index database

in the top 10, with Beijing, Shanghai and Taipei respectively in the 2nd, 7th and 8th place. London of Europe takes the top spot and Zurich is ranked 6th. This shows the strength of European cities. Cities from the two North American countries, the United States and Canada, New York, Los Angeles and Vancouver, are also in the top 10. The scores of the top 10 cities show that the gap is not huge.

The continental distribution of the top 100 cities by local element index also shows specific patterns in the (see Table 5.13). More than half of the cities in the top 100 are from Europe and America. There are 192 sample cities from Asia but only 18.23% of them made it into the top 100, with most of them from the eastern and southeast regions. Oceania has the highest mean because of its low number of sample cities and balanced development. It is followed by North America, with a high mean of 0.45. Overall, only African and South American cities have mean values that are lower than the world average. Looking at the coefficient of variation, African cities have the highest dispersion and the largest gap. North America and Oceania have lower coefficient of variation values and the performance of their cities is quite balanced.

5.3.2 *Patent Index*

A city is the carrier of new economies and the level of a city's technological innovation and speed of knowledge transfer often determine its development potential and level of innovation. In the long term, a city's efficiency in churning out technological innovation is representative of the development potential of its new economies. Deep accumulation of knowledge production is the "fertile soil" for new economies and new industries, which will ultimately affect and drive the direction and results of a city's economic development. The patent index is a most direct reflection of a city's level of technological innovation. International patents provide

Table 5.12 Global local elements index top 10 cities

City	London	Beijing	New York	Tokyo	Seoul	Zurich	Shanghai	Taipei	Los Angeles	Vancouver
Continent	Europe	Asia	North America	Asia	Asia	Europe	Asia	Asia	North America	North America
Score	1	0.956	0.889	0.870	0.857	0.838	0.816	0.786	0.781	0.775
Ranking	1	2	3	4	5	6	7	8	9	10

Source CASS city and competitiveness index database

Table 5.13 Local elements index: continental analysis and proportion in the top 100

Region	Sample size	Number (percentage) of cities in top 100	Mean	Coefficient of variation	Maximum		
					City	Score	World ranking
Asia	192	35 (18.23%)	0.383	0.464	Beijing	0.956	2
Europe	136	26 (19.12%)	0.395	0.389	London	1	1
North America	107	35 (32.71%)	0.450	0.375	New York	0.889	3
South America	28	1 (3.57%)	0.243	0.480	Sao Paulo	0.572	69
Oceania	9	3 (33.33%)	0.493	0.212	Sydney	0.683	27
Africa	33	0 (0)	0.106	0.820	Johannesburg	0.282	354
World Average	505	100 (100%)	0.377	0.482	London	1	1

Source CASS city and competitiveness index database

a comprehensive picture of a city's innovation quality, and therefore, conducting an analysis on the single core indicator of a "patent index" will provide a more in-depth explanation to the efficiency and quality of a city's technological innovation.

5.3.2.1 Overall Pattern: The Overall Standard of Global Cities is Low and Patents are Found Concentrated in Cities of Innovation

The patent index scores of global cities are generally very low. In the economic development environment led by innovation and technology today, this is something that the various countries in the world need to take note of. The world urban patent index mean is at a very low level of 0.013, and even so, there are still 415 cities with a value that is lower than the mean. This is more than 80% of all sample cities. The coefficient of variation is 4.229, which shows just how very imbalanced the standard of technological innovation in the world. Looking at the raw data on the number of patents (refer to Fig. 5.11), there is only one city with more than 10,000 patents awarded annually, only 22 cities with more than 1000 patents awarded, and 28 cities with more than 500 patents awarded. Most cities have less than 500 patents awarded, with the majority of cities in the less than 100 patents range. There are also 56 cities without a single patent awarded in a whole year. The awarding of patents in the world is generally weak, and the gap between cities wide.

Looking at the global top 10 cities of patent index (see Table 5.14), Japan shows the strongest performance, with Tokyo and Osaka topping the chart. Especially, no other cities in the world can match Tokyo. This is evidence of Japan's overall leadership in innovation. China's Shenzhen and South Korea's Seoul are following close behind. Beijing of China is in the 9th position. These are all typical innovative cities. It can be seen from this that Asian cities are leading the world in the number of patents and displaying more drive and strength in innovation. European cities, Paris

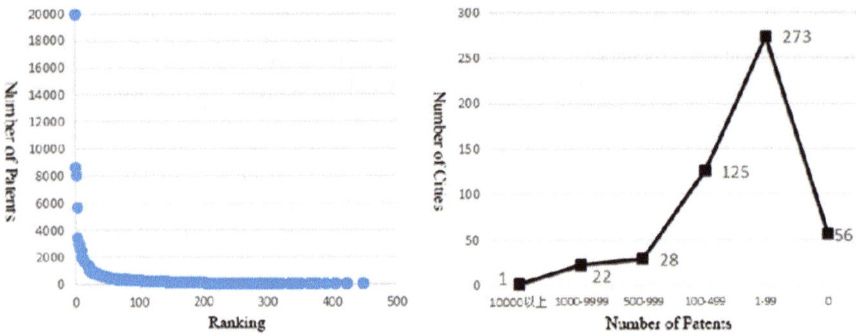

Fig. 5.11 Number of international patents awarded by segments and number of cities for different range intervals of patent quantities. *Source* CASS city and competitiveness index database

and Stuttgart, are in the top 10; North America's United States has three cities in the top 10. However, looking at the scores of the top 10 cities, the gap is very wide between them and there is a wide, empty and unfilled space between the values 0.5 and 1. Tokyo stands alone in a class of its own, separate from the cities trailing behind.

5.3.2.2 Regional Pattern: Major Cities in East Asia are Exceptionally Outstanding; Cities in Europe and America are Performing Well Overall

The patent index cannot represent the full technology and innovation prowess of a city or region. However, a patent index measured using the number of international patented inventions is the world's largest source of technical information. Patents account for 90–95% of the world's scientific and technological information. Therefore, the patent index is able to reflect a city's or region's development and accumulation of technological innovation within a period of time, the most direct indicator measuring technological innovation of a city or region. It can be seen from the two sets of kernel density distribution of the patent index that the scores of the various continents in the world are very low, with peaks that are close to zero. The kurtosis and skewness in Europe, North America and Oceania are closer to that of a normal distribution. The patent index distribution in Asia, Africa and Latin America is left-skewed compared to that of a normal distribution; these regions fare poorly in the patent index. Looking at the spatial distribution of the patent index, cities in Europe, America and East Asia have obvious comparative advantages, and the solitary spire representing Tokyo of Japan is extremely outstanding (see Fig. 5.12).

5.3.2.3 The Patent Index is Dependent on Innovation Resources. Companies and Universities are the Driving Forces

The patent index is an important measure of a city's technological innovation capabilities. Cities with high patent indexes tend to be cities of innovation, i.e. cities

Table 5.14 Patent index top 10 cities

City	Tokyo	Osaka	Shenzhen	Seoul	Paris	Houston	San Diego	New York	Beijing	Stuttgart
Continent	Asia	Asia	Asia	Asia	Europe	North America	North America	North America	Asia	Europe
Score	1	0.435	0.405	0.283	0.174	0.150	0.149	0.133	0.129	0.124
Original Value	19,942	8670	8078	5647	3479	2991	2974	2651	2563	2472
Ranking	1	2	3	4	5	6	7	8	9	10

Source CASS city and competitiveness index database

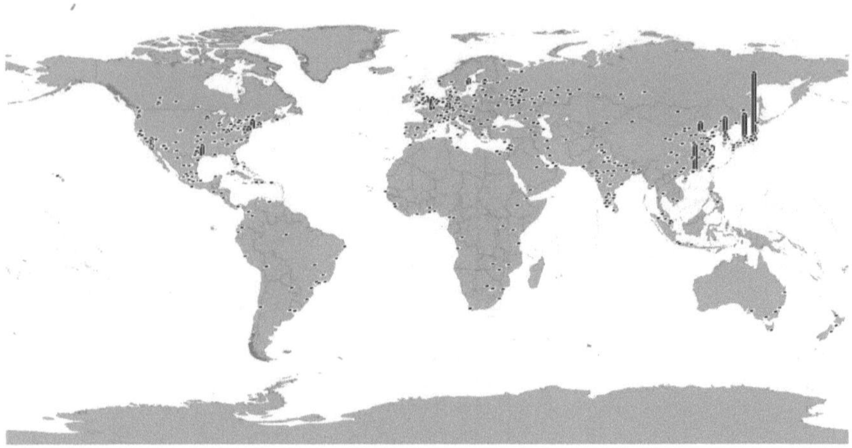

Fig. 5.12 Patent application index spatial distribution. *Source* CASS city and competitiveness index database

dependent primarily upon factors of innovation like technology, knowledge and culture etc. to drive their development. Among the many elements, the R&D teams of companies are the most important support for a city's technological innovation. At the same time, these departments are the main venues where patent inventions are taking place. We extracted the logarithm for the respective number of patents awarded, number of multinational corporations, number of Global 2000 companies and industry level, and focused our analysis of the top 300 cities in the ranking on the correlation between the number of patents awarded and the other three indicators above. The conclusion drawn from Fig. 5.13 is that the three factors, i.e. number of multinational corporations, number of Global 2000 companies and industry level, are key to the patent index score of a city.

5.4 Hardware Environment

Hardware environment mainly assesses the level of infrastructure and environmental quality of cities. Hardware environment is the connection established between different bodies and organizations, and the foundation for converting such connection into economic results more efficiently. The connections between bodies within the cities and between the cities are all dependent on hardware conditions, such as infrastructure etc., within and between cities. Therefore, Hardware Environment provided the means of connection for bodies in cities. Shortage of Hardware Environment hinders the sustainable development of a city by getting in the way of connection between city bodies. Hardware Environment is constructed from four lower-level indicators: PM2.5 emissions (measurement of urban environment quality), benchmark hotel prices (measurement of business costs),

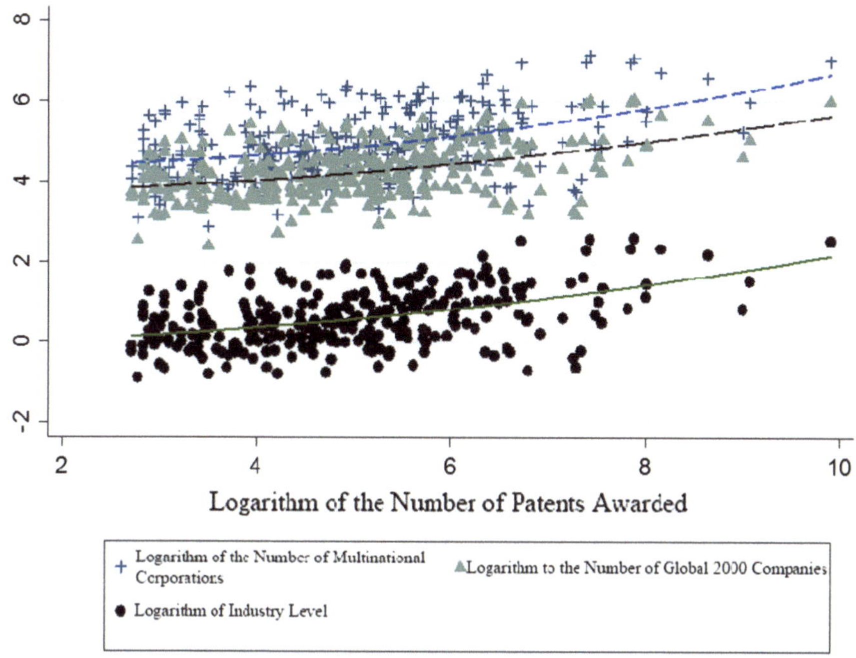

Fig. 5.13 Patent index versus university index and company strength index. *Source* CASS city and competitiveness index database

convenience of roads (representing the convenience of municipal facilities) and distance to sea (representing the natural location of a city).

5.4.1 Summary of Hardware Environment Index

5.4.1.1 Overall Pattern: The Index has a Close-to-Normal Distribution and World Cities have an "Olive-Shaped" Distribution

The hardware environment index mean of global cities is 0.603 and the median is 0.625. The median is higher than the mean, which means that more than half of the sample cities have a hardware environment index that is greater than the mean. The coefficient of variation is 0.207, which means that the hardware environment dispersion of world cities is not high and the scores of the cities are relatively uniform. The kernel density estimation (see Fig. 5.14) shows a Hardware Environment Index with a skewed distribution that is very close to a normal distribution. Looking at the Hardware Environment Index ranking by segments, there are few cities at the two extreme ends of the distribution. Most cities are concentrated in the middle range, very close to an "olive-shaped" city distribution. The Hardware Environment of the world cities is in an ideal state.

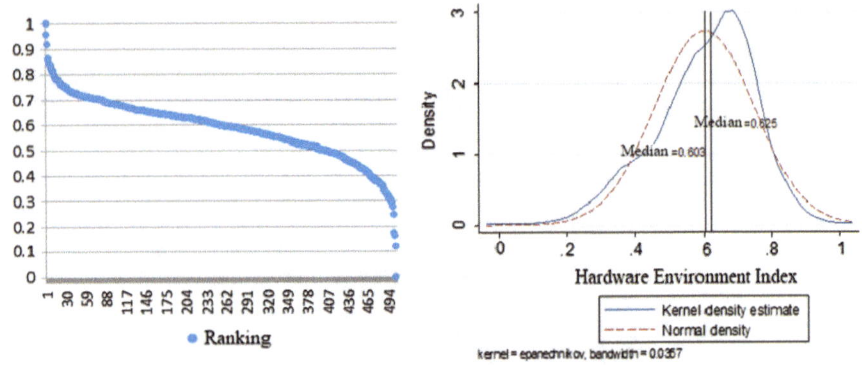

Fig. 5.14 Hardware environment index ranking by segments and kernel density distribution. *Source* CASS city and competitiveness index database

5.4.1.2 Regional Pattern: Hardware Conditions of Europe and America are Superior While Countries in Central Asia, Africa and Latin America are Still Lagging Behind

According to the hardware environment index distribution of global sample cities (see Fig. 5.15), the hardware environment of cities in Europe and America are superior. Most of these are in developed nations with higher levels of economic development, more advanced technologies and relatively sound infrastructure. Their residents enjoy a higher standard of living. In addition to being an important part of world economy, these countries also have a great impact on world economy and politics. With the exception of the four Asian Dragons, Japan, and central and eastern China, the hardware conditions of other Asian countries are relatively backward. The hardware environment of Indian cities is uniform, albeit on the low side. Due to historical reasons, Africa and Latin America are economically underdeveloped, with technology that is relatively backward and poor hardware environment foundations (especially some countries in Africa, which were still under some kind of colonial influence up to almost the end of the last century). These are developing countries in the process of rapid industrialization, impacted by the transfer of industries from western countries and pursuing economic development at the expense of the environment. The environmental quality in these regions is quite worrying.

Among the top 10 world cities by the hardware environment index (see Table 5.15), Frankfurt of Germany takes the top position, while El Paso of the US is ranked No. 2. Macao of China, with its natural location and superior infrastructure, is the top Asian city and third in the world rankings. Hobart of Australia is in the 4th place; Yaounde of Africa is No. 8. The scores of the top 10 cities are very close and the gap between them is not wide.

Among the top 100 cities by hardware environment (see Table 5.16), the performance of Oceania is the most outstanding, with more than half of its cities in this

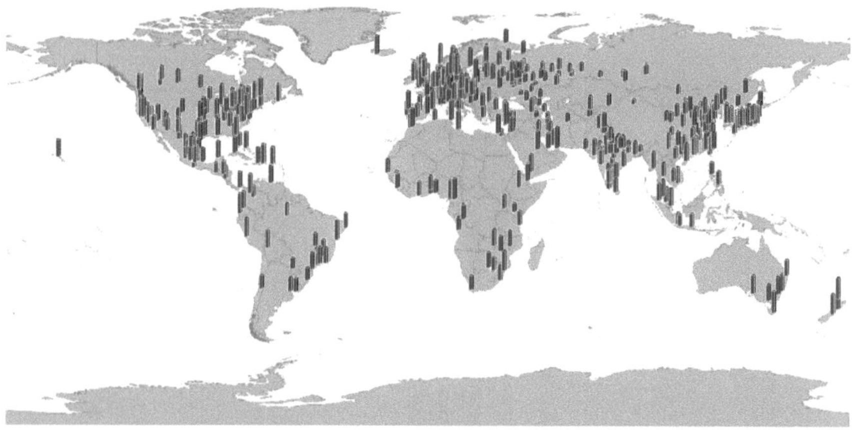

Fig. 5.15 Hardware environment index distribution of 505 cities. *Source* CASS city and competitiveness index database

range. It is followed by Europe, with more than a quarter of its sample cities making it into the top 100. South America and North America have a similar proportion of their sample cities in the top 100, both close to 22%. This proportion reflects the mediocre performance of North America headed by the United States and Canada. There are 24 Asian cities in the top 100, which is 12.5% of its total sample cities. They are mainly to be found in Japan, the four Asian Dragons, and the eastern coast of China. The economic foundation of these regions is fairly good. The markets are economically well-developed, there is ample capital in these cities and their infrastructure is sound. They are the first to complete industrial transformation and upgrading and to achieve sustainable development. However, cities in other parts of Asia as well as in Africa and Latin America, have a wide gap with the developed countries in terms of hardware environment, putting pressure on their economic development in the future.

5.4.2 PM2.5 Index[1]

The various sources of environmental pollution are harmful to the health of the people in a city. Pollution of the air, such as haze and dust etc. is the most direct manifestations of this. The report utilizes the PM2.5 index to measure the extent of

[1]The higher the composite urban competitiveness score, the higher the ranking. The higher the PM2.5 Index, however, the poorer the environmental quality and the lower the city's Environmental Quality Index scores. In order to facilitate the calculation of the composite index, we adjusted the PM2.5 Index. The current PM2.5 Index that we are using is actually a 1-PM2.5 index. Therefore, when the said index is higher, this means that the Environmental Quality index of the city is higher and the composite score is higher.

Table 5.15 Global hardware environment index top 10 cities

City	Frankfurt	El Paso	Macao	Hobart	Nicosia	Milan	Dubai	Yaounde	Wilmington	Christchurch
Continent	Europe	North America	Asia	Oceania	Asia	Europe	Asia	Africa	North America	Oceania
Score	1	0.925	0.904	0.891	0.889	0.889	0.878	0.860	0.850	0.849
Ranking	1	2	3	4	5	6	7	8	9	10

Source CASS city and competitiveness index database

Table 5.16 Global hardware environment index: continental analysis and proportion in the top 100

Region	Sample size	Number (percentage) of cities in top 100	Mean	Coefficient of variation	Maximum		
					City	Score	World ranking
Asia	192	24 (12.50%)	0.578	0.252	Macao	0.904	3
Europe	136	35 (25.74%)	0.589	0.287	Frankfurt	1	1
North America	107	23 (21.50%)	0.644	0.164	El Paso	0.925	2
South America	28	6 (21.43%)	0.622	0.193	Georgetown	0.829	16
Oceania	9	5 (55.56%)	0.767	0.119	Hobart	0.891	4
Africa	33	7 (21.21%)	0.619	0.204	Yaounde	0.860	8
World Average	505	100 (100%)	0.603	0.241	Frankfurt	1	1

Source CASS city and competitiveness index database

harm environmental pollution has on the health of people in cities. To make the composite index easy to calculate, we use a 1-PM2.5 index to represent the environmental quality of cities. The higher the index, the better the environment quality.

5.4.2.1 Overall Pattern: World Cities are Performing Well Generally and the List is Topped by Cities in Developed Countries

The environmental quality index mean of all cities is 0.859 and the coefficient of variation is 0.166 (see Table 5.17). This means that global environmental quality is quite good on the whole; the gap between cities is not big and dispersion is not high. The environmental quality index median is 0.901, which is higher than the mean. Nearly 70% of the cities have an environmental quality index that is higher than the world average.

The top 10 cities by the environmental quality index are all from developed countries (see Table 5.18). With the exception of Shizuoka of Japan, at No. 10, all the rest are from North America, Europe and Oceania. The city with the best air quality is Vancouver of Canada. Canada also has another city in the rankings, Ottawa, ranked No. 5. Also in North America, the Mexican city of Aguascalientes

Table 5.17 Environmental quality index

Indicator	Sample size	Mean	Standard deviation	Coefficient of variation	No. of cities below mean	Median
Environmental quality	505	0.859	0.142	0.166	159	0.901

Source CASS city and competitiveness index database

Table 5.18 Environment quality index top 10 cities

City	Vancouver	Aguascalientes	Melbourne	Sydney	Ottawa	Adelaide	Tucson	Krasnodar	Stavropol	Shizuoka
Continent	North America	North America	Australia	Australia	North America	Australia	North America	Europe	Europe	Asia
Score	1	0.998	0.996	0.994	0.991	0.990	0.989	0.989	0.989	0.989
Ranking	1	2	3	4	5	6	7	8	9	10

Source CASS city and competitiveness index database

takes the 2nd spot. Australia is the country with the most number of cities in the top 10, and because it has a relatively small number of sample cities, the cities that are in the top 10 make up one third of its sample cities. This is testament to the superior quality of air throughout Australia. The other three countries are from the United States and Russia.

5.4.2.2 Regional Pattern: Scores of European and American Countries are Close to the Maximum While those of Asian, African and Latin American Countries are on the Low Side

We categorized the countries of the world into developed countries and developing countries and charted the environmental quality index kernel density distribution (see Table 5.17) separately for Asia, Africa and Latin America, as well as for Europe, North America and Oceania. The scores of developed countries basically follow a normal distribution. The scores for cities in these countries are all higher than 0.5, with a peak that is closer to the maximum of 1. In comparison, the environmental quality of Asian, African and Latin American countries is less than that of Europe and America. Although the peak is right-skewed in the index range compared to a normal distribution, the dispersion of the cities is high. There is a significant portion of the cities below 0.5. The gap between cities is large and the environmental quality is not uniform (Fig. 5.16).

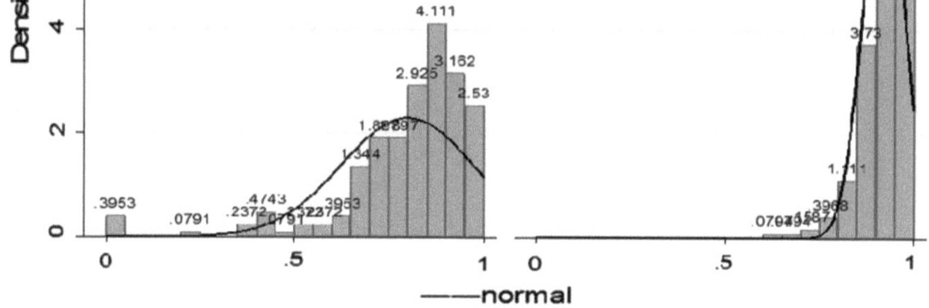

Fig. 5.16 Environmental quality index kernel density function and classification. *Source* CASS city and competitiveness index database

5.4.2.3 Environmental Quality and Industry Level are Correlated, Which is Clearer for the Last 100 Cities

The environmental Kuznets curve (EKC) shows an “inverted U” pattern: At lower levels of income, environmental quality rises as GDP per capita increases, and at higher levels of income, environmental quality decreases as GDP per capita increases. Specifically, when the level of economic development of a region is low, environmental pollution is low, but as the per capita income increases, environmental pollution will move to higher levels. The extent of environmental deterioration will increase with economic growth. Once economic development reaches a certain inflection point, environmental pollution will once again move from high to low as per capita income increases. The extent of environmental pollution will gradually ease and the quality of the environment will gradually improve. Since the inverted U pattern was proposed in 1991 by US economists Grossman and Krueger, this has been confirmed by empirical studies of samples from different countries and regions. Logarithms were derived from the sample cities’ PM2.5 emissions and GDP for curve fitting (see Fig. 5.17). It was found out that the inverted U EKC really does exist for the global samples made up of cities at different stages of development. Historically, developed countries have experienced events similar to that of the great smog in London and the photochemical smog of Los Angeles. In all instances, the PM2.5 index was at a high. With greater economic development

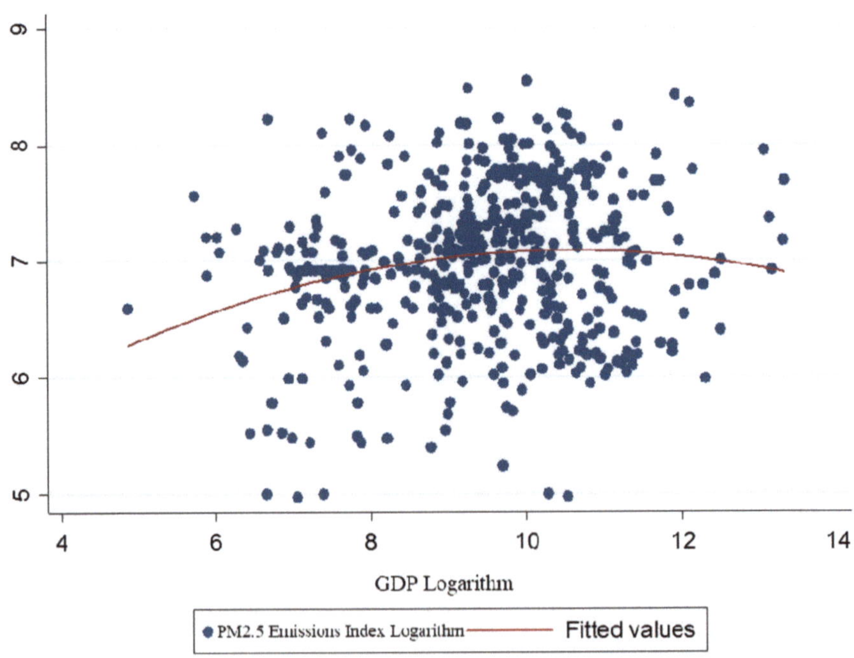

Fig. 5.17 Environment kuznets curve of 505 sample cities. *Source* CASS city and competitiveness index database

and years of tireless governance, London now has an annual average PM2.5 value of between 16 and 18 mcg per cubic meter and Los Angeles has an annual average of 13 mcg per cubic meter, significant improvements to air quality to become cities with good, clean air.

5.5 Software Environment

Software environment refers to the rules of conduct formulated and imposed by governments on the interactions between economic entities and for the protection of social development. Good systems can effectively lower transaction costs and increase transactional efficiency, and provide effective encouragement and restrictions to economic entities. This provides a good social environment for the sustainable development of cities. Software environment is constructed from four lower-level indicators: Crime rate (measurement of a city's public safety), language diversity index (indication of a city's cultural diversity), ease of doing business (extent of governmental regulation of commerce), and ratio of taxation by central versus local government (measurement of a cities' financial autonomy).

5.5.1 Summary of Software Environment Index

5.5.1.1 Overall Pattern: The Scores Show Nearly a Normal Distribution, and the Mean and Median are Close

We plotted the rankings of cities by segments (see Fig. 5.18, left) and the kernel density distribution (see Fig. 5.18, right) according to the software environment cores of the 505 sample cities. The software environment index rankings show nearly a diagonal line. The distribution of the 505 samples cities between the values

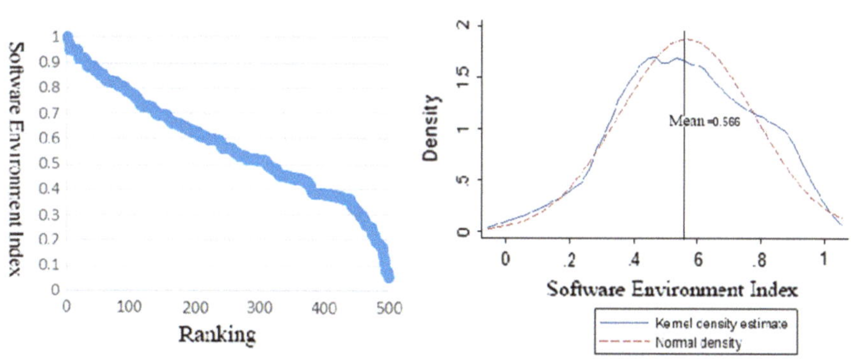

Fig. 5.18 Software environment index by segments and kernel density distribution. *Source* CASS city and competitiveness index database

of 0–1 is relatively balanced, meaning that the scores are reasonable. The rules for the distribution of the global institutional environment index are made clearer by the kernel density distribution. The index has a very close-to-normal distribution, with a software environment index mean of 0.566 and median of 0.563; the mean and median are quite close in values. The coefficient of variation is 0.375, so the gap between cities is not great. With reference to the graph, the index peaks between 0.4 and 0.6, a slight deviation from a normal distribution. If the institutional environment scores of cities in this portion rise, the world cities will have a more normal institutional environment distribution.

5.5.1.2 Regional Pattern: The Software Environment Index is High in Europe and America While Africa and Latin America are Lagging Behind

The Software environment score distribution of the sample cities highlights some characteristics of this index. The software environment of developed countries is very much superior and there is a wide gap between them and the developing countries (see Fig. 5.19). Most of the cities in the United States, Western Europe, Australia and New Zealand have a Software environment score higher than 0.8. The local governments of these cities are financially autonomous, have effective governmental business regulations, are more culturally inclusive and have a sound legal system. Countries in central and western Asia, Africa and Latin America all bear the marks of software environment "mishaps". Even so, improvements to software environment are a long and arduous process.

The top 10 positions in the rankings by software environment (see Table 5.19) are almost all taken by cities in the United States, which has six sports in the

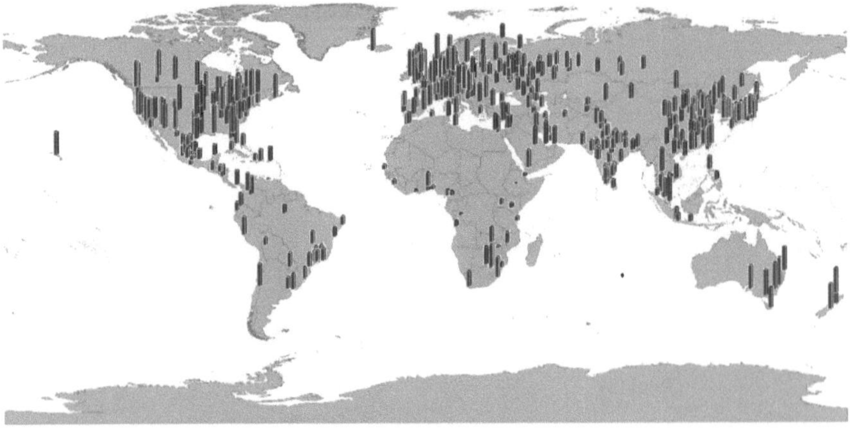

Fig. 5.19 Software environment index distribution of 505 sample cities. *Source* CASS city and competitiveness index database

rankings. This is clear indication of US superiority in software environment. The British capital London takes the first place in the world rankings for software environment. Sydney of Australia takes the third place. Asia's Singapore and Hong Kong of China are No. 4 and No. 6 respectively. Africa and Latin America do not have a single city in the top 10. With the exception of Hong Kong, which is one of the four Asian Dragons, no developing country has any city in the top 10. The software environment of countries that are still developing is quite poor and they lack the experience of developed countries in the development of market economy. Institutional elements such as government services, public safety, social justice, environmental protection and legal protection are far from perfect.

The distribution of the software environment top 100 cities highlights the problems (see Table 5.20). Almost 60% of the top 100 cities are North American cities, accounting for more than half all sample cities of the continent. This region is clearly exceptional in software environment. The performance of Oceanian cities is also outstanding, with all their sample cities in the top 100 and a mean far surpassing the world average. Its coefficient of variation is also the lowest and the performance of cities quite balanced. The performance of cities in Asia, Africa and Latin America is quite poor. Only 3.65% of Asian sample cities made it into the top 100. A few Asian cities with excellent performance in software environment like Singapore and Hong Kong are among them. The majority of Asian cities are outclassed by other cities. South America and Africa are almost totally left in the dust, except for only one city, Santiago, ranking 99th and barely making it into the top 100 cities. The world cities are cleanly split into two main groups in terms of software environment.

5.5.2 *Crime Rate Index*[2]

Public security is a basic need of people for production and development. It is a composite concept. Natural disasters, industrial accidents, food safety incidents, traffic accidents, fire hazards and contagious diseases are all factors jeopardizing public security. Among these, traffic accidents and fire hazards are sporadic events and are not dependable determinants of overall public security. Under the premise of data availability, crime rate is a reasonable and feasible gauge of public security. Taking the ease of calculation into consideration, "1-crime rate" is the index used to represent public security conditions. The higher the score, the better the social order of the city.

[2]The higher the composite urban competitiveness score, the higher the ranking. The higher the crime rate, however, the poorer the social security of the city and the lower the social security index of the city. In order to facilitate the calculation of the composite index, we adjusted the crime rate index and the current crime rate index that we have is actually 1-Crime Rate. Therefore, when the said index is higher, this means that the safety index of the city is higher and the composite score is higher.

Table 5.19 Global software environment index top 10 cities

City	London	Palo Alto	Sydney	Singapore	San Diego	Hong Kong	Cincinnati	Tampa	Cleveland	New Orleans
Continent	Europe	North America	Australia	Asia	North America	Asia	North America	North America	North America	North America
Score	1.000	0.982	0.972	0.953	0.951	0.951	0.950	0.950	0.950	0.950
Ranking	1	2	3	4	5	6	7	8	9	10

Source CASS city and competitiveness index database

Table 5.20 Global software environment index: continental analysis and proportion in the top 100

Region	Sample size	Number (percentage) of cities in top 100	Mean	Coefficient of variation	Maximum		
					City	Score	World ranking
Asia	192	7 (3.65%)	0.514	0.292	Singapore	0.953	4
Europe	136	25 (18.38%)	0.608	0.251	London	1	1
North America	107	59 (55.14%)	0.699	0.362	Palo Alto	0.982	2
South America	28	1 (3.57%)	0.428	0.333	Santiago	0.783	99
Oceania	9	8 (88.89%)	0.856	0.093	Sydney	0.972	3
Africa	33	0 (0%)	0.301	0.738	Johannesburg	0.770	105
World Average	505	100 (100%)	0.566	0.375	London	1	1

Source CASS city and competitiveness index database

5.5.2.1 Overall Pattern: The Index is Left-Skewed and Two Tenths of the Cities are Lower than the World Mean

The public security index mean is 0.959, and the coefficient of variation is 0.093. This means that public security conditions are quite good on the whole. It can be seen from the kernel density distribution (see Fig. 5.20) of the public security index (1-crime rate) that cities are concentrated in areas with high public security scores and the peak is left-skewed. Only a small number of cities are scattered in zones

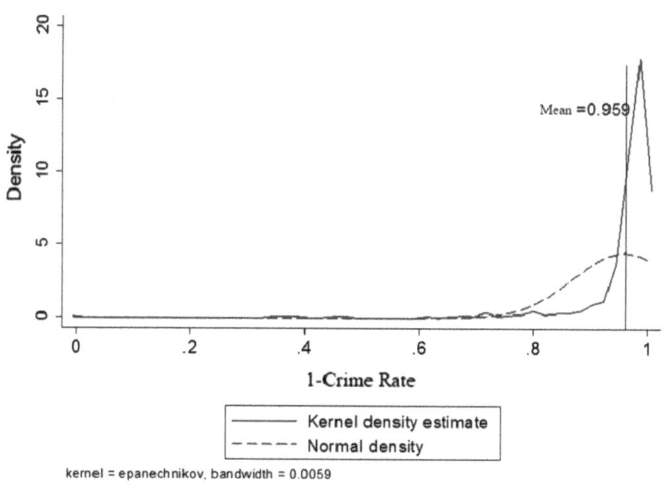

Fig. 5.20 Crime rate index kernel density distribution. *Source* CASS city and competitiveness index database

with low scores and the distribution is skewed towards the left with a long tail. From the numerical point of view, there are only about 20% of the cities with a mean that is below the world average and these cities are mainly to be found in North and South Americas and Africa.

5.5.2.2 Regional Pattern: Asian and European Mainland Fare Well Generally While the American and African Continents have Poor Public Security

The global top 10 cities by the public security index are all from Asia, especially Japan and China, with many of their cities making it into this list. The city with the lowest crime rate is Yokohama of Japan. Governments in Asia have created a safe and secure environment social and economic development. We classified the world cities by continents and plotted the public security index kernel density distribution of the Eurasia mainland, South and North Americas, Oceania and Africa (see Fig. 5.21). It can be clearly seen that the situation is very good in Eurasia. Crime rate is generally low and there is good public security. In comparison, public security in the American and African continents is troubling. Countries with the highest crime rates in the world are all located on these two continents. The United States, Canada, Brazil and South Africa are countries with the highest crime rates in the world. These countries have the worst problems of violence and the highest rates of gun-related deaths. A variety of criminal offenses have become the most prominent social issues that these countries are facing. In the United States, the number of people who died of gun shots has surpassed that of the number of deaths from terrorist attacks. The proliferation of firearms allows shooting incidents to

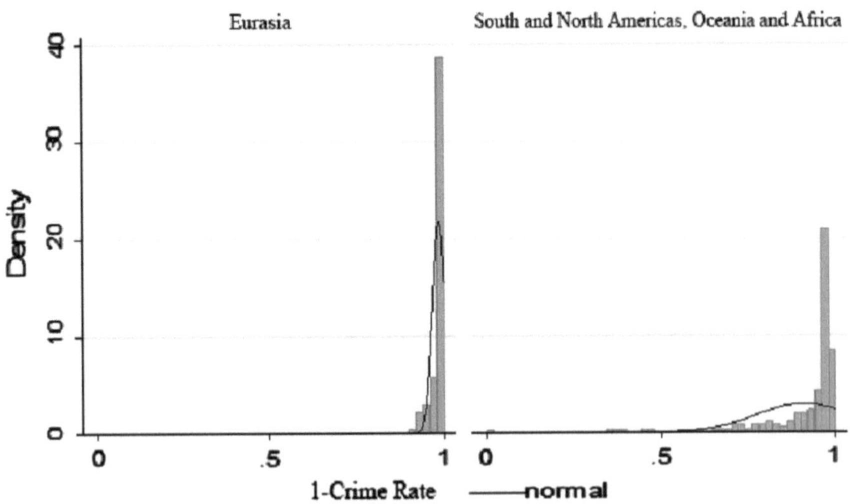

Fig. 5.21 Public security index (crime rate) kernel density function distribution. *Source* CASS city and competitiveness index database

happen frequently. Even so, the political system of these countries does not favor the control of firearms and the personal safety of citizens and public security remains a tricky issue.

5.6 Global Connection

The division of labor in society requires economic entities to have frequent contacts and interactions. Economic globalization leads to frequent and broad-based contact in the areas of politics, economy, society and culture between countries, cities, companies and even families. Economic connections and political, social and cultural connections influence one another. Ultimately, this ends in the congregation of industries within cities and the creation of markets for products and elements. Therefore, global connection has a great impact on the sustainable development of cities. The global connection index is constructed from three lower-level indicators: multinational corporation index (measurement of economic connection), international reputation index (examination of a city's reputation) and the number of air routes (representing level of external-facing infrastructure).

5.6.1 Summary of Global Connection Index

5.6.1.1 Overall Pattern: The Global Connection World Average is Low and the Gap Between Cities is Significant

We charted the Global connection scores of the 505 sample cities by segments (see Fig. 5.22, left) and the kernel density distribution (see Fig. 5.22, right). Only 11.3% of the cities have a global connection score higher than 0.5. Close to 20% of the

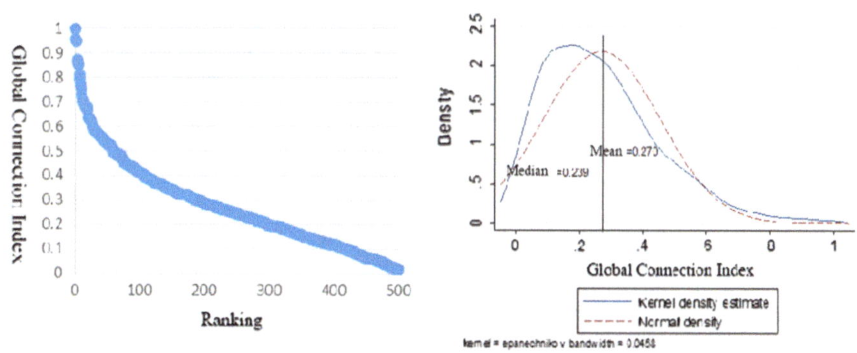

Fig. 5.22 Global connection index by segments and kernel density distribution. *Source* CASS city and competitiveness index database

cities have a score lower than 0.1. The global connection index mean is 0.27 and the median is 0.239. This further shows how low the overall scores of the cities are for this index. The global connection index coefficient of variation is 0.678, which shows that the dispersion between cities is quite large. The imbalance between the performances of cities constitutes a tricky problem. The distribution pattern of the global connection scores can be seen in the kernel density distribution. The peak of the frequency distribution is left-skewed with a long tail extending to the right. In contrast to normal distribution, the overall distribution of the global connection scores is left-skewed with high peaks. Close to 80% of the cities have a global connection score between 0 and 0.4. Only a small number of cities are doing well in on this indicator. The majority of cities are lagging behind.

5.6.1.2 Regional Pattern: Countries in Europe and America have Become Global Hubs. Countries in Africa and Latin America are Marginalized

The global connection index distribution of the sample global cities clearly illustrates the spatial distribution of the global connection of cities (see Fig. 5.23). Cities with higher scores are concentrated in three regions—Europe, North America and the Asia Pacific. The distribution in Europe is denser in cities with higher scores and these cities are concentrated in western and northern Europe. The Asian cities are concentrated in the west coast of the Pacific Ocean, Southeast Asia and the Middle East. Cities in North America with high global connection scores are mainly from the United States, with outstanding performance especially from cities on the east and west coasts. Africa and South America fare badly in global connection, with the exception of a few coastal cities. High global connection scores are also found in some cities in East Australia and in the New Zealand capital, Wellington.

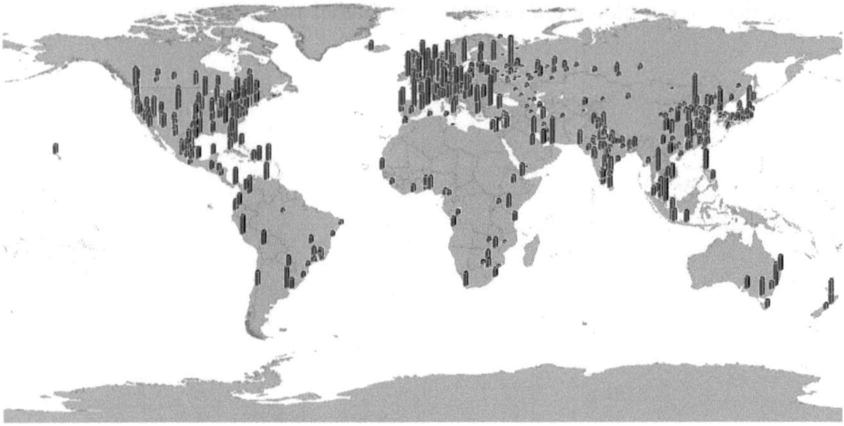

Fig. 5.23 Global connection index distribution of 505 sample cities. *Source* CASS city and competitiveness index database

Table 5.21 Global connection index top 10 cities

City	London	Paris	New York	Beijing	Moscow	Shanghai	Tokyo	Hong Kong	Istanbul	Frankfurt
Continent	Europe	Europe	North America	Asia	Europe	Asia	Asia	Asia	Asia	Europe
Score	1	0.959	0.949	0.872	0.861	0.852	0.813	0.795	0.770	0.754
Ranking	1	2	3	4	5	6	7	8	9	10

Source CASS city and competitiveness index database

Table 5.22 Global connection index: continental analysis and proportion in the top 100

Region	Sample size	Number (percentage) of cities in top 100	Mean	Coefficient of variation	Maximum		
					City	Score	World ranking
Asia	192	21 (10.94%)	0.225	0.750	Beijing	0.872	4
Europe	136	45 (33.09%)	0.307	0.701	London	1	1
North America	107	27 (25.23%)	0.337	0.471	New York	0.949	3
South America	28	4 (14.29%)	0.222	0.673	Buenos Aires	0.595	28
Oceania	9	2 (22.22%)	0.337	0.414	Sydney	0.584	30
Africa	33	1 (3.03%)	0.185	0.582	Johannesburg	0.453	76
World Average	505	100 (100%)	0.270	0.678	London	1	1

Source CASS city and competitiveness index database

Among the top 10 cities by Global connection (see Table 5.21), the highest number of cities are from Asia, taking half the spots. Among them, China's performance is the strongest, with high scores from Beijing, Shanghai and Hong Kong. Beijing is also the Asian city with the highest global connection score. Japan's Tokyo is ranked 7th on the list. The British capital London, and the French capital Paris are No. 1 and No. 2 in the rankings respectively. The Russian capital Moscow is in the 5th place, and Frankfurt of Germany is No. 10. The United States only has one city in the top 10, its largest city, New York, in the 3rd place.

Cities in Asia, Europe and North America make up 93% of the global connection top 100 cities (see Table 5.22). South America, Africa and Oceania are relatively backward. Cities in Europe and North America have the best performance in terms of the proportion of their cities making it into the list. Only 10.94% of Asian cities are in the top 100, meaning that there are very few Asian cities with high scores. Overall, Asian cities are still not on par yet with those of Europe and America. Looking at the global connection index mean and coefficient of variation of the different continents, North American cities have the highest mean and a coefficient of variation that is way below the world average. Asian cities have a mean that is lower than the world average and a coefficient of variation that is higher than the world average. This further shows that while the major cities in Asia are outstanding, the overall standard is poor and the gap between cities is very large.

5.6.2 *Airline Index*

Airlines offer efficient long-distance transportation and are changing the means and range by and in which the world communicates. International aviation hubs have also become key points for the globalization of an integrated national transportation

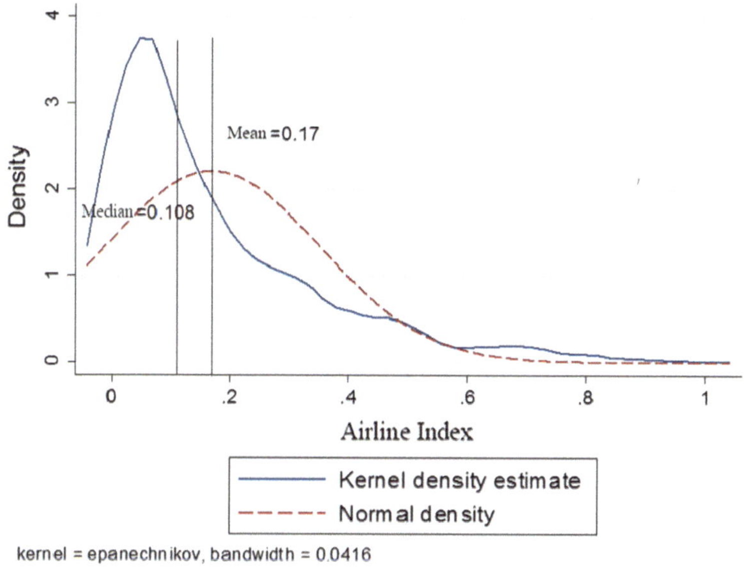

Fig. 5.24 Airline index kernel density distribution. *Source* CASS city and competitiveness index database

system. The most significant feature of a city which is an international aviation hub is the large number of air routes and the close links with world cities, which goes to say that the number of air routes of an airport reflects the standard of cities in the midst of worldwide communication and activities. The busiest global air routes are cross-North Atlantic routes between western Europe and North America connecting aviation hubs like Paris, London, Frankfurt, New York, Chicago and Montreal; western Europe to Middle East to Far East routes connecting the main airports of western Europe and the Far East cities of Hong Kong, Beijing and Tokyo while passing through important stops like Athens, Cairo, Tehran, Karachi, New Delhi, Bangkok and Singapore; North Pacific Ocean routes between the Far East and North America, which is the route across the open skies of the North Pacific Ocean from Beijing, Hong Kong and Tokyo to the west coast of North America such as Vancouver, Seattle, San Francisco and Los Angeles, and even extending to the east coast cities of North America. Honolulu, in the middle of the Pacific Ocean, is the main refueling stop on this route.

5.6.2.1 Overall Pattern: More than 60% of the Cities are Below World Average and the Airline Index is Severely Polarized

The global airline index has a mean of 0.17 and a median of 0.108, which shows that more than half the cities have a score that is lower than the world average. The reason for this is that a small number of the outstanding cities push the airline index

Table 5.23 Airline index top 10 cities

City	Paris	Istanbul	Frankfurt	Moscow	London	Beijing	Amsterdam	Hague	Utrecht	New York
Continent	Europe	Asia	Europe	Europe	Europe	Asia	Europe	Europe	Europe	North America
Score	1	0.882	0.852	0.833	0.764	0.764	0.751	0.705	0.682	0.682

Source CASS city and competitiveness index database

mean up. The 1.062 coefficient of variation also shows that there is a huge difference between the airline scores of global cities and that the gap between cities is very large. Figure 5.24 shows the global airline index kernel density distribution. From the graph, more cities are found to be in areas with low scores and the peak is very much skewed to the left. Only a small number of cities are scattered high score areas and the long tail extends towards the right. From a numerical point of view, more than 60% of the cities have a score lower than the world average. A few aviation hubs for intercontinental transit are highly active.

5.6.2.2 Regional Pattern: The Airline Routes of Developed Countries are Generally Busy. The Major Cities in Developing Countries have a Higher Index

Among the global top 10 cities of airline index, with the exception of New York of the United States, ranking No. 10; and Asian cities Istanbul and Beijing, respectively in the 2nd and 6th places, the other cities are all European cities with French capital Paris topping the rankings. Currently, the most developed global commercial aviation transportation regions are North America, Western Europe and the Asia Pacific. Many aviation hub cities are both regional and international aviation centers. They are also the aviation hubs within their own countries at the same time. The airline index top 10 cities listed in Table 5.23 are world aviation hubs, as well as host cities of the busiest airports in their respective countries.

Looking at the distribution of the global airline index top 100 cities (see Table 5.24), Europe and North America have the highest proportion of cities in the rankings, which is more than a quarter. The top 100 cities concentrate in developed countries of Europe and North America, especially in countries of the European Union like the UK, France and Germany, and countries within the North America

Table 5.24 Global airline index: continental analysis and proportion in the top 100

Region	Sample size	Number (percentage) of cities in top 100	Mean	Coefficient of variation	Maximum		
					City	Score	World ranking
Asia	192	31 (16.15%)	0.158	1.034	Istanbul	0.882	2
Europe	136	36 (26.47%)	0.210	1.048	Paris	1	1
North America	107	29 (27.10%)	0.182	1.036	New York	0.705	8
South America	28	2 (4.14%)	0.134	0.753	Sao Paulo	0.351	72
Oceania	9	0 (0%)	0.121	0.755	Sydney	0.282	108
Africa	33	1 (3.03%)	0.096	0.900	Casablanca	0.302	97
World Average	505	100 (100%)	0.170	1.062	Paris	1	1

Source CASS city and competitiveness index database

Free Trade Area (NAFTA) like the United States and Canada. These countries see the highest frequency in global trade. Therefore, the airline index scores are higher. Following them are some Asian countries, especially those in the Asia Pacific, which includes Japan, the eastern coasts of China and the four Asian Dragons, assembling the most active economies to form international trade centers. The cities in these countries also became global aviation hubs. However, the central and southern regions of Asia are mostly developing countries and most of them are quite underdeveloped. Together with Africa and South America, with the exception of a few cities with busy airports, most of these cities have airports that are relatively remote and unreachable. Oceania's performance is hampered by its location and although there are developed countries, its airline index is not high compared to those of Europe and America.

Part II
Topic Report Cities Network Along the Silk Road

Chapter 6
Analytical Framework

6.1 Defining the Silk Road

With the rise of China and the spotlight on the strategic position of the ancient Silk Road running through the Eurasian continent in recent years, countries with an interest in this region are all coming forward with strategic concepts for this region. Some of the more influential proposals come from Japan's "Silk Road Diplomacy", the "North–South Corridor" plan of Russia, India and other countries, the EU's "New Silk Road Plan", the US's "New Silk Road Strategy" and China's Belt and Road Initiative. Due to the vast area of land in this region, it plays an important part in world economics and politics. The implementation and promotion of the Silk Road strategy may lead to profound changes in the economic geography of Europe, Asia and Africa, and even the world. In this context, the systematic understanding of the historical evolution, current developments and future direction of the Silk Road has become the basic link between seizing the opportunities in the countries along the Silk Road and the economic and geographical developments in Europe, Asia and Africa.

In fact, since the successive introduction of Silk Road-related plans by many countries, especially since the issuance of the *Vision and Actions on Jointly Building the Silk Road Economic Belt and 21st-Century Maritime Silk Road* by the Chinese government in 2015, this has become an important theoretical and practical concern of the countries and regions along the Silk Road that has received widespread attention from the academia and governments. Many studies discuss the strategic implications, opportunities, challenges and responses concerning development along the Silk Road from different angles. But in any case, it is important to get an understanding of the Silk Road from the perspective of cities. As a category of spatial unit that brings together large populations and industry sectors, cities are important venues where human economic and social activities have been taking place since their inception, the backbone promoting the economic development of regions and countries. The rise of the Silk Road requires strong support from countries and cities along the routes. Examining the development of the Silk Road

© China Social Sciences Press and Springer Nature Singapore Pte Ltd. 2017
P. Ni et al., *Cities Network Along the Silk Road*,
DOI 10.1007/978-981-10-4834-0_6

from the perspective of city systems does not simply help us make use of the Silk Road's historical changes, current situation, influencing factors and direction of future development. There is also great significance in its promotion of the Belt and Road Initiative and the development of the countries along the routes to gain a comprehensive understanding of the development opportunities and challenges of the Silk Road, as well as to create a win-win-win collaboration between Europe, Asia and Africa.

Reviewing the history of mankind, countries and regions were connected along a variety of routes, which acted as physical vessels through which business and cultural exchanges were conducted, playing an important role in the promotion of mutual learning and open development of civilizations in countries along the route. As a strategic corridor connecting the three major continents of Asia, Europe and Africa, and the three oceans, i.e. the Pacific Ocean, the Indian Ocean and the Atlantic Ocean, the Silk Road has been bridging and facilitating cultural exchanges and trade between the East and the West since ages long past. Historically, the Silk Road is consisted of sea and land routes (see Fig. 6.1). The Silk Road on land refers collectively to the many historical routes first blazed by Zhang Qian in his capacity as an envoy to the Western Territories during the Western Han Dynasty in ancient China. It starts from Chang'an (Xi'an in modern day China), passes along the Hexi Corridor and the Tarim Basin, then goes through Central Asia and West Asia and ends finally in Europe. The Silk Road connects the cities of Xi'an, Lanzhou, Urumqi, Almaty, Bishkek, Dushanbe, Samarqand and Istanbul. The Maritime Silk Road was formed during China's Qin and Han dynasties and developed through the Three Kingdom period and the Sui Dynasty to its height during the Tang and Song dynasties. It includes maritime trade routes setting off from Guangzhou, Quanzhou and Hangzhou to the Arabian Sea and the east coast of Africa, and it connects cities

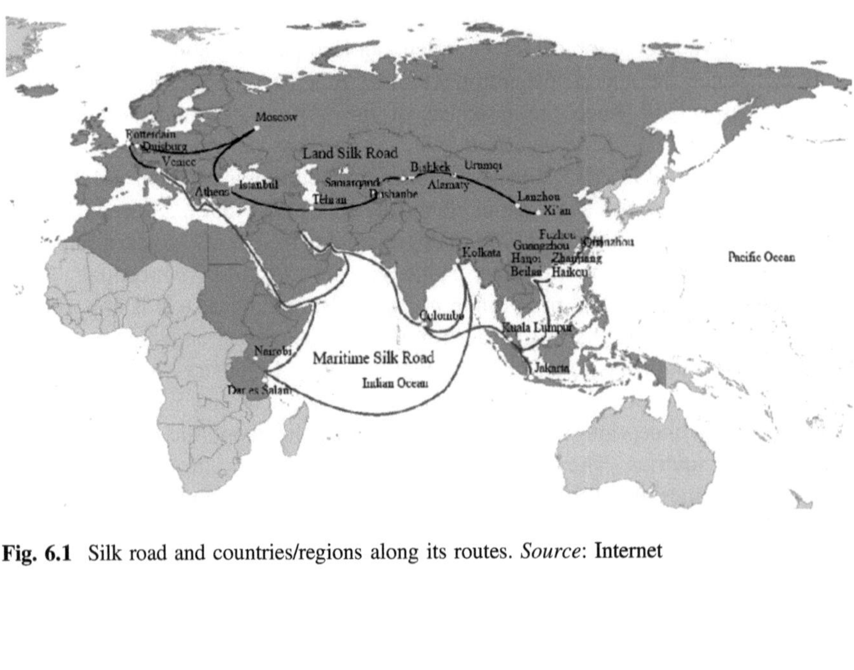

Fig. 6.1 Silk road and countries/regions along its routes. *Source*: Internet

like Jakarta, Kuala Lumpur, Kolkata, Colombo, Nairobi, Athens and Venice. The land and sea routes of the Silk Road are known collectively as the Silk Road. For hundreds and thousands of years, the countries along the routes connect and communicate through exchanges in property and treasures, plant and animal species, production and technology, scientific achievements and results, and culture and religion via the Silk Road and its cities, promoting friendly interactions between Asia, Europe and Africa as well as the development of world civilizations.

As science and technology advance, the economy and society develop, and globalization continues, the Silk Road has been given new meaning in present times. The contemporary Silk Road refers to the route of trade and cultural exchanges that is established upon the basis of the ancient routes and pinned by China's initiative of the "Silk Road Economic Belt" and the "21st Century Maritime Silk Road". The objective of the Belt and Road Initiative is to promote the joint development of trade and cultural exchanges in the countries along the routes. It is an open regional arrangement with cities of different scale, characteristics, and types connected by a few main transportation and trading routes and sub-routes to form a multi-staggered axial, zonal or meshed distribution.

For the purpose of defining the Silk Road, this report refers to the land and sea routes collectively as the Silk Road. The Silk Road is broadly defined to determine the overall places it passes through and the countries and regions involved (45 Asian countries, 43 European countries and 12 African countries), and to determine which cities in those countries are included. These cities are collectively known as Silk Road cities. Looking at the distribution of cities with a population of more than 300,000, the Silk Road covers several large regions with relatively dense distribution of cities in East Asia, South Asia and Europe. (see Fig. 6.2). When the Arctic and Antarctic regions are excluded, the regions covered by the network formed by Silk Road cities account for half of the world (Asia, Europe and Africa), covering approximately 53.6% of the land area on Earth.

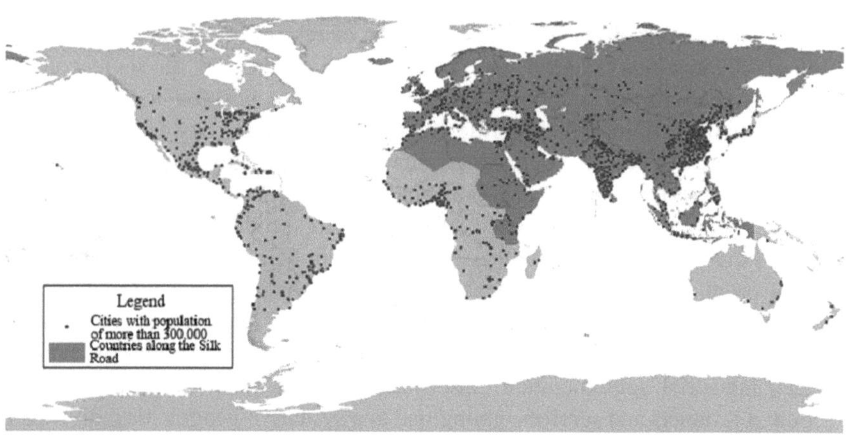

Fig. 6.2 Cities distribution of countries/regions along the silk road. *Source*: department of economic and social affairs, United Nations

6.2 Analytical Framework

As a political, economic, technological and cultural center of the modern society, a prominent feature of a city is its spatial agglomeration and operational openness. On the one hand, a city is the result of agglomeration, perhaps even a form of agglomeration caused by regional economic integration. On the other hand, cities connect with surrounding areas in production and other aspects. The different types of urban agglomeration at different levels and their connections are all set within a larger economic system. Its advanced form of development forms a complex city network system that will have an important impact on economic development.

6.2.1 Dimensional Analysis: Cities Network

A dimension is a specific perspective in understanding economic and social phenomena. As an advanced form of human social life, cities and their networks have been a manifestation of the development of human civilization and productivity since their emergence. Together, they are an important dimension by which the rise and fall of regions and nations can be explained. Among them, centrality and connection constitute the two main parts of the analysis of a cities network.

6.2.1.1 Centrality: Internal Development of Cities

Centrality shows the importance of a city in its network. Centrality is reflective not only of the capacity of a city to pool elements and provide goods and services to its surrounding areas, but also of the relative importance of a city amidst connections with neighboring regions. A central city is the service center of a city network and also a regional control and distribution center of resources, responsible for coordination, organization, control, and command in the region. In socioeconomic terms, the centrality of a city refers to the important position it takes through continuous connections and clustering processes between the city and other regions in the network. As nodes of a network, cities gather not only population, but also products and services, factors of production and industries, which all contribute to the development within the cities. Among them, products and services have evolved from being singular to diversified, and from being simple to complex. The scale of production, production density, amount of output per capita and growth rate shows the state of development in different cities. The factors of production involved are indicative of the extent of development in the cities in different aspects. Industrial agglomeration closely accompanies such factors and the production of products and services, giving rise to a system of geographical division of labor according to the natural resources and demand of each region.

In the clustering process of products, services, factors of production, and industries, city development is not just about the increment and expansion of wealth and economy. It is also indicative of innovation in the economic and social structures, and improvement in the standard of living and the input–output efficiency. In the open system of a city, the criteria of a centrality midst its fluid spaces do not only include the quantity of resources and output that it controls, but also include the quality of resources in circulation within. Compared to the economic size contained within a unit area of the city (GDP per unit land area), economic size measured in terms of output per capita, i.e. GDP per capita, is indicative of a city's extent of development. It is also able to compare population agglomeration against production agglomeration. Therefore, this report measures the centrality of the city network primarily using GDP per capita.

6.2.1.2 Connection Between Cities

Connection, when simply defined, means communication and contact. A more complex definition is an organic relationship between matters, one that is objective, universal and diverse. A cities network is a more complex system than a single city and it comes with an innate openness to internal and external connections. This connection spans products, services, personnel, capital, technology, etc. and also includes social connection such as culture and religion. In the midst of deepening connection between cities, a network structure is formed from the many instances in which cities become intersection points, routes become linkages, and the flowing people, commodities, capital and information become elements, and their organic connection. Within this network structure, connection takes place between cities in the areas of products, elements, industries etc. i.e. connection greatly reflects the status and ability of a city in controlling and allocating resources. Against the backdrop of continued globalization, cities are set within an enormous city network connected by the various flows of information, capital, labor etc. The Globalization and World Cities Research Network (GaWC) does not simply reflect the strength of a city's external relations, but is further capable of displaying the functional status of various cities as nodes in the "service flow" of the entire world network.

Multinational passageways of trade and cultural exchange connect cities, regions and countries along the routes. They involve connections in the economic, social, cultural and many other areas, and are comprised of three main categories of entities i.e. countries, cities and companies. Among them, cities are the core of connections between individual participants, organizations, institutions, etc. and of exchanges and cooperation between countries. In the city network, the strength, frequency and depth by which different cities connect with each other are different. There will be differences in the spatial range of connection. Therefore, the connection of a single city in the city network, in essence, shows its status and capabilities within the city network. Along with centrality, connection constitutes the core of city network analysis.

6.2.2 Supporting Factors: Hardware and Software

The city network is a specific type of spatial structure formed through the organic combination of city agglomeration and connection within and between cities. Its development and evolution is the result of the combined effect of many elements. According Neo-economic geography, increasing returns, transportation costs and the interaction between the flows of elements will result in the evolution of the economic spatial structure into a "centre–periphery" pattern. The increasing returns of space will result in the most essential economic force in industrial agglomeration. The agglomeration of elements and economic activities is brought about through promoting the sharing of external economies and there is frequent and continuous reinforcement together with the cumulative causation of forward and backward linkages to form specialized core areas and non-specialized peripherals. The contraction of time and space activated by the decrease in transportation costs will weaken the friction of economic activities and will continuously strengthen connection between regions. This includes accessibility enhancements from improvements to infrastructure such as transportation conditions, as well as reduction in transaction costs from improvements to software environment such as market regulations. In this process, there are both agglomeration and diffusion effects to the "centre–periphery" pattern. The formation, development and evolution of this particular spatial structure of a city network will be impacted by many factors, especially the influencing factors on development and connection between multinational and multiregional cities that are also increasingly complex. In summary, its supporting factors include both hardware and software aspects:

6.2.2.1 Hardware Factors

Natural environment: The natural environment is the material basis for human survival and socioeconomic development. Relatively superior natural and geographic conditions provide basic support for the birth and development of cities. Differences in the original endowments hidden within the natural environment imperceptibly have a fundamental impact on the course of a city's development.

Infrastructure: This includes economic and social infrastructure. Economic infrastructure such as transportation, postal and telecommunications, and energy supply play the role of material capital and are directly involved in the production process. Transportation, in particular, directly impacts accessibility between the cities. Social infrastructure such as science, education, culture and health and environmental protection impacts human, social and cultural capital, and is the foundation for adjusting and optimizing economic structure, improving investment environment, and promoting economic development.

Trade Demand: The wealth and prosperity of a country and its people, and its demand for foreign goods is a direct impetus for inter-city trade. The difference in demand preferences forms the foundation for mutually beneficial trade. Differences and complementarity in the trade demand of cities of a region constitute the initial impetus for the promotion of trade in goods and services. Diversified trade demand and its composition will lead to changes in the regional trade structure, further strengthening the industrial division of labor between cities and even countries.

Market Demand: Market demand is closely related to the size of economy, population and income level of a country or a region (city). Different aspects of different cities such as the size of economy, population and income of residents fundamentally determine the spatial distribution of market demand and affect the size, direction and model of the circulation of goods and services between cities.

6.2.2.2 Software Factors

Institutional Arrangement: A system is a standard restraining the behavior of individuals and organizations. It includes official systems such as laws and regulations, and informal systems such as customs. It is born out of the process of economic development and it affects economic development. Against the backdrop of economic globalization, the differences of a city in software environment such as management and services, differences at the national level such as investment and trade, as well as rules and institutional arrangements impact the agglomeration and connection regarding goods and services, factors of production and industrial agglomeration between cities of different countries.

State Relations: Relations between countries determine whether there is any connection or whether the connection is weak or strong between cities. This is especially true for foreign trade and cultural exchanges. When political relations between countries along the routes feature tension, hostility or harmony, the trade and cultural connections between cities will differ.

Political Situation: All development and connection between cities occur against the backdrop of specific global political situations. Global political situations and changes play an important part in remodeling specific regions, geopolitical situations, and state relations, thereby affecting the mobility of personnel, flow of elements and industrial changes between countries and cities.

Religion and Culture: As an informal institutional factor, religion and culture affect and restrict the economic actions of individuals and organizations in different regions. Countries and regions with different religious and cultural backgrounds have differences in religious exchange, cultural exchange and mutual learning, which produces different economic results.

To sum up, within the analytical framework of the city network and by focusing on development and connections, centrality (development within cities) and connection (connection between cities) make up the main body of a city network. Development provides support for the network in the form of agglomeration, connection establishes network connection in the form of spatial streaming, and the

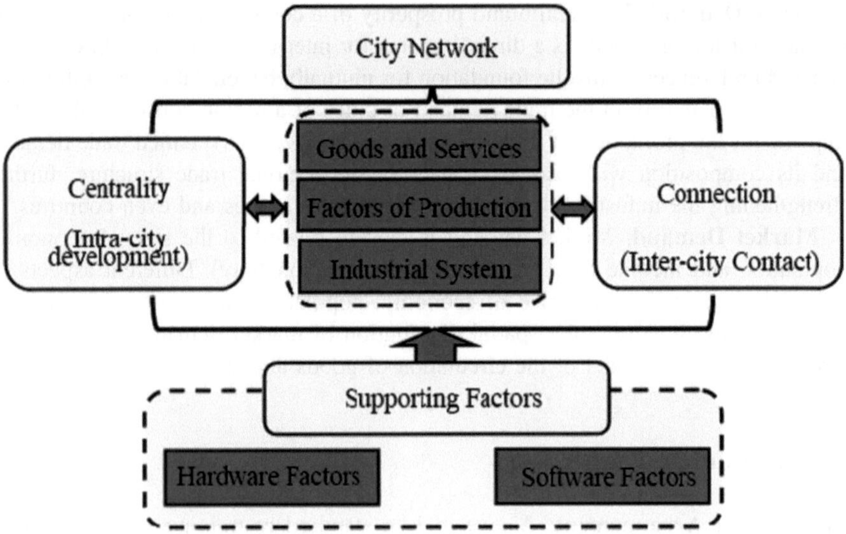

Fig. 6.3 Analytical framework

entire formation and evolution of the city network shall unfold through changes in development and connection contents such as goods and services, factors of production and industrial system etc. Furthermore, this kind of evolution are affected and supported by hardware factors such as natural conditions, infrastructure, trade demand and market demand, as well as by software factors such as institutional setup, state relations, political situation and religion and culture etc. They jointly constitute the analytical framework (see Fig. 6.3) of this report, and will be accommodated in the entire process of analyzing the historical evolution, current developments and future growth of the Silk Road from an urban dimension.

Chapter 7
Historical Evolution of the Ancient Silk Road

7.1 Development of the Ancient Silk Road

The Silk Road was first explored during the Western Han Dynasty (206BC–25AD), by Zhang Qian through a series travels across the Western Territories of China. At that time, China was the only producer of silk in the world. Prices were exorbitant and the product was easy to carry. Therefore, silk was the main commodity sold to the West. By the time of the Song and Yuan dynasties, maritime trade had reached its peak. As the Song, Yuan and Ming dynasties did not exert control over the Western Territories, the main trade route to West Asia and Europe was via the seas. The main commodity that was traded between the East and the West also changed from silk to porcelain. This East–West route closely connected the Chinese Mainland and Western Territories to Arabia and Persia. After a few centuries of continual development and evolution, the Silk Road extended all the way to the Mediterraneans. The eastern end of the Silk Road roughly extended to South Korea and Japan, and the western end reached France and the Netherlands. The maritime route covered even Italy and Egypt, and it became a "road of friendship" of economic and cultural exchanges between Asia, Europe and Africa.

The main territories covered by the ancient Silk Road on land were mainly the inland areas that lay between China and Europe. This region has an unusually dry climate and rainfall is extremely scarce. The main way of transportation was animals like camels and horses and stops along the route were needed for transit and replenishment of food supplies. Therefore, settlements along the Silk Road gradually became centers where people and goods gather, merchandise was exchanged and merchants made their transactions; and gradually, this led to the formation of a great number of ancient Western Territories cities along the routes. Major cities for maritime trade were mainly situated close to estuaries (mainly river ports rather than sea ports) along navigated river courses as the ships in those days had small

© China Social Sciences Press and Springer Nature Singapore Pte Ltd. 2017
P. Ni et al., *Cities Network Along the Silk Road*,
DOI 10.1007/978-981-10-4834-0_7

capacities and shallow drafts and river ports were more than enough to satisfy the requirements and safety needs. In addition, it was easier for ports located at estuaries to move the overseas supplies inland. In history, examples of strategically important Silk Road cities include Ningbo at the Yongjiang River, Quanzhou at the Jinjiang River inlet, and Guangzhou at the Pearl River Delta. The emergence of the ancient port cities of the Silk Road was not only the result of positive natural conditions, but also closely related to seaborne transportation and overseas trade.

7.2 Factors Influencing the Development of the Ancient Silk Road

A necessary guarantee for the development of the ancient Silk Road is political stability. A strong central government and its power to control areas along the Silk Road are what ensured the accessibility of the Silk Road and made it possible for Silk Road cities to develop and prosper. A stable and powerful central administration and its ability to have effective jurisdiction over the regions along the Silk Road ensures its smooth flow, thereby creating the necessary conditions for promoting the development and prosperity of the towns and cities along the route. Conversely, the pace and scale of development of the Silk Road towns and cities will be negatively impacted by inadequate control by the central government. Political and military factors have always been the main driving force promoting the development of towns and cities along the Silk Road. The developmental changes of the towns and cities are closely related to the development and operations of the central dynasty. With each rise and decline of the central dynasties, the setup changes according to the different scale of border expansion and the corresponding administrative system and cities that are strategic military strongholds. The developmental process of the towns and cities of this region also shows a lot of volatility.

Commerce and trade are the lifeblood of development for the ancient Silk Road. The rise and decline of towns and cities have a strong causal relationship to the rise and decline of trade along the Silk Road. Commerce is dependent upon the initiative of towns and cities, and the building of towns and cities is reliant on commercial interests. Along with the extension of the Silk Road and the development of trade along the Silk Road, market townships were formed in the areas with the most business activities. At the same time, the development of agriculture and animal husbandry made population agglomeration as well as handicraft industries and business travel supplies possible, enriching the variety of goods exchanged along the route, with agriculture and animal husbandry resources promoting the growth of many foodstuff trading and fur processing businesses in towns and cities. The ease of travelling on the Silk Road and trade activities along the route continued to develop, which led to the gathering of capital, goods and people at some of the better located towns and cities, hence driving the economic development of these towns and cities. Conversely, during times of trading decline along the Silk Road, trading also weakened in these towns and cities and the prosperity of the towns and cities along the Silk Road were definitely impacted.

Political necessity is the prerequisite for the formation of the Silk Road. The development and prosperity of the Silk Road is guaranteed by military strength. Once stability and peace in the Western Territories was under control and sustained, the economic and cultural interactions of China with the Western Territories and Europe would take place smoothly. If effective control over the Western Territories was lost, the Silk Road would be broken up. During Tang Dynasty, protectorate offices were established at Anxi and Beiting to provide military backing to the traffic routes to safeguard the close connection between the Chinese mainland and the Western Territories. The Silk Road continued to prosper and flourish during the Tang Dynasty. During the Song and Ming dynasties, as control over the Western Territories was lost, the routes gradually fell into disuse, and eventually, ceased to be used.

After the "An Lushan Rebellion" (755–762) during the Tang Dynasty, the country was greatly weakened and Tibetans occupied the Hexi Corridor and regions under the jurisdiction of the protectorates of Anxi and Beiting. The Silk Road was severed. At the same time, sea transportation grew popular and the economic center began moving towards the southeast. The Maritime Silk Road served as a replacement. In addition, the development of shipbuilding and navigation technology in China during the Tang Dynasty (618–907) also provided conditions for the opening-up and extension of routes to Southeast Asia, Straits of Malacca, the Indian Ocean, the Red Sea, as well as navigation routes to Africa. The Maritime Silk Road finally replaced the land route to become the main channel through which ancient China interacted with foreign lands. Zheng He made seven voyages west (1405–1433) successively in the early years of the Ming Dynasty, marking the peak period of the Maritime Silk Road. During the Ming and Qing dynasties, with the implementation of *haijin* (maritime trade ban) and the decline of China's navigation industry, the Maritime Silk Road, once a significant contributor to East–West exchanges, declined gradually as the maritime trade ban became increasingly stringent. Beginning in 1840, Western powers forced open the doors of China with powerful cannons. After two opium wars, China declined rapidly. Then, five countries in Central Asia became Russian territories. These two factors blocked China's path and journey to the West. The ancient Silk Road declined and was out of use by the end of the 19th century.

7.3 Development of Major Cities Along the Ancient Silk Road

During the development and evolution of the ancient Silk Road on land, a group of travelers' inns and coastal ports emerged and thrived to become major cities along the route. The development and connection of these cities are reflective of the state of development of the ancient Silk Road on land.

7.3.1 Silk Road on Land: Kashgar, Tehran and Istanbul

Kashgar, situated in southwestern Xinjiang, is at the intersection of the north and south routes of the ancient Silk Road. With the Tianshan Mountain to its north, the Pamir Plateau to its west, and eight different neighboring countries including Kyrgyzstan, Tajikistan, Afghanistan, Pakistan, and India, Kashgar has unique geographical advantages summed up by the saying, "five doorways to eight countries, one road between Europe and Asia". This is the No. 1 city of the ancient Silk Road leading from Central Asia and South Asia into China. It is also the access doorway to West Asia and Europe on land. During the Han Dynasty, Kashgar was known as Shule. Zhang Qian was here during his travels to the Western Territories. Ban Chao of the Eastern Han Dynasty was the administrator of the Western Territories and Kashgar was where he set up base. During the Tang Dynasty, it was one of the four townships of Anxi. During the early days of the Qing Dynasty, it was where the "Overall Administrator of the Eight Cities" diplomatic official to Kashgar was stationed. Since the hundreds and thousands of years past, Kashgar continued to be well-known as the center of politics, economics, culture and traffic south of Tianshan, and is an important town and international trading port where Chinese and foreign merchants congregate along the ancient Silk Road.

Tehran is a city with a long history. In the early years of the 9th century, it became a residential location, a suburb of Rey, a well-known city in those days, and was a resting place for ancient Silk Road merchants on the move. In the 13th century, Rey was destroyed by strong invasion forces and its role was taken over by Tehran. As this was the intersection between the main East–West road in northern Iran and the main road leading to the south, Tehran became a medium-sized city and trade center within a short period of time.

Istanbul is a military stronghold along the ancient Silk Road. During the development of Silk Road cities more than 2,000 years ago, Istanbul was where the land and sea routes of the Silk Road met. Historically, Istanbul was once the capital city of the Roman Empire, Byzantine Empire, Latin Empire, Ottoman Empire and the Republic of Turkey in its early days. The culture, language and religion of past rulers have been integrated into the city, and the thoughts, cultures and art of the people from the continents of Europe, Asia and Africa gathered here. Istanbul became an important meeting point of thoughts and culture from the East and the West, a shining treasure shared by Europe, Asia and Africa.

7.3.2 Silk Road by Sea: Fuzhou, Nairobi and Athens

Fuzhou is a famous historic city that goes hand in hand with the Maritime Silk Road. During the Tang Dynasty and the five Dynasties, there were frequent wars in the north and the land routes between China and the Western Territories were closed. The center of foreign economic and trade exchanges slowly shifted to the southeastern coasts. This situation created unprecedented opportunities that were favorable to the great development of cultural exchanges in Fuzhou and mainland China and overseas trade and transportation. Between the mid-Tang Dynasty and the five Dynasties, Fuzhou became an important port city and economic and cultural center of the Maritime Silk Road. During Song and Yuan dynasties, the shipping routes starting from Fuzhou reached Indochina, Malay Peninsula, Malay Archipelago and the Philippines in the south; various countries of South Asia and the countries and regions of India, Namburi, Guli, Arabia and Madagascar in West Asia and Africa. During the Ming Dynasty, Fuzhou was one of China's major shipbuilding bases. In the 24th year of Emperor Daoguang's reign during the Qing Dynasty (1844), Fuzhou became one of the five official trade ports of the country.

Nairobi is the capital of Kenya in East Africa, the farthest destination of the ancient Maritime Silk Road, and a major intersection city. Out of the seven voyages of Zheng He four led the great navigator to Kenya. As the transportation hub and economic leader of East Africa, Nairobi has developed into one of the four cities where a United Nations headquarters is located. It is the only city of a developing country with a UN headquarters and it also hosts UNEP and UN-Habitat.

Athens is the largest city and the economic, financial, industrial, political and cultural center of Greece. It is also one of the oldest cities in Europe and in the world. The ancient Greek Empire was a mighty and strong power for a period of time and its sphere of influence extended to the area around the Black Sea at one point, which opened up access to the supply of Chinese silk as well as resources from the East like furs and gold. As a core city in ancient Greece, Athens was the main point of intersection between the land and sea routes of the ancient Silk Road, already connected to China more than 2,000 years ago. Due to factors like flourishing trade and disruption by wars, Athens experienced many ups and downs in history.

7.4 Influence of the Ancient Silk Road

The ancient Silk Road paved the way for trade and communication between civilizations across the three major continents of Europe, Asia and Africa and brought together the cultures of ancient China, India, Greece and Persia. In addition to Chinese goods like silk and porcelain making their way to the West, techniques of silkworm-raising, gunpowder, compass, copper smelting, paper-making and printing. Also reached the lands of Central Asia, Iran and Rome one after another through the land and sea routes of the Silk Road. At the same time, goods and properties, astronomy, calendar, mathematics, medical science, music and arts etc. also flowed into China from Central Asia and the West via the Silk Road. The ancient Silk Road not only gave life to a few new cities and contributed to the continuous development of many existing cities along the route, it also promoted economic and social development of the countries and regions along the route through exchanges in goods, services, religion, culture and technology, thus putting in place significant historical foundation for the development of the present day Silk Road.

tended to the great development of cultural exchanges in Fuzhou and national China and overseas trade and transportation. Between the mid-Tang Dynasty and the five Dynasties, Fuzhou became an important port city and economic and cultural center of [illegible]

Chapter 8
Current Development of Silk Road Cities: An Emerging Irregular Cities Network

Through thousands of years of historical changes, the destiny of cities along the ancient Silk Road and the rise and fall of the countries they belonged to is closely linked with the destiny of the Silk Road. As the world situation shifts, there would be a thorough overhaul. After World War II, the countries along the Silk Road underwent different levels of development. At the western end of the Silk Road, the progress of cities accelerated further and took on post-modern characteristics as the economies of prosperous countries along the route recovered greatly and the economic power came primarily from the shift from industries to information. The urbanization of the many developing countries at the eastern and central parts of the Silk Road also saw rapid improvements, especially since the 1980s. There was rapid urbanization in the developing countries and this constitutes the majority of the world's urbanization today. Another important feature of urbanization in the current era is the prominent trend of metropolitanization and also the emergence of new forms of organizing urban space such as urban agglomeration and metropolitan belts. With this as a backdrop, the development and connection of cities along the Silk Road are shown to have developed some new characteristics.

8.1 Development of Cities Along the Silk Road

8.1.1 A Visual Presentation: Findings from Night Lights

As the major support for the economic and social development of countries along the Silk Road, the Silk Road cities have been developing rapidly after World War II and there are differences in the performance of cities in different regions. To get a visual understanding of the development of Silk Road cities, we first present the satellite image of night lights in these cities (see Fig. 8.1).

© China Social Sciences Press and Springer Nature Singapore Pte Ltd. 2017

P. Ni et al., *Cities Network Along the Silk Road*,
DOI 10.1007/978-981-10-4834-0_8

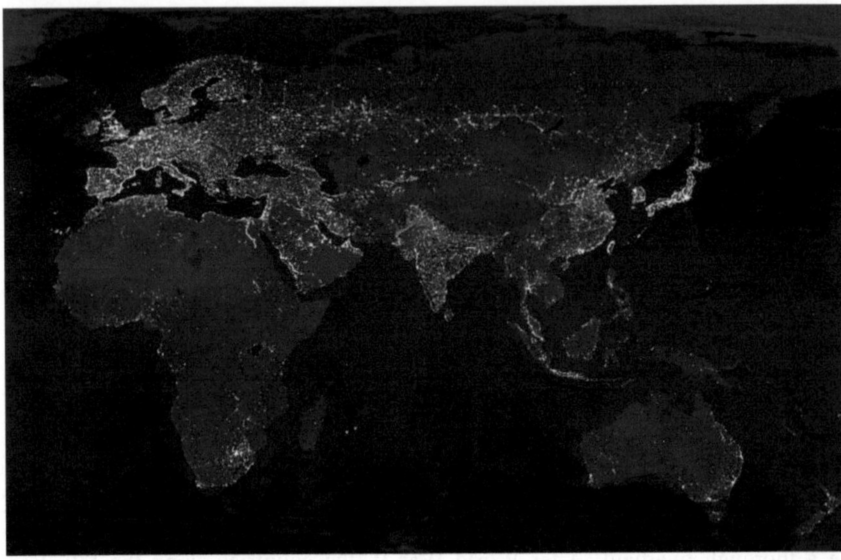

Fig. 8.1 Night Lights in Europe, Asia and Africa. *Source* NASA (http://visibleearth.nasa.gov)

It can be seen from the image that some cities along the eastern coast of China in the eastern part of the Silk Road as well as most of the European cities in the western section of the Silk Road are densely lighted. Some of the Southeast Asian countries, India of South Asia, the Arabian Peninsula and North Africa in the middle portion of the Silk Road are also densely lighted. The lights in the vast inlands of Eurasia are not uniform and have a scattered distribution. One can roughly make out two light belts. One belt passes through the Hexi corridor to reach Xinjiang, then through Central Asia into West Asia, and through Iran to Europe. The other light belt runs along the first Eurasian land bridge through the eastern and western parts of Russia. The brightness of the night lights in cities provides a visual reflection of the extent of economic agglomeration within the cities. The distribution of night lights as described above provides a visual indication of the uneven economic and social activities in the city spaces of the countries along the Silk Road.

8.1.2 Long-Term Development: Growth and Changes in City Population

The population of cities and their distribution are reflective of the degree of urbanization in a country. As a core feature of urban agglomeration, population growth and its changes are an important manifestation of a city's long-term development. Figure 8.2 shows the population distribution of cities along the Silk

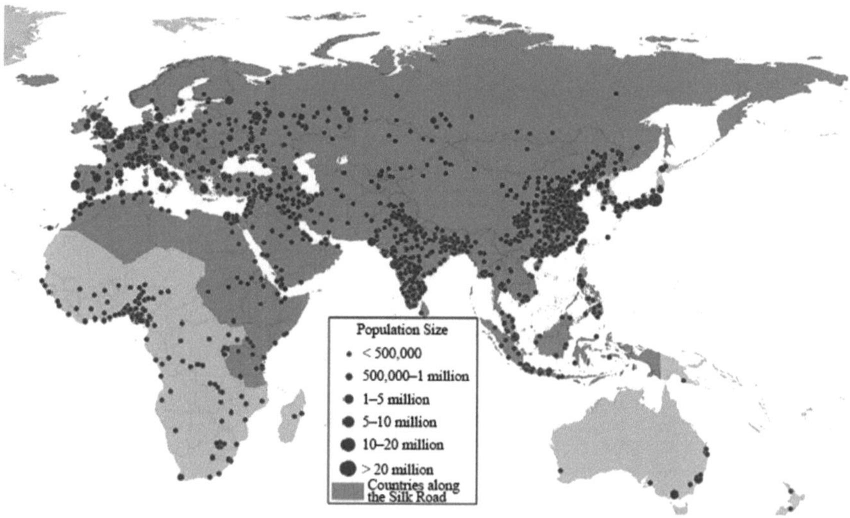

Fig. 8.2 Population distribution of Silk Road cities (1950). *Source* Department for Economic and Social Affairs, United Nations (http://esa.un.org/unpd/wup)

Road in 1950. From the image, it can be seen that city populations were distributed in China, Europe and India. Across the vast European inland, the population was generally quite small scattered. Looking at specific cities, London, Paris and Moscow were the top three cities along the Silk Road with an edge over the rest with their respective populations of 8.361, 6.283 and 5.356 million; Shanghai and Tianjin had a population of 4.301 and 2.467 million respectively and they were the two cities with the largest population in the eastern section of the Silk Road at that time. In comparison, the great majority of other Silk Road cities had a population of less than a million, in fact, most cities then had less than 500,000 people.

Following the rapid urbanization of Asian and African countries in the decades after war, the Silk Road cities also underwent rapid development, among which the most impressive growth came from their increasing population. Figure 8.3 shows the population distribution of the Silk Road cities in 2015, which has similarities with the 1950 distribution, as well as some new characteristics. On one hand, the size of cities in developing countries expanded rapidly in comparison with the developing countries in Europe, especially so in China and India. A visual representation of this phenomenon can be found in Fig. 8.4. On the other hand, some of the countries also saw rapid population growth in the non-hinterland areas of Europe and the emergence of large cities with populations of more than 1 million people, like Tashkent and Almaty. This goes to show that the urban agglomeration of these regions has grown further.

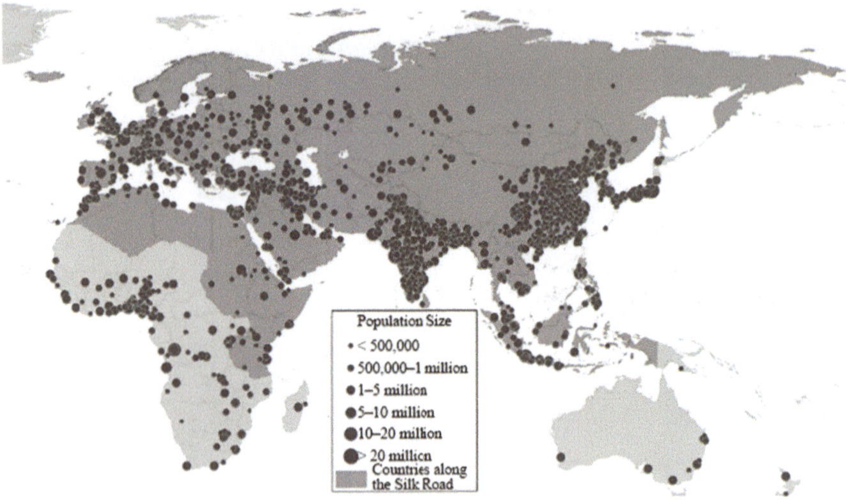

Fig. 8.3 Population distribution of Silk Road cities (2015). *Source* Department for Economic and Social Affairs, United Nations (http://esa.un.org/unpd/wup)

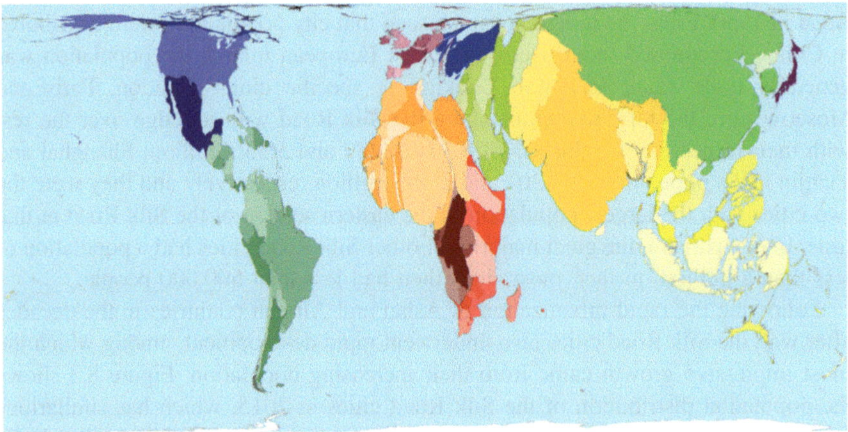

Fig. 8.4 2012–2015 global city population growth (Unit: million). *Source* http://www.sasi.group.shef.ac.uk/worldmapper/index.html. *Note* The larger the area of the countries in the figure, the higher the proportion of city population growth in the world during 2002–2015

Comparing the maps of the city night-time lights and city population distribution shows an overall match between the brightness of the lights and pattern, and the city population size and distribution, i.e. the distribution areas of urban population agglomeration are also where the night-time lights are brighter. The two maps jointly reflect the uneven agglomeration and development of Silk Road cities.

8.1.3 Patterns and Characteristics of Silk Road City Development

8.1.3.1 Overall Characteristics: a West-Raised U-shape Pattern

The development of Silk Road cities shows obvious spatial imbalance. Overall, the western and eastern ends are raised while the middle portion is sunken to form a U-shaped pattern. In order to conduct a systematic quantitative analysis on the development of cities along the Silk Road, we turned to the City and Competitiveness Index database of the Chinese Academy of Social Sciences and selected 301 sample Silk Road cities out of the 505 candidate cities. GDP per capita 2011 was used as the measurement of urban development level, and two cities, one form the eastern end and the other from the western end of the Silk Road (London and Shanghai), were picked to as benchmark cities. After plotting the scatter graphs of the GDP per capita and the spherical distance of the cities from Shanghai and London for the sample cities of the countries along the Silk Road, it was noted was that as the distance of a city from Shanghai (or London) increases, the level of economic development of Silk Road cities would decrease initially, then increase to show a west-raised U shape (Figs. 8.5 and 8.6).

In comparison, the development of Silk Road cities shows two peaks and a sunken middle section to form a U shape. The GDP per capita of the cities on the two ends of the distribution are different. The economic development of the Silk Road cities on the eastern end of the graph (East Asian cities relatively close to Shanghai) is generally lower than that of the cities on the western end (European cities relatively close to London). The majority of the cities in the Western section have GDP per capita upwards of USD20,000 and there are even many cities with GDP per capita of above USD40,000. In the eastern section, only a few of the cities

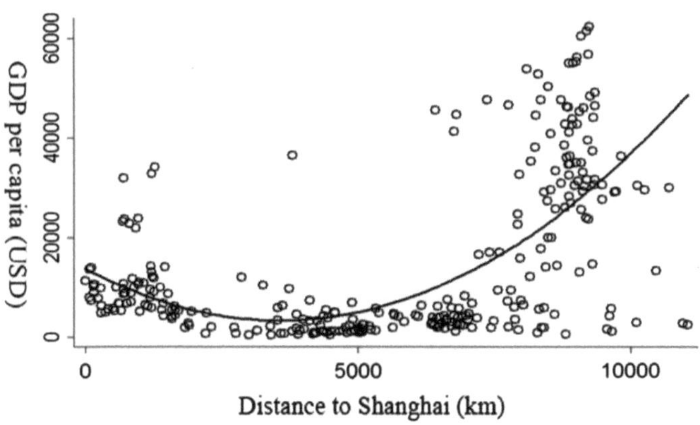

Fig. 8.5 GDP per capita and distance to Shanghai

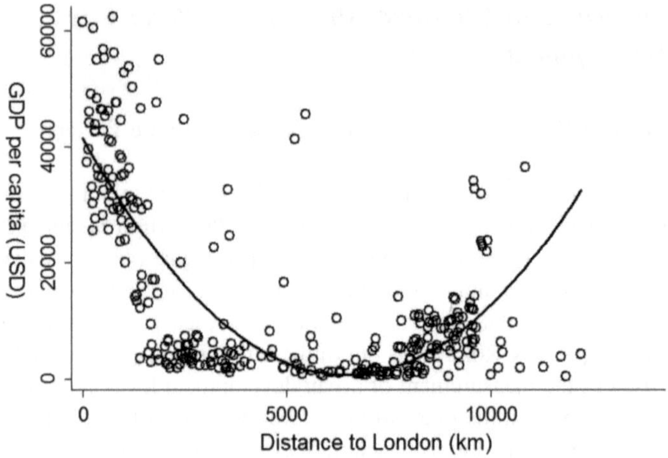

Fig. 8.6 GDP per capita and distance to London. *Source* CASS City and competitiveness index database

have GDP per capita of between USD20,000 and USD40,000. The majority of cities in the middle section of the Silk Road, cities in Central Asia, West Asia, South Asia and North Africa, have GDP per capita of less than USD20,000.

8.1.3.2 The Eastern Section: Fast Urban Development with Large Regional Gaps

The eastern section of the Silk Road mainly refers to the part of the Silk Road within China. The cities in this region are experiencing rapid development and there is a huge difference between the local regions. Table 8.1 shows the statistical characteristics of the urban development indicator. The average GDP growth of cities in the eastern section during 2009–2011 is generally high with a mean of 15.58%. The city with the fastest GDP growth has a value of 27.79% and cities in

Table 8.1 Statistical characteristics of the economic development indicators of cities in the eastern section of the Silk Road (2011)

	Mean	Minimum	Maximum	Coefficient of variation
GDP (million USD)	59435.53	7428.203	265768.4	0.86
GDP per capita (USD)	10371.53	2686.405	34117.64	0.65
GDP per land area (million USD)	52.66	3.12	567.10	1.49
2009–2011 average annual GDP growth (%)	15.58	−1.90	27.79	0.31

Source CASS City and competitiveness index database

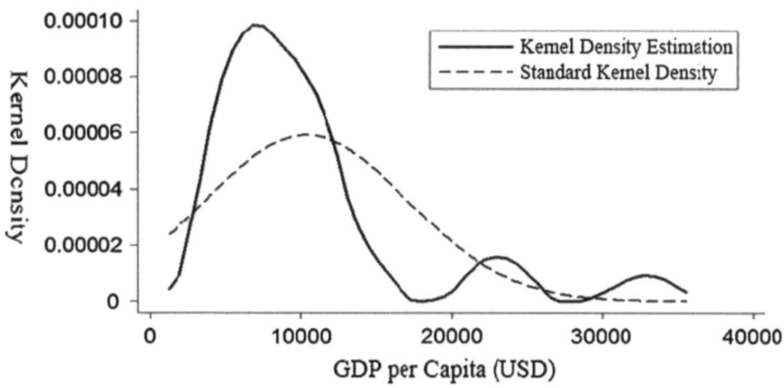

Fig. 8.7 Kernel density estimation of GDP per capita in the Eastern Section of the Silk Road. *Source* CASS City and competitiveness index database

the middle and western section have an average GDP growth mean of only 1.94% (the largest value is 22.13%; the smallest value is −11.71%). The economic growth rate across the countries and regions of the Silk Road are led by cities from the western section of the Silk Road.

Although the pace of urban development is generally fast, there is a relatively large gap in the size of the economies and economic density of the cities on the eastern section of the Silk Road. The coefficients of variation of the cities' GDP and GDP per land area are 0.86 and 1.49 respectively (see Table 8.1). The largest GDP per land area value is 181.68 times the smallest value, while the largest GDP per capita is 11.7 times the smallest value. By plotting the GDP per capita kernel density for the 69 sample cities in this section (see Fig. 8.7), the GDP per capita of the eastern section of the Silk Road have a positively skewed distribution with a long tail extending to the right. 44 of the cities have a GDP per capita that is lower than USD10,000. The GDP per capita of the major ancient Silk Road cities, Xi'an, Lanzhou, Urumqi and Quanzhou, are all within this low range. Cities like Hong Kong and Macao have a GDP per capita of more than USD30,000.

8.1.3.3 The Western Section: Slow Growth on a High Level

The western section of the Silk Road, mainly comprised of European countries and cities, is the intersection point for the land and sea routes of the Silk Road. The development of the cities shows the characteristics of high levels of urban development and small performance gap within the segment. It can be seen from the scatter graph of the cities' GDP per capita and distance to London in Fig. 8.6 that the GDP per capita of European cities (spatially near London) are generally higher. The GDP per capita mean in 2011 is USD23,424.38, way higher than the mean value of cities in the eastern section of the Silk Road (USD1,0371.53). However, as a result of the deep impact of the global financial and debt crises, the western section of the Silk Road has a significantly slower rate of economic growth compared to the cities in the eastern section. The average GDP growth mean during 2009–2011 is −0.89% and the economic growth of some of the cities are sluggish, some even in a state of stagnation. The average GDP growth of major Silk Road cities, Venice and Rotterdam, are −3.39 and −1.15% respectively, in negative growth.

8.1.3.4 The Middle Section: Low Development Level at Varied Development Stages

The middle section of the Silk Road is made up of Central Asia, West Asia, South Asia and North Africa, and it is covers cities of many developing countries, generally with low levels of urban development. These cities are sited in the sunken segment of the Silk Road U-shaped development pattern and they are in varying stages of development. Looking at the major economic development indicators of a few representative cities (Table 8.2), the level of development is generally low. With the exception of cities like Kuala Lumpur, Almaty and Istanbul with GDP per capita of more than USD6000, the rest of the cities, like Tehran and Jakarta, all have a GDP per capita of less than USD4000. Strategically significant Silk Road city, Dushanbe, has a GDP per capita of only USD849.47. In addition, it can be seen from indicators such as GDP per unit land area, average GDP growth, number of patent applications and number of multinational corporations, that the development of cities in the middle section of the Silk Road is quite unbalanced.

Table 8.2 Development of representative cities in the middle section of the Silk Road (2011)

City	GDP (million USD)	GDP per capita (USD)	GDP per land area (USD)	2009–2011 average GDP growth (%)	No. of Patent applications	No. of multinationals
Almaty	11145.30	7383.33	34.31	1.56	0	56
Dushanbe	533.75	849.47	4.28	7.29	0	51
Tehran	34908.09	3898.58	53.05	1.93	4	142
Istanbul	96566.91	7295.90	52.74	−2.33	332	441
Hanoi	8092.27	2306.92	8.79	9.39	11	237
Kuala Lumpur	15223.57	9602.51	62.48	1.17	161	494
Jakarta	34632.74	3785.31	52.79	2.86	12	510
Kolkata	29039.69	2191.25	155.02	9.30	5	110
Colombo	1498.95	2381.82	40.18	3.84	0	100
Nairobi	4259.23	1519.70	6.12	1.99	7	141

Source CASS City and competitiveness index database

8.2 Connections Between Silk Road Cities

With progress in science and technology and globalization, as well as the driving forces of industrialization, marketization and urbanization in different countries, profound changes have taken place in the relationships between cities. Especially in this wave of globalization with multinational corporations as main carriers, the global circulation of goods and services as well as the global allocation of factors of production stimulated development activities in many node cities along the Silk Road. Premium cities are connecting with other cities in the world with more openness, attracting and gathering the flow of people, materials, capital and information. In this process, connection between Silk Road cities also underwent a thorough overhaul, leading to complex and diverse characteristics.

We measured the connection matrix between Silk Road cities according to the interlocking network model of Taylor (2001) and the measurement system for world cities network connection (see Table 8.3), and utilized the statistical data extracted from the Forbes Global 2000 (2013) of 175 multinational corporations in services-producing industries distributed across 525 global cities. The total connection value and world cities network system connection of the different cities are aggregated, and the degree of connection between Silk Road cities and their positions within the network system are determined based on this.

8.2.1 "Over Head" Connection Is the Main Form of Connection Between Silk Road Cities

The calculation shows that among all the Silk Road cities, London and Hong Kong are the two major intersection cities with the most connections with other cities. Their total connection values are 71,636 and 56,362 respectively. At the same time, Paris, Singapore, Shanghai, Dubai, Beijing, Milan, Mumbai and Moscow are among the top 10 Silk Road cities in terms of their connection aggregate with other cities. These are generally premium cities that are the strongest performers in their countries, with outstanding agglomeration and diffusion. In comparison to other cities, the level of connection between these 10 cities far exceeds that of the other Silk Road cities. They are made up of London, Paris, Milan and Moscow as fulcrum points for the western section of the Silk Road, Hong Kong, Singapore, Shanghai and Beijing as the fulcrum points for the eastern section of the Silk Road, and Dubai and Mumbai as the fulcrum points of the middle coastal section of the Silk Road, connecting "over the heads" of the majority of cities in the middle section (see Fig. 8.8).

Based on calculation results of the city network connection using the UCINET software, a visualization of the connection matrix and centrality of 34 of the major cities along the Silk Road was produced (see Fig. 8.9). From the figure, it can be seen that connection is greatest for cities such as London, Paris, Singapore, Shanghai and Moscow from the eastern and western ends of the Silk Road (represented in the figure

Table 8.3 Measurement system of world cities network connection

Model	Indicator	Calculation method and process	Information source and samples
Interlocking network model	Global cities network connection	Suppose there are *m* advanced producer service providers out of *n* cities. The value of a company in the city is measured by the importance of the office in the said city in which the company's global office system is located. The entire city network is V, the service value matrix derived from the n × m arrangement. The standard setting of the matrix element, V_{ij}, is: $V_{ij} = \begin{cases} 0.\ \text{Noinstitutional network points} \\ 1.\ \text{General institutional or network points on a small scale} \\ 2.\ \text{General institutional or network points on a regular scale} \\ 3.\ \text{General institutional or network points on a large scale} \\ 4.\ \text{Regional headquarters} \\ 5.\ \text{Company headquarters} \end{cases}$ The calculation of the unit connection point, r_{abj}, between City a and City b via MNC j, as well as the aggregation of the urban connection value via all company unit connection points, r_{ab}: $r_{ab} = \sum_j r_{abj} = \sum_j V_{aj} \cdot V_{bj}$ Further aggregation is undertaken to obtain the total connection value of every city in the city network, N_a: $N_a = \sum_i r_{ai}, a \neq i$ Applying extreme value standardization on the N_a value of the sample cities to derive the connection index. The value of this index reflects the degree of connection and agglomeration in the world cities network connection. Its ranking will show the position of a city in the global city network	Statistical data from the Forbes Global 2000 (2013) of 175 multinational corporations in services-producing industries distributed across 525 cities

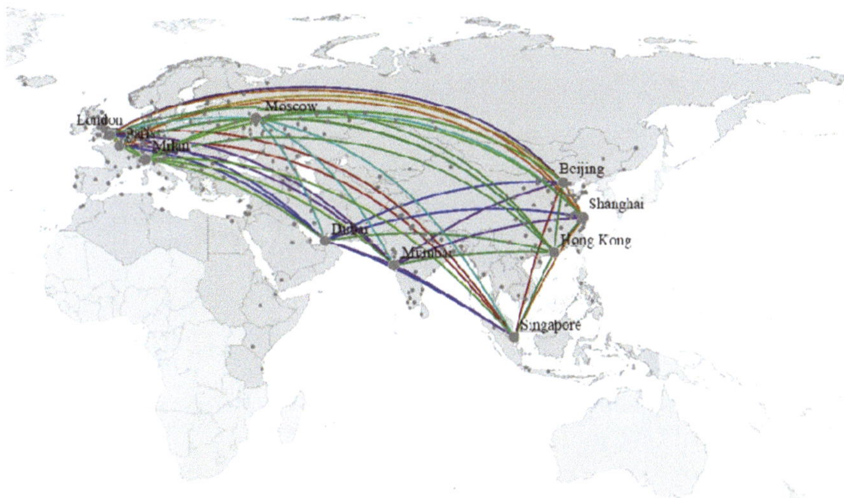

Fig. 8.8 "Over Head" connections between premium Silk Road cities. *Source* CASS City and competitiveness index database

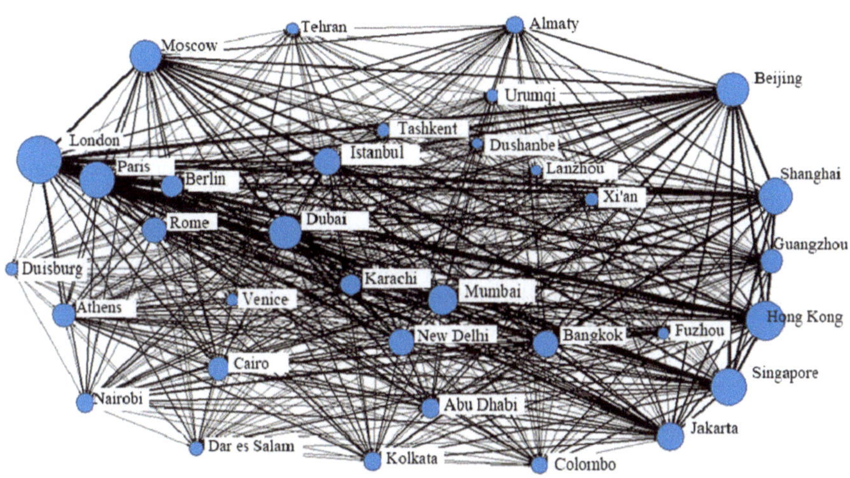

Fig. 8.9 Network connections of 34 major cities along the Silk Road. *Note* The thickness of the connecting lines between the cities represents the strength of connection between the cities; the size of the circles represents the centrality status of the cities in the city network

by thicker connection lines). Their centrality is relatively outstanding too (represented in the figure by larger circles). The connection of middle section cities like Tashkent, Almaty and Dushanbe with other cities is significantly weaker, and their centrality lesser. The premium services producing industries of major Silk Road cities are spatially characterized by "over head" connection.

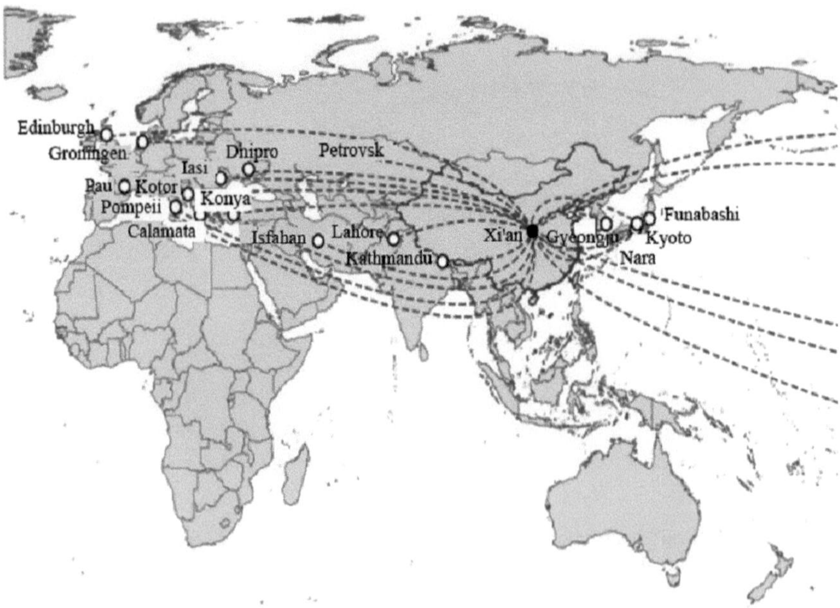

Fig. 8.10 Xi'an and its sister cities

In addition to the "over the head" feature for economic connection, an "over head" connection is also applicable in the friendly interactions and cultural exchanges between Silk Road cities. Taking the example of sister cities arrangements, the cities that entered into friendly partnerships with Xi'an and Shanghai are mainly distributed spatially in the western section of the Silk Road in Europe. Even though cities in Central Asia and West Asia are geographically nearer, the number of friendly partnerships formed between this region and Xi'an and Shanghai is extremely small (see Figs. 8.10 and 8.11). The connection between cities does not necessarily weaken as geographical distance increases.

8.2.2 High Level of Connection Between Major Cities in Sub-Regions and Unbalanced Local Connection

The unbalanced connection of the Silk Road cities is spatially obvious. The connections between regional premium cities are in the lead. From the distribution of cities according to the connection aggregation for the top 50 Silk Road sample cities (see Table 8.4), Asia and Europe have the absolute upper hand. The cities in some of the countries in this region have significant comparative advantage in global connection, while the overall performance of Africa is poor (only Cairo of Egypt made it into the top 50). Looking at the distribution across sub-regions, cities with

Fig. 8.11 Shanghai and its sister cities. *Source* CASS City and Competitiveness Index database

Table 8.4 Top 50 Silk Road cities in aggregate connections

Continent	Sub-region	City (ranking)	Number
Asia	East Asia	Hong Kong (2), Shanghai (5), Beijing (7), Taipei (27), Guangzhou (34)	5
	Southeast Asia	Singapore (4), Kuala Lumpur (14), Jakarta (20), Bangkok (24), Manila (36), Ho Chi Minh City (45)	6
	South Asia	Mumbai (9), New Delhi (21), Bangalore (33), Chennai (47)	4
	Central Asia	–	0
	West Asia	Dubai (6), Istanbul (16), Tel Aviv (37), Beirut (46), Riyadh (48)	5
Europe	Western Europe	London (1), Paris (3), Amsterdam (13), Brussels (15), Dublin (28), Luxembourg (44), Manchester (49)	7
	Northern Europe	Stockholm (23), Copenhagen (35), Helsinki (50)	3
	Central Europe	Frankfurt, (11), Warsaw (17), Vienna (18), Zurich (19), Munich (25), Prague (26), Hamburg (30), Dusseldorf (32), Budapest (40), Berlin (41)	10
	Eastern Europe	Moscow (10), Kiev (42)	2
	Southern Europe	Milan (8), Madrid (12), Barcelona (22), Rome (29), Lisbon (31), Athens (38), Bucharest (43)	7
Africa	East Africa	–	0
	North Africa	Cairo (39)	1

Source CASS City and competitiveness index database

closer connections to other Silk Road cities are mainly found in East Asia, Southeast Asia, South Asia and West Asia. In Central Asia, inter-city connection very limited and none of the cities from this region made it into the top 50. In comparison to other cities in this region, Almaty, as the finance and education center of Kazakhstan and the rest of the Central Asian cities, has a relatively busy connection compared with other cities in the Silk Road and is ranked 67th in the ranking of the Silk Road sample cities. In Europe, the connection of Western Europe, Central Europe and Southern Europe cities with other Silk Road cities is greater compared to that of Eastern Europe and Northern Europe. Out of the 29 cities from the European section of the Silk Road in the top 50, 24 are in these three sub-regions. In Africa, the connection of East African cities and the other cities is generally inadequate. The city with the most connections is Nairobi (62nd in the ranking). Its performance, however, is lower than that of Casablanca (54th in the ranking) and Tunisia (60th in the ranking). It can be seen that Silk Road cities have "over head" connection due to a general lack of premium cities in Central Asia, Eastern Europe, East Africa and North Africa, as well as an overall collapse in urban connection.

8.2.3 Significant Inadequacies in the Breadth and Depth of External Connection of Local Cities

In the countries along the Silk Road, some of the cities have limited connections with other countries and cities; some are even cut off from the outside world. If we take a city's scope of external connection, measured by whether or not one city has connection with the other Silk Road cities, and the proportion of sample cities with connections, we discovered through calculations that there are 9.3% of the sample cities with less than 50% external connection with other Silk Road cities in producer services. This also means that this category of cities is only connected with less than half of the Silk Road cities. Among them, cities like Isfahan and Mashhad of Iran and Thimphu of Bhutan have extremely low levels of external connections, which shows that cities of this category have very limited external connection in the area of global services-production with other cities along the Silk Road, with a noticeably closed-door attitude towards economic development.

8.3 Relationship Between Centrality and Connection of the Silk Road Cities Network

Centrality and connection constitute the core ingredients of a specific city network. In reality, in the context of globalization, a portion of the cities in the city network have an accentuated centrality, forming asymmetric control and capabilities in allocating resources as a result of the connection between goods and services, factors of production and industry agglomeration, which results in further self-strengthening of these cities with greater agglomeration. At the same time, major cities in the network perform differently from the other cities in terms of connection. There exists an important relationship between centrality and connection in the Silk Road city network.

8.3.1 *Positive Correlation Between Connection and Income Level*

There is an important relationship between connections and the income level of a city. To a certain extent, income level determines the basic requirements for connections between a city and other cities during economic and social interactions. A study on the relationship between GDP per capita and national income of Silk Road cities shows a positive correlation between the two (see Fig. 8.12), i.e. cities with relatively high GDP per capita or national income per capita are generally perform well in global connection.

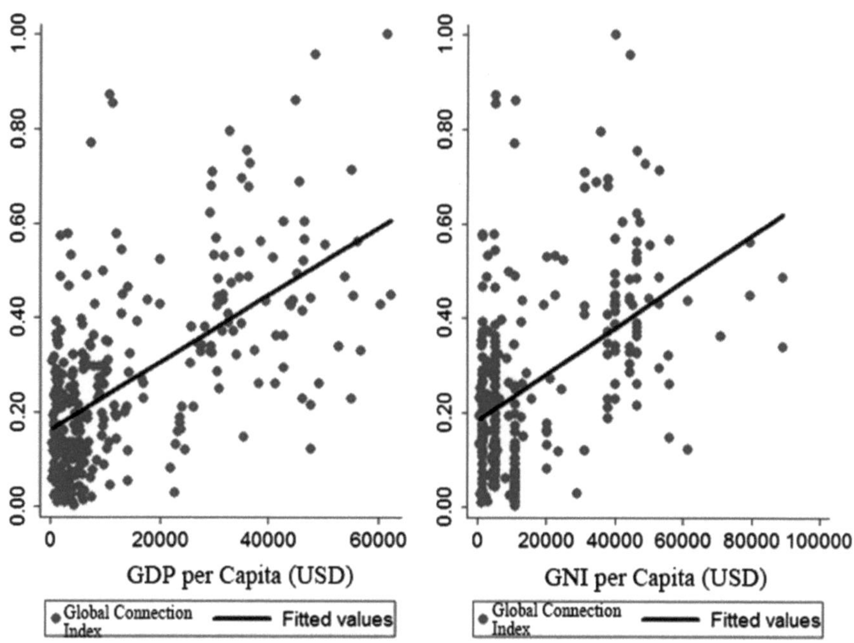

Fig. 8.12 Global connection index and income of Silk Road cities. *Source* CASS City and competitiveness index database

8.3.2 *Economic Density Is the Key Support for Connections*

The total amount of wealth accumulated per unit of land area in a city, i.e. GDP per land area is the full expression of a city's economic development and agglomeration. It is the economic foundation and support for the incidence of connection between a city and other cities. Looking at the relationship between global connection and GDP per land area of Silk Road cities, there is a positive correlation between them (see Fig. 8.13): Cities with lower GDP per land area correspond to lower levels of global connection, while cities with higher GDP per land area correspond to higher levels of global connection.

Specifically, Silk Road cities with GDP per land area that is lower than USD50 million/km^2 in 2011 have a global connection index mean of 0.179. Those with GDP per unit land area of between USD50–100 million/km^2 have a global connection index mean of 0.369, significantly higher than that of the first group. And the corresponding global connection index mean of cities with GDP per land area of between USD100–200 million/km^2 nd more than USD 200 million/km^2 are significantly higher than the first two groups of cities, as high as 0.403 and 0.599 respectively.

8.3.3 *Tiered Difference in the Global Connection Between Cities of Different Sizes*

Looking at global connection and city size of Silk Road cities, the global connection of medium and small cities are generally lower, while large cities, especially the massive ones, are generally superior in terms of global connection (see Table 8.5).

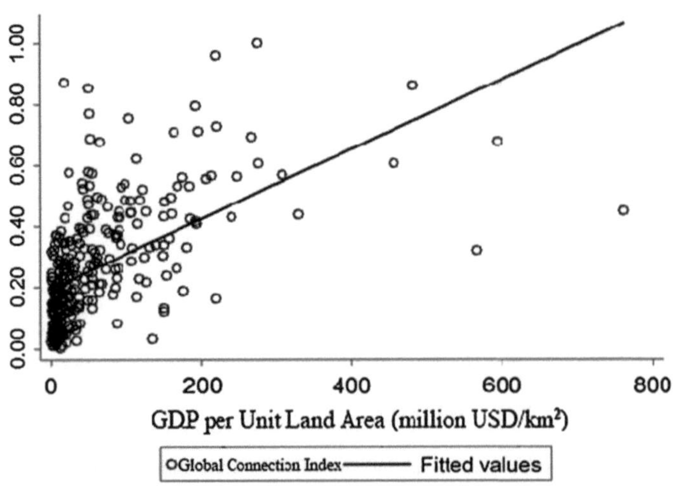

Fig. 8.13 Correlation between global connection and GDP per Unit Land Area. *Source* CASS City and Competitiveness Index database

Table 8.5 Correlation between global connection and population of Silk Road cities

Population	No. of cities	Global connection index mean
<500,000	59	0.232
50,000–1 million	62	0.252
1–5 million	121	0.249
5–10 million	41	0.289
10–20 million	15	0.453
>20 million	3	0.682

Source CASS City and competitiveness index database

Looking at the incremental relationship between global connection index mean and city population in the above table, the level of global connection between Silk Road cities shows a tiered difference. This difference is even more apparent in the gap between cities with a population of below 100 million and those with a population of above 100 million. Cities like Shanghai, Beijing, Istanbul, Paris and Moscow, with a population of more than 100 million have global connection scores of 0.85, 0.87, 0.77, 0.96 and 0.86 respectively.

8.4 Pattern and Characteristics of Silk Road Cities Network

Examining the situation of all Silk Road cities, the profile of a Silk Road city can be produced. Urban development serves as the supporting point of intersection, and urban connection as its key nodes. In comparison to a city network that is generally laid out in a pattern of concentric circles, this Silk Road city network that makes up "Half of the World" takes a unique form.

8.4.1 Emerging Irregular Network

The city network made up of global Silk Road cities presents significant irregularities. The two ends of the route are led by premium node cities, with one line connecting Beijing, Hong Kong and Singapore on one side, one line connecting Singapore, Mumbai, Dubai, Milan, Paris and London on another side, and another line connecting London, Moscow and Beijing, forming a triangle (see Fig. 8.14).

On one hand, the cities on the two ends of the west-raised U-shaped developmental pattern with higher levels of development make up the core connecting points of the Silk Road city network. The close connection that these cities have with the other Silk Road cities supports the main framework of the Silk Road city network, and plays the role of an intersection point city. On the other hand, in the

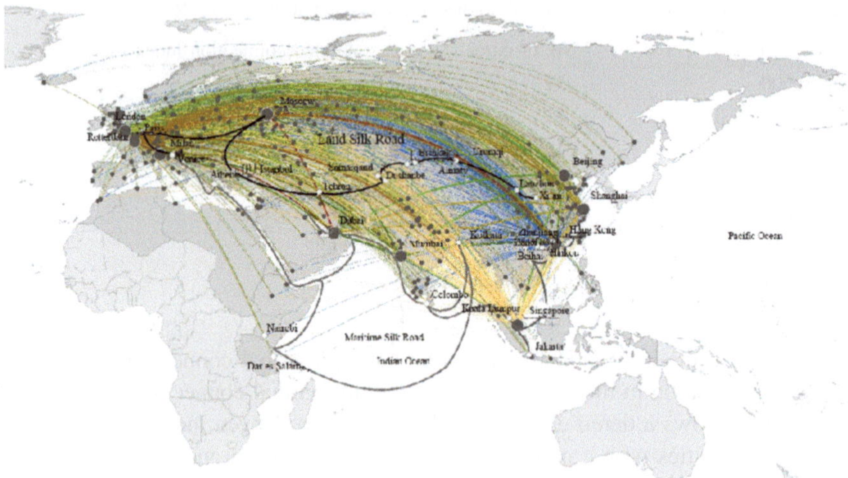

Fig. 8.14 Silk Road cities network. *Source* CASS City and competitiveness index database

development pattern of cities along Silk Road that are literally referred to as "sea-strong, land-weak", like Mumbai and Dubai, premium node cities along the Maritime Silk Road, are unable to support the irregularities of the southern end of the Silk Road city network. As the Eurasian inland and hinterland lacks the support of cities with high connection, the left side of the Silk Road city network is weaker overall.

Even though there are irregularities in the Silk Road cities network, the profile of the network is becoming clear. According to the global cities network connection performance of the different Silk Road cities, cities like London, Paris, Singapore, Hong Kong and Shanghai are core cities of the highest level in the entire Silk Road cities network, and the capitals or largest cities of the remaining Silk Road countries are the intermediary central cities in the urban system (see Fig. 8.15). In this system, cities are at different stages of development, with different levels of connection, and the status of cities of different levels are not same. There is obvious hierarchy in the geospatial range of its diffusion.

In the central and eastern regions of China along the Eastern section of the Silk Road, the characteristics of urban integration development are starting to emerge and connection between cities has become increasingly close. A multicenter-periphery connection structure with Shanghai, Beijing and Hong Kong as the centers is emerging. In the western section of the Silk Road between the European cities, urban development has advanced. In the group of cities of which London and Paris are the centers, there is high connection among them and they form a multinational urban belt. Among the Central Asian and West Asian cities of the middle section of the Silk Road, there are connections between urban development and other cities on the axis to show a dot-axial structure transmitted through spatial streaming.

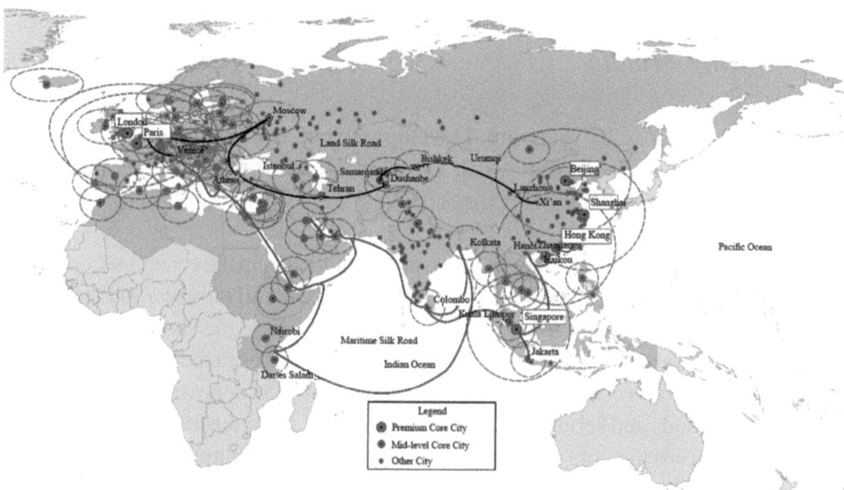

Fig. 8.15 Silk Road cities system. *Source* CASS City and competitiveness index database

8.4.2 The Middle Section Is Marginalized and the Two Ends Centralized

The Silk Road city network has the characteristic of "the center is the periphery; the periphery is the center", i.e. the geographic center of the Silk Road is not the center of the city network, and the geographic periphery is not the periphery of the city network. This is different from city networks that generally have geographic centers as their core, the diffusion axis as the connecting line, and are surrounded by hinterland.

Looking at spatial form, the Central Asia, West Asia and East Africa regions constitute the geographic center of the entire Silk Road. However, as urban development in this region is generally in a state of collapse, these cities are yet to be capable of assuming the role of supporting the entire Silk Road city network, and are hence relegated to being periphery regions of the Silk Road city network. In contrast, the geographic periphery of the Silk Road, East Asia, West Asia, Western Europe and Southern Europe, has taken on the role of being the fulcrum that is supporting the entire Silk Road city network to become the bona fide center of the Silk Road city network. Therefore, the urban center of the Silk Road city network is at the two ends while its geographical center is the periphery in the network. The U-shaped curve of Silk Road cities urban development, as well as the "over the head" characteristic of Silk Road cities' urban connection jointly determined the spatial structure of Silk Road cities' urban development, where the roles of the center and periphery are exchanged.

8.4.3 *Networks at the Two Ends and Axial Form in the Middle*

8.4.3.1 Significant City Network Development at the Eastern And Western Sections with Overlap Of Multiple Center-Periphery Structures

As the pace of China's infrastructural construction increases in the eastern section of the Silk Road city network, especially in the opening of high speed railways and the gradual establishment of the network transportation system that forms the skeleton for the high speed railway, the space and temporal distances between cities in the eastern and central regions of China are in contraction, and there are increasing connections between cities in the areas of goods and services, factors of production and industrial division of labor. Massive cities form the core of the city network and the medium and small cities and towns on the periphery as well as their hinterland became the "multicenter-periphery" overlapping the connection structure of the periphery. Spatially, the "at one with east and central" urban development is supported by the Yangtze River Delta, Pearl River Delta and Beijing–Tianjin–Hebei urban regions (Ni Pengfei 2015).

In the European region of the western section of Silk Road, urban development has advanced to become the Paris-Lyon-Le Havre urban belt along the downstream of the Seine River, the Rhine-Ruhr urban region and the Greater London region etc. These urban regions have comprehensive regional infrastructural network which includes sophisticated railway and highway facilities that form the structural skeleton of the urban space. At the same time, central cities like London and Paris have a core role to play in the formation and development of urban regions and they have become gravitational centers of population and industrial agglomeration, creating urban groups made up of large, medium and small cities through the cooperative division of labor and organic connection.

8.4.3.2 Local Dot-Axial Structure Dominates the Middle Section

The central region, of Central Asia, West Asia and East Asia, through which the Silk Road passes, is mainly made up of the cities of developing countries. This region has a large concentration of oil exporting and resource providing countries. Their industrial structures are relatively simple, the overall development of these cities is not great, and connections are dominated by a local dot-axial pattern. Beginning from the starting point of the Silk Road on land, at Xi'an, passing through cities like Baoji, Tianshui, Lanzhou, Wuwei and Zhangye to reach Urumqi, the cities along the route are connected by the 2nd largest mainland bridge between Europe and Asia, the Land and Sea Lanzhou–Xinjiang Line, a clear example of the dot-axial spatial structure. This section has a complex terrain and relatively dispersed population distribution. The restrictions of longer distance are greater and the limitations on overall connection between cities are greater. What is lacking

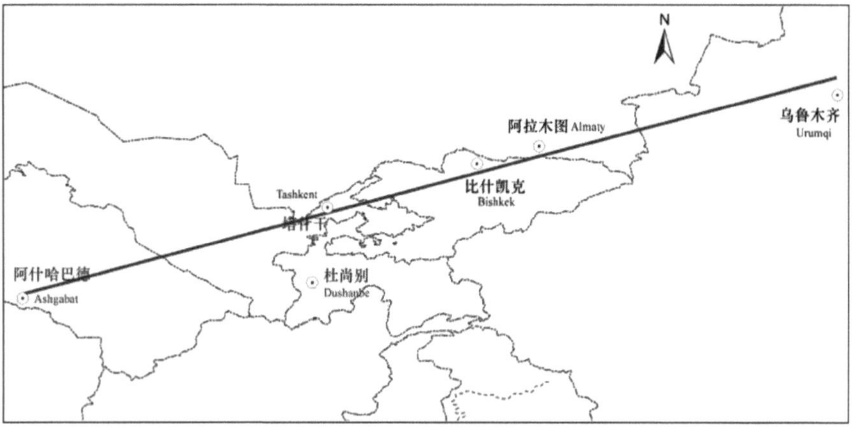

Fig. 8.16 Development axis of Silk Road cities in Central Asia. *Source* Yang Shu and Wang Shusen (2015)

currently is a core city that can be the driving and diffusion point for the entire area. After entering Central Asia, from Kazakhstan's Almaty to passing the Turkmenistan capital, Ashgabat, in one line to the capital of Kyrgyzstan, Bishkek, and Uzbekistan capital, Tashkent, as well as Tajikistan capital, Dushanbe, this axial line spatially connects the six major economic centers in the central part of Asia (see Fig. 8.16) to form the most densely concentrated regional belt in Central Asia in terms of population distribution. This region extends westward into West Asian cities to reach the Turkish city of Istanbul. The local dot-axial spatial connection pattern can be seen throughout the regional belt.

Looking at cities from the central section of the Maritime Silk Road, a portion of the port cities like Kolkata, Colombo and Nairobi etc. is linked to the other cities by the shipping routes as the main axis of connection and such connections are made up of commodities like petroleum and minerals. Connections in the areas of factors of production and industrial division of labor are relatively limited.

The multiple forms of the above Silk Road local network, urban belt and dot-axial connection are intertwined with the unique form of the Silk Road where "the center is the periphery; the periphery is the center", which condenses and reflects the basic characteristics of urban development and connection in the Silk Road and presents them as the early shadow of an irregular city network through a hierarchical system.

8.5 An Interpretation of the Silk Road Cities Network

The formation of an irregular city network in the Silk Road is supported and impacted by many factors. In the city network that spans Europe, Asia and Africa, there are differences between the regions and countries along the routes in the areas of physical geography, economic infrastructure, social development and political system etc. The many geographical, economic, social and cultural factors are intertwined and they have a major impact on the Silk Road city network pattern.

8.5.1 Impact of Hardware Factors

Hardware elements like natural geographic conditions and infrastructure are important foundation with impact on the progress of the Silk Road city network, and are the basic support for urban development and the establishment of connection between cities. In the webbed regions at the two ends of the Silk Road that are Europe and the eastern regions of China, coastal plains and hills are the basic geographical features. The ecological environment of a region such as natural geographic conditions, climate and temperature are all relatively superior. At the same time, public roads, railways and airline routes are all densely distributed and infrastructure relatively complete, and there is a pattern of network development for the transportation system. This laid the foundation for supporting the city network at both ends of the Silk Road. In comparison, as the geological features of the region are complex in the many landlocked countries of Central Asia and West Asia in the central section of the Silk Road, the overall ecological environment is relatively poor and the land areas expansive. The populations are very much dispersed and the size of the local markets is limited. Urban development and connections between cities are affected. In addition, there is inadequate supply of transport infrastructure such as roads, railways and airlines in the region, restricting the connection between cities and hindering land connections such as trade and logistics between the cities at two ends of the Silk Road.

By comparing the connection and airline network distribution (see Fig. 8.17) and railway network distribution pattern (see Fig. 8.18) between Silk Road cities, it can be seen that the reason why Silk Road cities have a pattern of an "over the head connection" with a collapsed central section of the city network was basically determined by the infrastructure like railways and airlines. At the eastern and western ends of the Silk Road, railway and airline networks are densely laid out to provide support for the close connection between cities with high intersections. In the expanse of the central section regions, everything is sparsely distributed, whether it is the airline or railway network, directly restricting connection between the cities on the two ends and the cities in the central section of the Silk Road. In the urban development axis of Central Asian cities, for example, even though there is an interdependent relationship between the cities on the axis, geographic conditions and transport infrastructure are poor and the connection of these cities are limited, so what exists is a type of one-way spatial relationship connected by a single axis.

Looking further at the Hardware Environment Index scores of the Silk Road sample cities (see Fig. 8.19), European and East Asian cities enjoy higher degrees of convenience in hardware and infrastructure. In the central section regions, however, hardware environment of the cities are lower than that at the two ends,

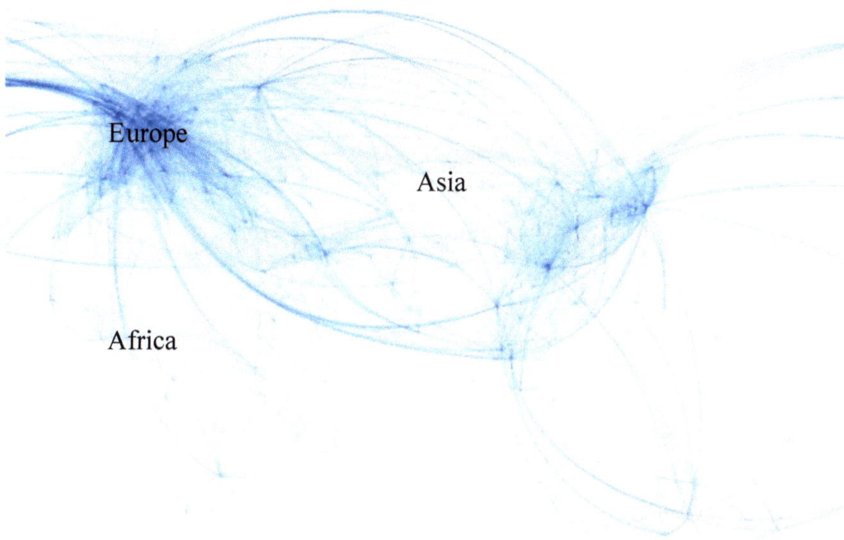

Fig. 8.17 Aviation network of European, Asian and African cities. *Source* Internet

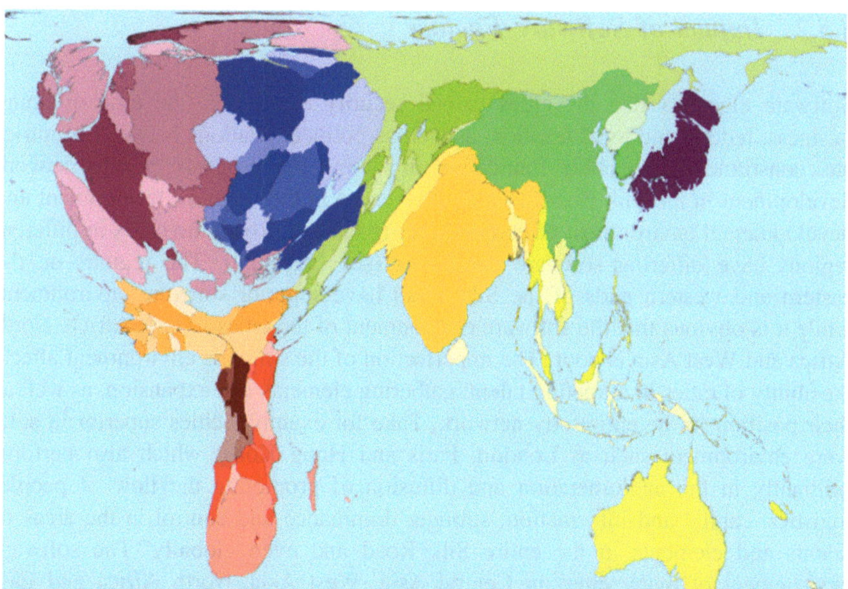

Fig. 8.18 Railway network across Europe, Asia and Africa. *Source* http://www.worldmapper.org/

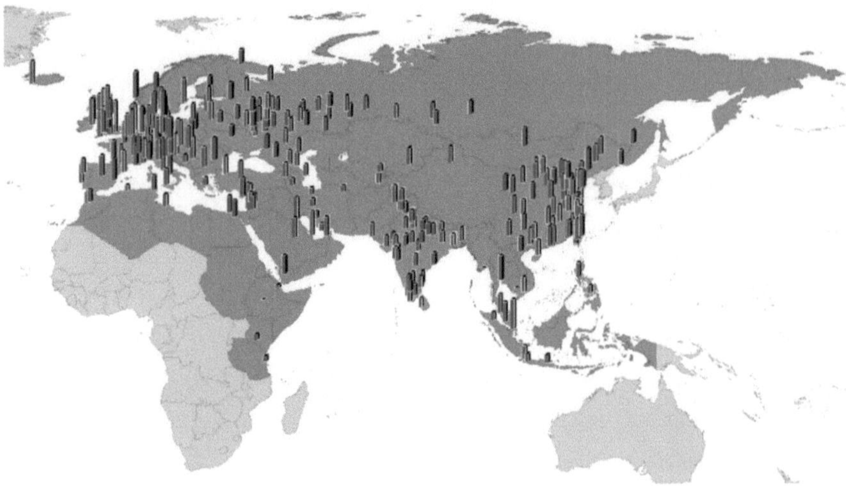

Fig. 8.19 Hardware environment index of Silk Road cities. *Source* CASS City and competitiveness index database

and the differences within the region are uneven, especially in cities of East Africa, India, Central Asia and West Asia, where the hardware environment is in urgent need of improvement.

8.5.2 Impact of Software Factors

Software elements like the cities' social security conditions, the ease of doing business, federal and local taxation, as well as political relations between countries etc. constitute the invisible foundation impacting the progress of city network development in the Silk Road. Due to differences in the stage of development and developmental environment of countries along the Silk Road, the cities in different regions have differing software conditions (see Fig. 8.20). The regions on the eastern and western ends of the Silk Road have superior software environment, while it is obvious that the software environment of the cities in East Africa, North Africa and West Asia is poor. The imperfection of the software environment affects the ability of cities in attracting talent, gathering elements and expansion, as well as their position in the entire city network. Take for example, cities superior in software environment such as London, Paris and Hong Kong, which also perform brilliantly in the agglomeration and diffusion of promoting the flow of people, logistics, capital and information, stronger dominance and control in the areas of talents and elements in the entire Silk Road and even globally. The software environment of many cities in Central Asia, West Asia, North Africa and East Africa, such as ease of doing business and livability, are generally poor. The

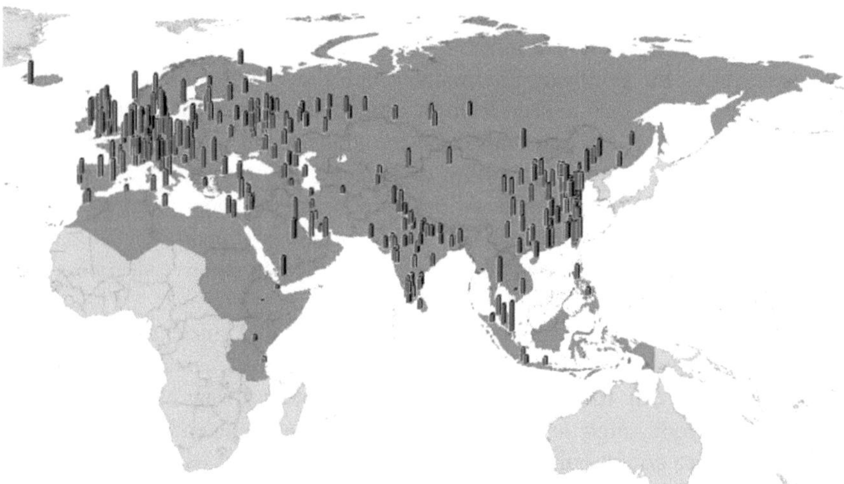

Fig. 8.20 Software environment index of Silk Road cities. *Source* CASS City and competitiveness index database

agglomeration and diffusion capabilities of cities are limited and are inadequate for the purpose of supporting the city network of the entire Silk Road.

With increasing globalization, the impact from the gap between hardware and software environment on the city network of the cities is increasingly prominent, especially software environment, which is becoming an important factor affecting connection between cities in the Silk Road. Take a look at the scatter plot relationships between global connection and the software and hardware environment indexes of the Silk Road (see Fig. 8.21). Cities with a certain level of advantage in hardware and software environments perform better in global connection. In the

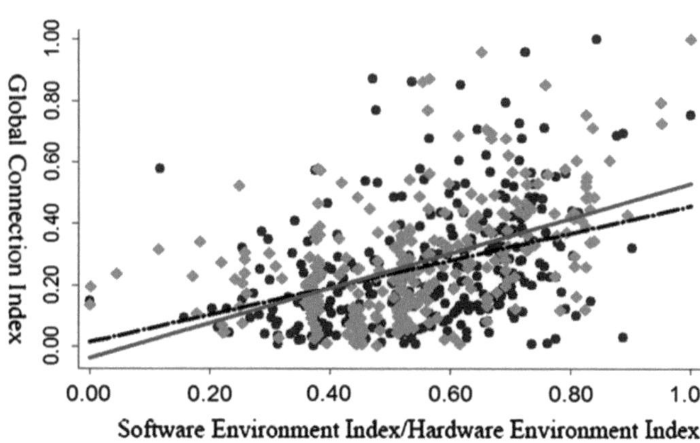

Fig. 8.21 Global connection vs. hardware environment and software environment of Silk Road cities. *Source* CASS city and competitiveness index database

figure, the gray color line is the fitted line representing the Software Environment Index and Global Environment Index in the scatter plot. The dotted line is the fitted line representing the Hardware Environment Index and Global Environment Index in the scatter plot. It can be seen from this that both software and hardware environments respectively have an impact on the global connection of the cities, fulfilling two basic conditions supporting the material environment and institutional environment of global connection. At the same time, compared to hardware environment, the software environment of Silk Road cities supports the global connection of cities more (represented in the figure by the comparative steepness of the fitted lines).

In summary, the city network pattern has a consolidated impact on the hardware environment, software environment, as well as income level, economic density and population of the Silk Road. Cities with hardware and software environments that are relatively good, high levels of income and population and economies of a considerable size do not only stand out in terms of centrality within the entire Silk Road city network, but also generally have a higher level of global network connection, control and dominance in the region and even over global resources, playing the role of network nodes and links connecting with other cities. It is precisely because of the enormous gap between the hardware and software factors of different regional cities along the Silk Road spanning "Half of the World", that an initial profile of the Silk Road city network can be mapped, albeit with irregularities.

Chapter 9
Prospects of the Silk Road Cities Network

9.1 Opportunities and Challenges

Sustainable prosperity of cities and an open, cooperative and win–win city network are important supports to national and regional ties for development. Since the pioneering Eurasian people began to explore the Silk Road more than 2000 years ago, the rise and fall of cities along the Silk Road have been closely linked to the development of the countries and the flow of trade along the route. In a historical context that is intertwined with irreversible globalization, accelerated regional economic integration, and the ongoing industrialization, urbanization and marketization processes in developing countries, the Silk Road cities network that branches out and connects half of the world will continue to evolve and see opportunities as well as challenges in infrastructures networks, institutional environment, trade in goods and services, flow of production factors, and industrial network construction.

9.1.1 *Infrastructure Connection*

An integrated and well-connected infrastructure network is the material foundation for the opening-up and development of cities and win–win cooperation. The history of the Silk Road shows that the basic connection of infrastructure such as transportation and communications networks, is not only essential to the flow of labor, commodity, capital and information among cities, but also a critical tangible condition for viability and vitality of the Silk Road.

From the camels and horses in ancient times to the contemporary railways and ferries, every major improvement in infrastructure has strengthened the trade ties and cultural exchanges between cities along the Silk Road. Therefore, the further evolution of the Silk Road Cities Network relies primarily on the prioritization of infrastructure connection. Based on the current international and national situations, infrastructure connection is in a period of great development opportunities. First, the

© China Social Sciences Press and Springer Nature Singapore Pte Ltd. 2017

P. Ni et al., *Cities Network Along the Silk Road*,
DOI 10.1007/978-981-10-4834-0_9

financial support for transportation and other infrastructure is gradually put in place. The well-developed cities in Europe in the western part of the Silk Road and those in China's coastal regions in the east already offer good infrastructure in the sectors of transportation, communication, electricity, etc. China, in the eastern section of the Silk Road, is vigorously promoting the construction of economic corridors, one through Mongolia to Russia, one to Pakistan, and one connecting Bangladesh, India and Myanmar, as well as building land and sea connections towards the west and the south via node cities. At the same time, the launch of the USD40 billion Silk Road Fund (SRF) and the USD50 billion Asian Infrastructure Investment Bank (AIIB), which are dedicated to projects concerning the development of Central Asia, also provide funding for building the infrastructure networks that connect the two ends of the Silk Road as well as the cities in between. Second, there is strong demand for infrastructure improvement in developing countries along the routes. Since many countries in the middle section of the Silk Road are in the early or middle stage of industrialization and urbanization, the demand for infrastructure is strong as cities developing towards higher income levels. The strong demand for infrastructure connection will form an internal driving force, creating conditions for the construction of bridges, oil and gas pipelines, cross-border cables and information networking. Third, the rapid development of science and technology, such as high-speed railway, will provide technical support for the infrastructure networks among cities along the Silk Road. Therefore, with high-speed railways as backbones and other land routes and major sea routes as supplement, it is technically feasible to establish a transportation network that connects the cities in East Asia, Central Asia, West Asia, East Africa, West Africa, and Europe.

However, since the Silk Road runs through Europe, Asia and Africa, it covers a wide geographical span comprised of complex and diverse landforms and natural environment, such as mountains, plateaus, deserts, seas, etc. Such natural environment and spatial distance are the primal factors that constrain the building of infrastructure networks connecting cities along the Silk Road when compared to those in other parts of the world. At the same time, due to the huge investment required for infrastructure building, long investment cycle, and the irreconcilable interests of all parties, there is still a long way to go in building an integrated city infrastructure network based on existing economic conditions along the Silk Road.

9.1.2 Institutional Environment

As a soft environment factor, the integrated institutional mechanism is indispensable in developing cities network along the Silk Road. It helps reduce transaction costs, promote the flow of commodity and services, the circulation of production factors and the division of labor among cities in different countries, and enhance the efficient allocation of resources. On the contrary, institutional barriers such as investment and trade barriers, market access restrictions, and national segregation that impede the flow of goods, services and resources, will affect the integration process.

There are opportunities as well as challenges in the current and future development of an integrated system regarding city development and city network along the Silk Road. First, the time-honored 'Silk Road spirit', i.e., the spirit of peace and cooperation, openness and inclusiveness, mutual learning and shared benefits, serves as the valuable spiritual legacy and historical foundation in eliminating institutional and cultural barriers, promoting the formation of an integrated system. Second, several integrated organizations and free trade agreements were formed in various regions in Europe, Asia, and Africa after World War II. They have created strong conditions for the elimination of trade and investment barriers. The increasing people-to-people cultural exchanges also have positive impact on mutual understanding, trust and cooperation among the cities along the Silk Road.

However, there are many realistic problems in promoting the institutional integration among cities along the Silk Road. On the one hand, the key region and the most difficult region of the integration is the middle section of the Silk Road, including Central Asia, West Asia, East Africa and North Africa, where the conflicts between some countries are endless, the concept of peaceful development has not been solidified, different expectations or ineffective governance and implementation in promoting the integration exist (Li Yongquan 2015), unresolved national disputes in various areas are seen in some countries. Besides, being the forefront of power wrestling, these regions have greater political risks, which create additional uncertainty for the future development. All of these factors thus limit the communication and connections at the city level throughout the Silk Road. On the other hand, although Russia and other countries have attempted to establish a customs alliance and other agreements in Central Asia as well as free trade areas in China and Southeast Asian countries in recent years, the differences in consensus and the degree of participation make it difficult for these trade zones to benefit the entire region, and even lead to regional divide to some extent. The lack of a free trade area that covers Eurasian and African cities along the Silk Road limits the progress of the institutional integration.

9.1.3 *Trade in Goods and Services*

Finished goods and services are the two main components of economic output, and the important venues of economic connections between cities (Braun 2015). Limited by the production capacity and transportation conditions, tea, silk, spices and other simple goods were shipped by camels, horses, wood boats and other means of transport among cities along the ancient Silk Road. Along with the advancement of science and technology, the development of productive forces, and the aggregation of population, the demand for goods and services increase gradually, the needs become more diversified, and therefore, commodity production becomes more profuse in the urban areas along this trade route. In addition, the railway, air and sea transport, and other infrastructure continue to improve, the content of goods and services has been greatly expanded in the city networks along the Silk Road. Especially the completion of the first and the second Eurasian land bridges greatly supported the flow of commodities, such as crude oil, non-ferrous metals, steel, agricultural products, iron ore, and coal, among the cities along the railway lines.

The historical development of the goods and service circulation and the city connection along the Silk Road shows that the trade in goods and services between cities has been constrained by infrastructure and institutional factors and effectively promoted with every major infrastructure improvement in this region. At present, the trade of goods and services is facing an important opportunity for the cities along the Silk Road. On the one hand, China, India and other developing countries are undergoing rapid industrialization and urbanization processes. The continuous increase of urban population and income level will be the foundation of a broad market for final products. The differences in prices, quality and other aspects of commodities also drive the trade among the cities. On the other hand, the countries in the eastern part of the Silk Road are faced with the developmental challenges in production capacity and economic restructuring, while the countries in the western part are trying to stride away from the impact of the financial crisis and to find new opportunities. These countries have the internal driving force to explore markets for goods and services in the cities with greater development potential in the middle section of the Silk Road. However, due to the differences in the natural environment and in respective economic and social conditions of these three parts, to facilitate the flows of goods and services among the cities along the Silk Road still sees many difficulties in both soft and hard environments, such as the lack of infrastructure connection and trade facilitation.

9.1.4 Flow of Production Factors

The unobstructed flow and efficient allocation of talent, capital, technology and other factors of production between cities ensure the development of a region's potential and foster the vitality of growth. During the ancient times, due to the restraint of infrastructure and production capacity, the content and form of the flow of resources were relatively simple, and the flow of merchants, currency and technology was relatively slow among the cities along the Silk Road. After the Industrial Revolution, especially in the modern era, with the rapid development of production forces, the continuous improvement of technology and the deepening of globalization, the content of flows, including talent, capital, technology and other production factors, has been greatly expanded. The cities along the Silk Road began to obtain factors of production on the domestic and international markets.

The long history of trade along the Silk Road shows that the flows of production factors transform the local prospects, improve transportation and other infrastructure, enhance the competitiveness of the region, increase the collaboration and division of labor among the cities, and enhance the city's position in the industrial value chain of the region. With the deepening globalization and the accelerated economic integration of the region, the flow and transnational allocation of production factors among the cities along the Silk Road are facing important opportunities. On the one hand, the countries along the Silk Road are endowed with natural resources that are mutually complementary among one another, possessing a strong potential in resource sharing and a broad area for cooperation. This creates the basic condition for the flow of production factors between cities along the Silk Road. On the other hand, along the route, the high-end node cities that gather more multinational corporations are displaying their advantages in attracting global production factors. And the flows of production factors begin to shift from cities in developed countries to big cities in emerging economies, from cities in the coastal areas to the node cities in the hinterland. This complementary and cooperative feature in resource transfer and sharing provides the opportunity to build a resource network covering all cities along the Silk Road.

9.1.5 Development of Industrial Network

From the longitudinal perspective, an industrial network is a chain of industries, of which the evolution is closely related to the formation and development of industry. Over the 2000 years before the industrial revolution, the economic development of the cities along the Silk Road was extremely slow. From the exchanges of simple goods to the exploitation and sales of commodities, such as natural resources and energy, the Silk Road has transformed from the "route of goods" to the "path of energy". Into the era with highly developed production forces and deepening globalization, the industrial system has undergone profound changes in Eurasian and African cities. The countries along the Silk Road have developed competitive division of labor, which is based on their comparative advantages in their own natural resource endowment. As a supporting carrier of national economy, the cities have undergone drastic industrial restructuring. Among them, the developed European cities in the western part of the Silk Road are in a leading position in high value-added industries, such as global finance, innovative manufacturing, and professional services; the cities of the emerging economies in the eastern part of the Silk Road develop as the world's manufacturing centers due to labor and other resource advantages; the cities in the middle section of the Silk Road that covers Central Asia, South Asia, North Africa, and East Africa, are strong performers in oil mining, resource export and other traditional industries.

Along with the further development of the global value chains and the restructuring of the global industrial landscape, the cities along the Silk Road have great prospect in industrial cooperation because of their distinctive natural resource conditions, highly mutual complementary economic features, and various gradients in economic development. The cities of the emerging economies in the eastern part of the Silk Road, such as Shanghai, Beijing, etc., see rapid economic growth and have abundant capital and labor resources. These cities, with increasing talent and market demands, are displaying their advantages in attracting multinationals, enhancing its position in global industry, especially in the manufacturing sector. They also expand their overseas operations and investment markets eastwards and westwards based on a balanced maritime and land strategic planning. The European cities in the western part of the Silk Road are in the post-industrial age. With developed economy and advanced technology, these cities are restructuring the regional industrial system and seeking cooperation with foreign countries, relying on their advantages of relatively matured technology and high-end factors. The cities in the middle section of the Silk Road, an area covering Central Asia, West Asia, North Africa and East Africa, have rich deposits of natural resources and energy supplies despite their simple economic structure and underdeveloped industries. Their strong desire to develop local economy, seeking international capital and investment in technology, will prompt the increased exploitation of the energy and other natural resources. By leveraging the technological advantages of European cities in the western part of the Silk Road, the huge market demand for energy resources from such emerging economies as China and India in the eastern section of the Silk Road, along with the integrated land-and-sea transport corridors, these countries can carry out collaboration amidst division of labor, improve the industrial system, and be fully integrated into the global value chain. With their own advantages in natural resources and industrial division of labor, the cities in each section can promote the development of the Silk Road from a "route of goods" to a "path of energy" and then to "the passage of division of labor and collaboration", supporting the sustainable development of the industrial network in the entire Silk Road region.

9.2 Trends and Outlook of the Silk Road Cities Network

Along with the advancement of infrastructure connection as well as the continuous improvement of the regulatory environment, the content, degree and scale of urban development and connection will change accordingly in the areas along the Silk Road; along with this change, the Silk Road Cities Network, which covers "half of the world," will continue to evolve in shape and in structure, and play an important role in reshaping the economic landscape of Eurasia and Africa and the urban system of the world.

9.2.1 Development Trends

Expansion of Europe The European region, or the western part of the Silk Road, has a higher degree of development in urban network; in the future, there will be a network spillover effect, showing the development trend of outward expansion. European countries and cities, due to the high degree of industrialization, urbanization and aggregation, will gradually display the spillover and catalyst effect on countries and regions along the Silk Road, which will then extend to the North

African countries along the Mediterranean coast, and the West and Central Asian regions near East Europe.

The Increasing Clustering in East Asia With the accelerated advance of industrialization and urbanization in the major developing powers in the eastern part of the Silk Road, such as China(Ni Pengfei 2015, 2016), the urban system will undergo profound changes: the population size and economy scale will further expand, especially in some big cities with better economic geography; many mid-sized and small cities (towns) within the urban areas will see increasing population density and more frequent economic activities; new cities will also be formed. At the same time, along with the extension of the transportation network, the economic ties and division of labor between the major cities will be expanded to the satellite cities in East Asia, opening up the west and south regions. The numbers of cities, urban population and economic output in East Asia indicate a trend of increasing geographical density.

The Rise of India and Africa As two important underdeveloped areas along the Silk Road, India and Africa are in a stage of rapid development, with stronger potential for future economic growth. Among them, India rises as a large emerging economy with huge population size, vast domestic market, and progressive industrialization and urbanization. Africa, especially the cities along coastal areas, also sees elevated economic scale with the transformation in their national resources and the advancement of industrialization. Especially in the context of globalization, the core cities in this region, such as Delhi of India, Cairo of Egypt, and Nairobi of Kenya, will have stronger connection to the global community and uplift the regional development by playing their agglomeration effect.

The Decline of Central Asia Central Asia is an important region along the Silk Road in the Eurasian hinterland; with the established Silk Road, which connects Europe and East Asia at both ends, and the improved transportation infrastructure that connects international railways and land routes, the Central Asian countries already have much-improved hardware environment to support their urban development. However, due to the disadvantage of its deep-inland geographical location and the long-term constraints from the harsh natural and geographical conditions, on top of the relatively backward infrastructure and divergent institutional environment, when compared to the two ends of the Silk Road, Central Asia is likely to be marginalized. In the long run, the region can share the advantages of the network spillover from both ends, but in the near term, it may suffer the siphon effect and face greater risks for a decline in comparison with other regions along the Silk Road.

The Disintegration of the Middle East Situated among the "two oceans, three continents, and five sea," the Middle East holds the strategic location in the Silk Road Cities Network, connecting the East and the West as well as the three continents: Europe, Asia and Africa. This region is part of both the land-based Silk Road and the maritime Silk Road. Because of the considerable differences in resource distribution, geographical location and development environment, the countries in the Middle East are very different in their respective status and connection to the whole Silk Road Cities Network. With the improved hardware environment and software environment along the Silk Road, either the advantage or disadvantage of the cities within the region will be strengthened. The global connection of the regions centering on Dubai and Istanbul will be further enhanced, while the impediments of the cities in other regions, particularly those suffering sectarian strife and warfare, could be solidified. The future development of the Middle East will be polarized.

9.2.2 The Changing Landscape: "Three Networks and Four Belts"

In the future, the urban network of the Silk Road will mark a diversified evolution under the development trends of the expansion of the two ends, the rise of India and Africa, the decline of Central Asia and the disintegration of the Middle East. With the deepening globalization and the formation of division of labor along the value chains, the European cities at one end of the Silk Road will have solid cities networks, while the East Asian core cities at the other end of the Silk Road will have enhanced capacity in the control and allocation of global resources, the pattern of the urban development along the Silk Road will change from a lopsided U shape, in which the western part is elevated, to a symmetrical U shape. At the same time, with the rise of India and Africa, the relative position of South Asia and West Africa will be heightened. The urban landscape of other areas in the Silk Road Cities Network will be mapped out along the main traffic routes as belts and clusters.

In the context of globalization, digitization and rapid development of communication and transportation, the dominant spatial form of Silk Road Cities Network will no longer be a geographical one but a mobile one. In such a network system, a city, on the one hand, accumulates and creates wealth and maintains its influence by becoming a node in the flowing space(Taylor 2001;Ni Pengfei et al. 2011). On the other hand, the city's functional attributes, scale and rank, are represented by the production and reproduction created by the spatial flows that travel through the city. Their development and evolution will have an important impact on shaping the structuring the urban networks(Qin Chenglin and Sang Mancheng 2015;Tang Zilai et al. 2015). In the future, the Silk Road Cities Network will evolve into a landscape of "Three Networks and Four Belts."

9.2.2.1 Three Networks

On the basis of the preliminary outline of the Silk Road Cities Network and with the improvement of the transportation infrastructure, the urban network development will become more prominent at both ends of the Silk Road and the southern area, featuring the East Asian Cities Network, the European Cities Network and the South Asian (Indian) Cities Network.

The East Asian Cities Network With the establishment of transportation network that is supported by China's high-speed railways, the spatial and temporal distances between cities in the eastern and central regions of China are greatly shortened, and an integrated network is in the making, which is supported by the Yangtze River Delta, Pearl River Delta and the Beijing–Tianjin–Hebei city clusters. At the same time, Shanghai, Beijing and other cities with great development potentials are rising rapidly; together with Tokyo, Seoul and other major cities in East Asia, these cities will support and lead the future development of the Eastern Silk Road and the adjacent regions, facilitating the flows of goods and services, factors of production and the division of labor between cities. The East Asia Cities Network, a multi-tiered and composite connection network that is centered on the mega cities and extended to the small- and mid-size satellite cities and towns as well as their hinterland in this region, is thus formed.

European Cities Network The European cities in the western part of the Silk Road are highly urbanized, forming Paris-Lyon-Le Havre urban agglomeration along the lower reach of the Seine River, Rhine-Ruhr metropolitan region, and the Greater London metropolitan region. In the future, cities with outstanding competitiveness, such as London and Paris, will continue to be in dominant positions in the global circulation of goods and services, factors of production and the industrial network development, and their role as the core of urban agglomerations will become increasingly prominent. They will be the gravitational center that attracts the population and industries; through the collaboration and division of labor between cities, they will become a multinational urban agglomeration consisting of large, mid-sized and small cities. At the same time, since the European industrial structure is developed horizontally with classification and clusters and vertically in chain-type hierarchy, the hinterland of the European urban agglomeration also extended to North African cities along the Mediterranean coast.

South Asian Cities Network With the rise of India, a populous developing country and the progressive construction of the China-Pakistan economic corridor, a cities network is taking form in South Asia. This cities network is supported by such core cities as Mumbai, New Delhi, Bangalore, and Karachi, connected by transportation network in all directions and linked by the flows of talents, commodities and capital. At the same time, the core cities of this cities network, together with the other cities with strong global connection, such as Singapore, Jakarta, and Bangkok, will support the formation of the South Asian Cities Network, and promote the consistent network development of the coastal areas in the middle section of the Silk Road Cities Network.

9.2.2.2 Four Belts

The First Eurasian Land Bridge Cities Belt With the improved railway and other transport infrastructure, in the future, the cities network to the north of the Silk Road will develop into a cities belt, spanning from the eastern part of Russia, connecting the Siberian cities that are relatively densely-populated along the First

Eurasian Land Bridge Railway, and extending eastward to the European metropolitan region. This belt takes the First Eurasian Land Bridge as the transportation artery, linking several node cities in northeast China, southern Russia and northern Europe through numerous branch lines in all compass directions, and forming an extended belt of urban agglomeration.

The New Eurasian Land Bridge Cities Belt With the future development at both ends of the Silk Road in sight, the New Eurasian Land Bridge Cities Belt is taking shape. This extensive metropolitan region is developed on the basis of ancient land-based Silk Road, extended via international railways and high-speed railways along the Second Eurasian Land Bridge as well as the branch lines throughout the Eurasian inland, and anchored at the major cities along the way, including Zhengzhou, Xi'an, Lanzhou, Urumqi and other cities in Central Asia(Wei Ling and Dai Jiangwei 2015). This belt will serve as the key overland link connecting the East Asian Cities Network and the European Cities Network.

Maritime Silk Road Cities Belt This belt is developed on the foundation of the ancient maritime Silk Road; by taking the sea route as the main axis, this belt starts from the coastal cities in eastern China and connects other major economic regions, including ASEAN, South Asia, West Asia, East Africa, North Africa, and Europe. It is a maritime cities belt, connecting the cities and metropolitan areas around the South China Sea, the Pacific and the Indian Ocean. This belt will become an important maritime link that connects the East Asian cities network, the South Asian Cities Network and the European Cities Network.

The West African Coast Cities Belt Along with the rise of Africa and the spread of the Silk Road Cities Network into Africa, a cities belt will be formed among the countries along the west coast of Africa, where the population density is higher and the natural and geographical conditions are better. This belt, supported by the capitals and other large cities of these coastal countries, is a metropolitan complex that extends along the coastline and reaches into the hinterland of Africa.

9.2.3 Global Economic Structure Supported by Silk Road Cities Network

9.2.3.1 Extended Networks: Asia–Europe–Africa City Triangle

With the diversified and deepening interactions, the relationship among the cities along the Silk Road will change from the current linear connection to a multi-tiered and composite connection network. That is, the entire urban system along the Silk Road is changed from a simple framework composed of two cities networks at two the ends and an linear connection between node cities in the middle section to an open and complex structure, which contains multi-facet networks in society and culture, goods and services, production factors, and industrial ties, and is based on the established infrastructure intercourse and integrated institutional system. The development of connection, including the content, degree and pattern of exchange,

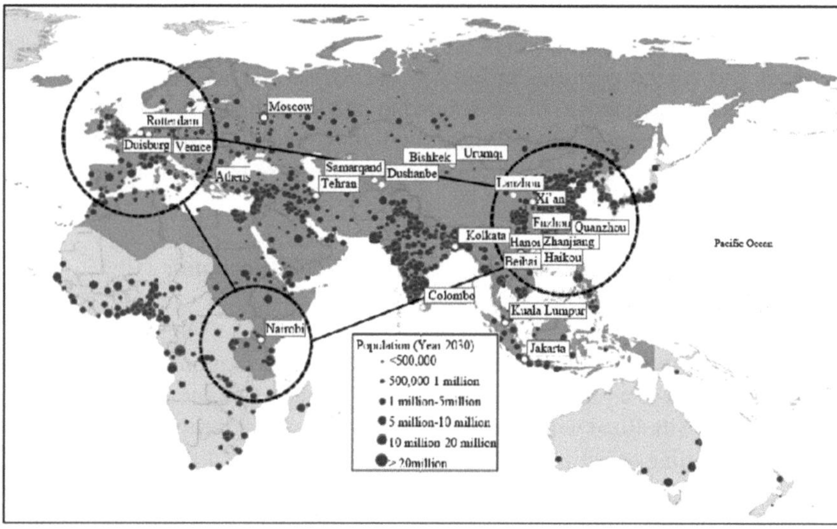

Fig. 9.1 Asia–Europe–Africa City Triangle *Source* population data from the World Urbanization Prospects 2014

among the cities along the Silk Road will have profound impact on the evolution of urban systems in Eurasia and Africa. Thus, an expansive metropolitan complex is developing, in which the main cities along the Silk Road serve as the nodes of the system, the land bridges as the centerline, high-speed rails as catalyst, air transport as accelerator, sea routes as engine. It covers land, air, and marine areas simultaneously, advancing from scattered cities to city belts; through the flows of goods and services, exchanges of production factors, and connections of industrial system, chains of cities are clustered into a network complex. Based on the cities networks along the Silk Road, the Asia–Europe–Africa megalopolis is formed as a triangle of metropolitan regions pillared by the East Asian economic zone, the European economic zone and the African economic zone (See Fig. 9.1).

9.2.3.2 Expanded City Belts: Accelerating the Integration of Sea Nations and Landlocked Countries

The multiple overland and sea routes of the Silk Road, together with its developing open cities networks, will compensate the geographical disadvantage of the landlocked countries in Eurasia and Africa. Since the space–time contraction effect resulting from the better connection achieved through transportation infrastructure building will significantly shorten the geographical distance between the landlocked countries and those coastal developed countries in Eurasia and Africa, the landlocked cities in the underdeveloped countries thus have the chance to increase their contacts with the developed regions through a variety of networks and routes, to share development opportunities and to receive spillover benefits. In the long run, as the gap in development level narrowed, the integration of the landlocked countries and coastal countries in Eurasia and Africa will accelerate. Through the organic connection among the cities along the Silk Road, the mutual benefit between inland countries and coastal countries is enhanced and an "open, cooperative and win–win" growth and development structure is thus achieved.

9.2.3.3 Multipolar Support: Reshaping the World Economic Landscape

The Silk Road Cities Network will play an important role in promoting a multipolar world economy. The urban development and the strengthened connection among the cities along the Silk Road will reshape the economic environment of Asia inland and Africa. The pulling effect of the Silk Road Cities Network lifts up the economic collapse regions, such as the African and the Eurasian hinterland, in the world economic landscape, while weakens the constraints from long distance and gradually eliminates the blockage caused by segmentation in urban development; the Cities Network, which has core cities as the main wealth producer supplemented by key small and medium-sized cities, is geared toward clusters connection. Through demonstrating the aggregating and diffusing effects, the Cities Network will increase the economic density of the developing countries along the Silk Road as well as their share in the world economy, and shapes a multipolar world economic structure underpinned by North America, the European Union, East Asia, and South Asia.

References

Braun, Gerhard O. 2015. Some theoretical issues on the reconstruction of the Silk Road economic belt. *Journal of Urban and Regional Planning* 01: 133–147.

Li, Yongquan. 2015. *The Silk Road economic belt*. Beijing: Social Science Literature Press.

Ni, Pengfei. 2016. *China urban competitiveness report no. 14-New engine: Multi-center city network system*. Beijing: Social Science Literature Press.

Ni, Pengfei. 2015. *China urban competitiveness report no. 13-Giant HAND: Holds up a new map of urban China*. Beijing: Social Science Literature Press.

Ni, Pengfei, Kai Liu, and P.J. Taylor. 2011. The Urban Connectivity in China: A measurement based on the interlocking network model. *Economic and Social System Comparison* 6: 96–103.

Qin, Chenglin. 2015. Sang Mancheng. Urban network and urban economic growth. *Study and Practice* 04: 6–11.

Tang, Zilai, Can Li, Yang Xiao, et al. 2015. Analysis of the relationship between the world economic structure and the world city system. *Urban Planning Forum* 1: 1–9.

Taylor, P.J. 2001. Specification of the world city network. *Geographical Analysis* 33: 181–194.

Wei, Ling, and Jiangwei Dai. 2015. A Perspective on the Agglomeration of China in the Silk Road economic belt—Based on the study of city rank-size distribution. *Journal of Lanzhou University (Social Science Edition)* 2: 1–7.

Part III
Specialized Analysis

Chapter 10
Global Connection and Technological Innovation

Human history is a history of technological innovation. Advance in science and technology has improved the economy, living standard and human society. With thriving science and technology, deepening economic globalization and intensifying international competition, technological innovation will be a common trend to drive urban development worldwide. The position and prospect of any country or city in the global arena will also depend on its competence in technological innovation. Increasing attention has been on how to grasp the new situation, to seize the international economic and technological high ground, to increase productivity, and to accelerate new urbanization. This chapter analyzes the distribution characteristics and development trend of technological innovation around the world to illustrate that global connection is an important factor in technological innovation for a city.

10.1 Spatial Distribution and Trends of Innovation Worldwide

10.1.1 North America and Western Europe Dominate Global Technological Innovation

The world sees unbalanced development in technological innovation, with big differences between cities, countries and regions. The average of number of patent applications of the 500 cities around the world is 266, but the standard deviation reaches 1126 with a variation coefficient of 4.2.

The 500 cities can be categorized into five groups based on their rankings by the number of patent applications. The comparison shows that (see Fig. 10.1), the average number of patent applications of the top 100 cities is higher than that of the cities ranked between 100 and 200, while the mean of the former is about eight

© China Social Sciences Press and Springer Nature Singapore Pte Ltd. 2017

P. Ni et al., *Cities Network Along the Silk Road*,
DOI 10.1007/978-981-10-4834-0_10

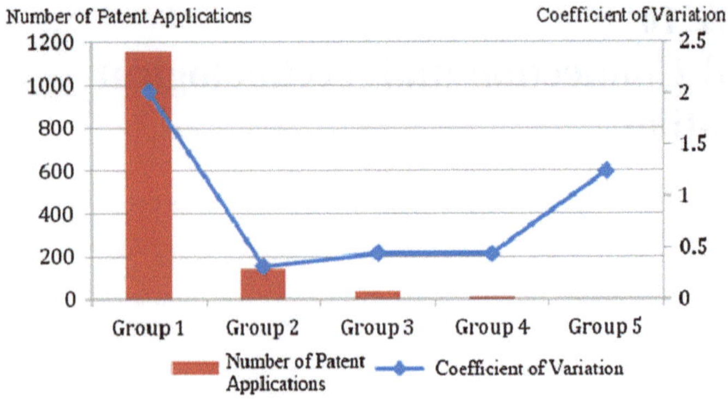

Fig. 10.1 Patent applications of cities worldwide. *Source* CASS city and competitiveness index database

times more than that of the latter. The patent applications of the cities ranked below 200 are much fewer. This shows that cities differ greatly in the capability of technological innovation, which is stronger and more active among the top 100 cities. Furthermore, among the top 100 cities in the patent application rankings, 28 cities are in Europe, 38 in North America, 32 in Asia, including 12 Japanese cities such as Fukuoka, Chiba and Shizuoka, two cities in Oceania, namely, Wellington of New Zealand and Melbourne of Australia.

Comparing the numbers of patent applications by the breakdown of continents (see Fig. 10.2), the mean of North American and European cities is relatively higher at 318 and 183, respectively, and with smaller standard deviation, 562 and 431, and the coefficient of variation 1.8 and 2.4, respectively, indicating that North American and European cities have stronger capability for technological innovation. Although Asian cities have an average of 383 patent applications, the standard deviation reaches 1731, with a coefficient of variation at 4.5, indicating a greater difference in

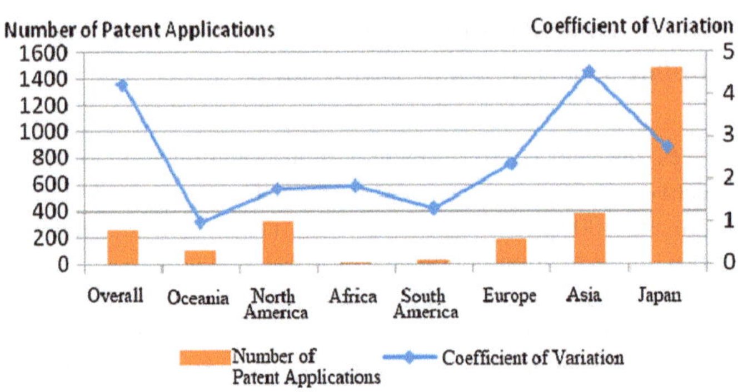

Fig. 10.2 Mean of patent applications and coefficient of variation. *Source* CASS city and competitiveness index database

technological innovation between cities. Besides, it is mainly Japanese cities that have strong capability for technological innovation, while other cities are generally weak in this regard, so are the cities in Oceania, Africa and South America.

Therefore, from whichever perspective, the studies show technological innovation are unevenly distributed around the world, with high concentration in the developed countries and regions of North America, Western Europe and Asia (Japan); North America and Western Europe are dominant powers. The result is consistent with the 2thinknow Innovation Cities Top 100 Index of 2014, which concludes that the most innovative cities are highly concentrated in the United States, Western Europe and other developed countries and regions.

10.1.2 Clustering Features of Technological Innovation

Within a country or a region, world technological innovation centers are mainly concentrated in metropolitan areas, particularly in the metropolitan areas in North America and Western Europe, as shown in Table 10.1. Among the top 100 cities by the number of patent applications, 28 out of the 38 cities in North America are located in the northeastern area, the Great Lakes Megalopolis and the west coast San Francisco-San Diego megalopolis of California. Wherein, there are eight cities in either the northeastern coastal area or the west coast San-San megalopolis and 12 in the Great Lakes Megalopolis. Among the top 100 cities of technological innovation, 19 out of the 28 European cities are located in the London-centered and Paris-centered metropolitan areas; out of the 32 Asian cities, 12 are located in Japan's Tokyo metropolitan area and two in China's Shanghai-centered Yangtze River Delta region.

10.1.3 Technological Innovation is Becoming the Benchmark Function of the World Cities

With technological innovation becoming one of the core functions of a modern city, some cities, such as New York, London, Singapore, Tokyo, and Seoul, are stepping up in planning and building global or regional innovation centers, which further highlights and strengthens the role of technological innovation in leading and supporting urbanization. For example, the Britain initiated the national strategy "United Kingdom Technology City" in 2010 and the United States developed the grand blueprint "Eastern Silicon Valley" in 2012, which are endeavors to develop world cities like London into a technological innovation center so as to claim the "global innovation leadership." The reality also supports that the international metropolis are usually cities with stronger technological innovation capacities, as shown in Table 10.2.

Table 10.1 Distribution and rankings of the top 100 innovative cities

Metropolitan area	City (ranking)
Northeastern/Atlantic coast, United States	New York (8), Washington (11), Boston (32), Philadelphia (65), Baltimore (86), Portland (35), Wilmington (22), Arlington (54)
United Kingdom	London (15), Bristol (72), Manchester (87), Plymouth (94)
Northwestern Europe	Brussels (83), Stuttgart (10), Berlin (24), Hamburger (28), Frankfurt (37), Mannheim (50), Hanover (53), Essen (74), Munich (92), Dortmund (99), Paris (5), Lyon (59), The Hague (46), Rotterdam (67), Amsterdam (82)
Great Lakes Megalopolis, North America	Toronto (56), Chicago (36), Montreal (91), Minneapolis (39), Quebec (97), Pittsburgh (84), Cleveland (49), Cincinnati (31), Columbus (81), Indianapolis (66), Ottawa (80), Windsor (77)
West coast San Francisco-San Diego megalopolis, United States	San Jose (13), San Francisco (21), Los Angeles (48), San Diego (7), Oakland (United States) (44), Seattle (58), Riverside (60), Palo Alto (23)
Pacific coast metropolis, Japan	Tokyo (1), Osaka (2), Yokohama (12), Kyoto (14), Kawasaki (18), Shizuoka (25), Chiba (27), Nagoya (33), Kobe (40), Fukuoka (61), Hamamatsu (68), Hiroshima (75)
Yangtze River Delta, China	Shanghai (16), Hangzhou (78)

Source CASS city and competitiveness index database

Table 10.2 Numbers of patent applications and rankings of selected cities

City	No. of patent applications	Ranking
Tokyo	19942	1
Paris	3479	5
London	1688	15
Beijing	2563	9
Shanghai	1624	16
New York	2651	8
Chicago	704	36
Washington	1926	11
Singapore	831	29
Seoul	5647	4

Source CASS city and competitiveness index database

10.1.4 Growing Technological Innovation Capability of Hub/Node Cities

Although cities stronger in technological innovation are mainly located in the core economic regions of the world, there are a growing number of cities in non-core areas showing strong capacity in technological innovation, such as Shenzhen of

China and Bangalore of India. One attribute of these cities is a stronger local demand or better external connection. Especially, the degree of convenience in external accessibility gradually becomes an important determinant to a city's capacity in technological innovation. Bangalore, the emerging city of technological innovation in India, for example, is where a lot of sci-tech and industrial parks are built close to the airport. Thus, cities in peripheral areas rely on infrastructure such as international air, railway and highway networks to strengthen their function as a transportation hub and enhance the capability to attract global innovation resources that are conducive to building their capability for technological innovation.

10.2 Global Connection and Technological Innovation

The globalization of technology as well as global cooperation and production in technology drives technological innovation toward the path of globalization. Jiang Xiaojuan (2004) points out that the globalization of technologies will inevitably require increased openness of each country's sci-tech systems. The *2005 World Investment Report* also states that with the heightened competitions and the greater degree of technical complexity, innovation is deemed to rely more on external knowledge base. Thus, among many factors that influence a city's capability for innovation, global connection is extremely important, especially for the cities in the inland areas. For example, cities with stronger technological innovation ability, such as New York, Chicago, Seoul, Paris, Tokyo, London, Shanghai, Beijing, and Singapore, dominate the top 10 slots in global connection rankings.

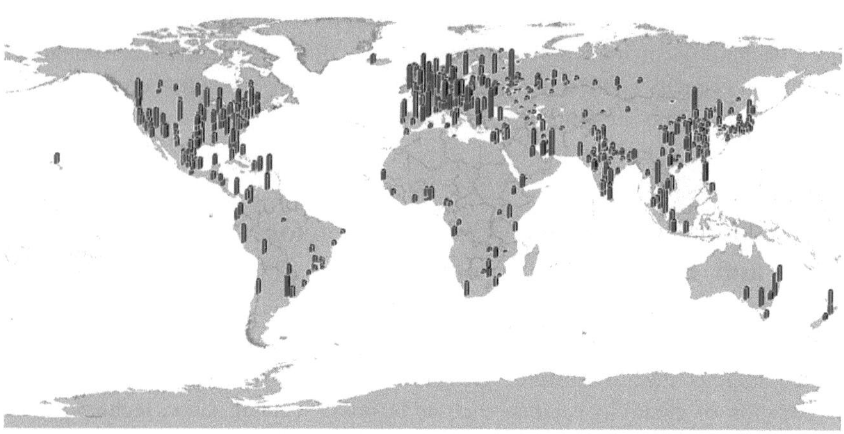

Fig. 10.3 Distribution of global connections between cities. *Source* CASS city and competitiveness index database

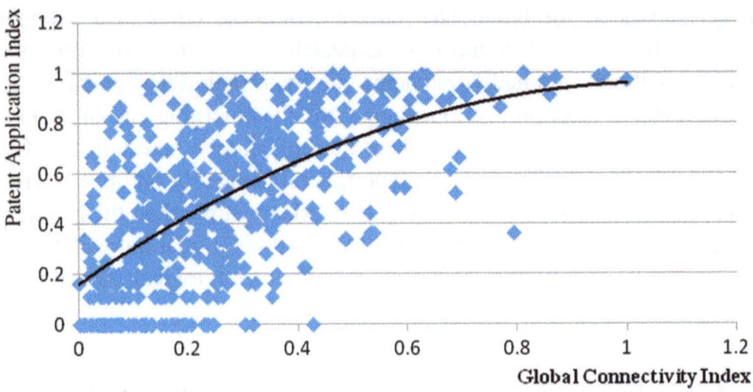

Fig. 10.4 Patent application index and global connection index. *Source* CASS city and competitiveness index database

To verify the correlation between global connection and technological innovation, we analyze the spatial distribution characteristics of the global connection index, as shown in Fig. 10.3. Among the top 100 cities, 27 cities are in North America, 45 in Europe, 21 in Asia, four in South America, two in Oceania and one in Africa. The spatial distribution pattern of global connection scores is similar to that of urban technological innovation in the given previously.

Furthermore, the scatter plots of the index of patent applications and the index of global connection (see Fig. 10.4) suggest a strong correlation between global linkage and technological innovation. The slope of the trend curve indicates the correlation coefficient of the two reaches 0.6, suggesting the global linkages do have some intrinsic impact to a city's technological innovation. In our opinion, the significant correlation is because global connection may have an impact on the city's technological innovation at least in two dimensions: the development of innovation capacity and the translation of technological innovations, which will be discussed separately in Sects. 10.3 and 10.4.

10.3 Global Connection, Creativity Factors and Technological Innovation

The ease of transportation can reduce transport costs and easy transaction can reduce trading rate. Therefore, greater external connection will facilitate the aggregation of creativity factors, such as business, capital, labor, technology and information, and the integration of global innovation resources, providing essential guarantee for innovative urban development and enhanced capacity for innovation.

10.3.1 Global Connection, Creativity Factors, and Technological Innovation

Enterprises and research institutions are important elements of urban innovation systems. A city's ability for innovation depends, to a great extent, on its ability to gather and integrate these innovative elements, which is why an international metropolis is usually a technological innovation center. The higher the concentration of innovation or research institutions and other enterprises a city has, the stronger the city's ability for technological innovation. At the same time, more exchanges and communication, formal or informal, of ideas and knowledge between enterprises and research institutions, will contribute to regional innovation systems and innovation efficiency. As shown in Fig. 10.5, the top 100 cities in the patent application rankings are divided into four groups: the first group are cities in the top 50 for both the number of firms and the number of universities they host; the second group are cities in the top 50 by the number of firms but not in the top 50 by the number of universities; the third group are cities in the top 50 by the number of universities but out of the top 50 by the number of firms; and the fourth group are the cities in neither of the two lists. We find that the average number of patent applications for the first, second, third and fourth groups are respectively 2,093, 731, 522, and 132.

As shown in Fig. 10.6, when the cities are grouped by global connection, the result shows that a city's global connection is significantly correlated to the number

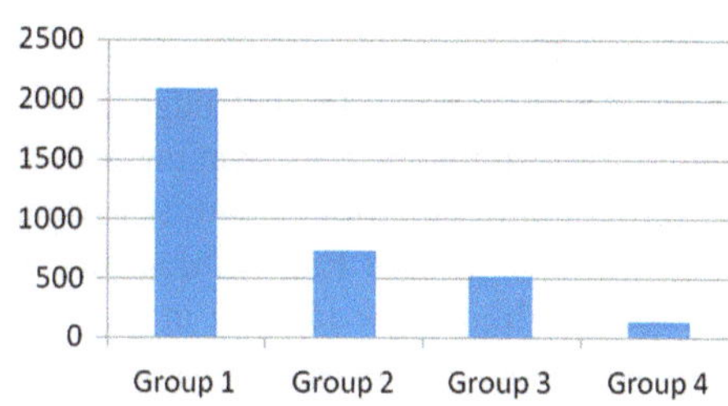

Fig. 10.5 Aggregation of innovation factors and cities' innovation capability. *Source* CASS city and competitiveness index database

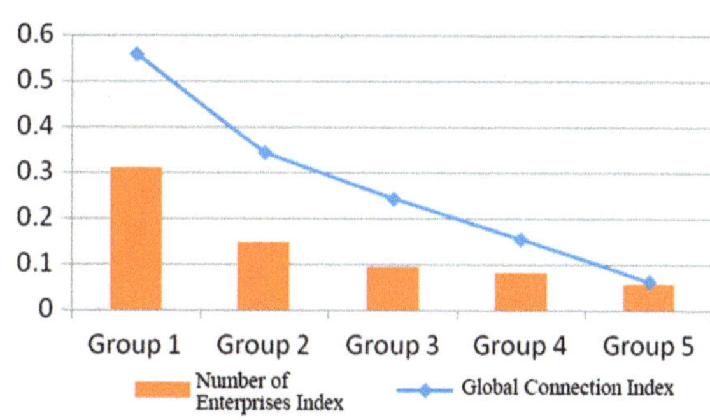

Fig. 10.6 External connection and enterprise conglomeration. *Source* CASS city and competitiveness index database

of Forbes Global Top 2000 firms it hosts. Therefore, we believe that external connection can enhance a city's ability to gather and integrate innovative resources, thus improve the city's ability for innovation; particularly for those cities in need of resources, external connection, of which aggregation effect optimizes local resource allocation, may be the dominant factor in enhancing its capability for innovation.

10.3.2 Global Connection, Cultural Diversity and Technological Innovation

Innovation, an interactive process among people, is inseparable from society. An inclusive and innovative culture gathers global innovative talents and information. Therefore, an open and vibrant culture is an important source for a city's ability in innovation (Ma Haitao et al. 2013). For example, EU culture Commissioner Vassiliou points out that "Cultural diversity and creativity is one of the most dynamic industries as well as an impetus of innovation and development in Europe; cultural diversity is a distinctive feature of the European Union." The United States is a nation of immigrants who naturally constitute a very prominent diverse culture for the country. Thus, the United States, as a country strong in technological innovation, bears a significant multicultural character. This conclusion can be verified by the strong correlation between the patent application index and the language diversity index. More than three languages are used in the top 10 cities for patent application; five or even more languages are used in cities like Tokyo, Shenzhen, Paris, Houston, San Diego, New York, and Stuttgart. By dividing the world's 500-plus cities into five groups based on their technological innovation scores (see Fig. 10.7), the language diversity index shows that a city with stronger ability for technological innovation often is more clearly a city of cultural diversity.

By grouping the cities according to their rankings in global connection from high to low, the result (see Fig. 10.8) shows that the higher the ranking in global connection, the higher the ranking in language diversity. This suggests that, although there are some "conflicts" between different cultures of various regions around the world, with growing interactions, more cultural exchanges between countries will

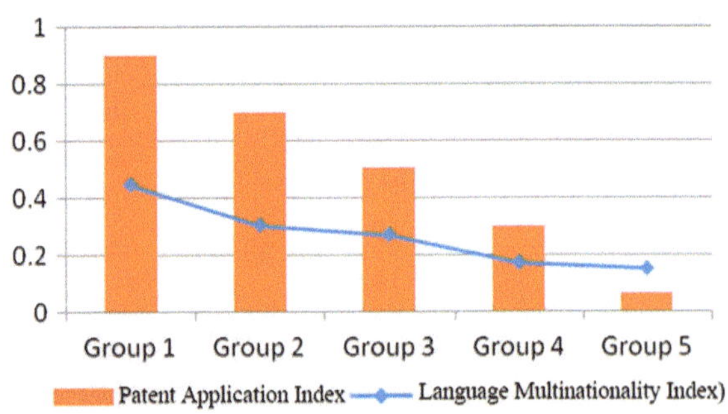

Fig. 10.7 Patent application and cultural diversity. *Source* CASS city and competitiveness index database

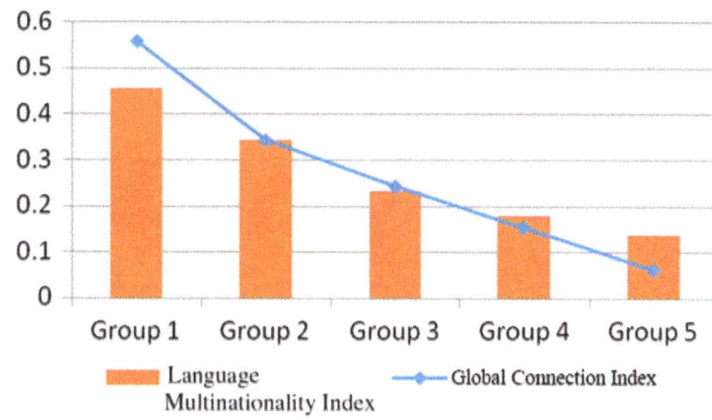

Fig. 10.8 Global connection and cultural diversity. *Source* CASS city and competitiveness index database

bring a variety of cultures into a city. Cultural interaction and assimilation will prompt the urban development into the stage of multiculturalism. Therefore, global connection is conducive to developing an open and diverse urban culture and further enhancing a city's capacity for technological innovation.

10.4 Global Connection, Market Size and Technological Innovation

10.4.1 External Connection Reduces Constraints on Technological Innovation due to Insufficient Market Demand

Market demand is an important factor in translating the results of technological innovation; it provides a platform where innovations are transformed into practical productivity. Thus, the market size is a major factor in transforming technological innovations for a country or region (Xu Kangning and Feng Wei, 2010). In general, the market size impacts technology innovation in the following aspects: (1) On the one hand, the market size affects the technology spillover effects among enterprises as it influences the level of business conglomeration (Yang Haochang et al. 2015); on the other hand, it strengthens competition, forcing enterprises to continue with technological innovation and transformation (Melitz and Ottaviano 2008). (2) According to Schmookle's (1966) "demand drives invention" theory, technological innovation and the transformation of innovation achievements are geared toward profits, which is only possible in a sizable market. (3) Market size determines the specified division of labor in a society. As labor requires more specialized skills, it is easier to promote technological innovations. This hypothesis is supported by Ades and Glaeser (1999), Chaney and Ossa (2012) and many other theoretical and empirical studies. According to market demand, we divided the cities into five groups and found that the greater the market demand, the more the city's patent applications. On the contrary, the less the market demand, the fewer

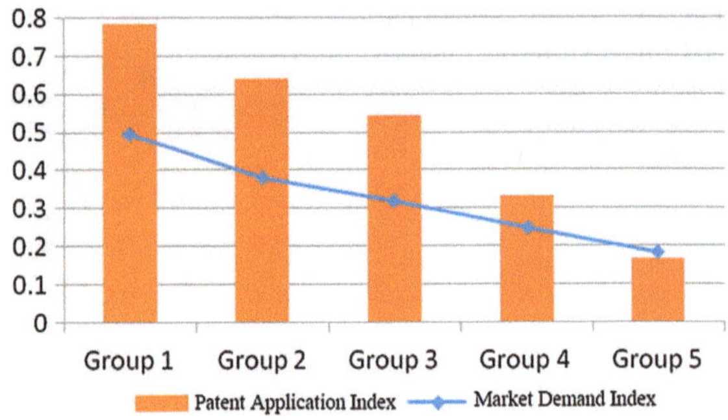

Fig. 10.9 Market size and patent applications. *Source* CASS city and competitiveness Index database

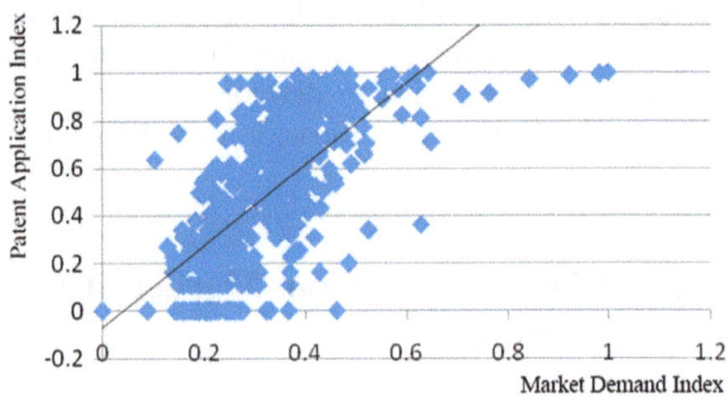

Fig. 10.10 City size and technological innovation. *Source* CASS city and competitiveness index database

the city's patent applications, as shown in Fig. 10.9. This shows that market demand is indeed an important factor, and a significant one that affects the technological innovation in a region.

Although the market demand is crucial for innovative activities in an area, the market demand and technological innovation are not exactly correlated to each other at a city level, as shown in Fig. 10.10. Some cities with smaller local demand may also have a strong capacity for technological innovation. For example, among the top 100 cities in patent application ranking, 45 cities have market demand ranked below 100. Among them, 14 cities have market demand ranked below 200, such as Washington in the United States; Suwon City, Daejeon, Seongnam, Incheon, Daegu and Ansan in Republic of Korea; Hangzhou, Changsha of China; and Taipei. This is because market demand is not the only factor for a city's technology innovation; another critical factor is the global connection, which will weaken the impact of the local market demand on technological innovations.

In a relatively closed economy, a city's market size will be limited by administrative boundaries. However, with the advance of globalization and increased connection, the definition of market size is no longer confined to the local market within a city's boundary but more related to external market demand. As a result, external market demand gradually replaces local market demand (Neal 2011). The impact of external connection on a city's technological innovation capacity is growing, and even greater than that from the local market demand in some cities.

For example, Brussels is ranked 83rd in technological innovation; although its domestic market demand is at the 304th position, its global connection index is among the top 27. Frankfurt, ranked 37th in technological innovation, is among the top 10 of global connection, although 110th in local demand rankings. Bangalore, ranked 42nd in technological innovation, is among the first 73 in global connection although 254th in local demand ranking. Taipei, ranked 79th in technological innovation, is among the top 50 in global connection although 138th in local demand index. These all explain why local demand might influence a city's innovation capability, but there is no absolute correlation between the two. Besides, an innovation-oriented global city is often an important node in a global city network or the accessible link within an urban agglomeration.

10.4.2 Threshold Feature of Global Connection on Innovation Transformation

Global connection can lower the constraints from local market size, thus speeds up the transformation of technological innovations. However, this catalyst effect is characterized by a certain threshold: since a big local market is less restricting to technological innovation, the effect of global connection in promoting technological innovation would be smaller; for cities with a relatively smaller market, since the market size is a determinant in transforming technological innovations, global connection has a more significant effect in weakening the constraint of local market size; for cities with particularly small local market demand, global connection has difficulty in weakening the the fundamental constraint of market demand on innovation, thus the effect in promoting technological innovation may also be relatively small. In order to verify this assumption, we divide the 500 cities into five groups according to their local market size to study the impact of global connection on technological innovation.

According to Fig. 10.11, global connection and technological innovation are positively correlated for cities with different market demands. The impact of global connection on technological innovation becomes more significant when a city's market demand becomes smaller. More specifically, the slope of the trend line added to the scatter plot suggest that among the top 100 cities with high market demands, such as Tokyo (Japan), Paris (France), New York (the United States), London (United Kingdom), and Seoul (Republic of Korea), the marginal effect of global connection index over the patent application index is approximately 0.324; for the cities ranked 101–200 in market demand, such as Mumbai (India), San Diego (Chile), Frankfurt (Germany), and Nanjing (China), the marginal effect of global connection index over the patent application index is approximately 0.422; for the cities ranked 201–300 in market demand ranking, such as Pittsburgh (United States), Lima (Peru), Lyon (France), St. Petersburg (Russia), and Halifax (Canada), the marginal effect of global connection index over the patent application

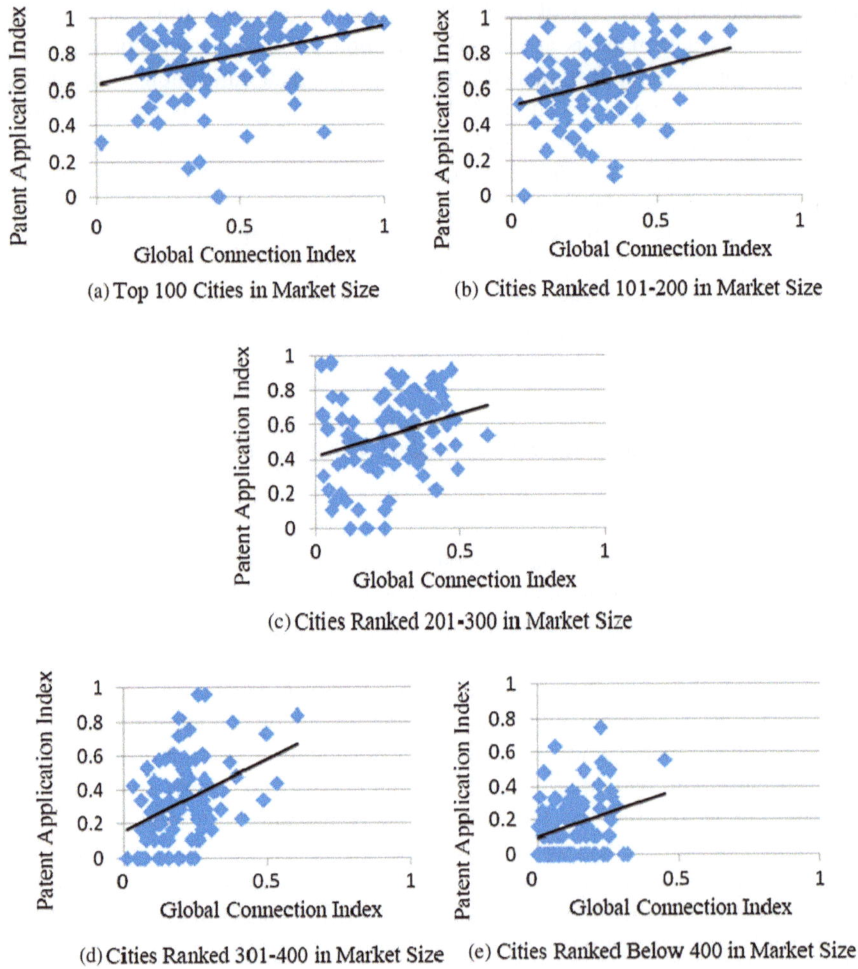

Fig. 10.11 Global connection and technological innovation for cities with different market sizes. *Source* CASS city and competitiveness index database

index is approximately 0.488; for the cities ranked 301–400 in market demand, such as Pretoria (South Africa), Bucharest (Romania), Aberdeen (United States), Brussels (Belgium),and Yangon (Myanmar), the marginal effect of global connection index over the patent application index is as high as 0.845. However, when market size is too small, the Global connection will have limited effect on technological innovation, for example, the cities ranked below 400 in market demands, such as Voronezh (Russia), São Bernardo do Campo (Brazil), Veracruz (Mexico), Faridabad (India), the marginal effect of global connection index over the patent application index is approximately 0.584.

10.5 Conclusion

The globalization of science and technology, an objective process, improves the efficiency in the global configuration of technological resources. In this context, strong global connection is the driving factor of the city's active participation in globalizing science and technology. Moreover, the analyses in this paper show that to strengthen the global linkage will enhance the city's technological innovation capability in two ways: to integrate the innovative elements and to promote transformation of scientific and technological achievements. Especially for those cities that lack innovation elements and have smaller market size, their capacity for innovation is greatly dependent on the support of global connection. Therefore, to grasp the new trend of and to fully involve in the world's technological innovation, it is necessary to strengthen global connection.

References

Ades, A., and E. Glaeser. 1999. Evidence on growth, increasing returns and the extent of the market. *Quarterly Journal of Economics* 114 (3): 1025–1045.

Chaney, T., and R. Ossa. 2012. Market size, division of labor, and firm productivity. *Social Science Electronic Publishing* 90 (1): 177–180.

Haitao, Ma., Fang Chuanglin, and Wang Shaojian. 2013. Basic feature of the global innovative city and its implication for China. *Urban Planning Forum* 1: 69–77.

Haochang, Yang, Li Lianshui, and Liu Jun. 2015. Influence and regional difference of local market size on technological innovation capability. *China Technology Forum* 1: 27–32.

Kangning, Xu, and Feng Wei. 2010. Upgrade of the biochemical industry based on the local market size: alternative path of technological innovation. *China Industrial Economics* 11: 58–67.

Melitz, M.J., and G.I.P. Ottaviano. 2008. Market size, trade, and productivity. *Review of Economic Studies* 75 (1): 295–316.

Neal, Z.P. 2011. From Central places to network bases: A transition in the U.S. urban hierarchy, 1900–2000. *City & Community* 10 (1): 49–75.

Schmookler, J. 1996. *Invention and economic growth*. Boston, MA: Harvard University Press.

Unctad, B. 2005. *World investment report*. Geneva: United Nations Publication.

Xiaojuan, Jiang. 2004. Understanding globalization of science and technology - enhanced resource reconfiguration, collaboration and innovation. *Management World* 6: 4–13.

Chapter 11
Urban Characteristics, National Characteristics and Global Connection of Primate Cities

11.1 Introduction

The global urban system has become a hot research topic in recent years, starting with the term "world city". The term "world city," coined by British designer Geddes in 1915, refers to those cities that host the world's most important business activities. In the 1960s, British scholar Hall thought that a "world city" is the top international metropolis operating as an economic, political and cultural center of the world or most countries. In 1981, Kuhn started studying the urban system based on the new international division of labor theory. Subsequently, Friedman put forward his famous "world city hypothesis" and the "world city hierarchy", both of which are regarded as a major theoretical framework for urban development studies. In 1991, American sociologist Sassen defined the concept "global city" as significant production point of specialized financial and producer services, such as New York, London and Tokyo. In 1989, Custer suggested that globalization, information technology and networking created a new "mobile space" instead of "local space"; a city's status mainly depends on its strength in networking. And a global city is a key node in the global network. In 1995, British scholar Taylor proposed the concept of "world city network", breaking the long-standing hierarchy theory and emphasizing the importance of networking and partnerships between cities. Therefore, a world city (global city) is not an isolated regional leader, but its capacity in associated productivity.

With globalization deepening, the role and functions of global cities have become increasingly prominent. As a node in the global network, a city can no longer remain isolated or detached, but need to relate to and cooperate with other cities. The traditional cities of developed countries now coexist and compete with cities of emerging countries. This study thus focuses on the global cities network, especially the relationship between the attributes of primate cities and the national characteristics of the countries they each represents. This chapter also analyzes a sample of 505 cities around the world, which basically represents today's cities in

© China Social Sciences Press and Springer Nature Singapore Pte Ltd. 2017
P. Ni et al., *Cities Network Along the Silk Road*,
DOI 10.1007/978-981-10-4834-0_11

different regions and at different levels of development. We examine the "global connection index" of the global urban competitiveness index (GUCI) of these 505 cities so as to explore the deeper ties between them.

11.2 Literature Review

In 1939, American scholar Jefferson proposed the concept of "primate city", which is the largest city in a country or region, disproportionately larger than the next largest city. The previous studies on primate cities mainly focused on the degree of primacy, which is a measurement of the city's significance in its country or region, reflecting the range and degree of influence, the level of driving capacity and the population size of the city. Ades and Glaeser (1994) explored what constitutes a primate city at the national level, and found that political factors have a greater impact on the degree of primacy than economic factors. Bertinelli and Strobl (2003) examined 39 developing countries and found that the urban primacy index mostly (except Brazil, India and other large countries) falls between 0.20 and 0.45 in 1999, and was basically on an upward trend from 1960 to 1990. Studies on primate cities started in the 1980s in China. The initial studies were focused on the degree of primacy, introduced by Yan Chongmin et al. (1981) Their studies examine the primacy ranking of each province in the period from the founding of the People's Republic of China and the reform and opening-up (1949–1978), aiming to explore what boosts urban population growth in administrative centers; Gu Chaolin (1992) analyzed the primacy index of the cities in each province, and categorized the provincial urban system into three basic types: bipolar, balanced and core-bound, with a simple analysis of the relationship between each type and its level of economic development; Wang Mingfeng (2000) surveyed the primacy index of the major provincial cities from 1984 to 1997 and found that the changes in the degree of primacy gradually decreased, suggesting that the distribution of provincial urban systems became more balanced. Recent researches on the degree of primacy have been extended to new areas. Lu Xuefa et al. (2007) advanced the concepts of economic primacy index, industry primacy index, science and technology primacy index, talent primacy index and cultural primacy index.

In addition to the abundant researches on primacy, the academic communities home and abroad also have conducted more studies on the development of primate cities. Ghosh (1986) studied the development of primate cities in Asia, proposing that such cities should abandon the uneven development for balanced growth. Das and Dutt (1993) examined the characteristics of India's urban index and primate cities. Tammaru (1999) studied the relationship between differentiated urbanization and primate city development in the former Soviet Union and Estonia. The Chinese researchers, Chen Zhao and Lu Ming (2015), presented a paper that shed light on the determinants of a country's primate city by examining data of a variety of countries, and found that a nation's population size directly determines the size of its primate city, while globalization and urbanization also increase the primate city's share in its country's total population. Yao Yongling and Tang Yanzhe (2015) studied how the internal structure of a metropolitan area is determined by the ways the primate city connects with its surrounding cities. They establish an interconnection matrix among cities within 12 Chinese metropolises; through the matrix, the connection paths are identified and an interconnection structure established; based on the connection structure, the centrality and power of the primate city of each metropolitan area is calculated and the function of the primate city is analyzed.

Thus, the studies of a country's primate city have grown in quantity and depth, yet the studies on the correlation between a primate city and its global connection are rarely seen in traditional literature, as the study on the characteristics of a primate city's global connection is a relatively new field. This chapter will focus on the features of the primate city's global connection at the global level in order to get some new findings.

11.3 Characteristics of Global Connection Demonstrated by Primate Cities Worldwide

A primate city refers to the largest city in terms of population size in a relatively independent geographical scope (such as a country, region, etc.) or in a relatively complete urban system. Among the 505 cities, we choose cities with the largest population size in each country and derive a sample of 119 countries.

11.3.1 Primate Cities with the Best Global Connection at the National Level

Of the 119 primate cities, 111 have both the largest population size and the highest global connection in their respective countries, accounting for 93%. The remaining eight primate cities do not have the best global connection, and they are the primate cities of Germany, Italy, China, Malaysia, India, Ecuador, Australia and New Zealand. Seven out of these eight cities, with the only exception being China, have the largest population size and the second highest global connection in their respective countries; while the city with the highest global connection is often the city with the second largest population (see Table 11.1). It suggests that, at the global level, a primate city is the top city in the urban system and usually serves as the national economic center with more advanced and influential production and service industries compared to other cities in the same country. This function of a primate city is based on the economies of scale, of which the key mechanism is that economic agglomeration facilitates labor productivity (World Bank 2009; Lu Ming 2013). And this is precisely what brings along the global exchanges and contacts. Therefore, a primate city is the best representative city with the highest global connection of a country.

Table 11.1 Countries and primate cities not having leading global connection

	Country	City	National ranking by population size	Global connection index	National ranking by global connection
1	Germany	Berlin	1	0.62232	2
		Frankfurt	2	0.753997	1
2	Italy	Rome	1	0.678049	2
		Milan	2	0.694094	1
3	China	Chongqing	1	0.322168	12
		Beijing	3	0.871796	1
4	Malaysia	Penang	1	0.192367	2
		Kuala Lumpur	2	0.497166	1
5	India	Mumbai	1	0.573754	2
		Delhi	2	0.577317	1
6	Ecuador	Guayaquil	1	0.270702	2
		Quito	2	0.301168	1
7	Australia	Melbourne	1	0.457233	2
		Sydney	2	0.583782	1
8	New Zealand	Auckland	1	0.357354	2
		Wellington	2	0.382184	1

Source CASS city and competitiveness Index database

11.3.2 Economic Scale is a Determinant of Global Connection of a City

In 114 countries, the city of the largest economic scale also has the highest global connection and this accounts for 96% of the 119 countries studied. In the five countries of Germany, Italy, China, Ecuador and New Zealand (see Table 11.2), the city with the largest GDP does not have the highest global connection. The scatter plot showing the cities with the largest GDP and their global connection index (see Fig. 11.1) indicates a positive correlation, that is, the economic scale is a key determinant of global connection for a city.

Table 11.2 Global connection of cities with the largest economic scale of their countries

Country	City with highest GDP	Global connection ranking	City with highest global connection	GDP ranking
Germany	Berlin	2	Frankfurt	5
Italy	Rome	2	Milan	2
China	Shanghai	2	Beijing	2
Ecuador	Guayaquil	2	Quito	2
New Zealand	Auckland	2	Wellington	3

Source CASS City and Competitiveness Index database

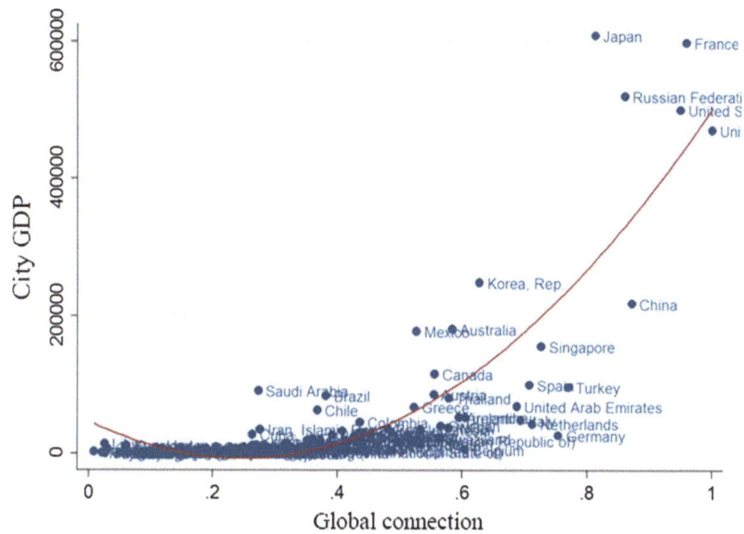

Fig. 11.1 GDP and global connection of some cities. *Source* CASS City and Competitiveness Index database

At the city level, the larger the economy, the more obvious the effect of agglomeration. The effect of economies of scale that attracts business conglomeration, builds industry chains, strengthens international connections between enterprises, and thus increases the global connection of larger cities.

Further, the analysis and data above shows that among the 505 cities from 119 countries, the primate cities are basically the largest economic centers of their respective countries. This illustrates the high correlation between the population size, economic scale and global connection of cities worldwide. Generally speaking, the city with the largest population size and economic scale usually has the highest global connection in its country.

11.4 Global Connection of Primate Cities of Major Countries

Because there are many countries, we are unable to assess the global connection of each country's primate city. In this study, we selected 14 most representative countries—the United Kingdom, France, Germany, Italy, Russia, Japan, the Republic of Korea, India, the United States, Canada, Mexico, Brazil, Australia and China, covering all continents and countries of different levels of development, and including the developed countries of traditional capitalism and emerging market economies.

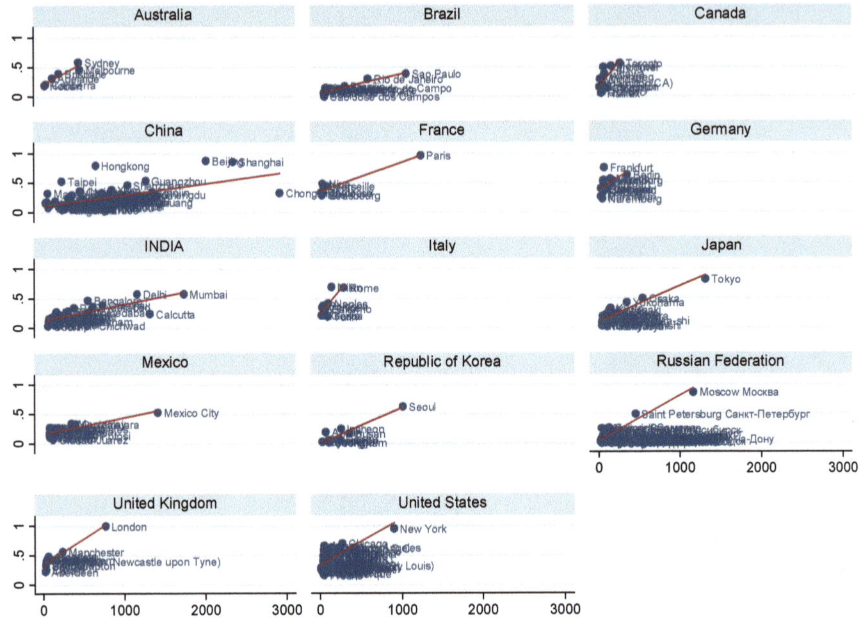

Fig. 11.2 City population size and global connection. *Source* CASS City and Competitiveness Index database

The scatter plot with a fitted curve between the city's population size and global connection index shows that the two are highly correlated in these countries. Thus, the following study is focused on the prominent features of the primate cities' global connection of these countries.

As shown in Fig. 11.2, this study examines the primate cities of 14 countries on four continents.

Finding 1: The primate cities of developed countries remain in dominant positions, while those of the emerging market economies in Asia are growing rapidly. The chart shows the features of major countries' primate cities by charting the global connection index from GUCI (see Table 11.3): the global connection scores of the primate cities of the 14 G20 countries are relatively high; their mean score is three times higher than that of the average of the 505 sample cities. It can be said that the primate cities of these countries are the best representatives of global cities. In terms of trend and pattern, the traditional cities in developed countries, particularly those primate cities in Europe and America, with their great economic, social and cultural advantages and years of sophistication and experiences in hardware and software environments, are still major centers in the global network system. But the rise of the primate cities in emerging market economies is noteworthy. Shanghai of China and Seoul of the Republic of Korea are ranked 6th and 23rd, respectively, in global connection. Mumbai of India is also among the top 40 of the world. This phenomenon indirectly suggests that the emerging market economies, leveraging

Table 11.3 Global connection index and ranking of primate cities of major countries

City	Country	Continent	Global connection index	Ranking
London	United Kingdom	Europe	1.0000	1
Paris	France	Europe	0.9585	2
Berlin	Germany	Europe	0.6223	24
Rome	Italy	Europe	0.6780	17
Moscow	Russia	Europe	0.8605	5
Shanghai	China	Asia	0.8524	6
Tokyo	Japan	Asia	0.8131	7
Seoul	Republic of Korea	Asia	0.6272	23
Mumbai	India	Asia	0.5738	34
New York	United States	North America	0.9495	3
Toronto	Canada	North America	0.5551	40
Mexico City	Mexico	North America	0.5261	53
Sao Paulo	Brazil	South America	0.3814	118
Melbourne	Australia	Oceania	0.4572	75

Source CASS City and Competitiveness Index database

their comparative advantages in the international division of labor and enhanced manufacturing capabilities, have become the world's important sites for business conglomeration; against this context, the primate cities of the emerging market economies are gradually becoming key nodes in the global network.

Finding 2: The aggregation and enhanced connection of services strengthen the global connection of the primate cities. The analysis of the global connection of the primate cities shows that economic connection of the primate cities, that is, the interconnection of multinational firms, is higher than that of the rest of the cities worldwide. For example, London, New York, Tokyo, and Shanghai are the top four cities, and Paris, Moscow, and Seoul are also among the top 10 (ranked 8th, 9th, and 10th respectively) at the global level. Among these cities, London, New York, Tokyo, and Shanghai have more than 1000 multinational firms (see Fig. 11.3), indicating that multinational companies have their headquarters set in the primate cities with regard to various factors, including exchanges on production inputs, technology use, and convenience, and thus contribute to the industrial agglomeration and financial conglomeration in the primate cities. New York, for example, brings together 11 financial headquarters and becomes a global financial center; Tokyo has 18 industrial headquarters and becomes the world's largest industrial city. Thus, the aggregation of service business deepens a city's connection with the rest of the world, and thus builds its competitiveness.

Finding 3: Infrastructure is a key factor in improving primate cities' global connection. Urban infrastructure is characterized by the physical form of infrastructure in an urban system. Infrastructure is the fundamental carrier of economic and social activities in a city; advanced and hi-tech infrastructure is essential for the development of connection between cities. Examining external connections, one of

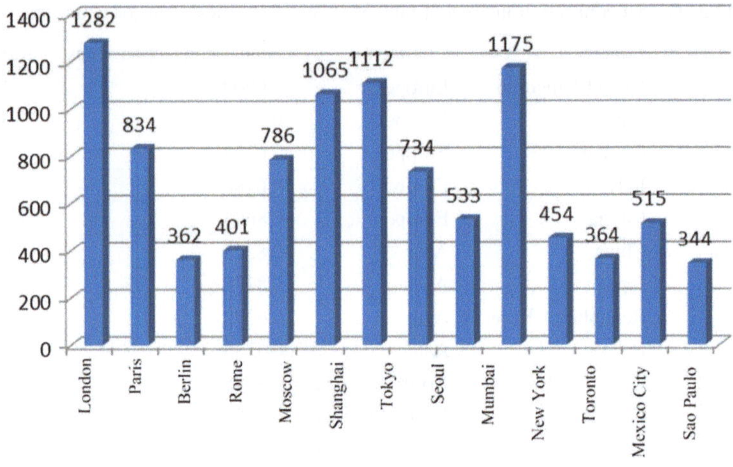

Fig. 11.3 Number of multinational firms in major primate cities, *Source* CASS City and Competitiveness Index database

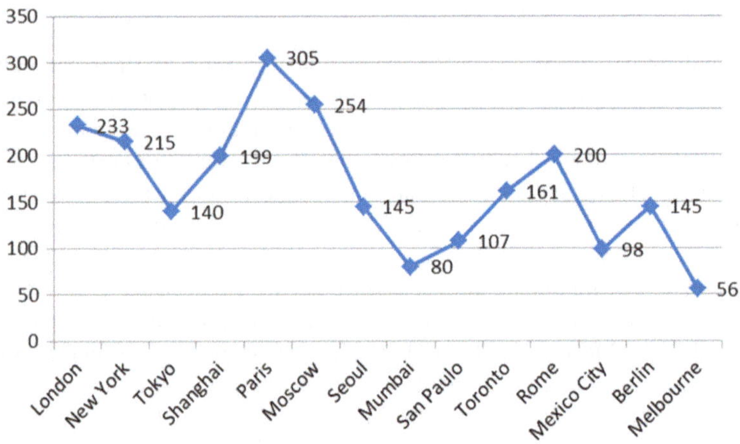

Fig. 11.4 Number of air routes in major primate cities. *Source* CASS City and Competitiveness Index database

the relevant indicator showing a primate city's infrastructure conditions, the average number of air routes, has a average of 167 for the 14 primate cities covered here, which is three times the world average which is 51. These primate cities have more air routes than other cities worldwide (see Fig. 11.4). Thus, the 14 primate cities become international metropolises, where the flows of materials, population, business, capital, and information converge, basically because they are also the world's most important transportation hubs (international airports). So, the global connection and the future improvement of a primate city are closely related to infrastructure building.

11.5 National Characteristics and Global Connection of the Primate Cities

11.5.1 Selection and Calculation for Interaction Between Cities: Introduction to Revised Gravity Model

The gravity model is used to measure the degree of spatial interaction. Derived from the seventeenth-century physicist Newton's Law of Gravity, the gravity model of economics is widely used in international trade and regional economic studies. American scholar Reilly (1929) is the first to apply this model in economic studies and he proposed the famous retail law of gravitation, in which the ratio of a city's retail sales to that of two cities *i* and *j*, is proportional to the population of the two cities, but inversely proportional to the square of the distance to the two cities. Later, Converse (1930) expanded Reilly's theory and applied the model to the measurement of the interactions between cities in regional development. Zipf (1949) and Isard (1965) further interpreted and applied the theory, and derived a more consistent gravity model, of which the basic form is as follows:

$$I_{ij} = G\frac{Q_i Q_j}{r_{ij}^b}$$

In this equation, I_{ij} is the gravitation between two cities *i* and *j*; r_{ij} is the distance between the two cities; Q_i and Q_j are a social economic measurement (such as population, economic scale, etc.), G is the gravitational coefficient, b is the gravitational attenuation index.

In the recent studies on the connection between cities, Q is not just the population or GDP, but also a comprehensive index, such as the quality of a city, in the modified gravity model. Therefore, this paper also employs this modified gravity model, in which Q is the city's global connection index, r_{ij} is the distance between two cities, the gravitational coefficient G is set to 1, while the gravitation decline index b is set at 1/2.

11.5.2 Characteristics of Connections Between the Primate Cities of Major Countries

Employing the gravity model and the data from the database of global competitiveness, we calculate the connection between the 14 primate cities mentioned above, with specific information shown in Table 11.4.

After carefully examining Table 11.4, we obtain the following three findings:

Finding 1: Geographical relation is still a fundamental characteristic in the connection between the primate cities. The most noticeable result derived from the gravity model is that the geographical relation still dominates the connection

Table 11.4 Connection between major primate cities based on the gravity model

	London	Paris	Berlin	Rome	Moscow	Shanghai	Tokyo	Seoul	Mumbai	New York	Toronto	Mexico City	Sao Paulo	Melbourne
London	–	5.111	2.042	1.786	1.722	0.889	0.832	0.667	0.677	1.272	0.735	0.557	0.391	0.352
Paris	5.111	–	2.013	1.954	1.654	0.849	0.791	0.635	0.657	1.191	0.687	0.526	0.377	0.338
Berlin	2.042	2.013	–	1.226	1.335	0.579	0.536	0.433	0.450	0.739	0.429	0.332	0.234	0.225
Rome	1.786	1.954	1.226	–	1.197	0.605	0.555	0.449	0.495	0.776	0.447	0.352	0.266	0.245
Moscow	1.722	1.654	1.335	1.197	–	0.888	0.809	0.664	0.696	0.943	0.552	0.437	0.302	0.327
Shanghai	0.889	0.849	0.579	0.605	0.888	–	1.653	1.816	0.689	0.743	0.443	0.395	0.239	0.434
Tokyo	0.832	0.791	0.536	0.555	0.809	1.653	–	1.503	0.569	0.741	0.444	0.402	0.228	0.411
Seoul	0.667	0.635	0.433	0.449	0.664	1.816	1.503	–	0.481	0.566	0.338	0.301	0.177	0.309
Mumbai	0.677	0.657	0.450	0.495	0.696	0.689	0.569	0.481	–	0.487	0.285	0.241	0.186	0.265
New York	1.272	1.191	0.739	0.776	0.943	0.743	0.741	0.566	0.487	–	2.245	0.861	0.413	0.336
Toronto	0.735	0.687	0.429	0.447	0.552	0.443	0.444	0.338	0.285	2.245	–	0.511	0.234	0.199
Mexico City	0.557	0.526	0.332	0.352	0.437	0.395	0.402	0.301	0.241	0.861	0.511	–	0.233	0.207
Sao Paulo	0.391	0.377	0.234	0.266	0.302	0.239	0.228	0.177	0.186	0.413	0.234	0.233	–	0.153
Melbourne	0.352	0.338	0.225	0.245	0.327	0.434	0.411	0.309	0.265	0.336	0.199	0.207	0.153	–

Note since the original values of the connection between primate cities are too small, the values in this table are the original values multiplied by 100
Source CASS City and Competitiveness Index database

between primate cities. In Europe, the connections between London, Paris, Berlin and Rome is relatively high (London has the highest 5.111 with Paris, and 2.042 and 1.786 with Berlin and Rome, respectively, substantially higher than with other cities. Berlin and Rome have similar situations.) In Asia, Shanghai, Tokyo, and Seoul obviously form a community (Shanghai has connection scores of 1.653 and 1.816 with Tokyo and Seoul, respectively, higher than that with other cities). In North America, New York and Toronto are highly connected (New York has a connection score up to 2.245 with Toronto). Thus, the geographical factor is a fundamental determinant in the interaction between cities. The countries in geographical proximity often see convergent economic behaviors and it is easy to form close regional cooperation. The economic relation is connected by geographical closeness, which, in turn, can foster the development of economic blocs or the integration of regional economies. From the connection characteristics mentioned above, the connection between the primate cities of countries within an economic bloc is significantly higher than that with cities outside the bloc. Thus, the integration of regional economies is the main form and content of the current world geo-economy. The world economy is now divided into three competing core economic blocs, namely, the European economic zone with France and Germany as the centers; the Pacific-rim economic zone with Japan and South Korea as the lead; and the US-led Western Hemisphere economic zone. This regional integration contributes to the urban development in that the cities have crossed the boundaries of their own countries and formed a diversified city network, especially the polycentric mega-city network. The London–Paris–Berlin city network, the Shanghai–Seoul–Tokyo city network, and the New York–Toronto city network are all developed around multiple cities, which is characterized by the development of clusters of smaller cities, intensive networking of a variety of resources within a space, and regional collaboration.

Finding 2: A country's high-end industry capacity is the cornerstone of the connection between the primate cities. Based on the analysis of Table 11.4 and Finding 1, geo-relation is still the most fundamental connection between cities. It can be said that regional connection is basically out of geographical factors. Multinational firms are the most prominent actors of the geo-economy between cities. Multinational corporations are the product of capital internationalization, technological revolution and the deepening international division of labor; they are the main carriers of internationalization, with advantages in monopolization, ownership, and location that attracts foreign direct investment; they have affiliates throughout the world, forming an integrated network in production, sales, technology, new product development and other aspects.

When put together, there is a positive correlation (see Fig. 11.5) between the primate city's global connection index and the country's high-end industry index (Forbes Global Top 2000 distribution of headquarters in different countries), indicating that the connection between cities is established by the high-end industries created by the multinational enterprises of a country.

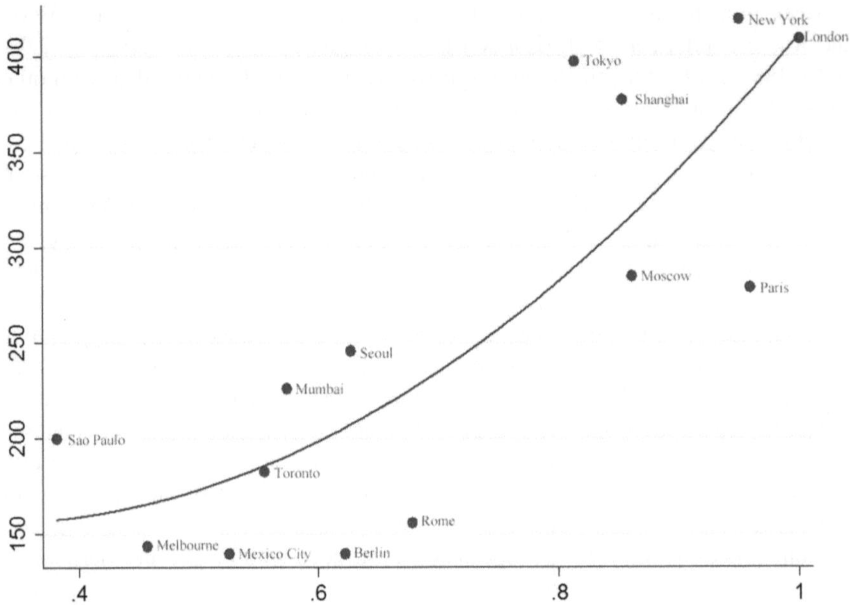

Fig. 11.5 Primate city global connection index and the national high-end industry index. *Source* CASS City and Competitiveness Index database

First, the cross-border businesses operated by multinational companies strengthen the ties between countries, drive and deepen the collaboration in production, exchange, circulation, consumption, technology and R&D. Besides, the interactions between countries nowadays are mostly represented by the interaction and cooperation between primate cities. There are 536 Forbes Global Top 2000 companies across the United States, and 419 are in New York, accounting for 78%. It shows that the multinational enterprises connect various countries; more precisely, the multinational enterprises strengthen the exchanges, cooperation, and competition between primate cities.

Second, multinational firms facilitate more efficient circulation and reasonable allocation of goods, services, capital and other economic resources within a region; they have complete production and sales systems worldwide to promote the circulation and allocation of goods, services, capital, information, human resources and other production factors or products. The industrial upgrade brought about by the transnational corporations is the key to a city's prosperity. The primate cities interact with one another through multinationals, deepening their global connection and thus enhancing the vitality of the cities. Of these 14 primate cities, the global connection index is highly correlated with the GDP growth and GDP per capita, with correlation coefficients at 0.702 and 0.716, respectively, indicating that the global connection is bound to bring along the rapid economic growth and higher living standards in these cities.

All in all, the global operation of transnational corporations and the rapid development of high-end industries with multinational companies as the core are the basic links that connect the primate cities, forming a stable, value-bound city network, and fostering the prosperity and development of metropolises.

Finding 3: The connections between primate cities collectively manifest the demand for trade between countries. Regarding the origin of cities, researchers believe that the medieval cities in western Europe were developed in two situations: small cities (towns) were mainly developed from agricultural activities, while big and mid-sized cities (also known as the "central place" cities) were formed because of long-distance transport for trading activities. In modern days, the relationship between cities cannot do without the demand for trade between countries. By fitting the scatter plot using the calculated data that indicate the connection between Shanghai and 13 other cities listed in Table 8.4 and the total bilateral trade between China and the countries where these 13 cities belong (the same is done for the United States), we find that for either China and other countries (Shanghai and other cities), or the United States with other countries (New York and other cities), high connection between cities corresponds to high trading demand between the countries (Fig. 11.6).

The connection between cities and the demand for trade between countries is a two-way interactive relationship. The demand for trade between countries requires trade operators—multinationals and related commercial entities; they need big cities so as to operate efficiently; they also need support services to ensure business development, thus stimulate the growth of supporting service industries, especially the financial industry, shipping industry, etc. is important. The interaction with the trade industry greatly enhances a city's competitiveness. While these international trade hubs not only drive the rapid development of industrial innovation and production but also activate revolutionary global consumption, the cities thus continue

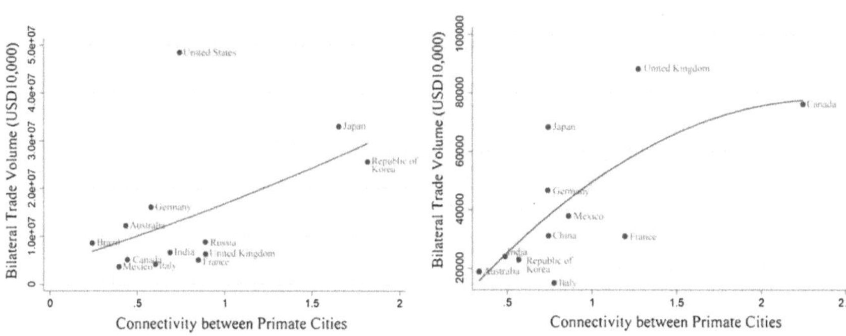

(a) China and Other Countries (b) United States and Other Countries

Fig. 11.6 Connection between cities and trade between countries. The data of bilateral trade between China and other countries are derived from *China Statistical Yearbook 2013*. The data of bilateral trade between the United States and other countries are derived from *Statistical Abstract of the United States: 2012*(US Census Bureau, in which the data between United States and Brazil are missing. *Source* CASS City and Competitiveness Index database

to grow. Our studies show that a primate city, the product of a highly industrialized country, is also an international trade center; the key link between these cities is the trading relationship between the countries.

In turn, the close links between the primate cities and the higher degree of interaction reflect these cities are at about the same level in urban development, the comprehensive economic strength, the attractiveness for talents, information exchange capacity, international competitiveness, technological innovation, transportation capacity; these "common features" are exactly the "pillars" that support the trading activities between the countries. Therefore, the collective expression of the trade between countries is the extensive connection between their primate cities; while behind the close connection between the cities is the "mutual demands", that is, the trade.

11.5.3 Characteristics of Connection Between Primate Cities of Major Economies: King, the Declining Giant, and the Challenger

In this section, we will further explore the characteristics of the representative cities based on the result of the connection between the primate cities of the world's major countries shown in Fig. 11.4.

11.5.3.1 The King: New York, Representative of the Developed Countries, Its Past, Present and Future Global connection

New York consistently dominates the top slot in the global rankings of primate city connection at the global level (excluding Mumbai). In addition to close linkage with other cities on the same continent, primate cities on all continents score the highest in the connection with New York and this involves the primate cities of Britain and France of Europe, Japan and South Korea of Asia, Australia of Oceania, and Brazil of South America. This finding indicates that New York remains the center of the global network, linking the whole world. First, New York City is the largest city of the United State, situated in the northeast of the country with the largest population. It is a culturally diverse city, home to immigrants from 97 countries and regions around the world and where 800 different languages are used. New York is one of the three major financial centers of the world; up till the end of 2008, New York controlled 40% of the world's financial capital to claim the title of the world's largest financial center. The New York Stock Exchange owns the world's largest total capital of listed companies, with a global market value of USD 15 trillion. Among Fortune Top 500 companies, 73 are located in New York. Second, New York is a key industrial city in the United States; the New York state has 13 industrial clusters, covering computer hardware and electronics, machinery and systems, and finance and insurance. In terms of employment opportunities offered in the United States, New York state ranks first in optoelectronic manufacturing, second in defense electronics manufacturing, and third in high-tech manufacturing. New York is also the cultural center of the world. Times Square, a hub located in the Broadway theater district, is known as the "crossroad of the world."

New York was originally an ordinary port city but by riding the trend and following the law of economic development, strategically adapting to the historical context and adopting a comprehensive approach, it has developed into a global city characterized by an internationalized economy, known as an international business center as well as a culturally diverse and inclusive place that has a reasonable industrial structure and highly inclusive population. New York is not only the city with the highest global connection but also the key command center in the global city network. Its king role in the global network is closely associated with the overall economic strength of the United States. Historically, London of the United Kingdom was the world's oldest and largest financial and trade center and shipping hub since the Industrial Revolution, claiming the very center of the entire global network. With the decline of the United Kingdom after World War II, London has become a declining giant; the second industrial revolution infused the United States with economic vitality, which helped New York replace London and become the central city of the world with the largest trading volume, the most concentrated capital, and the most competitive capacity, and it has remained in this leading position to this day. Being the most crucial link in the global network, New York is always at the very center because of its high connection either to the cities in the traditional capitalist countries or to the cities of the emerging countries.

With the United States in a long economic downturn, the impact of financial crisis and the booming cities of the emerging market economies, New York will encounter a great challenge as for its future status as the global center. In the knowledge age, to keep the leading role in the global connections, New York will need to successfully transform into a capital city or even a global financial center driven by service industries and smart production. In other words, to realize its vision as an all-inclusive intelligent city and Idea City is the key for New York to keep the leading role in global connections.

11.5.3.2 The Challenger: Shanghai, Representative of the Emerging Economies, Its Past, Present and Future Global Connection

London and New York are both top global metropolises, and dominated the global network most of the time in the twentieth century. However, in the 21st century, when the economic development in the United States and the EU become increasingly difficult, both cities face new challenges once and again. The most prominent one is the city prosperity brought about by the thriving emerging market economies, among which, China is the most noteworthy. In the late twentieth century, China's economy started to take off; its average annual GDP growth rate (1978–2006) reached 9.7%, and the country maintained double-digit growth for years, achieving lasting and rapid economic growth, which is known as the "China miracle." China's share in the world economy rose to 12% in 2013 from the 1.8% of 1978. As China's economy took off, Chinese cities also leapt forward.

Looking back at Table 11.4, we can see that Shanghai has comparable connections with the cities in western Europe, New York of the United States in North America, and Moscow of Russia in the Eurasian region. The connection score with London is 0.040, New York 0.051, and Moscow 0. 030). Shanghai is 8th in the global connection rankings, which making it comparable to the established international metropolises. Shanghai is located at the mouth of the Yangtze River, and bordered in the south by the Hangzhou Bay. It is one of the centers of economy, transportation, science and technology, industry, finance, exhibition and shipping in China. Its 2014 GDP is ranked first among all cities in China, second in Asia; and as of 2013, Shanghai had a population of more than 25 million. It is known as the "showpiece of China's economy." Shanghai has the world's busiest container port that tops the global ranking in cargo throughput and container throughput.

From the perspective of historical development, Shanghai was part of the prosperous and fertile Jiangsu and Zhejiang region in ancient China. During the early modern era, Shanghai was divided into various foreign concessions. After the founding of People's Republic of China, Shanghai enjoyed a special status in China as a municipality directly under the central government, but had few interactions with the world as the country's door remained closed. After the implementation of the reform and opening-up policy and thanks to the preferential policies for the Pudong special economic area, Shanghai saw massive economic growth and urban development at unprecedented speed. In recent years, with the rapid economic development of emerging countries, Shanghai has taken advantage of the economic reform and the rise of China and developed into a representative metropolis of emerging market economies. On the one hand, among the cities of the emerging countries, Shanghai serves as the linking point and a platform for communication between the cities of these countries; international organizations of emerging market economies open their offices in Shanghai, such as the headquarters of the BRICS Development Bank and Shanghai is in the leading position among these countries; on the other hand, Shanghai is also the link between emerging market economies and the western developed countries.

With the shift of the world economic center, Shanghai, as a new rising power, challenges the once-dominant powers in the global network. The future representative of emerging market economy is stepping onto and sharing the stage with the elite world cities with greater efficiency and a broader vision, which all begin with global connection.

Chapter 12
Global Connection and Doing Business

12.1 Introduction

Behind the deepening economic globalization, the multinational company is an important impetus in driving the global economy (Pengfei et al. 2011). The multinationals' worldwide resources configuration, related production and business activities constitute the core of the global city network. The aggregation of the multinational's headquarters or regional offices and international organizations indicates a city's global connection, which largely determines the status and level of development of a city in the global network, and is the most important factor for a city to become a global city. Thus, multinationals is an important dimension to measure a city's connections to the rest of the world. In addition to the multinational companies, infrastructure network, represented by the volume of airline flights, is another important dimension to measure a city's global connection. The infrastructure global network represents a city's basic capacity of global connection.

A business-friendly environment is also an important factor of urban development as well as a manifestation of a city's governance capacity. The core in building a sound business environment is the government's planning and implementation of regulations on the founding and operation of a local firm. The business environment discussed in this study mainly refers to the government's service and regulatory systems covered in the World Bank Group's Doing Business Report. According to the World Bank, a sound business environment is marked by an established regulation system that promotes market exchanges, protects public interest, and removes unnecessary barriers business development. Or to put it in another way, it means a society has a sound market system of low transaction costs and a fair market regulation framework.

A sound business environment is important for a city because it encourages domestic private investment (World Bank 2004).[1] And another important factor is

[1]According to the World Bank's study on 80 countries, a foreseeable policy upgrade alone can increase the possibility by 30% about the enterprise's investment increase.

© China Social Sciences Press and Springer Nature Singapore Pte Ltd. 2017

P. Ni et al., *Cities Network Along the Silk Road*,
DOI 10.1007/978-981-10-4834-0_12

that it attracts more foreign direct investment (Yao Shujie et al. 2006; Yao Shu-jie and Wei Kai-lei 2007), which means that a business-friendly city is more likely to be preferred by multinationals. A city's business environment and global connection is positively correlated.

This report is to study a city's global connection from the perspective of business environment. A sample of 131 cities is obtained from a combined survey of 505 sample cities and 189 economies from the World Bank's *Doing Business Index*. And based on this sample of 131 cities, we examine the following questions: what are the distribution characteristics of the doing business index displayed in the primate cities around the world? How is business environment related to the city's population size and level of economic development? From the perspective of global connection, how is the business environment related to the global connection of multinationals and global infrastructure network?

12.2 Comparison of Primate Cities in Doing Business

First, the selection of sample cities and data is as follows:

About sample cities: A total of 131 cities are selected from the 505 cities in the city and competitiveness index database of the Chinese Academy of Social Sciences as sample cities in this chapter. Cities selected here are the largest city in each country; for most of the countries involved, only one city is selected from each of them if the country's capital city is the city with the largest economic scale; for other countries, two cities are selected mainly based on the following principles: (1) Based on the 2014 World Bank Doing Business Report, one additional city is chosen from each economy with more than 100 million population. In line with this, we select two cities, the capital city and the city with the largest economy (except the capital), from each of the countries whose population size is over 100 million (World Bank 2014). Specifically, these countries are Brazil, China, India, Indonesia, Japan, Mexico, Nigeria, Pakistan, Russia and the United States. (2) For some major countries, if the capital city is not the city with the largest economy, we will choose the capital city and the city with the largest economy as sample cities. This involves Canada, Australia, and South Africa. After this selection process, we combine the 505 sample cities with the 189 sample economies from the World Bank Doing Business Report and choose 131 sample cities for this study.

Data on business environment: The rankings by the doing business index among the 189 economies of the world are provided in the WDI database. Economies are ranked from 1 to 189 according to their ease of doing business. A high ranking means the regulatory environment is more conducive to the founding and operation of a local firm. Ease of doing business indicators are used to analyze economic performance as well as to explain what, how and why a regulation reform is effective. The economies are ranked by their average score in 10 areas of business regulation that affect the entire life cycle of business operation; within these 10 areas, the indicators for a business-friendly environment are:

(1) administrative efficiency for starting a business; (2) urban planning and zoning under construction permits; (3) land management quality under property registering; (4) the importance of getting credit; (5) indices on the extent of disclosure, extent of director liability and ease of shareholder suits; (6) the taxation trends before and after the financial crisis under the paying taxes; (7) the judicial efficiency that guarantees freedom of contract under the enforcing contracts; (8) the effect of bankruptcy law under resolving insolvency. In our study, the index of the sample city is obtained by non-dimensionalizing the Doing Business value to between 0 and 1.

Data on global connection: In this study, multinational connection and infrastructure network are taken as important indicators of a business-friendly environment. The raw data on multinational connection is mainly drawn from the Forbes Global 2000 index. The specific calculation method is to add up the scores assigned to a city's listed companies, wherein global headquarters score 5 points, intercontinental headquarters 4 points, national headquarters 3 points, regional headquarters 2 points and city office 1 point. Finally, the multinational connection of each city is set between 0 and 1 by the dimensionless approach. The infrastructure connection is mainly measured by the numbers of air routes, which are collected from the websites of some airports, with related data from Wikipedia and the website of the International Air Transport Association.

Data from other studies: Our analysis, in addition to the doing business index and global connection index, also includes gross national income (GNI) per capita, GDP per capita, population size, etc. GNI per capita represents the level of economic development of the country or region the city belongs to. GDP per capita represents the level of a city's economic development. Population size represents the size of a city; a larger population size suggests a higher degree of diversity and a bigger city size.

12.2.1 Comparison Based on the Economic Development at Regional Level: The Developed Regions Perform Better than the Developing Regions

Based on the World Bank's doing business index, and the distribution of the sample cities by continents, we calculate the average degree of ease of doing business of the sample cities within each continent. Generally speaking, developed regions score higher than developing regions. At the continent level, Oceania ranks the highest Europe is the second, followed by North America. These continents not only have higher overall average scores but also see a rising trend in their doing business rankings. Asia has average business environment and regressed in 2014; South America and Africa have relatively poor performance in this aspect.

We also select the top three cities in Doing Business within each continent. The best performers of Asia, Singapore, Hong Kong, and Seoul, are also placed high in

Table 12.1 Doing business scores of representative cities by continent

Continent	Doing business score mean (2013)	Doing business score mean (2014)	Top 3 cities	Doing business score (2013)	Doing business score (2014)
Europe	46.6	38.7	Copenhagen	5	4
			Oslo	9	6
			London	10	8
North America	71.5	65.9	Washington	4	7
			New York	4	7
			Ottawa	19	16
Oceania	8.3	7.3	Wellington	3	2
			Sydney	11	10
			Canberra	11	10
Asia	84.5	87.8	Singapore	1	1
			Hong Kong	2	3
			Seoul	7	5
South America	105.6	102.1	Bogota	43	34
			Lima	42	35
			San Diego	34	41
Africa	133.4	133.2	Johannesburg	41	43
			Cape Town	41	43
			Tunisia	51	60

Sources World Bank database

the global rankings; they are part of the emerging market economies in Asia. Since the average doing business score of Asian cities is not at the top of the list, it indicates that there is a big gap among the Asian cities. North America is in a similar situation; except those better performers in the United States and Canada, the rest of the cities are not placed high in the rankings. In addition, the representative cities of Europe and Oceania belong to developed economies, where the rest of the representative cities are among the top 10, indicating that these cities should be in the forefront in the global ranking. Examining the situation in South America and Africa, we see the top three cities within these two continents are ranked below 30 globally, indicating that the business environment are generally poor in Africa and South America (see Table 12.1).

Considering that the doing business index may be associated with the level of national economic development, we constructed scatter plots with GNI per capita and the doing business index of the 131 sample cities (Fig. 12.1). The scatter plots show a positive correlation between the two indicators. It also shows that the primate cities of developed countries have much better business environment. However, a business-friendly environment is not necessarily found in the primate cities of highly developed countries, which means a sound business environment is a prerequisite for enhancing the level of economic development. The correlation

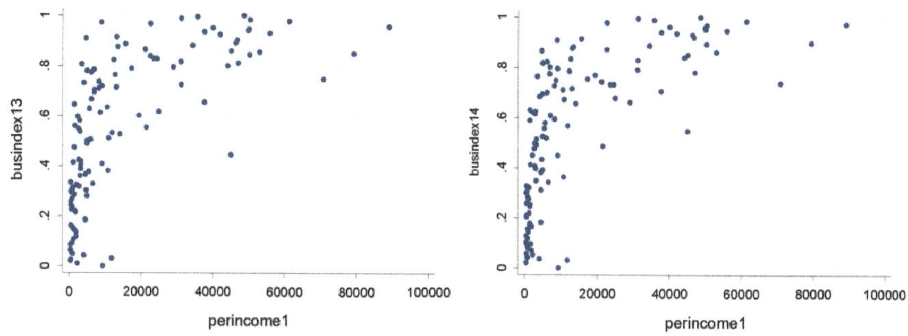

Fig. 12.1 Doing business index (2013, 2014) and GNI per capita. *Sources* World Bank database and CASS city and competitiveness database

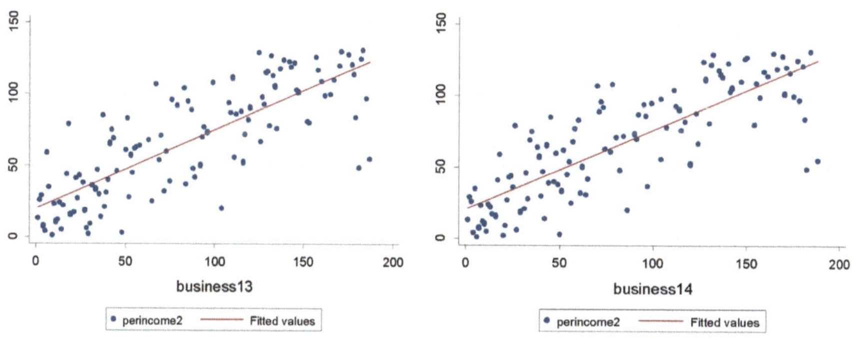

Fig. 12.2 Relationship between doing business index (2013, 2014) and urban GDP per capita. *Sources* World Bank database and CASS city and competitiveness database

coefficient derived from Pearson correlation analysis is −0.6852 in 2013 and −0.6824 in 2014, which means there is a correlation between the two factors.

We then proceed to draw scatter plots to study the relationship between GDP per capita and the doing business scores of the cities and find a positive correlation between the two factors: the higher the ranking by the doing business index, the higher the ranking by GDP per capita. The correlation coefficient between the two indexes is 0.8057 in 2013 and 0.8186 in 2014, which also shows a rather significant positive correlation (Fig. 12.2).

12.2.2 Comparison Based Urban Development Level: High-Income Cities Outperform Low-Income Cities

Analysis based on the level of urban development shows that high-income cities perform significantly better than low-income cities in terms of the doing business index. The top ten cities in GDP per capita ranking perform better in business environment, with nine of the ten cities ranked in the top 30. While among the bottom 10 cities in GDP per capita ranking, nine are placed below 120 (see Table 12.2). From this we can see that a city's GDP per capita and ease of doing business may be highly correlated, the higher the level of economic development, the better its performance in the doing business index, and the lower the level of economic development, the poorer the performance in the doing business index.

Based on the data of the 131 sample cities, a scatter plot is constructed to reflect the relationship between the doing business index and GDP per capita (Fig. 12.3). The scatter plot does not show a very clear correlation between the two indicators. Based on our observation, high-income cities always have a business-friendly environment, but such an environment does not always exist in a high-income city. A business-friendly environment is an essential driving factor for a high-income city. Based on Pearson correlation analysis, the correlation coefficient between the

Table 12.2 Top 10 and bottom 10 of GDP per capita and their business environment

Top 10 of GDP per capita	Doing business index (2013)	Doing business index (2014)	Bottom 10 cities in GDP per capita ranking (122–131)	Doing business index (2013)	Doing business index (2014)
Washington	4	7	Ulan Bator	76	72
London	10	8	Dacre	178	161
Zurich	29	20	Harare	170	171
New York	4	7	Blantyre	171	164
Amsterdam	28	27	Addis Ababa	125	132
Reykjavik	13	12	Maputo	139	127
Oslo	9	6	Yangon	182	177
Vienna	30	21	Surabaya	120	114
Paris	38	31	Lome	157	149

Sources World Bank database and CASS city and competitiveness database

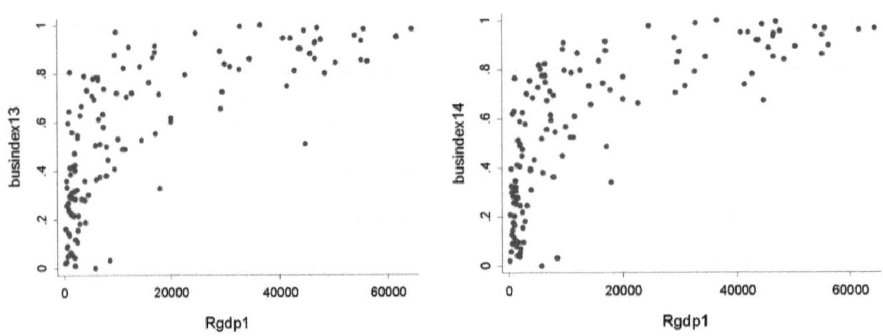

Fig. 12.3 Doing business index (2013, 2014) GDP per capita. *Sources* World Bank database and CASS city and competitiveness database

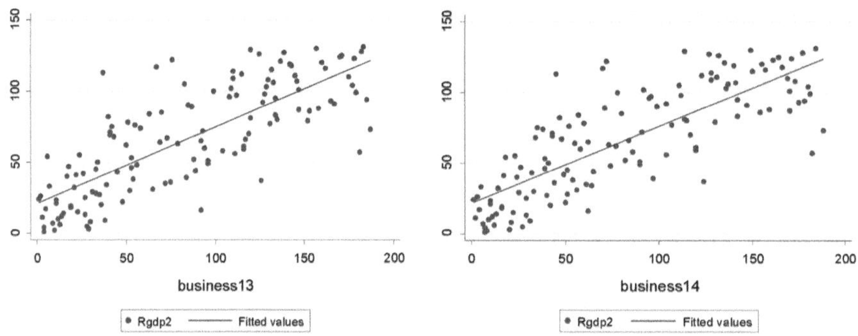

Fig. 12.4 Doing business index (2013, 2014) and GDP per capita rankings. *Sources* World Bank database and CASS city and competitiveness database

doing business index and the GDP per capita is −0.7165 in 2013 and −0.7176 in 2014, indicating that there is indeed a correlation between the two, the higher the city's GDP per capita, the better its environment for doing business.

We proceed to draw scatter plots to study the relationship between the GDP per capita ranking and the doing business index of cities and find that there is a positive correlation between the two, with a correlation coefficient 0.7846 in 2013 and 0.7971 in 2014. This also shows that a better business environment can help low-income cities catch up with high-income cities, even though a more business-friendly environment alone is not enough (Fig. 12.4).

12.2.3 A Comparison Based on City Size: City Size and the Ease of Doing Business are not Correlated

A comparison based on city size shows that the business environment may be irrelevant to city size. Based on our survey of cities by population ranking (see Table 12.3), some of the top ten cities, like Tokyo and Paris, have good business environment, others, like Mumbai and Karachi, have poor business environment. Among the bottom ten cities, there are also cities with sound business environment, such as Wellington and Zurich, and cities with poor business environment, such as Sarajevo and Georgetown. Therefore, we derive a preliminary conclusion that a city's population size may be irrelevant to their business environment.

For a more comprehensive analysis of the relationship between city size and business environment, we present a scatter plot with the data of the 131 sample cities (Fig. 12.5). It shows no regular distribution. The Pearson correlation coefficient is 0.0493 in 2013 and 0.0433 in 2014. This basically confirms the finding stated above, that is, a city's population size and its business environment are not correlated.

Since the World Bank's doing business index is based on a number of lower-level indicators, it may be more reasonable to analyze the correlation between

Table 12.3 Business environment of the top ten and the bottom ten cities in population size ranking

Top 10 of population size	Doing business index (2013)	Doing business index (2014)	Bottom 10 of population size	Doing business index (2013)	Doing business index (2014)
Shanghai	96	90	Zurich	29	20
Beijing	96	90	Sarajevo	131	107
Mumbai	134	142	Ljubljana	33	51
Mexico City	53	39	Nicosia	39	64
Karachi	110	128	Georgetown	115	123
Tokyo	27	29	Nassau	84	97
Paris	38	31	Wellington	3	2
Delhi	134	142	Gaborone	56	74
Moscow	92	62	Brussels	36	42
Sao Paulo	116	120	Reykjavik	13	12

Sources World Bank database and CASS city and competitiveness database

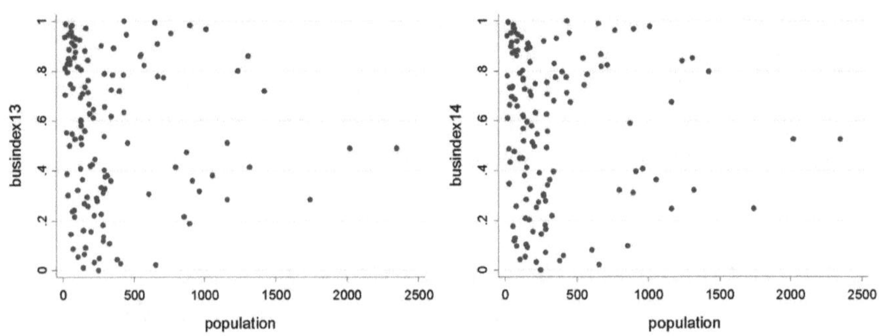

Fig. 12.5 Doing business index (2013, 2014) and city population size. *Sources* World Bank database and CASS city and competitiveness database

population size ranking and doing business index ranking. Therefore, we construct the following correlation analysis and scatter plots, and draw fit curves (Fig. 12.6). They show no regular pattern and the correlation coefficient is −0.1492 in 2013 and −0.1252 in 2014, which also shows no close correlation between the two variables.

12.2.4 New Findings

From the above analysis, we draw the following conclusions.

Finding 1: Developed regions, including Europe, America, and Oceania, have better business environment than developing regions such as Asia, Africa and Latin America. In general, cities of developed economies have much better business

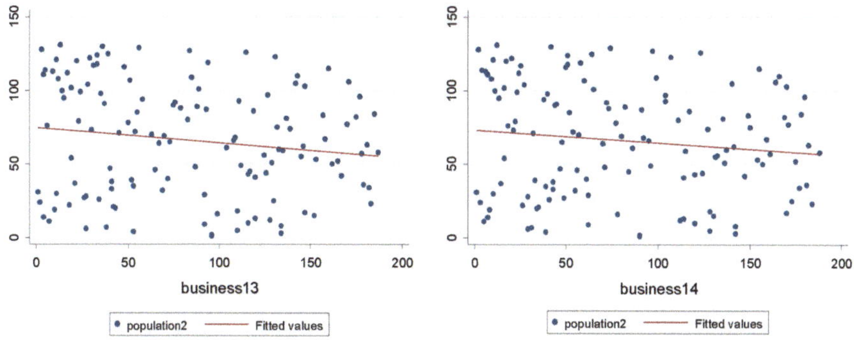

Fig. 12.6 Doing business index (2013, 2014) and population size ranking. *Sources* World Bank database and CASS city and competitiveness database

environment than those of developing economies. However, each region has its own specific characteristics. With a higher level of overall development, the cities of Oceania and Europe overall have better conditions for business operations, while the cities in Asia and North America differ greatly in this aspect. Asian cities, such as Hong Kong, Singapore, and Seoul, rank high by the doing business index globally; US and Canadian cities of North America also have relatively high rankings. However, the other cities on these two continents are not outstanding performers and the cities in South America and Africa are lagging behind.

Finding 2: Three types of cities have the best business environment. The first type is emerging cities with a high degree of economic freedom, such as Singapore, Hong Kong and Wellington. After being British colonies for a long time, these cities claimed independence after World War II and now enjoy a very high degree of economic freedom and are highly internationalized. The second type is big cities of developed countries in Europe and America, such as New York, London and Paris, which usually have large economic scale and sound economic development. The third type is medium-sized cities in Northern Europe, such as Copenhagen, Oslo and Helsinki. They are the wealthiest cities in Nordic countries; although the population size is small, they have high levels of economic and social development.

Finding 3: Big cities and small cities do not differ significantly in their business environment but this environment is indeed better in high-income cities than in low-income cities. Big cities may have good or bad business environment and so do small cities. But GDP per capita or the level of economic development, may be an important factor of a favorable business environment; business environment is significantly better in high-income cities than in low-income cities.

12.3 Doing Business and Global Connection of Primate Cities

Among the 131 sample cities, we select the top ten cities of the doing business index in 2013 and 2014 and the top ten cities in the rankings of multinational connection and the number air routes (Table 12.4). An analysis of these cities shows that although a city may be in more than one top 10 lists, the distribution of each set of cities show clear features. The top 10 cities in the doing business index are mostly from developed economies but they have different population sizes. There are mega cities like New York and London and medium-sized city like Wellington and Copenhagen. According to the global connection index, the top 10 cities are from both developed economies emerging market economies, including Beijing, Shanghai and Moscow. However, a common feature of these cities is that they are generally truly big cities as well as very influential in global finance and economy.

12.3.1 Relationship Between Doing Business and Multinational Global Connection of Primate Cities

In static terms, the two have only a weak correlation between them; business environment is not an important factor for multinationals to settle down in a city.

One of the findings in our study is that global connection is not closely related to business environment, with a very weak positive correlation between the two. When choosing a city to settle down, multinational companies may show a slight

Table 12.4 Top 10 of doing business index and global connection index

Ranking	Doing business 2013	Doing business 2014	Multinational connection	Infrastructure connection
1	Singapore	Singapore	London	Paris
2	Hong Kong	Wellington	New York	Moscow
3	Wellington	Hong Kong	Tokyo	London
4	New York	Copenhagen	Shanghai	Beijing
5	Washington	Seoul	Singapore	Amsterdam
6	Copenhagen	Oslo	Beijing	New York
7	Kuala Lumpur	New York	Hong Kong	Dubai
8	Seoul	Washington	Paris	Brussels
9	Oslo	London	Moscow	Rome
10	London	Helsinki	Seoul	Shanghai

Sources World Bank database and CASS city and competitiveness database

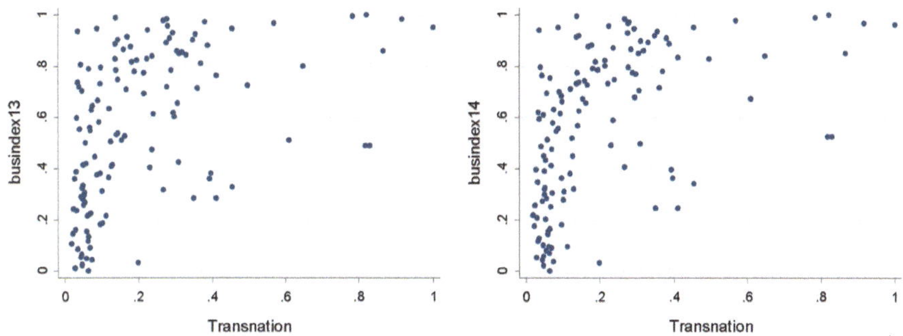

Fig. 12.7 Doing business index (2013, 2014) and multinational connection index. *Sources* World Bank database and CASS city and competitiveness database

preference for favorable business environment, but his is clearly not an important factor. In Northern Europe and Oceania, there are quite a few cities with business-friendly environment yet they are not favored by big corporations and these cities have multinational connection scores, ranked near the bottom of the list. Big cities in some emerging market economies, such as China, Russia and India, have high multinational connection scores but their business environment is just about average.

For a comprehensive analysis of the relationship between a city's business environment and its global connections, we make a scatter plot with the data of the 131 sample cities (Fig. 12.7). From plot we see no clear correlation between the two factors. Moreover, we can see that: (1) Cities with poor business environment are generally not favored by big companies and have low global connection scores. (2) Although multinationals do not prefer cities with the worst business environment, they do not particularly look for cities with exceptionally good business environment. A city with an average environment for doing business is actually quite acceptable. (3) In terms of global connection, most cities score below 0.2 for multinational connection but have a favorable environment for doing business in almost all aspects. This means that although there are many cities fit for business operation with top global ranking, they are not chosen by the multinational companies. We calculated the Pearson correlation coefficient between the multinational connection index and the doing business index of the 131 sample cities and the result shows that the correlation coefficient is −0.4671 in 2013 and −0.4877 in 2014, indicating a weak correlation between the two.

Since the World Bank's doing business index is based on an array of lower-level indicators, a correlation analysis of the multinational connection ranking and doing business index is probably a more scientific approach. Based on this, the following correlation analyses are conducted by drawing scatter plots and fit curves (Fig. 12.8). Through the correlation analysis, we find a positive, though relatively weak, correlation between the two factors. With the correlation coefficient being 0.5696 in 2013 and 0.5987 in 2014, it also shows that although to some extent, the multinationals will consider the business environment, it is not a strong factor in

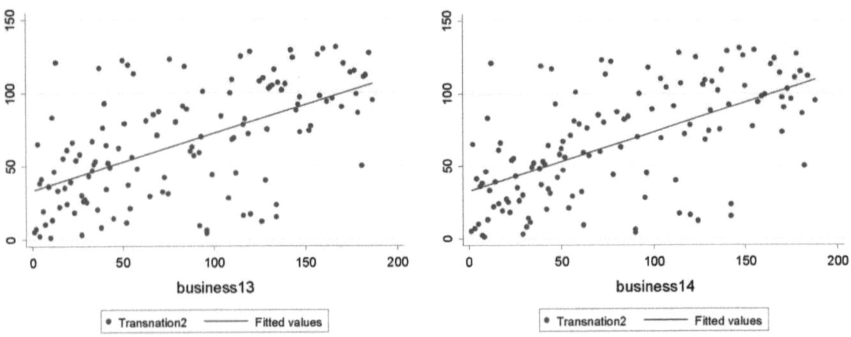

Fig. 12.8 Doing business index (2013, 2014) and multinational connection index. *Sources* World Bank database and CASS city and competitiveness database

their decision-making process. Some cities ranking high by the doing business index are not selected by multinational companies and examples include Wellington, Copenhagen, Oslo, etc. Similarly, some cities doe not have favorable business environment but are ranked high in terms of multinational connection and these include Shanghai, Beijing, Moscow, etc.

From a dynamic perspective, multinational firms may help improve the local business environment.

The second finding of our study is that from a dynamic perspective, all the regions with higher degree of global connection see continuous improvement in their business environment. Although the analysis of this chapter reveals no close correlation between the local business environment and global connection, multinationals may still have their impact on the local business environment. Because of the scale of large companies, local governments often give them preferential policies and in order to attract large enterprises, local governments may take initiative to improve the business environment. After settling down, big companies usually take the upper hand over smaller ones in their negotiation with the local government and they are more likely to put pressure on local governments to launch more open policies and looser control over economic activities. And this explains why a multinational is not quite concerned about the business environment: compared to other factors, the business environment is where a multinational company exerts its impact.

We examine the doing business index of the top 10 cities for multinational connection (see Table 12.5) and Beijing and Shanghai have the same score for the World Bank's data are for economies, not cities. With this in mind, we added Madrid, ranked 11th, in this analysis. These 11 cities also happen to be all the cities scored 0.5 or higher in nondimensionalized multinational connection. The analysis shows that among these 11 cities, seven are trending up in doing business ranking and Moscow and Madrid, in particular, moved up by 30 and 19 places respectively. Only three cities moved down slightly in ranking. Singapore remains at the top of the list. Since the change in business environment is reflected by the change in

Table 12.5 Change in doing business rankings of top 11 cities of global connection

Ranking	City	Doing business 2013	Doing business 2014	Change
1	London	10	8	2
2	New York	4	7	−3
3	Tokyo	27	29	−2
4	Shanghai	96	90	6
5	Singapore	1	1	0
6	Beijing	96	90	6
7	Hong Kong	2	3	−1
8	Paris	38	31	7
9	Moscow	92	62	30
10	Seoul	7	5	2
11	Madrid	52	33	19

Source World Bank database

cities' rankings on this indicator, we add up the numbers in the "change" column and find that the 11 cities moved up by 66 places in sum. So basically, we can conclude that the top cities in multinational connection, generally are on the rise in terms of business environment.

In order to fully depict this phenomenon, we conducted a statistical analysis of the changes of all the 131 sample cities in doing business index from 2013 to 2014, combined with the data of their multinationals connection, and then plotted their correlation (Fig. 12.9). Based on our observation, the top 60 cities in multinational connection ranking, their doing business index are distributed toward the right, meaning the cities with better multinational connection, their doing business environment is improving. But for those cities ranked after 60th in multinational connection, their doing business index scores basically remain the same. Using the multinational connection index of the 131 sample cities as the baseline, sample cities are divided by the median into two groups. We then analyze the cities ranked from 1st to 65th, add up their changes in the rankings, and get the sum of 294, indicating a significant improvement; while the accumulative value in change of doing business for those cities ranked 66th–131st in multinational connection is −20. This further confirms the conclusion that in those cities ranked higher in multinational connection index, when the large companies settled in and have the capability to negotiate with local governments, they could prompt the local governments to be more open in regulation; from the perspective of local governments, in order to attract large companies, they may also actively improve their own environment.

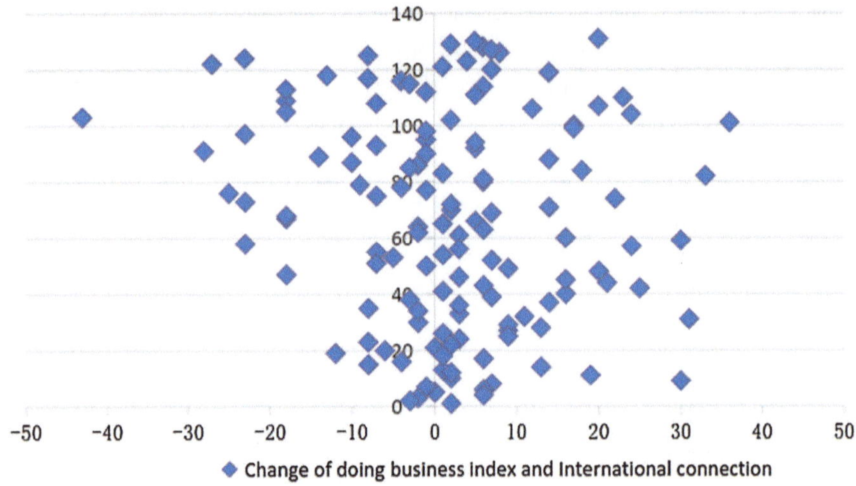

Fig. 12.9 Change of doing business ranking and global connection. *Sources* World Bank database and CASS city and competitiveness database

12.3.2 Doing Business and Infrastructure Global Network of the Primate City

From a static perspective, there is a weak correlation between the two; a business-friendly environment is not an important factor for the improvement of air transport infrastructure. One of the findings in our study is that there is no close correlation between infrastructure connection and business environment; there is a weak positive correlation between the two. To a city with a good business environment, it has stronger ties with the rest of the world economically. Thus its air travel infrastructure is more likely driven to improve, but this is clearly not an important factor. In Northern Europe and Oceania, many cities have favorable business environment but average or even low number of air routes. Some major cities in the world's prominent emerging market economies, such as China and Russia, have much more air routes and high infrastructure connection scores. However, the business environment in these cities is not outstanding.

To have a more comprehensive analysis of the relationship between doing business and infrastructure connection, we make a scatter plot (Fig. 12.10). It shows a correlation, though not very significant, between the two factors. Moreover, we find: (1) a city of poor business environment tends to have fewer air routes but a business-friendly environment does not promise more routes. (2) In terms of infrastructure connection, more air routes generally indicate a better business environment. This means that a good business environment may be a basic condition for better infrastructure connection. We calculate the Pearson correlation coefficient between the multinational connection index and the doing business

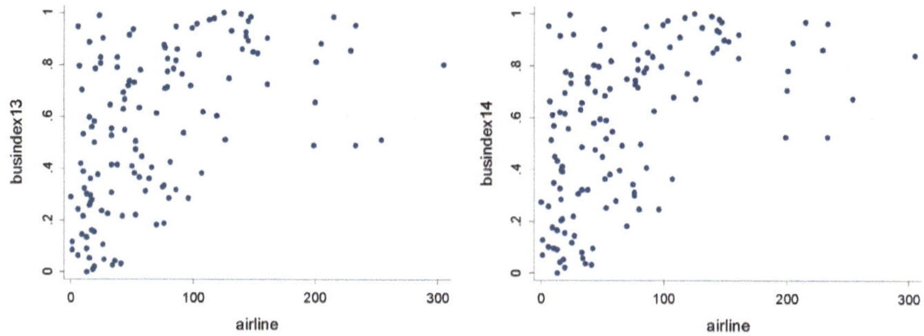

Fig. 12.10 Doing business index (2013, 2014) and numbers of air routes. *Sources* World Bank database and CASS city and competitiveness database

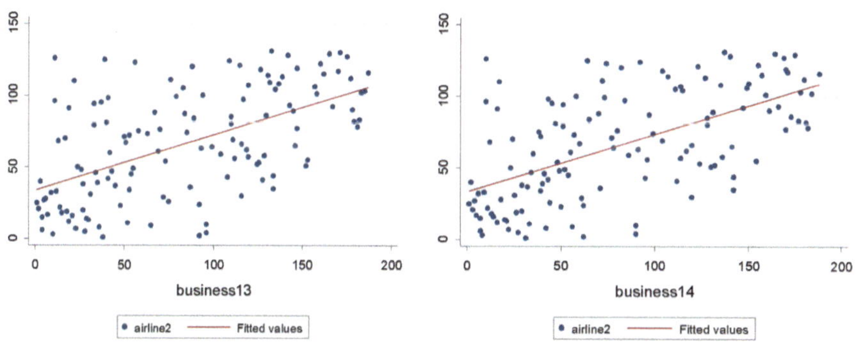

Fig. 12.11 Doing business INDEX (2013, 2014) and multinational connection index. *Sources* World Bank database and CASS city and competitiveness database

index for the 131 sample cities and The result shows a correlation coefficient of −0.5011 in 2013 and −0.5326 in 2014, suggesting weak correlation.

We further explore the relationship between the doing business index and the number of air routes by conducting relevant analysis and making scatter plots (Fig. 12.11). Based on our observation and correlation analysis, there indeed is a positive correlation between the two, but this correlation is relatively weak. The correlation coefficient is 0.5580 in 2013 and 0.5881 in 2014, indicating a positive but weak correlation. There are cities at the top of the rankings of business environment but with a low number of air routes. Examples include Canberra and Reykjavik. Similarly, there are cities with poor business environment but high in the rankings by multinational connection and examples are Shanghai, Beijing and Moscow.

In dynamic terms, good air transport infrastructure may help improve the business environment.

In terms of the relationship between infrastructure connection and business environment, we see that from a dynamic perspective, all the regions with more air

Table 12.6 Top 10 cities in infrastructure connection and change in their doing business rankings

Ranking	City	Doing business 2013	Doing business 2014	Change
1	Paris	38	31	7
2	Moscow	92	62	30
3	London	10	8	2
4	Beijing	96	90	6
5	Amsterdam	28	27	1
6	New York	4	7	−3
7	Dubai	23	22	1
8	Brussels	36	42	−6
9	Rome	65	56	9
10	Shanghai	96	90	6
11	Madrid	52	33	19

Source World Bank database

routes see continuous improvement in their business environment. Although the analysis of this chapter suggests that a city's business environment is not closely correlated to its infrastructure connection, good infrastructure can did enhance a city's ability to conduct international exchanges, which has its impact on the local business environment.

We selected the top 10 cities in infrastructure connection to observe the changes in doing business index (see Table 12.6). Since the World Bank's doing business index is for economies, not cities, Beijing and Shanghai have the same score. With this in mind, we added Madrid, which is ranked 11th, in this analysis. The analysis shows that among these 11 cities, nine are trending up in the doing business ranking; Moscow and Madrid, in particular, moved up by 30 and 19 places respectively. Only two cities show a slight decline in their rankings. Singapore remains at the top of the list. Since the change in business environment is reflected by the change of rankings on this indicator, we add up the changes in the rankings of the 11 cities and get a sum of 72. So basically, we can conclude that the top cities in infrastructure connection are generally on the rise in terms of business environment.

In order to fully reflect this phenomenon, we conducted a statistical analysis of the changes in doing business index of all the 131 sample cities from 2013 to 2014, combined with the data of their multinational connection, and constructed scatter plots (Fig. 12.12). Based on our observation, the top 60 cities in multinational connection ranking, their doing business scores are distributed toward the right, suggesting the business environment is improving in the cities with better infrastructure global connection. But there is not much change in the doing business scores of those cities ranked after 60th in multinational connection. Using data of the 131 sample cities by air routes as the standard, sample cities are divided by the median into two groups. We then analyze the cities ranked from 1st to 65th, add up the changes in their doing business rankings, and get the sum of 316, suggesting a

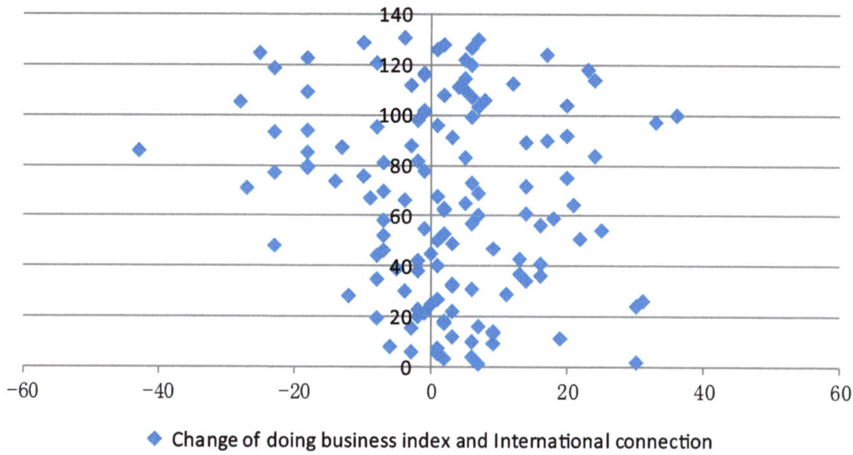

Fig. 12.12 Changes in doing business rankings and global connection. *Sources* World Bank database and CASS city and competitiveness database

significant advancement; while the sum of changes in doing business rankings is −42 for those cities ranked 66th–131st in multinational connection. This further confirms the conclusion that the business environment is becoming better in those cities with better air transport infrastructure.

12.3.3 Comparison of the Relations Between Two Types of Global Connection and Doing Business: There is a High Correlation

Examining the relationship between business environment and multinational connection and the relationship between business environment and infrastructure connection, these two relationships, in general, are very similar, indicating a high correlation between them as shown in the following aspects:

First, both pairs are weakly correlated and both show some deviations. The correlation coefficients are between 0.55 and 0.6. And, based on the scatter plots, the two relationships have similar patterns. In other words, some cities have a certain degree of deviation between the global connection and business environment. To verify this pattern, we take the medians of doing business rankings and global connection rankings as axes to divide the scatter plot into four domains. Then, it is easy to find that although most of the sample cities are scattered in the upper right and the lower left domains, there are still some cities in the upper left and lower right domains, wherein are the cities that deviate in terms of the relationship between business environment and global connection.

Second, from a static perspective, the two pairs show nearly identical patterns. In other words, a city with a poor business environment has fewer multinational connections and air routes; a city with favorable business environment may either have good or bad multinational connection and more or fewer air routes; and a city with more multinational connections and air routes has better business environment. This series of patterns show noticeable correlation between the two pairs.

Third, the two pairs show similar patterns too in a dynamic perspective. Examining the changes in the doing business index from 2013 to 2014, the top 50% of the sample cities in multinational connection see great improvement in their doing business scores, while the latter half of the sample cities see a decline in their scores. Changes in the doing business index and the air traffic rankings show the same pattern. The dynamic analysis again proves the high correlation between the two pairs, that is, the increased numbers of multinational enterprises and the improved aviation infrastructure contribute to the business environment in a city.

12.4 Analysis on Reasons

12.4.1 Reasons for the Weak Correlation Between the Two Types of Global Connection and the Doing Business Index Might have to do with City Characteristics

In order to analyze the deviation in the relationship between the city's global connection and ease of doing business, we identify three types of cities based on these features of the 131 sample cities, and examine the characteristics of these cities. Since business environment and global connection (including multinational connection and infrastructure connection) are weakly correlated, while the multinational connection and infrastructure connection are strongly correlated, we divided the 131 sample cities into three categories: type 1 is cities with high rankings in doing business and global connection; type 2 is cities ranked high in doing business but mediocre in global connection; type 3 is cities ranked high in global connection but mediocre in doing business. For the convenience of analysis, we included GDP as an indicator to measure the scale of the cities; we also included GNI per capita to measure the per-capita income level of the economies to which the cities belong. The reason to include these two additional indicators is that we believe that the global connection of a city may be related to its GDP, and the business environment may be associated with GNI per capita because the regulatory environment may be influenced and constrained by the level of economic development (Acemoglu 2008). Details are given in Table 12.7.

Type-1 cities are global centers located in developed economies. Among the sample cities, cities of this type are among the top ten in doing business, multinational connection, and infrastructure connection. London and New York are

Table 12.7 City rankings in doing business and global connection by city type

	City	Doing business index	Multinational connection index	Infrastructure connection index	GDP	GNI per capita
Type 1	London	8	1	3	5	23
	New York	7	2	6	4	7
	Singapore	1	5	25	13	13
	Hong Kong	3	7	21	9	26
	Seoul	5	10	17	7	35
Type 2	Copenhagen	4	41	27	47	4
	Oslo	6	36	32	39	1
	Helsinki	9	46	33	43	12
	Canberra	10	83	126	56	10
	Reykjavik	12	121	68	86	24
Type 3	Shanghai	90	4	10	6	73
	Beijing	90	6	4	8	73
	Moscow	62	9	2	3	50
	Sao Paulo	120	16	30	20	52
	Delhi	142	23	35	32	106

Sources World Bank database and CASS city and competitiveness database

mega cities of developed economies in Europe and America, and have leading positions in the global cities network. Singapore, Hong Kong and Seoul are the most developed cities of Asia. Meanwhile, New York, London, Hong Kong and Singapore are the world's top four financial centers. They have the largest GDP globally. Their GNI per capita also indicates that these cities are in highly developed economies.

Type-2 cities are highly-developed medium-sized cities in Northern Europe and Oceania. Cities of this type are among the top 15 in doing business but in middle or lower range in multinational connection and infrastructure connection. Among them, Canberra is a representative of Oceania, while Oslo, Copenhagen, Helsinki and Reykjavik are the representative of the Nordic cities. These cities share some common features: they belong to developed economies which have a high degree of social development and are ranked high in GNI per capita in the world; in terms of population and GDP, these cities are not really and with relatively limited influence in the world.

Type-3 cities are cities ranked top 15 in multinational connection but perform averagely or poorly in business environment. They belong to emerging economies. Among them, Beijing, Shanghai and Moscow have very important positions in the global cities network, while Sao Paulo and Delhi are major cities in their respective regions. In terms of GDP, Beijing, Shanghai and Moscow are leading cities in the world; Sao Paulo and Delhi are also in relatively high positions. However, in terms of GNI per capita, Delhi is near the bottom of the rankings and the other cities are in the middle range. This suggests that although they are big cities at the global and regional levels in the emerging economies of which the economy and society are still developing, doing business in these big cities has not reached the level of that in the developed economies.

12.4.2 Contributor to the Strong Correlation Between Multinational Connection and Infrastructure Connection

Analysis shows that the relationships of business environment with both types of global connection have very similar patterns. This means that these two types of connections are highly correlated. Basically, the global connection index measures the linkages between transnational corporations, and the infrastructure linkage is represented by the number of air routes. The inflow of multinational companies will drive a city to improve the local aviation infrastructure; and better aviation infrastructure becomes an important factor that attracts multinational companies.

We present a scatter plot with multinational connection and the number of air routes, of which the respective rankings are also analyzed with fitted curves (Figs. 12.13 and 12.14). Based on observation and correlation analysis, we find that multinational connection and air transportation have a strong positive correlation. The correlation coefficients also confirm this: the correlation coefficient of multinational connection and air transportation is 0.8079, and that between the two rankings is 0.8398, which demonstrate the identical characteristics of the two in their relationship with the doing business. In other words, multinational connection and infrastructure connection, which is represented by air transportation, is essentially highly correlated.

Accordingly, multinational connection and infrastructure connection share similar patterns and have similar impact on business environment. Multinationals are not quite concerned about business environment when selecting a city to build

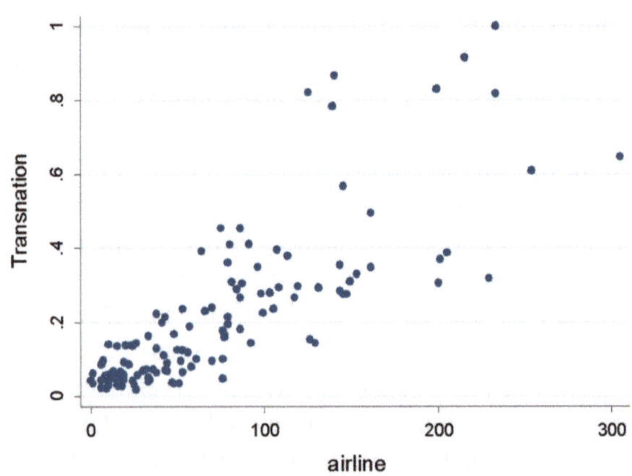

Fig. 12.13 Multinational connection and number of air routes

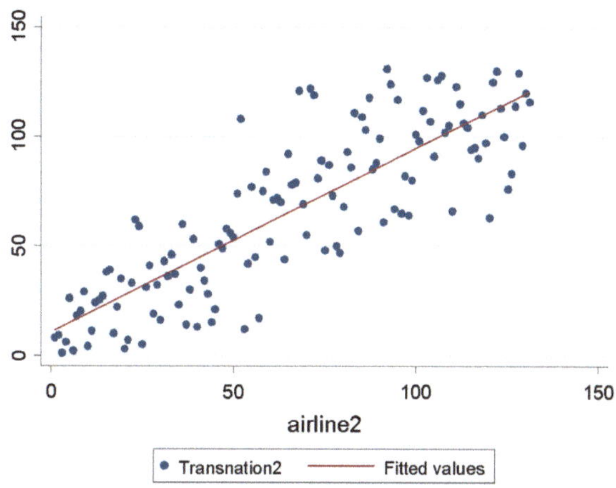

Fig. 12.14 Multinational connection and ranking in number of air routes. *Sources* World Bank database and CASS city and competitiveness database

their branches. However, from a dynamic perspective, the inflow of multinationals and the enhancement of aviation infrastructure can improve a city's business environment.

12.4.3 Influential Factors for Doing Business and Global Connection: An Empirical Analysis Based on Multiple Regressions

The above analyses indicate not only a weak correlation between the business environment and global connection but also the possible contributing factors in the correlation. The factors can be divided into two categories, one is the indicator of the level of economic development, including GNI per capita, representing the level of development of a country or a region, or urban GDP, representing the level of development of a city; and the other category is the indicator representing the size of a city, namely, urban scale index. Meanwhile, our correlation analysis also shows a weak correlation between global linkages and business environment. Based on this, we used multiple regression analyses to verify the relation between these variables.

Because a strong multi-collinearity might exist between GNI per capita and GDP as well as between multinational connection and infrastructure connection, we apply separate regression analysis on these two sets of indexes. Our validation method is as follows: first, we analyze the factor affecting business environment, which is then taken as a dependent variable (to simplify the analysis, only the doing business index of 2014 is used as a dependent variable); based on previous analysis, GDP per capita, GNI per capita, the city population size and the two types of global connection are used as independent variables. Because the doing business index is a

Table 12.8 Influencing factors for doing business index

Variables	Doing business 14			
	(1)	(2)	(3)	(4)
Rgdp2	0.965[a] (0.128)	0.947[a](0.118)		
perincome2			0.986[a] (0.110)	0.994[a](0.107)
population2	−0.159 (0.0993)	−0.176[c] (0.0958)	−0.137 (0.0916)	−0.136 (0.0909)
Transnation2	0.271[b] (0.136)		0.313[a] (0.116)	
airline2		0.310[b](0.125)		0.309[a] (0.113)
Constant	10.64 (8.464)	10.36 (8.315)	5.043 (8.021)	4.693 (7.994)
Observations	131	131	131	131
R-squared	0.647	0.653	0.688	0.689

Standard errors in parentheses
[a]$p < 0.01$, [b]$p < 0.05$, [c]$p < 0.1$

ranking list, each independent variable used in this analysis is based on its rank among the primate cities. The results are shown in Table 12.8:

According to the results of regression analysis shown in Table 12.8, the GDP per capita (Rgdp2) and GNI per capita (perincome2) are significantly positive at the 1% level; population size (population2) in Eqs. (1), (3), (4) is not significant, only in the Eq. (2) is significantly negative at the 10% level, which is consistent with the result of our previous correlation analysis, once again validating the business environment is related to the level of development but substantially independent of city size. At the same time, multinational global connection (Transnation2) and infrastructure global network (airline2) are positively correlated, but in the Eqs. (1), (2) only at the 5% level is significantly positive, showing a weak correlation between the business environment and the global connection.

12.5 Conclusions

This paper analyzes the distribution characteristics of doing business environment, and its relation with population size and economic development. We further study the relation between two types of global connection and business environment from the perspective of global connection. Based on our observation and analysis, the conclusions are as follows:

In terms of the distribution of business environment, we find that: (1) the distribution exhibits strong regional characteristics. Cities in developed regions such as Europe have better business environment than cities in developing regions. (2) The cities with the best business environment are those in emerging economies of Asia, big cities in developed countries of Western Europe and North America, and medium-sized cities Nordic countries. (3) Business environment is not related to a city's population size. A sound business environment is necessary for a low-income city to develop into a high-income city. All high-income cities perform better in terms of the doing business index.

In terms of a city's business environment and multinational global connection, we find that: (1) there is a weak correlation between the two; big enterprises are not too much concerned about business environment; because of their scale, these companies often enjoy preferential treatment given by local governments, or they can rely on their own global connections. (2) Although multinationals are not too much concerned about business environment, their inflow does enhance the local business environment; also, they have the capability to improve the local business environment once they settle down in a city.

In terms of a city's business environment and the infrastructure connection, we find that: (1) there is a weak correlation between the two factors. (2) From a dynamic perspective, good air transport infrastructure can help enhance a city's connection with other regions and cities, which, in turn, can improve the city's business environment.

By comparing two types of global connection versus the business environment, we obtain the following findings: (1) the strong positive correlation and similarity between infrastructure connection and multinational connection lead to a high correlation between these two types of global connection versus business environment. (2) Although a strong correlation between the two types of connection, they present a weak correlation with the ease of doing business environment. Global connection is often influenced by a city's GDP, and the business environment is often influenced by the city's GNI per capita, wherein two types of cities will see a deviation in the relationship between global connection and business environment. One is highly-developed medium-sized cities located in Northern Europe and Oceania; this type of cities has a sound business environment but a lower degree of global connection. The other one is the major big cities in emerging economies and this type of cities have a higher degree of global connection but less desirable business environment. (3) According to our report, the cities with larger GDP usually have a higher global connection, with a relatively good infrastructure, to attract more multinational companies settled. For these cities, although from a static point of view, the business environment is not at the forefront in the world, but because of the promotion of global connection, the improvement of business environment in these cities is more obvious than other cities.

References

Acemoglu, D.A. 2008. Growth and Institutions. In *The new palgrave dictionary of economics*, ed. Steven N. Duralauf, and Lawrence E. Blume. Basingstoke: Palgrave Macmillan.

Pengfei, Ni, Kai Liu, Taylor Peter. 2011. Chinese city connection: A measurement based on the interlocking network model, *Comparative Economic and Social Systems* 12.

Shu-jie, Yao, Kai-lei Wei. 2007. Economic growth, foreign direct investment and export trade: An empirical analysis. *Quarterly Journal of economics* 3.

World Bank. 2004. *Doing business in 2005: Removing obstacles to growth.* Washington, DC: World Bank.

World Bank. 2014. *Doing business in 2015: Going beyond efficiency*. Washington, DC: World Bank.

Yao, Shujie, Genfu Feng, and Kailei Wei. 2006. A study on the relationship between foreign direct investment and economic growth. *Economic Research* 12: 35–46.

Chapter 13
Large Enterprises in North America: Where They Locate and Why

The locational decisions of large enterprises are a far more complex issue than would appear at first glance. One would naturally assume that large enterprises would want to be located in our largest cities. If many large firms and headquarters functions are situated in the same large cities business and social interaction will be most easily accomplished. After all the largest cities have the advantages of economies of agglomeration, large populations of skilled workers, first-class universities and cultural institutions, the greatest access to talented professionals, air and telecommunications connectivity to all parts of the globe and with all of the other firms with which they have relationships of cooperation or competition. However, the issue is actually more involved than would appear at first glance. Along with the advantages, large cities are also fraught with congestion, pollution, crime, and diseconomies of agglomeration. Many large cities are simply too large, impersonal and dysfunctional to work well, in spite of efforts to create neighborhoods and congeniality.[1]

In actuality, many firms have located their head offices and much of their economic activity in cities that are considerably smaller than the ones we see discussed in the media. In this paper we will examine the locational decisions of firms in the contemporary economy and the factors that are primary in their decision-making process.

13.1 The Setting: The Earlier Period

However, before examining the viability of our largest cities as locations of economic activities and how firms make their locational decisions it is clear from recent research that one must give attention to the period of time, the context, in which these cities and firms operate, the characteristics of this period, the sectors that are

[1] Joel Kotkin, "The Problem with Mega-Cities", http://www.forbes.com/sites/megacities/2011/04/04/the-problem-with-megacities.

© China Social Sciences Press and Springer Nature Singapore Pte Ltd. 2017

P. Ni et al., *Cities Network Along the Silk Road*,
DOI 10.1007/978-981-10-4834-0_13

most relevant to it, and the demands they make for factors of production and other assets. Clearly, the *context* in which firms operate today is dramatically different that it was a few decades ago. Until a half century ago manufacturing was the principal activity in many economic regions. A few such as New York and London had moved from making things to providing the capital and professional services to those that still did. For the vast majority of urban regions economic success required that they had to provide the assets, connections, factors of production, and production space that the firms required. In this context the determinants of urban or regional competitiveness were 'hard' determinants—a good port, rail and highway connection, industrial plant and equipment, capital availability, suitable labor, and proximity to raw materials. City leaders did what they could to induce other levels of government to make investments in these assets that would enhance the attractiveness of the city to manufacturing firms. Many industrial cities, while producing industrial products in great profusion, unfortunately also created the conditions that would give rise to labor unionization movements, many of which were marked by bloody battles; slum housing and districts where poorly paid workers lived—close to the factory; air quality that created lung and other ailments that gave rise to the clean city and environmental movements beginning in the 1980s; the corruption of city politics and government; the powerful abridgement of democracy; and great disparities in wealth—only some of which was returned to the community by wealthy individuals and families in the form of contributions to art museums, libraries, performance centers, hospitals and so forth.

With regard to the *characteristics* of that earlier period, while it was certainly not autarkic, international trade did not play the same role that it does today. Nonetheless, the US economy had a trade surplus from 1893 until the early 1970s. For many European countries international trade was dominated by imports of primary goods from colonies and former colonies, and exports to manufactured good to them. Transportation costs limited access to distant domestic markets so, while not of overwhelming importance, international trade did give support to the manufacturing firms of the industrialized countries. These conditions also fostered the development of national monopolies and oligopolies and the rise of more interventionist governments, whether to clear the way for this growth or to establish some social control over the attendant abuses and inefficiencies.

War is a great stimulator of technological progress and the First World War was no exception. Standardization of manufacturing processes, the mind-numbing monotonous efficiency of the Fordist system of mass production, the rapid urbanization of most industrialized societies, the development of the skyscraper building prior to 1914 that allowed for a spatial concentration of firms and economic activities, massive migration of Europeans and others to the 'lands of recent settlement', the US, Canada, Australia and New Zealand, and the gradual emancipation of both women and racial minorities all stamped a character on this earlier period of industrialism that made it dramatically different from that which went before and that set the stage for the equally dramatic changes that would follow the Great Depression and the Second World War.

At the beginning of the 20th century, the principal *sectors* involved in economic production were resource extraction, resource processing, and manufacturing. Iron, copper, lead, bauxite and other minerals, and timber and food-stuffs were dominant. Here firm size varied by sector, with farming being relative small scale and mining and manufacturing soon becoming dominated by large firms. For most of these sectors firm location, no matter how large the firm, was determined largely by proximity to the basic material being worked on. Inexpensive river and lake transportation allowed production and manufacturing sites throughout the US Great Lakes to develop and to flourish in these industries—Chicago, Pittsburgh, Cleveland, and Hamilton, among others are testament to this phenomenon. In the case of the transformation of bauxite into aluminum cheap hydro-electric power mandated that production be located in places such as Washington and Quebec. Milling of wheat was also situated close to rail-heads on the Great Lakes for shipping to ports around the world; as rail service reduces transportation over land, milling shifted from the port cities to cities closer to the production areas. Labor was to a significant degree supplied by immigrants who tended to settle in port cities or in the places where the economic activity of the day was being conducted. So labor flowed to production sites rather than firms having to locate where the labor was.

The *demands* imposed by firms for the assets that were necessary for production, started as being a demand for labor with certain specific skills, many of which were artisanal or at least skills that had been handed down from generation to generation. Products from hats to iron objects evolved in their needs for labor as technology advanced, and standardized production and deconstructed complex tasks into mass production in which each laborer no longer needed to be skilled and was asked to do just one simple task time after time after time throughout the work day. This deskilling of labor had powerful impacts on the relationship between factory manager and the workers. Workers lost whatever bargaining power they had had and were often massed at the factory gate with the first dozens or hundreds to get through the gate able to be employed that day.

Capital was provided by wealthy 'landed' individuals before stock and capital markets developed to their current capacity and degree of efficiency. The large enterprises were then able to develop a degree of monopoly power in the market that allowed auto-financing and accumulation of capital by the owners. Corruption in the relationship between business and local government facilitated transfer of land to companies and whatever changes in regulations and land use mandates they required.

Prior to the inter-war period, these 'hard' determinants of competitiveness governed firm decision-making with regard to location of production facilities. Essentially, firms went to the choice locations. All of the great cities of this time were situated on ocean shores, lakes, and navigable rivers. This era was brought to its end by the dislocation of the Great Depression and by the consequences of World War II, which included dramatic increases in technology of production, transportation and communication, the growth of the state in Western nations, increased power of organized labor, the resort in most economies to a system based on markets and democracy, and the dramatic development of financial markets. The contemporary economic world differs dramatically from this earlier one. Naturally firms have had to change their approaches to locational decision-making.

13.2 The Setting: The Contemporary Period

The dramatic developments just noted above greatly transformed the economic setting for economic activity and for the firms that conduct it.

The *context* that confronts firms today is dramatically different in most ways than the one that preceded it, but in some ways little has changed. While heavy manufacturing virtually invited workers to seek to form a bargaining agent—a union, in the service-dominated contemporary economy some workers are more mobile and their skills give them some leverage, while others work in low-level retail and food service industries in which they are often treated like disposable objects. In neither case is the fervor to unionize as strong as it had been. Hence, union membership in the US is about one third of what it was thirty years ago, as a share of the workforce. However, the tension over distributive shares is as strong today as it was in the 1930s. In the interim, the business class has been able to convince the congress to pass regulations and tax policies that have continued to concentrate an increasing share of total income in the hands of the top 5% of the population. This has made the distribution of income and inequality a powerful force in contemporary US politics. See, for example, Joseph Stiglitz's book, *The Price of Inequality*. This followed on the heels of the Occupy Wall Street movement.

Air quality and industrial pollution have become international issues, first with the United Nations' Kyoto meeting in 1997 and now with the Paris meeting in November 2015. The same thing has happened to other issues, such as slum housing, public health, access to education, and jobs that have become internationalized. These issues are now recognized as being endemic to countries throughout the developing world. Some consequences of economic activity have become less onerous, while others have simply become globalized.

The principal *characteristics* of the earlier economy, trade and technological progress have certainly increased their role in economic life and have increased the pace of their growth. The Trade Agreements Act of 1962 kicked off a series of bi-national, regional and global trade liberalizing agreements that dramatically altered the relationship between firms and production sites throughout the world. De-industrialization, a shift of production and assembly functions to developing countries in Asia, Latin America and Africa—globalization, and a gradually growing difference in economic growth rates between the industrialized and developing economies reconfigured the global economy.

Advances in transportation communication, and production technologies, as well as an increase in the pace of their advance has led to the rise of many new products and industries and the decline and even disappearance of others.

Communication by Skype, cell phone and computer have revolutionized the way in which individuals involved in production and design communicate with each other and the degree to which they require frequent face-to-face contact. Individuals thousands of miles apart can collaborate as effectively as though they were on different floors of the same high-rise corporate tower. It is increasingly easy now to transfer employees from one country to another for less than permanent moves, and the migration of skilled workers from one country to the other means that firms can work to attract this highly mobile work force to whatever location in the company structure it is felt is in need of this labor.

In short, the global economy is now more fluid, flexible and malleable than it was in the earlier period. This works greatly to the advantage of firms that operate on the international stage and to the highly mobile and skilled cohorts of the labor force; however, it causes considerable difficulty in terms of stagnant incomes and reduced employment opportunities for the rest of the population.

In the contemporary situation the principal *sectors* for much of the industrialized world are not longer manufacturing and primary goods production. In fact, many of the cities of the developing world are beginning to enhance their competitiveness in sectors such as finance, professional services, and technology-related activities. Pittsburgh and Turin are two examples of industrial cities that found themselves abandoned by traditional specialization in steel and automobile production and have had to re-focus their economic activity in areas such as medical technology, information and computer science, and other high-technology activities. Other cities such as Denver and Charlotte have been able to develop competitiveness in these areas while being devoid of the 'hard' determinants of competitiveness that marked the earlier period—ports, access to raw materials, etc. We will discuss below the rise in the importance of 'soft' determinants, such as public safety, education and culture, and so forth. This shift is largely due to the requirements of the educated and skilled labor force that is the *sine qua non* of today's competitive urban economy.

It is interesting to note that firms in these recently important sectors have less need to concentrate in our largest cities. Large bio-pharmaceutical, information-communications, and specialty manufacturing firms normally have many centers of production, distribution, research and decision-making and these entities are typically scattered throughout the national and international economic space. In some sectors clustering is important, but in others that are dominated by corporate centers and top-down transfers of knowledge, such as bio-pharmaceutical, clustering is often quite unimportant. So, it is clear that the specific sectors that are of greatest importance to the current economy have powerful impacts on the requirements that firms demand from potential production sites.

Factor of production *demands* of contemporary firms have become both more complex and simpler at the same time. Capital is now provided by a vast array of sources from banks, to governments, to venture capital funds, to individual entrepreneurs, to the stock market and to entirely new options such as crowd-sourcing. This has greatly increased the availability of capital to existing firms and to start-ups as well. Almost all urban areas are now promoting incubator centers and venture capital for start-up firms focusing on new products and new technologies as a key item in their approach to enhancing competitiveness, employment and revenues. We have already noted the enhanced mobility of skilled and educated labor, things that have increased the availability of needed labor but that have also increased its options and bargaining power to the detriment of the firms.

Abuses of power and market position by firms and banks have increased the demands on the part of the public for closer government scrutiny of firm operations. Automobile recalls, the role of financial institutions in the near collapse of the world economy in 2008, awareness of the ability of firms in food production to gain favorable regulatory treatment, and other similar abuses have made the public aware of its need to assert its demands for a game that is 'less rigged'. Over the longer run this cannot work favorably for the business community.

The multi-faceted situation of the contemporary world economy is one of a much more open operational environment for firms, one that will have powerful impacts on the process of decision-making with regard to firm entity location, and one that has the potential of making operations a bit more difficult or constrained, in part due to past transgressions and abuses of the business community. We will now explore this question in the remaining pages of this paper.

13.3 Decision-Making *re* Location Today

Apple allocates its production over 95 countries, from Malta and the Philippines with less than 30 tons to China with just over 37 million tons, and with another 12 countries with over 1 million tons each. Toyota produces in 18 countries and has joint ventures or licensing arrangements with another 10. Some of this is done to gain access to the local market and some to curry favor with the host government, but for the rest the reason has to be linked with economic rationality and cost effectiveness. This is where we get to the decision-making for location of facilities and the factors than enter into it.

We must begin by asking: "What do firms seek out today when making plant location decisions?"

1. **Aspects of firm and city competitiveness**

The discussion above gives us some ideas as to what firms include in this decision-making process. The crucial element for firms today is a labor force that is skilled, and educated; at the same time this labor is highly mobile. Firms must work to attract the appropriate labor and then it must work to retain it. It is important to differentiate between these workers and those of the era of heavy manufacturing. The high-technology sector workers of today typically have university education rather than the high school education of blue-collar workers. They also have more discretionary time that they can devote to more work or to leisure activities. Blue-collar workers had little time away from the job. Labor had to struggle many years top gain the 40-h workweek and annual vacations. It is therefore understandable that today's skilled workers demand an array of amenities such as recreation sites, cultural and educational facilities and opportunities, pleasant parks, public security, health care, congenial housing, and public transportation. If firms are not able to provide these amenities, the highly mobile workers will simply move to another employment location.

It is clear then that the locus of power has shifted a bit in favor of these workers and that firms must now cater to some of their needs by locating their operations in cities that offer skilled and mobile workers what they require. The movement out of the city center was chronicled in 1991 by Joel Garreau, in his book *Edge City*. Garreau noted that corporations were then establishing corporate campuses in suburbs on the periphery of the metropolitan area, in part because this was where most of their employees wanted to live. Some were new towns, some were intersections of major highways and some were existing cities or towns. Key to this was, of course, the increased ownership of automobiles, their daily use and the need for parking spaces for them. This was not congenial to the traditional large city. By reducing commuting time and cost, this new configuration of employment and residence increased economic efficiency and the incomes of workers.

More recently, Joel Kotkin has written about the 'flight from the city' and the rise of alternative urban spaces: midopolis, nerdistan and small towns. The midopolis is essentially Garreau's Edge City. Nerdistan encompasses the many large research university towns which are blessed with the sort of recreational, entertainment, cultural, artistic, and other amenities sought out by the highly skilled and mobile work force. When these workers begin to have a family they often seek out an alternative to the large, bustling, traditional city center; Austin, Boulder, Madison, Salt Lake City, among many others are attractive to them. Workers with families want these amenities, even if they work long hours, for their children. Hence, firms in these sectors establish facilities, if not head offices, in these amenity-rich cities. Finally, Kotkin notes that many firms find it possible to be competitive in small towns, at least in those with universities, good health care facilities, and small town amenities. Ithaca, New York, is such place, with Cornell University, many start up firms and the small town environment of a city with only 30,000 non-student residents. The bottom line here is to say that the array of places in which firms can locate facilities has broadened dramatically in recent years. This has an advantage to firms as they can now tailor-match facilities with the relevant work force in places that are congenial to both.

The notion that smaller cities can be as attractive to firms and as competitive in the global economy as our largest cities deserves further analysis. In research I have conducted with my colleague Daniele Ietri, we have verified that smaller cities have many features that are desired by skilled workers and by the firms that seek to employ them (Kresl and Ietri 2016). Many smaller cities have high quality research universities with all that means for skilled graduates, faculty consultants, start-up firms, athletics, and intellectual and cultural environment a very good mix for a younger skilled work force. Social capital is more easily developed as is public–private sector collaboration. In a recent paper two researchers found that while it was true that larger cities have historically been the sites of advanced research and technological progress, this advantage has been diminishing in recent decades and this advantage over smaller cities has been eroded. Firms seeking to generate technological advances no longer have to put city size at the head of the list of desired attributes (Packalen and Bhattacharya 2015).

This raises the issue of the determinants of competitiveness and how they relate to the location decisions of firms. We have already differentiated between 'hard' and 'soft' determinants of urban competitiveness. "Hard' determinants are typically physical things such as ports, intermodal transportation centers, aggregations of factories and other production facilities, housing stock, research facilities, and deposits of raw materials (Kresl and Ietri 2015). These were the basis of development of production centers, and our industrial cities, in the nineteenth century and the first three-quarters of the twentieth. Changes in technology made some centers no longer competitive while others rose in significance. For example, in the first part of the 19th century Cincinnati was the center of pork production in the US—'porkopolis'. But when rail transportation proved more competitive than river shipping after the Civil War, pork production shifted to Chicago, as did the claim to the title 'porkopolis'.

After the de-industrialization crisis that hit Europe and the US in the 1970s, 'soft' determinants replaced 'hard' determinants as the basis for corporate locational decision-making. These determinants include public security, recreation assets, health care, cultural and educational institutions, parks, bike lanes and walking paths, lively entertainment and good restaurants. Pittsburgh is a smaller city that has reconfigured itself from a center of 'hard' determinants to one of 'soft' determinants as the basis of its economy was transformed from steel production and manufacturing to health care, medical technology, computer science and robotics. There are scores of other cities, large and small, that have been able to accomplish this transition so they can remain attractive to the desired work force and to the firms that seek to employ them. This is indicative of the fact that cities, of all sizes, have become more active in creating the sort of economic environment that will ensure that they remain attractive and competitive.

2. **Traditional approaches to firm location**

The traditional approach to firm location has focused on several standard elements, elements that affect the cost of production and distribution. This case is made compellingly by Bhat, Paleti and Singh, who show that a multivariate approach to analysing firm location decisions is most positively predictive (Bhat et al. 2014). As we shall see, some of these elements do not work in the way one would intuitively believe they would. This is in part due to the fact that the contemporary economy functions in a way that is different from that of the earlier period, as noted above. For example, one would think that labor cost would be a powerful factor in the decision as to where to place a plant. Costly labor would reduce profit and would drive firms away. However, today the work force is highly skilled and highly mobile. Labor fluidly moves from one site to another as the attractiveness of each is altered over time. This would cause the cost of labor to be continually moving toward an equilibrium structure over the geographic area being considered by the firm. So the firm in the relevant sector would then be less likely to use labor cost as a major determinant in its plant location decisions.

Low tariffs and trade barriers would allow a firm to import its raw materials and intermediate products and this would make the location attractive, but this would allow for more competition from other firms for this market. On the other hand, high tariffs and trade barriers would induce firms to increase their direct investment in this area. If the local market is insufficiently large it would not be attractive to firms that wanted to sell nationally their products made as a consequence of their investment. So trade liberalization or the lack thereof will have an impact that will be specific to the individual situation, and cannot be said to be favorable or unfavorable to the host area. Its attractiveness to a firm will depend largely on the sector in which the firm functions and its objectives in making a direct investment.

Market size will be very important for firms such as automobiles in which production and assembly plants are typically situated in large economies and do not exclusively focus on low-cost exports to industrialized markets. Aircraft and telecommunications equipment are produced with components from many countries, in part to induce host governments to give the firm orders for the product. But as we noted above, Apple produces goods in almost 100 countries, including Malta with its miniscule local market. Nonetheless major plants are always located in large market countries, such as China, Mexico, and India.

Large cities do, of course, have economies of agglomeration, economic features that are possible only when the city is a major player in the global economy. The ability to support a major internationally connected airport hub is considered to be a great benefit to firms that require face-to-face interaction with partners that are at great distance. The availability of large numbers of suppliers of professional and other services, and of firms that can supply the wide array of inputs required are also only available in our largest cities. However, our largest cities are also host to a wide array of diseconomies of agglomeration, such as environmental pollution, traffic, congestion, social pathologies, crime, a harried pace of life, and cultural and recreational amenities that may be difficult to gain access. These economies and diseconomies make large cities attractive or disagreeable to skilled and mobile workers and, depending on the industrial sector, agglomeration may work to favor or hinder the city in its effort to become attractive to firms when they make decisions about plant location.

In recent years much has been made of clustering as an incentive for firms to seek sites in certain locations. Beginning with Alfred Marshall's notion of the 'industrial district', economists have recognized the benefits that come from having many firms in the same economic activity located in close proximity. The benefits of the face-to-face transfer of information that comes from even casual interaction of workers are thought to be at times enormous. When in clusters, firms can also join together to seek funding and other support for common projects and initiatives such as research funding, infrastructure improvements, expansion of university and research facilities, and lobbying with government for a wide array of regulatory changes and fiscal measures. Hence, in many sectors in which firms are open to and clearly benefit from exchange and interaction with workers from other firms the existence of a cluster can be a powerful inducement for the firm to situate one or more of its entities in such an environment.

Firms are also responsive to government subsidies and other incentives and to local tax rates. As shown by Howell, early stage grants, especially to smaller firms, can make financing constraints less severe (Howell 2015). She suggests that it is more productive to give many smaller grants to firms that are trying to get a product to market than to offer a few large grants to firms that are thought to be the "best" firms. The former assures that some of the grants will be successful whereas the latter approach risks losing all on wrong decisions as to which firms and the most likely to be successful. However, if these grants are used to induce firms to locate somewhere firms that respond to these sorts of incentives are often induced, at some moment in the future, to move to another location because of better incentives. This has been shown to be a factor of importance for firm location decisions within a defined geographic space, such as a state or province (Calcagno and Thompson 2005). It is also the case that grants, such as those of the US federal government Empowerment Zone program, can be shown to alter the industrial mix in a region in which they are awarded. Specifically, the grants are most positive in their impact on firms in the retail and service sectors, while there is a negative impact on firms in the transportation and finance, insurance and real estate sectors (Hanson and Rohlin 2011). The result will be a change in the industrial composition of the regional economy. Firms will respond to tax and other incentives, but the result for the region may not be the one that is desired unless care is taken as to how the incentives are structured. The Australian government has "channeled significant financial and other resources towards building technology incubators, innovation centers and science parks" in an effort to make Australian firms more significant as generators of new technologies and as participators in innovation. This has induced firms to move to specific favored locations but Australian firms still lag in relation to innovation and technology development in other parts of the world. The point here is that progress does not happen quickly and that it is difficult to guess the best ways to promote it and to use available government funding.

What grants and incentives can do that is very important for firms in their location decision-making is to work to reduce the cost of fixed investment. This is typically the single largest outlay for the firm in a new location and is the item where one finds the most intense competition among cities that are vying for the facility. This includes land, rail and other transportation linkages, and the construction of new production facilities. While funding for these is not always a local initiative, the city can work with the firms to secure contributions from the state and, with the state, the national government and its agencies. With many cities seeing this as a way to attract new investments, firms can 'shop around' to find the package that is best for them.

In the earlier period it was crucial for the new firm to have these rail and water connections to markets and to inputs such as raw materials. In recent decades technology has transformed the reality of connectivity, but not its importance to firms when seeking sites for facilities. This has clearly been the case for a city such as Chicago that was the center of the nation's rail system as well as being the key to water transport from the Atlantic Ocean, via the St. Lawrence River and the Great Lakes through the 'Chicago connection' to the Illinois and Mississippi Rivers to the Gulf of Mexico. In the Post-WWII years air travel grew rapidly and Chicago became a hub in this system, and it was also key in the trucking system and in intermodal truck-rail linkage for shipments between the East and the West coasts. Many other cities have seen their competitiveness enhanced or diminished by their participation, or lack thereof, in this new model of connectivity. The sophistication of intermodal sea-land shipment has also advanced considerably, and union acceptance and other factors have made cities such as Seattle and Barcelona advance in relation to other less accommodating cities such as Vancouver and Genoa and Marseilles.

The innovations in electronic communication have generated a new world in connectivity. Cities everywhere are lobbying governments and telecommunications providers for broadband, offering the fastest speed of connection and the largest capacity, since they know how important this is to firms seeking to operate under the most efficient form of connectivity. In a study of 6000 firms in New Zealand, Grimes, Ren and Stevens found an increase in overall productivity of 7–10% following broadband adoption. This was especially important for firms that were large, foreign owned, urban, focused on R&D, and had firm-specific ICT knowledge and high general management capability. Such firms were more likely to purchase goods on the internet, to have a web-page, to enter new export markets and to make sales over the internet than were firms without broadband. While access to broadband is not transformative for a firm, (Grimes et al. 2012) the impact is "material and significant".

13.4 Final Thoughts

Finding the best place to locate the next facility of a large firm, or even the first of a start-up, has become a very complex and sometimes confusing activity. In the earlier period, prior to the crisis in manufacturing of the 1970's 'hard' determinants of competitiveness dominated the decision—proximity to inputs, a suitable work force, good transportation and good sites for the facility. We see today many of the results of this decision-making in the abandoned and rusting production facilities that were suitable for the earlier period but are totally unsuitable for the contemporary economy. Many of the firms of the earlier period have disappeared to be replaced by others in other sectors or by others that use different technologies. The contemporary economy has become dominated by 'soft' determinants—public security, health care, parks and other amenities, and educational, cultural and recreational assets. Whereas in the earlier period the firms were in charge, now the firms must accommodate themselves and their location decision-making to the life-style and work preferences of a work force that is highly skilled and highly mobile.

Most large firms produce goods in many facilities, often in many countries. Presumably each location is optimal in some way. At the lowest level of sophistication, firms may site a facility simply to curry favor with the government or to gain some concessions from it. Government may be more passively involved since they impose a trade regime, fiscal structure, and investment in infrastructure and fixed capital irrespective of the wishes or even the presence of the firm. We have found that fiscal incentives can have results other than those that are desired. These measures may just re-position production facilities from one region in the country to another with no overall benefit. They may also alter the sectoral composition of national output in ways that were not desired.

A very important aspect of the contemporary economy is that the balance of power has shifted in many instances from the firm to the workforce. The highly skilled and highly mobile worker has options that were not available to the worker of the earlier period. Many workers today can choose to work wherever the environment is suitably congenial. Firms now have to induce these relatively scarce workers to accept employment with them by offering a working and living situation that they find congenial, not just for themselves but also for their family. If firms are otherwise indifferent to where the facility is to be situated they are perfectly pleased to accommodate the workforce.

Firms in industries that are not characterized by proprietary information and strong head office and relatively weak subsidiary relationships find it very desirable to locate some of the facilities in sectoral clusters, in which the firm benefits from profitable interaction, knowledge sharing, and joint action with regard to finance, marketing, and research, among other things.

Finally, it has become clear that the firm no longer has to confine its location decision-making to large cities to the exclusion of smaller ones. Research has shown that smaller cities have many positive features that are lacking in larger cities, although they do lack the latter's agglomeration effects. On net basis, in many situations for many firms in a variety of sectors siting in smaller cities brings benefits to the work force and to the firm. Clearly, many firms do need the easy access to a globally connected airport, to a deep supply of relevant professional services, to big finance, to high rise buildings that will accommodate high level employees and departments, and to world-class research universities and research facilities.

For most firms, the decision to locate a facility in some specific place is a very complex and important decision. In the contemporary economy new sets of considerations have emerged as being important, and the will continue to emerge; the firm must always be sensitive to the characteristics of this new environment.

References

Bhat, Chandra R., Rajesh Paleti, and Palvinder Singh. 2014. A spatial multivariate count model for firm location decisions. *Journal of Regional Science* 54 (3): 462–502.

Calcagno, Peter T., and Henry Thompson. 2005. State economic incentives: Stimulus or reallocation? *Public Finance Review* 32 (6): 651–665.

Grimes, Arthur, Cleo Ren, and Phillip Stevens. 2012. The need for speed: Impacts of internet connectivity on firm productivity. *Journal of Productivity Analysis* 37: 199.

Hanson, Andrew, and Shawn Rohlin. 2011. The effect of location-based tax incentives on establishment location and employment across industry sectors. *Public Finance Review* 39 (2): 195–225.

Howell Sabrina. 2015. Financing constraints as barriers to innovation: Evidence from R&D grants to energy startups, research paper, Harvard Lab for economic applications and policy.

Kresl, Peter Karl, and Daniele Ietri. 2016. *Smaller cities in a world of competitiveness*. Abingdon: Routledge.

Kresl, Peter Karl, Daniele Ietri. 2015. Urban competitiveness: Theory and practice, Ch. *4*, Abington: Routledge.

Packalen, Mikko, Jay Bhattacharya. 2015. Cities and Ideas, NBER working Paper No. 20921.

Chapter 14
The Conjunction of Networked Agglomeration and Location Factor in Chinese Cities: Taking FDI and Domestic Investment as an Example

14.1 Introduction

Taylor has contended that according to Jacobs (1969), 'cities in networks' have existed for thousands of years (Taylor 2012). Cities can be regarded as the original form of cooperation, agglomeration and international trade in human society and economy. Cluster and agglomeration processes within cities, combined with network/city connectivity processes between cities (Taylor 2012), have improved economic productivity by generating integrated markets, labour pools, new technologies and innovations. There is no doubt that agglomeration and network effects together make contemporary cities the critical inter-connected nodes for human reproduction, creativity and economic growth. Contrary to late twentieth century predictions of the "end of geography" (O'Brien 1992) and "death of distance" due to the rise of advanced telecommunications and linked technological breakthroughs (Cairncross 2001) generating the "network society" (Castells 1996), the United Nations (2013) has predicted that 64.1 and 85.9% of the developing and developed world respectively, will be urbanized by 2050. And as predicted a century ago by Gottman in relation to the United States, most of this population growth will occur in big cities that are spilling over metropolitan boundaries to form extensive globalizing 'mega-city regions' consisting of many functionally inter-linked geographically proximate large and small urban settlements (Gottman 1961; Scott 2001; Hall and Pain 2006).

Many scholars have dedicated themselves to explaining urban agglomeration phenomena (for example, Marshall 1920; Isard 1956; Helsley and Strange 1990; Krugman 1997; Glaeser 2010). In 1920, emphasizing the importance of specialization, Marshall articulated three sources of agglomeration economies: labour pooling, scale economies of intermediate input and tacit knowledge spillovers. In contrast, Jacobs (1984) has argued that it is local diversification that drives agglomeration externalities, emphasizing as priorities heterogeneity versus homogeneity and parallelism versus hierarchism respectively. Jacobs has asserted that

© China Social Sciences Press and Springer Nature Singapore Pte Ltd. 2017

P. Ni et al., *Cities Network Along the Silk Road*,
DOI 10.1007/978-981-10-4834-0_14

knowledge spill-overs generated across diverse industries are more active and innovative than those generated across specialized clusters. Ellison and Glaeser (1999) found that in North America the distribution of diversification and specialization is not random but highly concentrated in big cities with four-digit sectors.[1] Meanwhile, it has been found that larger cities tend to be more diversified and specialized in service sectors as opposed to manufacturing whilst many cities also show a significant path dependence tendency and location inertia (Henderson 1991; Kim 1995). This conclusion has been endorsed by research into advanced business (producer) services (APS) clustering in North West Europe where two distinctive urban processes have been identified: Process A—'mega-city region economic expansion' and Process B—'mega-city regions of proximate cities' (Taylor and Pain 2007; Pain 2008a). Process A is distinguished by functionally polycentric multi-sector clustering which generates Jacobsean economic enveloping and upgrading of towns and cities surrounding a major globally networked city, whereas process B is distinguished by morphological urban polycentricity and sectoral specialization which generate more static, less globally networked, regions (Pain 2008a).

Both Jacobs (1969) and Castells (1996) have emphasized city agglomeration as a process that involves flows between cities. Among such flows, investment inputs, throughputs and outputs, are significant in the reproduction of capital, the allocation of resources and so the stimulation of business activities and employment that diffuse technology, knowledge etc. (Domar 1946; Romer 1986; Barro 1989; Anderson 1990). Foreign direct investment (FDI) and domestic investment (DI) are therefore valuable indicators that can shed light on agglomeration economies in urban areas and city regions. FDI is a relatively new form of investment under prevailing globalization, characterized by transnational practices, international exchange, complex ownership, long-tern intentions and so forth. It is also argued that FDI generates technology and information diffusion, elite and skilled-labour flows, complementary capital and export incentivization with international attributes (Noorzoy 1979; De Mello 1999; Kim and Seo 2003). FDI by multinational corporations (MNCs) especially, contributes to job generation, trading and the transfer of capital, skills and technologies (Borensztein et al. 1998; Blomström and Sjöholm 1999; Liu 2008). Mello (1999) has denoted that FDI has positive incentives for domestic firms by upgrading their capital stock. It is estimated that 30% of the productivity growth of manufacturing in the UK was affected by FDI between 1985 and 1995 according to Barrell and Pain (1997). However, the positive effects of FDI are not permanent and some scholars are skeptical as to the compelling importance of FDI flows into domestic markets. Industrial organization theorists have expressed concerns that the MNC strategy of increasing FDI to compete for control of global value chains weakens the economic sovereignty of host countries because the competitiveness of indigenous firms is diminished (Caves 1971; Dunning 1981). Aitken and Harrison have found that fiercer competition introduced

[1]The standard industrial classification by 4 digit codes in the US, established in 1937.

by foreign firms, crowds out the market share of domestic firms. Hejazi and Pauly's analysis of the effects of inward FDI in Canada discovered negative impacts of FDI on the domestic market. There is a contradiction then between this skeptical interpretation of FDI and theorization of cities and mega-city regions as an economically vibrant process made possible by flows within global networks of firms and FDI.

14.2 Explaining the Urban Agglomeration Process: Location or Network?

This contradiction is important considering the spatial implications of agglomeration/cluster processes within cities and network/connectivity processes between cities as noted in North West European mega-city regions (Taylor and Pain 2007). Fingleton's (1999) spatial auto-correlated error model estimating regional economic convergence found technology spillovers across 178 European regions. Van Oort (2007) has estimated the effects of agglomeration economies on neighbouring regions by means of a spatial dependence model which has found significant spatial dependence of the growth externalities of cities. Jocobs et al. (2011) have asserted that the spillover of complementary knowledge across diverse urban industries is the most important source of innovation and agglomeration economies. Their analysis of a sample of 459 cities across the world found that advanced maritime producer services tend to be attracted to the cities where their clients or advanced service providers locate. However, in contrast, Boschma (2004) has argued that knowledge externalities are geographically bounded due to privileged access to information flows, knowledge transfer and interactive learning. And in terms of American firms specifically, Henderson (2003) has found that the spatial implication of agglomeration economies is restricted according to the characteristics of industries: positive technology spillovers for high-tech firms, but not for manufacturing firms. The source of externalities and their spatial implications has become of key interest in relation to agglomerated activities such as FDI and DI with contrasting perspectives presented by the two main theoretical schools explaining the spatial agglomeration of economic activities: location factor analysis (city endogenous growth) and connectivity analysis (the city network paradigm).

Diversified location factors are highlighted as endogenous drivers, such as local market size, labour pool, accessibility, industrial configuration, institutional context, high-tech clusters, cultural atmosphere and urban landscape such as universities, urban lifestyles and diversity (Florida 2002). Turok (2004) has conceived the focus of urban development strategy as transferred from spatial policy to the exploitation of indigenous strengths. According to the urban competitiveness literature, location factors are critical in boosting industrial innovation and upgrading capacity which are seen as core competitiveness factors under processes of product differentiation and globalization (Porter 1990). However, over-emphasis on the competitiveness of nations and firms gives rise to a missing space between the national level and the firm level. The city level is regarded as a suitable 'wedge' to fill this space due to predominant agglomeration effects under pervasive neoliberalism and the intermediate role of cities between the nation and active actors, firms and institutions. Amongst others, Boschma (2004) has asserted that, like firms, cities compete with each other under conditions of strong economic specialization in similar markets. Along the lines of Jacobs' analysis (1969), it is variety that leads to knowledge creation, and learning has extended from an organizational to a territorial level. Generally, the capacity to attract investment through location factors is one significant aspect to explain economic competitiveness. It is argued that the impacts of FDI depend on the absorptive capability of the domestic markets of host countries (Agosin and Machado 2007; Mahroum et al. 2008). Specifically, human capital, financial markets, and technology gaps are critical location factors explaining the determinants of absorptive capacity (Glass and Saggi 1998; Alfaro et al. 2004; Mahroum et al. 2008). For instance, Blomstrom et al. analysis of the effects of FDI in the UK (1999) has found positive effects in England but negative effects in Wales and Scotland. They have attributed this result to the technology gap between foreign firms and domestic firms.

On the other hand, there are those who criticize the epidemic of urban attribute (location factors) analysis and econometric studies in explaining urban development (Berry 1964). They deem that markets stem from social networks intrinsically whilst market regulation reflects hints, trust and rules generated by mutual communication of producers' and marketers' networks. It is argued that the network is an invisible space where ideas, thoughts, innovations and learning can be generated and shared (Powell et al. 1996). Nevertheless, this theoretical debate does not mean that the two analytical approaches are mutually exclusive. In fact, they can be seen as complementary since networks underline connectivity whilst location factors provide endogenous thinking. Berry (1964) has claimed that urban geography essentially focuses on 'cities as systems within systems of cities', which indicates that we need to look at cities in a broad perspective emphasizing their connectivity, such as investment relationships between cities. His view is broadly in line with the emphasis on inter-city relations of Jacobs (1969). However, the networks of cities are spiky; cities hold different centralities according to headquarter-subsidiary structure and distinctive functions (Wall and Van der Knaap 2011). Moreover, due to fuzzy production modes, different specializations, and the division of labour, the economic and functional relationships between cities tend to be more complementary than competitive, benefitting from scale economies, knowledge exchange and synergies (Capello 2000; Meijers 2007). Especially under globalization, big cities are more globally connected and have more relations with other big cities than with their neighbouring cities (Pain 2008b; Pain and Van Hamme 2014). Johansson and Quigley (2004) have agreed that agglomeration and networks are complementary to each other in terms of knowledge diffusion and productivity gains. Nevertheless, we cannot ignore the links between knowledge diffusion and investment because investment, especially FDI, is regarded as an important pipeline to diffuse knowledge. Therefore, it is necessary to observe the agglomeration of urban activities such as the agglomeration of FDI in a network way. Accordingly, this paper tests the pipeline function of networks in FDI agglomeration. In addition, the dispersal of production modes and the concentration of specialized services is evidence that location factor analysis and network analysis cannot be separated when we analyze the economic activities in cities, especially capital flows. Burt (2009) has highlighted that competition is a relationship issue other than the competition of economic players themselves. Specifically, it is argued that establishing linkages and resultant collaboration networks can help firms to obtain access to external knowledge and boost regional internal productivity as an outcome (Powell et al. 1996; Nicolini et al. 2003). Cooperation with external partners is tremendously meaningful for capability in product development, particularly in business markets (Håkansson and Snehota 1989; Pain 2008b). The introduction of social network analysis (SNA) complements the traditional focus on attributes and location factors; it emphasizes the relationships among actors instead of the actors themselves, and aims to incorporate topology to illustrate the structure of networks (Borgatti and Foster 2003).

Accompanying accelerating urbanization and integration in global markets, China has become both the second biggest economy and the biggest FDI host country in the world. Through a time series analysis, Tang et al. (2008) have asserted that FDI has a positive effect on Chinese economic growth and the domestic market, though DI has less impact on FDI. In addition, Ouyang and Fu (2012) have noted the inter-regional spillover of FDI from the highly urbanized eastern coastal areas of China to inland areas, meanwhile the capacity of inland cities to absorb spillover profits is mainly based on their manufacturing and mining capacity. This paper does not only follow a series of previous studies of location factors and 'crowd-in' or 'crowd-out' of FDI and DI, but it attempts to explain the agglomeration of FDI and DI, and the role of Chinese cities in investment networks. It thereby contributes to the literature tackling Chinese 'off the map' inter-city network research by articulating the development patterns and driving mechanisms of FDI and DI in China. Practically, the results could help urban actors to develop strategies that reflect a network vision and endogenous mechanisms. The first part of this paper introduces the development of FDI and DI in China in 2012, including size, geographical distribution, and sector composition. And it explores the relationship between cities and sectors, and compares the similarities of cities in approaching sectors. In the second part of the paper, cities and their investment are regarded as nodes and edges in networks respectively in order to carry out SNA to analyze the characteristics of investment networks. In the third part, a Negative Binomial Regression model is used to identify significant location factors that attract FDI and DI. Finally, the results are reflected upon and tentative policy recommendations are proposed.

14.3 Data and Methodology

Modelling data are derived from FDI markets,[2] ORBIS,[3] and China Data Online.[4] There were 948 Greenfield FDI projects flowing in mainland China (excluding Hong Kong, Macao, and Taiwan) in 2012 and 17508 DI contracts recorded in ORBIS in 2012. We set the cities where source companies' headquarters are located as source cities to simplify intricate headquarter-subsidiary structures, especially for large and fund management companies. However, by virtue of complicated ownerships and missing data, it is impossible to exclude the DI investments of firms which share ownership and are under the control of the same owners. Thus, in future empirical research it is worth delving further to understand the characteristics of investment connectivity, such as estimating the stability and structure of investment relationships, between headquarters and subsidiaries, between subsidiaries and subsidiaries, between independent firms, and between firms with shared ownership or board membership,. In the DI database, information on personal investments and the companies that have unclear headquarters and/or have ceased to operate is absent. The problem of missing addresses of source companies in the ORBIS database is dealt with by reference to information from Bloomberg and companies' official websites. As for the location factor process, raw numbers are logged and outliers are eliminated at the outset. Afterwards, variance inflation factor (VIF) and robust standard errors are adopted to control multicollinearity and skewness respectively. The cities included are provincial-level cities (Beijing, Shanghai, Tianjin, and Chongqing), vice-province cities, and prefecture-level cities according to Chinese administrative jurisdiction.

Netdraw is utilized to explore the relationship between sectors and destination cities by multidimensional scaling (MDS).[5] In the SNA analysis, since the FDI network is a two-mode network, and due to a lack of outward investment data for Chinese cities, only a non-metric MDS technique is adopted to display power and similarities of nodes by means of visualization. Therefore, the focus of the networking analysis is a DI one-mode network. Firstly, the values of vertices are dichotomized and diagonal values are not considered in order to comply with principles of SNA and pay more attention to relationships rather than the strength of ties and self-investment. The SNA analysis is divided into three parts to illuminate the general pattern and individual roles in the DI network: cohesion analysis,

[2]FDI Markets is a central bank of information on the globalization of business. The service tracks crossborder greenfield investment across all sectors and countries worldwide, with real-time monitoring of investment projects, capital investment and job creation.

[3]ORBIS is an online database by Bureau van Dijk that contains information on over 170 million companies worldwide, with an emphasis on private company information.

[4]China Data Online is an online database by China Data Center in University of Michigan that contains comprehensive statistical data of China.

[5]MDS is a means of visualizing the level of similarity of individual cases in a dataset. It refers to a set of related ordination techniques used in information visualization, in particular to display the information contained in a distance matrix.

centrality analysis, and subgrouping analysis. Cohesion analysis includes the calculation of density, transitivity, reciprocity, geodesic distance; in centrality analysis, degree, closeness and 'betweenness' are adopted[6]; while subgrouping analysis is a bottom-up approach (cliques partition) and top-down approach (blocks and cut points, factions partition, and 'core-periphery' pattern).[7]

Since FDI and DI data are only valid for 2012, cross sectional data only are available for modelling. A negative binomial regression model is used to explore the relationship between location factors and investments since FDI and DI are over-dispersed count outcome variables. The probability mass function of the negative binomial distribution is $f(k;r,p) \equiv \Pr(X=k) = \binom{k+r-1}{k} p^k (1-p)^r \mathit{for}\, k = 0, 1, 2, \ldots$ p is the probability of occurring investment; k is the number of investment projects; r is non-investment.

14.4 Results: Agglomerated Network Patterns and Significant Factors

1. **FDI Development and Sector Composition**

Since the introduction of open policy and economic reform, massive international capital has been flowing into China. Meanwhile, foreign capital is equipped with knowledge and production modes which can be transferred to indigenous firms to improve China's productivity and integration into global markets. Especially in the eastern areas of China, due to labour market advantages and geographic location advantages, coastal cities have formed relatively comprehensive industrial systems and account for the major share of national exports as a global manufacturing centre. Currently, China has been the largest FDI host economy in the world. This paper looks at the FDI distribution in 2012 when the world economy started to revive following the 2008 global economic crisis. Figures 14.1 and 14.2 show the top 64 FDI source cities (which invest more than 3 projects when the mean is 2.5) and the top 30 destination cities (which receive more than 5 projects when the mean is 4.6, excluding two outliers Beijing and Shanghai). It can be seen that most FDI source cities are agglomerated in North Western Europe, the US and Japan, whilst most top destination cities are agglomerated around the Chinese coastline, the

[6]Degree evaluates the amount of each node's direct linkages; closeness is each node's sum of geodesic distances with other nodes in the network; betweenness evaluates the extent of each node locating in others' geodesic distances.

[7]Core-periphery is an ideal pattern which divides row and column into two categories. In an ideal pattern, nodes in a core block connect with each other completely so its density is 1. Nodes in a periphery block have no connections with each other so its density is 0 while they may have some connections with core nodes.

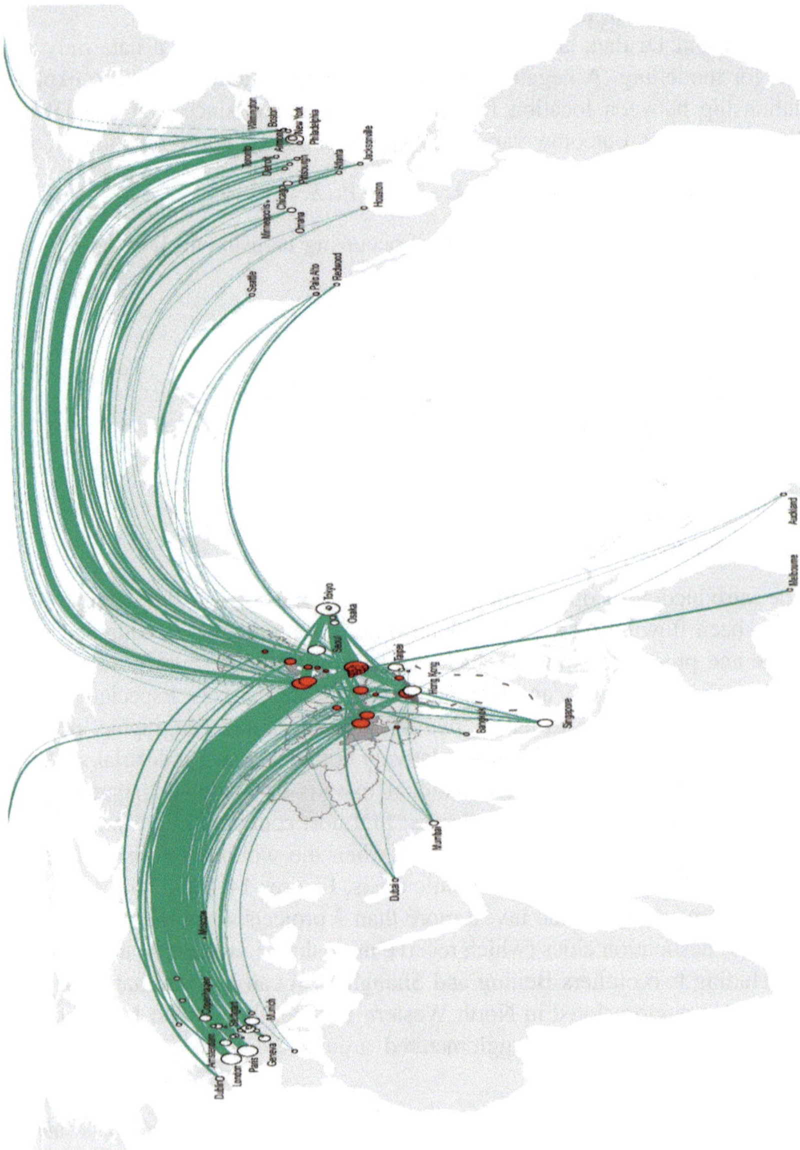

Fig. 14.1 Top FDI cities in the world (based on FDI markets data analysis)

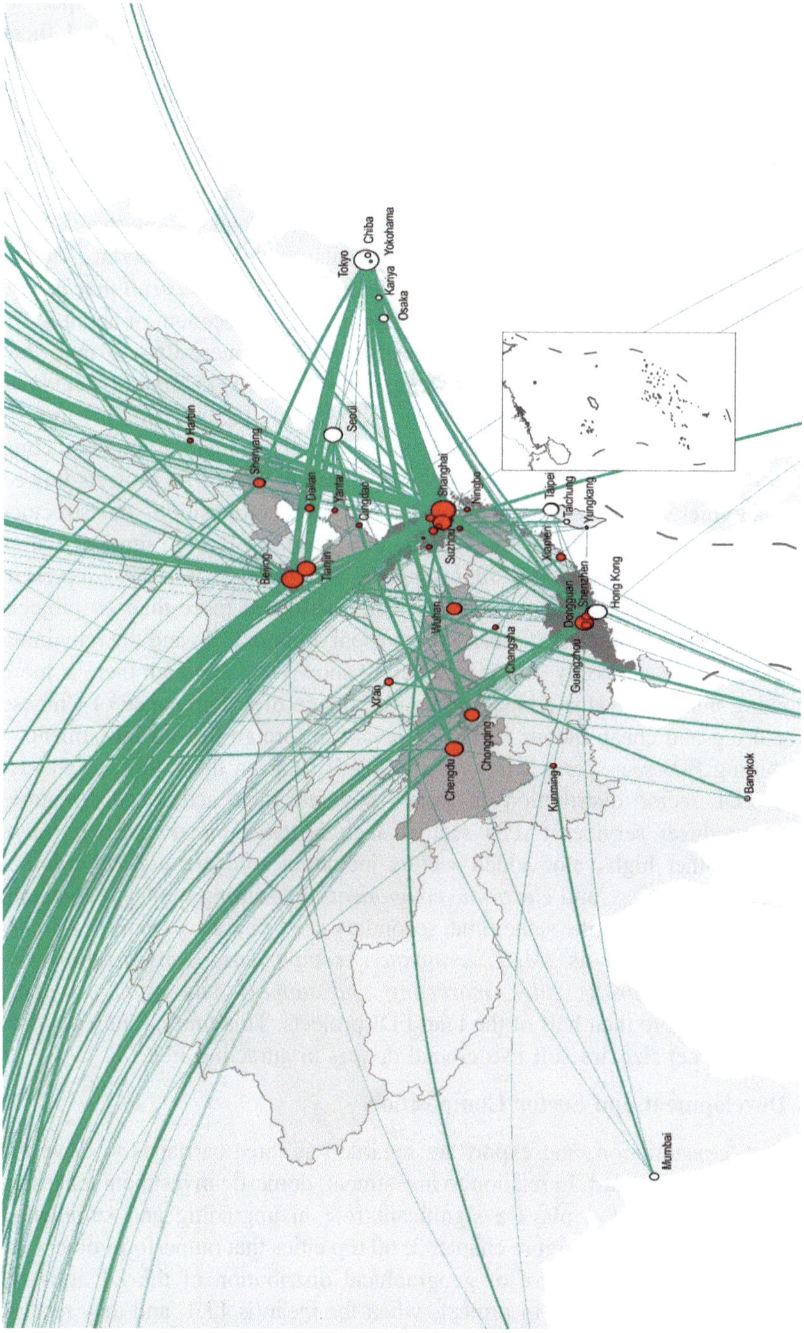

Fig. 14.2 Top FDI destination cities in China (based on FDI markets data analysis)

Bohai Economic Rim, the Yangtze River Delta and the Pearl River Delta. In addition to traditional western global cities, Seoul, Singapore, and Taipei, as emerging Asian global cities, are also listed in the top 10. On the other hand, there are few star cities located in other areas, especially western China. However, some cities in the western and central areas of China are rising, such as Chengdu, Chongqing, Wuhan, Xi'an, and Changsha.

Regarding FDI sector composition (Chart 14.1), there are 38 sectors that absorbed FDI in 2012. Nevertheless, an obvious gentrification pattern is displayed: the top three sectors (*business service*, *financial service*s and *automotive components*) take account of about 30% of all investments; another 12 important sectors that absorb more than 26 investments (the mean is 25) (from *industrial machinery, equipment and tools* (*IMET*) to *electronic components*) take account of about 55%; 23 sectors account for the remaining investments. It is interesting to note that foreign investors put the spotlight on *business services* (No. 1), *financial services* (No. 2) and other high value-added sectors (No. 6, No. 13, and No. 15) though heavy industry sectors and manufacturing sectors still play a major role in attracting FDI. With respect to FDI activities' structure (Chart 14.2), all FDI projects flowed into 17 activities. However, by contrast with sector composition, the structure shows considerable disparities between different activities: the top three activities (*manufacturing*, *sales, marketing and support*, and *business services*) represent 72% of all projects; other major activities which absorbed more than 10 projects (from *retail* to *maintenance and services*) represent around 25%; and the remaining seven activities attracted only 3%. It is therefore shown that although there is more FDI flowing into high value-added sectors, the image of a dominance of Chinese manufacturing and cheap labour remains relevant in foreign inward investment.

Combining FDI sector and activity status sheds light on the following characteristics: FDI sector distribution is more scattered than activity distribution; advanced producer services (APS) sectors such as *financial services*, *business services* and other high value-added sectors including *software and information technology* (*IT*) *services,* and *electronic components* are starting to play a dominant role in attracting FDI. At the same time, secondary sector industry sectors still play a significant role, such as *IMET*, *automotive components*, *transportation and chemicals*; *manufacturing*, *sales, marketing and support,* and *retail* activities, which make up more than half of the total FDI projects. This finding indicates that labour and market size are still two crucial drivers in attracting FDI.

2. **DI Development and Sector Composition**

Investment, consumption, and export are regarded as three carriages to drive the Chinese economy forward. In relation to investment, domestic investment makes up the major proportion and plays a significant role in upgrading and stimulating reproduction. As shown in Figure chapter 3, 60 top cities that outperform others are selected to illustrate the pattern of geographical distribution of the DI network. These cities invest more than 14 projects when the mean is 13.1, and they receive more than 48 projects when the mean is 47.8, excluding three outliers, Beijing,

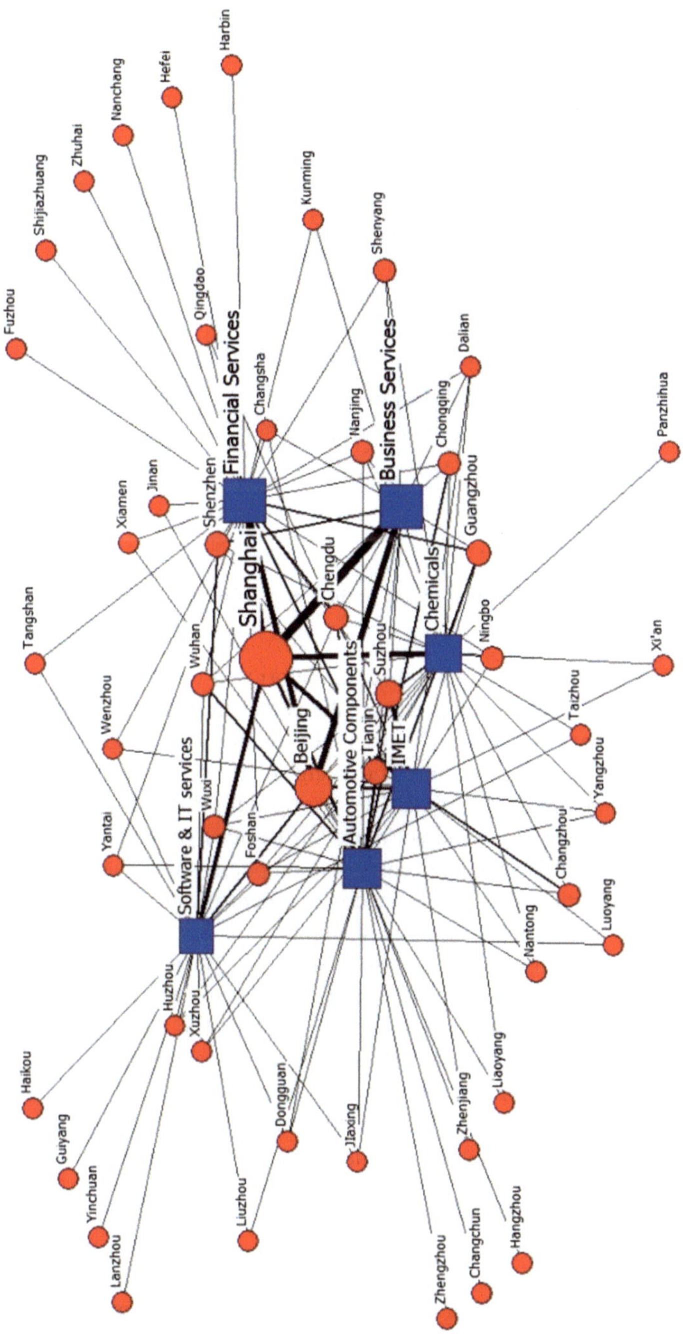

Chart. 14.1 FDI sector composition (based on FDI markets data analysis)

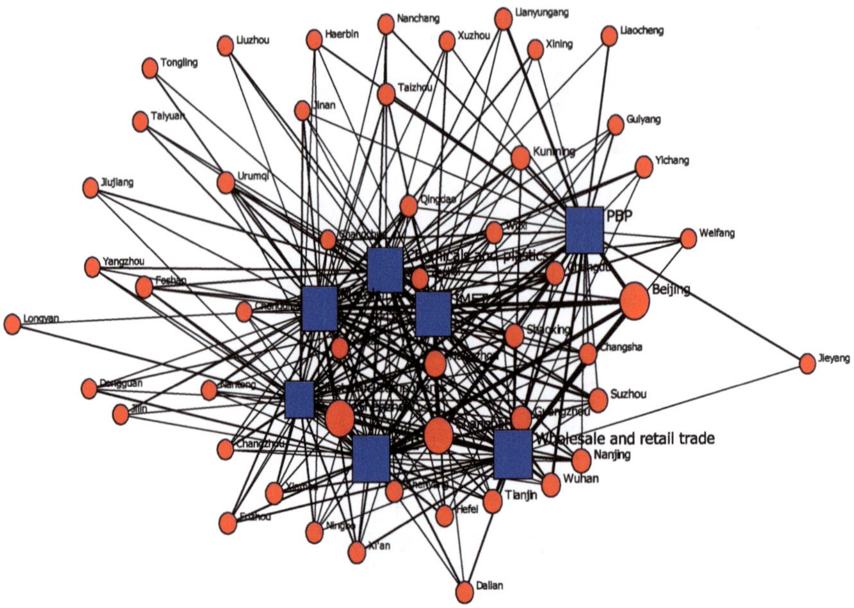

Chart. 14.2 FDI activity composition (based on FDI markets data analysis)

Shanghai and Shenzhen. It is shown that the majority of these top cities are located in the coastal areas, agglomerated around the Bohai Economic Rim, the Yangtze River Delta and the Pearl River Delta, similar to the FDI geography. However, besides these three city regions, the Mid-Yangtze River region and the northeast region are catching up. In addition, Chongqing and Chengdu, as two hubs in western China, are rising up to attract more DI. Besides geographical distribution, as shown in Chart 14.3, investment profile also pinpoints some characteristics of DI development in China: firstly, there is obvious gentrification in investment size between the top three cities (Beijing, Shanghai, and Shenzhen) and the others; secondly, only the top four cities (Beijing, Shanghai, Shenzhen, and Guangzhou) have an overwhelming capacity to outsource investment while the others depend heavily on inward investment (also illustrated in Fig. 14.3: the white rim indicates the scale of outsource while the red rim indicates the scale of inward investment); self-investment plays a fairly important part in many cities, especially in cities whose ranking is relatively low. The top 30 cities' investment graph is shown in Chart 14.4, which indicates a steeper disparity between the top three cities and the others.

By contrast, DI sector distribution is relatively even; the top three [Metals, Chemicals and Plastics, and Pharmaceutical and Biotechnological Products (PBP)] in 40 DI sectors make up about 24% in total (Chart 14.5); meanwhile Wholesale and Retail Trade, semiconductors and consumer electronics (SCE), and IMET also receive more than 1000 projects; the other 10 outstanding sectors that receive more

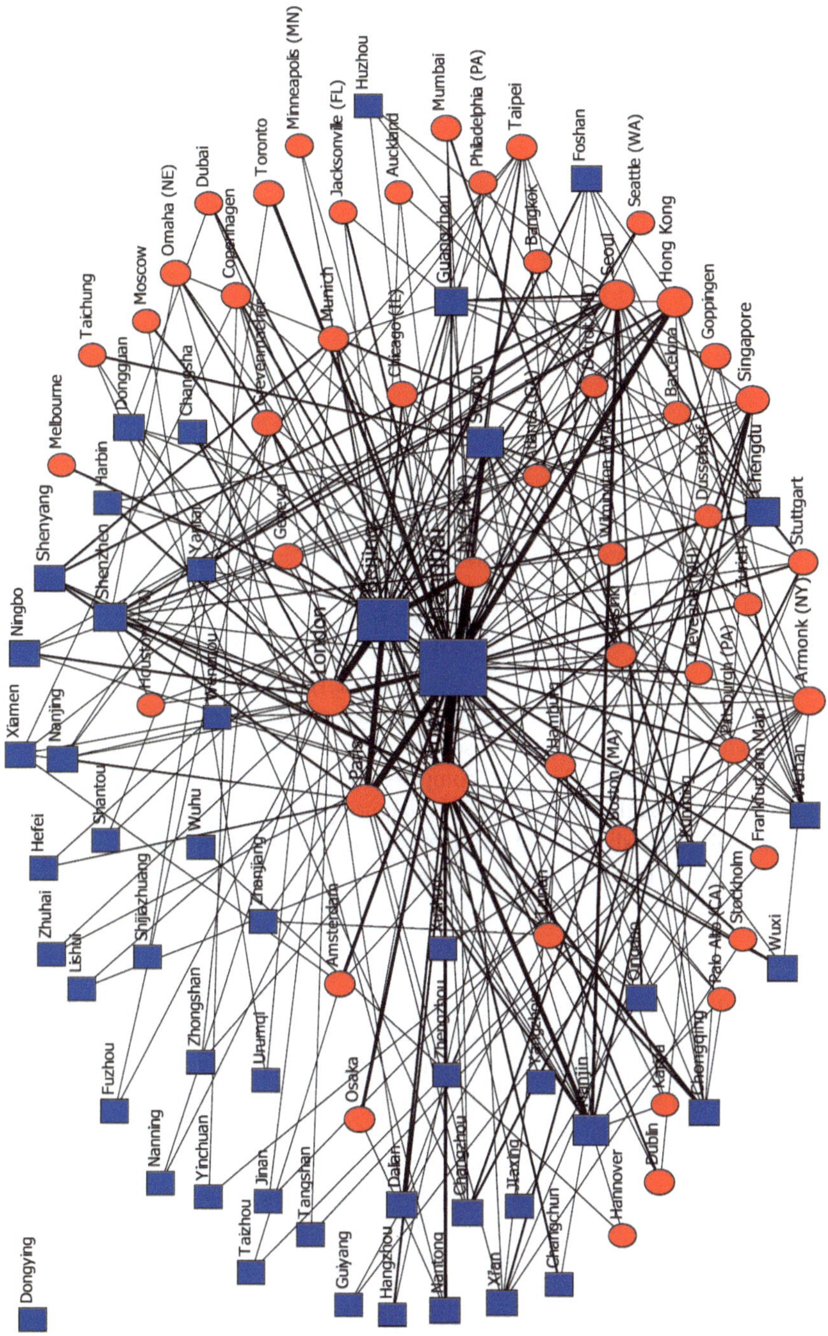

Chart. 14.3 11 DI profile of top 15 cities (based on ORBIS database analysis)

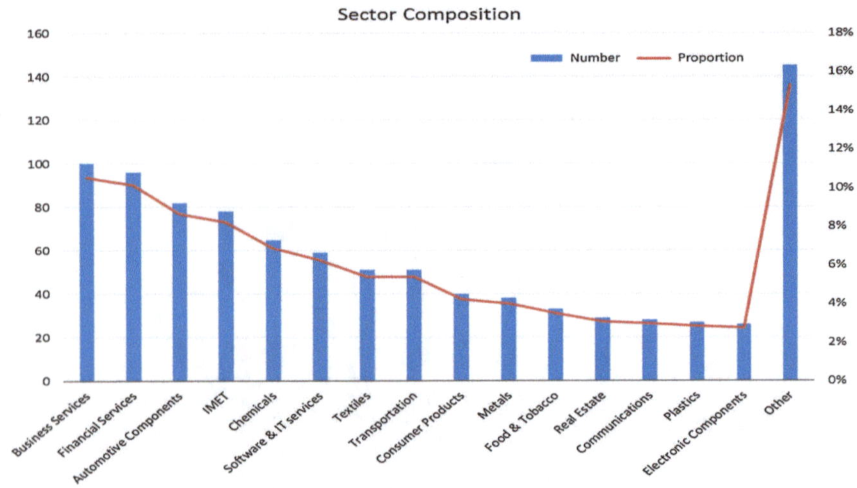

Fig. 14.3 Top 60 DI cities in China (based on ORBIS database analysis)

than 442 when the mean is 438, constitute around 36%. This finding denotes that natural resources, cheap labour and market size are still three dominant stimuli for DI since four out of six top sectors receive more than 1000 projects and eight out of 10 outstanding sectors strongly rely on those three factors. However, only a small number of high end sectors and APS sectors that have high added-value, lead (PBP ranks No. 4; SCE ranks No. 5; Financial service ranks No. 9; Real Estate ranks No. 13), while other value-added sectors such as Software and IT services, Aerospace, and Business Services comprise the remainder. In short, domestic investors are still mainly confined to manufacturing and heavy and light industries that are resource-intensive and labour intensive, revealing that China's DI ability is still not sustainable even though China has become the second largest economy in the world.

3. **Adjacency Between Cities and Sectors**

In this section, top destination cities and top sectors are selected to form a matrix so as to explore the adjacency between cities and sectors. Node size is determined by the number of projects. In order to uncover general patterns of relationships between cities and sectors, the top 50 FDI destination cities and the top six sectors (both taking over more than 50%) are dropped to form a matrix. Given the results of DI development and sector composition, the top 50 DI destination cities (more than the mean 48 projects) and the top seven sectors (both taking over more than 50%) are selected to form a matrix. As shown in Fig. 14.4, *IMET* and *automotive components* are proximate and share many destination cities. The other four sectors are relatively independent and surrounded by individual city groups. In addition, some top cities are proximate to not just one top sector, indicating that they have a more comprehensive and balanced FDI sector composition. For instance, Shanghai is

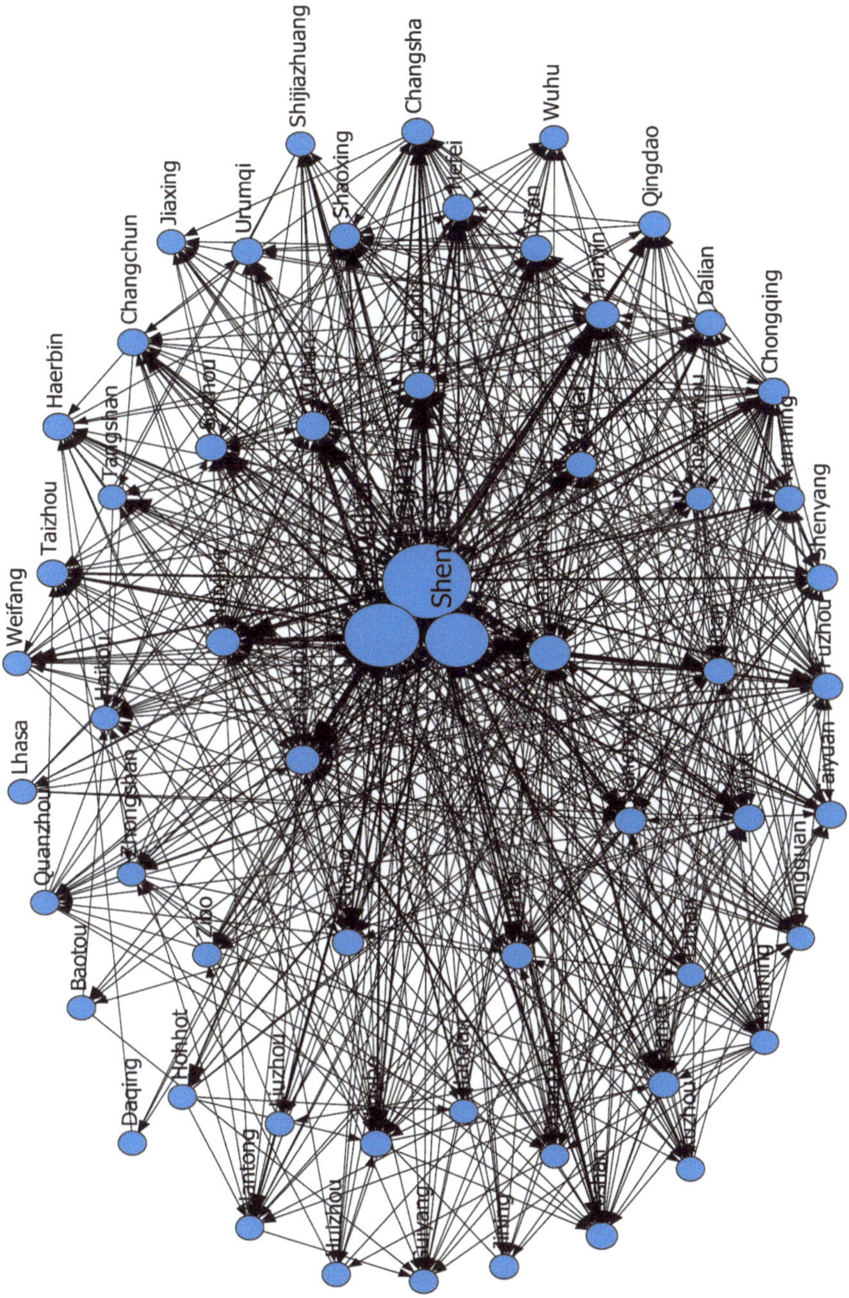

Chart. 14.4 Top 30 Chinese cities' investment profile

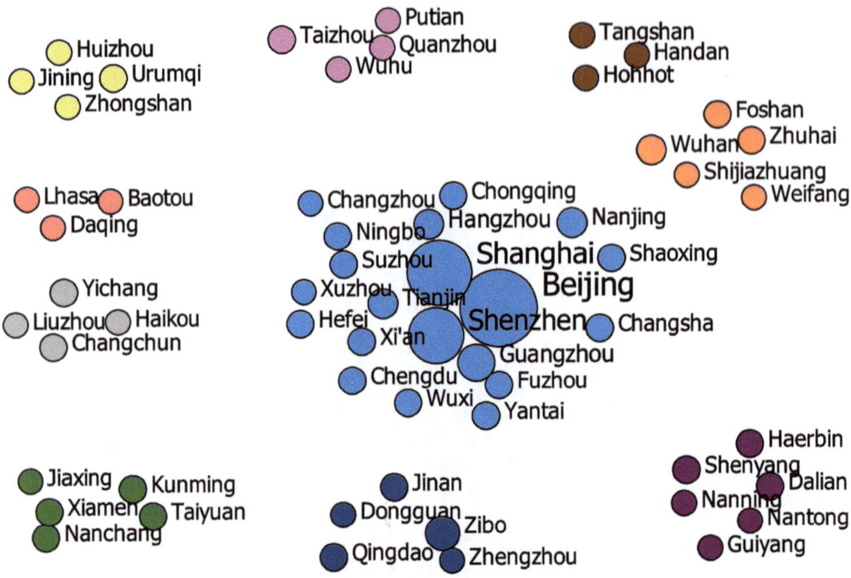

Chart. 14.5 DI sector composition (based on ORBIS database analysis)

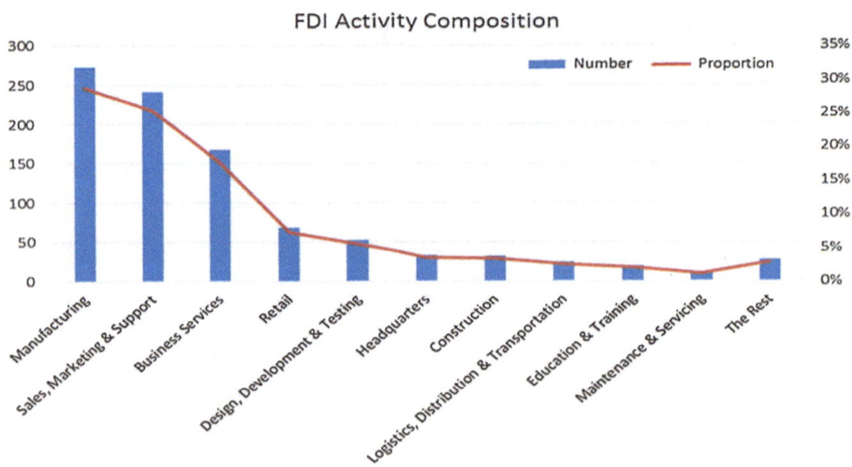

Fig. 14.4 FDI city-sector MDS layout (based on FDI markets data analysis)

located in the core position which is surrounded by all sectors; meanwhile, it is apparent that cities in the central area have very thick ties with sectors which express their power in this network. In addition, cities that are proximate to each other have a similar relationship with sectors. For instance, as shown in Table 14.1, major cities like Tianjin and Suzhou share a very similar investment profile, whilst

Table 14.1 FDI and DI MDS examples

Sector city	Automotive components	Business services	Chemicals	Financial services	IMET	Software and IT services
Suzhou	6	2	4	3	17	1
Tianjin	5	2	3	5	2	1
Huzhou	0	0	1	0	1	1
Xuzhou	0	0	1	0	1	1

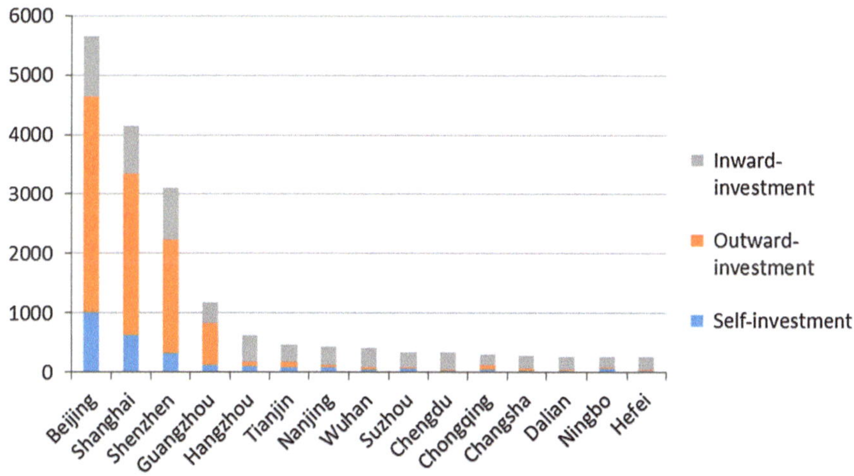

Fig. 14.5 DI city-sector MDS layout (based on ORBIS data analysis)

Huzhou and Xuzhou share the same relationships with sectors. The proximity between cities illuminates the degree of similarity of profile since they are receiving investments from similar sectors. Regarding DI, MDS layout shown in Fig. 14.5, *IMET, metals*, and *chemicals* and *plastics* share similar destination cities while the others are relatively independent; it is found that there are no cities locating in the center of sectors any more, which indicates that most cities have DI profile preferences; in addition, powerful nodes like Beijing, Shanghai, Shenzhen, and Guangzhou are more scattered rather than clustering in the FDI-sector network, which means that big cities have more dissimilarities in the DI-sector network (Table 14.1).

4. **Agglomerated Network Pattern and the Position of Cities in Networks**

Several SNA methods are generally carried out to unravel investment networks, mostly the DI one-mode network. For purposes of clean mapping and symmetry for the FDI network, the top 50 source cities and 50 destination cities are selected, based on the number of projects, to form a two-mode matrix; for the DI network,

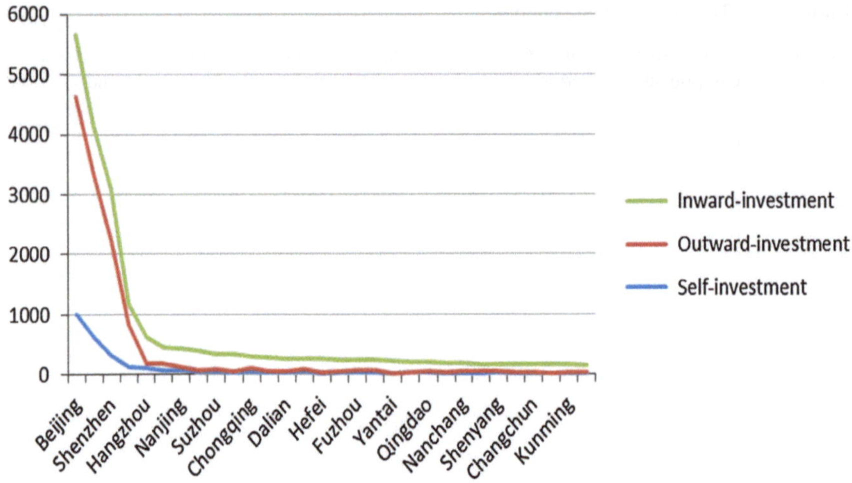

Fig. 14.6 FDI city–city MDS layout (based on FDI markets data analysis)

the top 60 cities are selected to form a one-mode matrix based on the number of projects. Regarding the FDI network, due to its two-mode attribute and lack of outward FDI, only the MDS technique is used to discern the similarities of cities. As shown in Fig. 14.6, cities are clustered in the centre and are similar to each other in investment profile with Tokyo, Paris, and London as source cities for example, and Beijing and Shanghai as destination cities. In contrast, the other two Chinese mega city formations Shenzhen and Guangzhou are very different from each other. It is interesting to note here that there are some special nodes that are located far from their groups, which indicates that they have relatively unique investment preferences like Huzhou, Foshan, and Chengdu as destination cities, and Houston as a source city.

In terms of DI network, city similarities evaluated by MDS are presented in Fig. 14.7 and all the results concerning its cohesion and centrality are shown in Table 14.2. It can be seen that Beijing, Shanghai, and Shenzhen are overlapped, which means that they have very similar roles in connecting other cities. In addition, cities in a central place have much denser ties with others. A good fit starts at only 60% in two dimensions, reaching 81% in nine dimensions, which means that more factors can explain the similarities of cities besides their adjacencies and closeness. Comparing the complete network, the DI network is a centralized network that has loose ties with peripheral cities in terms of degree centralization, density, and average degree. However, it is still a small world network since any city can get connected within two steps, and the longest geodesic distance is three. In terms of degree, this not only indicates the power of cities but it also highlights the different roles of cities. For instance, Guangzhou and Nanning are 'outsiders' as their out-degrees are much higher than their in-degrees. Chengdu is a 'sinker' as its in-degree is much higher than its out-degree. Ningbo is a 'communicator' since its

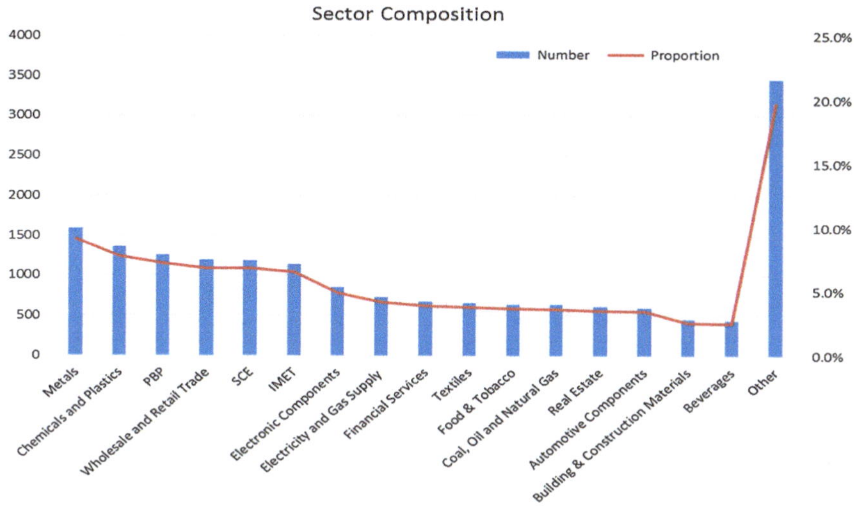

Fig. 14.7 DI city–city MDS layout (based on ORBIS data analysis)

in-degree equals its out-degree. In terms of closeness, Beijing, Shanghai and Shenzhen are overwhelmingly powerful in approaching all others. There are some interesting nodes that have a large gap between in-closeness and out-closeness, like Guangzhou and Nanning which can out-approach all others easily but are difficult to be approached by all others. With respect to betweenness this can explain the extent to which nodes can pass through the geodesic path between two cities. The cities with high values play a 'broker' role in this network. Among four cities, Guangzhou's value is relatively low, which indicates that its broker power is limited in a subgroup rather than the overall network like Beijing, Shanghai, and Shenzhen. It is surprising that Jinan performs much better than the same level of cities, illustrating its powerful broker role in the network. In addition, Nanning is special again in terms of its poor 'bridging' capacity. Transitivity is expressed by a clustering coefficient which calculates the density of its open neighborhood. Such cities have low values since their linked cities have less dense ties with each other. The cities with high value like Shaoxing, Dalian, Suzhou and Changsha have ego networks that are more cohesive and have high reachability. In terms of asymmetric value of overall network and individuals, the DI network is a reciprocate network, particularly in big cities.

Besides cohesion and centrality analysis, this paper also adopts several subgrouping methods to investigate whether there are some factions in the DI network. Firstly, clique[8] partition, as a bottom-up approach, is carried out. It is interesting to look at co-membership across cliques which can denote the capacity of cities in

[8]A clique is a sub-set of a network in which the actors are more closely and intensely tied to one another than they are to other members of the network.

Table 14.2 Cohesion and centrality of cities in the DI network (based on ORBIS data analysis)

Top 20 cities	In-degree	Out-degree	In-closeness	Out-closeness	Betweenness	Transitivity	Reciprocity
Beijing	41	58	75	58	653.348	0.226	0.707
Shanghai	39	55	77	61	501.621	0.239	0.679
Shenzhen	30	57	87	59	336.1	0.235	0.526
Guangzhou	19	53	100	63	132.086	0.254	0.309
Tianjin	20	35	98	81	131.653	0.324	0.41
Hangzhou	26	27	91	89	97.975	0.337	0.359
Chongqing	17	32	102	84	83.293	0.324	0.256
Nanjing	23	27	95	89	61.336	0.366	0.389
Ningbo	17	17	100	99	33.318	0.442	0.308
Changsha	15	19	104	97	19.319	0.454	0.214
Nanning	5	28	116	88	2.8	0.393	0.138
Fuzhou	15	23	105	93	39.166	0.375	0.267
Suzhou	21	16	97	100	38.367	0.472	0.48
Wuhan	23	15	93	101	55.878	0.376	0.226
Jinan	14	20	105	96	94.694	0.354	0.214
Chengdu	24	12	93	104	26.186	0.403	0.2
Dalian	13	16	105	100	18.14	0.496	0.318
Nanchang	15	15	103	101	40.171	0.413	0.364
Shaoxing	18	9	98	107	11.23	0.494	0.174
Changzhou	15	16	102	100	28.67	0.451	0.292

Density = 0.247, Av-degree = 14.322, degree centralization = 0.779, Av-distance = 1.807, diameter = 3, asymmetric = 0.274

bridging cliques. When clique size is set at five, 32 cliques are found. The rank of co-membership is as follows: Beijing (32), Shanghai (29), Shenzhen (16), Nanjing (11), Guangzhou (8), Tianjin (8), Hangzhou (7), Chongqing (3), Changsha (3), and Xi'an (2). When clique size is set at six, eight cliques are found. The rank of co-membership is as follows: Beijing (8), Shanghai (8), Shenzhen (8), Guangzhou (6), Nanjing (3), Hangzhou (3), Tianjin (3), and Chongqing (2). Secondly, through block and cut-point[9] analysis, no blocks and cut-points are found in the DI network. Lastly, this paper carries out factions partitions clustering analysis through Tabu optimization and core-periphery pattern in order to find closely connected subgroups in the DI network. Through iterating algorithms in each analysis, they have a similar result, indicating that instead of several cohesive subgroups existing in the DI network, there is one major relatively firm and cohesive subgroup (of core players). Figure 14.8 illustrates the combination of core-periphery pattern (fitness = 0.578) and 10 factions when poor fit and faction number are relatively low, iterating from five factions to 18 factions. The factions are distinguished in 10 colours; blue nodes are core players while other colours are peripheral players; the only difference is that Jinan, Wuhan and Nanchang are core players in core-periphery analysis but are dropped in the dark blue faction, whilst Xuzhou is a peripheral player but is dropped in the light blue faction (core faction). When geographical proximity is considered, the nodes that exist in the same factions in a network sense and are close to each other in a geographical sense can be explained as geographical factions or cohesive city regions: such as Huizhou and Zhongshan located in both the yellow faction and the Pearl River Delta, Putian and Quanzhou located in both the purple faction and Fujian Province, Tangshan and Handan located in both the brown faction and Hebei Province, Foshan and Zhuhai located in both the orange faction and the Pearl River Delta, Haerbin, Dalian and Shenyang located in both the dark purple faction and northeast region, Jinan, Qingdao and Zibo located in both the dark blue faction and Shandong Province, Shanghai, Hangzhou, Nanjing, Suzhou, Ningbo, Shaoxing, Changzhou, Wuxi and Xuzhou located in both the core faction and the Yangtze River Delta, Bejing and Tianjin located in both the core faction and the Bohai Rim Economic Zone, and Shenzhen and Guangzhou located in both the core faction and Pearl River Delta. Therefore, among the regions, the Yangtze River Delta is a more cohesive and balanced region since it has more core players agglomerated in its region while the other two are more loose and centralized urban regions.

5. **Identifying Significant Factors**

Besides SNA methods that analyze the relationships and roles of cities in networks, location factor analysis is the other fundamental dimension that can explain agglomerating FDI and DI in different cities. Next, Negative Binomial Model is considered to explore the relationship between location factors and investments. As

[9]Cutpoints are the nodes that divide a graph into two disconnected sub-graphs. The divisions into which cutpoints divide a graph are called blocks.

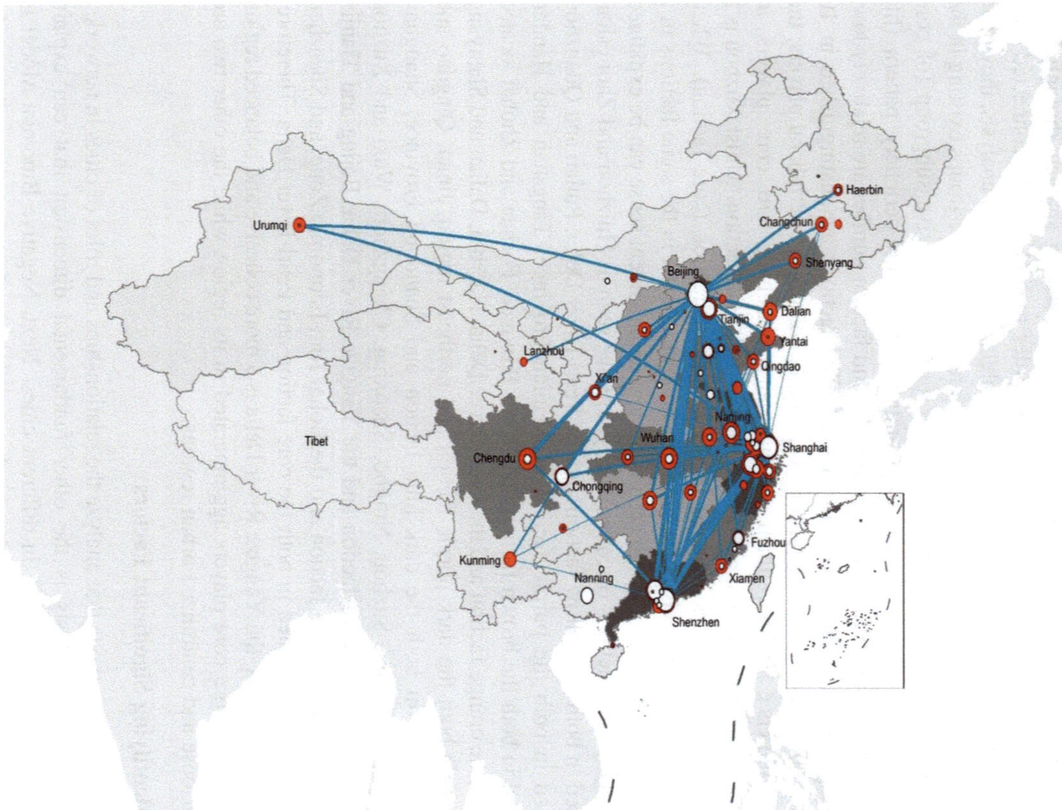

Fig. 14.8 Faction partitions in the top 60 cities (based on ORBIS data analysis)

shown in Table 14.3, 14 models have been used to identify factors significant to FDI. In M1, DI is identified as very significant to FDI when the model fit is 16.2%. In M3, population growth rate is negatively related to FDI while population density is positively related to FDI when the model fit is 13.1%. In M4, the average number and wages of employees are both very significant to FDI when the model fit is 20.7%. In M5, we can see that only employees in secondary sector industries, as opposed to primary and tertiary sector industries, is very significant to FDI when the model fit is 19.3%. In M6, banking and insurance is significant to FDI instead of (anticipated) scientific research. In M7, fixed assets investment is detected as a very significant contributor to FDI when the model fit is 24.7%. In M8, gross industrial output of foreign funded enterprises is identified as a very significant factor for FDI when the model fit is 14.4%. In M9, students enrolled in higher education institutions is very significant to FDI when the model fit is 11.4%. In M10, the area of paved roads is identified as a very significant factor to FDI when the model fit is 23%, meanwhile electricity consumption is also considered a significant factor to FDI regardless of its significance level of 5% since it is also identified in M12, M13, and M14. In M11, dummy variable 'inland/coast' location is very significant to FDI when the model fit is 3.8%. In M12, the average wages of employees (significance level of 1%), employees of secondary sector industry (significance level of 1%), gross industrial output of foreign funded enterprises (significance level of 5%), students enrolled in higher education institutions (significance level of 5%), and electricity consumption (significance level of 5%) are identified again in different significant levels when the model fit is 27.8%. In M14 with the dummy variable inland/coast, all the significant factors identified in M13 with the same significance level plus inland/coast (significance level of 5%), are significant to FDI when the model fit is 28.5%. In the overall final model with fixed effect of Province, gross industrial output of foreign enterprises and students enrolled in higher education institutions are identified as two very significant factors to FDI again, whilst population density and electricity consumption are identified at a 5% significance level.

Based on the results of these FDI models, it can be deduced that highly skilled labour, foreign capital accumulation (path dependence), and market size are three key drivers in FDI agglomeration. It is also found that DI has a crowd-in effect on FDI. Meanwhile, the strength of secondary sector industry, including manufacturing, light industry, and heavy industry, is still a basic condition attracting FDI, which may be explained by the fact that the majority of FDI still flows into manufacturing-related sectors that are labour intensive and resource intensive. It is interesting that financial services have become a significant factor in the agglomeration of FDI projects, suggesting that the capital source of FDI projects tends to be localized in supply. In addition, the size of fixed assets investment and paved roads not only indicates the dynamics of local economies but also demonstrates the local capacity of reproduction and developed infrastructure to some extent. Therefore, the dynamics of the local economy and a well-developed industrial base and urban infrastructure are critical to agglomerate FDI. With respect to geographic

Table 14.3 FDI model results

Model	(M1)	(M2)	(M3)	(M4)	(M5)	(M6)	(M7)	(M8)	(M9)	(M10)	(M11)	(M12)	(M13)	(M14)
Dependent variable	FDI	FDI	FDI	FDI	FDI	FDI	FDI	FDI	FDI	FDI	FDI	FDI	FDI	FDI
DI	0.0112***													
	(5.30)													
Land area		−0.426												
		(−1.10)												
Developed land area		0.00120												
		(0.84)												
Population growth rate			−0.0937**											
			(−3.04)											
Population density			0.00374***									0.000554	0.000422	0.00139*
			(7.48)									(1.62)	(1.39)	(2.50)
Av. Employees				0.0202***										
				(4.16)										
Average wage staff workers				0.000118***								0.0000897***	0.0000758***	0.0000232
				(6.35)								(4.07)	(3.70)	(0.54)
Employ. prim					−0.123									
					(−1.49)									
Emply. secon					0.0529***							0.0190**	0.0175**	−0.0141
					(8.04)							(3.13)	(2.71)	(−0.47)
Employ. tertia					−0.000128									
					(−0.03)									
Electric power gas water						−0.192								
						(−0.60)								
Banking and insurance						0.950**								
						(3.27)								
Scientific research						−0.150								
						(−0.90)								
						0.339								

(continued)

Table 14.3 (continued)

Model	(M1)	(M2)	(M3)	(M4)	(M5)	(M6)	(M7)	(M8)	(M9)	(M10)	(M11)	(M12)	(M13)	(M14)
Environmental management														
						(0.92)								
Fixed assets investment							0.00143***							
							(7.01)							
Sigcontr							0.000759*					−0.000976	−0.000903*	0.00173
							(2.18)					(−1.79)	(−2.17)	(1.04)
Loans							0.0000695							
							(0.87)							
GIO. HK								0.0000718						
								(0.24)						
GIO. Foreign								0.00135***				0.000227*	0.000206*	0.00554***
								(4.53)				(2.36)	(2.24)	(5.32)
Student. HE									0.0874***			0.0170*	0.0233*	0.101***
									(5.25)			(2.25)	(2.53)	(3.53)
Student. SE									0.00884					
									(0.98)					
Area paved roads										0.000618***		0.0000615	0.0000743	0.000242
										(8.47)		(0.62)	(0.78)	(0.57)
Elec. consump										0.00167*		0.000715*	0.000635*	−0.00273*
										(2.44)		(2.24)	(2.23)	(−2.25)
Post.tele										0.000142				
										(0.68)				
Indcoast (dummy)											2.043***		0.533*	
											(4.01)		(2.32)	
Model Specification	Negative Binomial	Negative Binomial	Negative Binomial	Negative Binomial	Negative Binomial	Negative Binomial	Negative Binomial	Negative Binomial	Negative Binomial	Negative Binomial	Negative Binomial	Negative Binomial	Negative Binomial	Province Fixed
McFadden R2	0.162	0.006	0.131	0.207	0.193	0.161	0.247	0.144	0.114	0.23	0.038	0.278	0.285	
R2														0.99
Constant	−0.828***	1.712***	−1.112**	−3.863***	−1.125***	−1.383***	−1.345***	−0.448*	−0.700**	−1.763***	0.0762	−3.760***	−3.620***	−3.768**
	(−4.06)	(3.81)	(−3.28)	(−8.50)	(−5.54)	(−5.13)	(−8.09)	(−2.32)	(−2.70)	(−7.01)	(0.24)	(−6.58)	(−6.59)	(−2.92)
lnalpha constant	0.906***	2.085***	1.138***	0.470*	0.476*	0.904***	−0.167	0.994***	1.265***	0.251	1.827***	−0.379	−0.421	
	(4.46)	(11.83)	(7.39)	(2.31)	(2.07)	(4.91)	(−0.75)	(4.81)	(6.55)	(0.97)	(11.66)	(−1.45)	(−1.82)	
N	234	185	234	234	233	234	224	230	230	231	234	221	221	221

Encode average number of employees (Av. Employees), employees primary industry (Employ. prim), employees secondary industry (Emply. secon), employees tertiary industry (Employ. tertia), newly signed contracts by foreign capital (Sigcontr), gross ind. output HK funded firms (GIO. HK), Gross ind. output foreign funded firms (GIO. Foreign), student enrolment higher education (Student. HE), student enrolment secondary education (Student. SE), electricity consumption Per capita (Elec. consump), post and telecommunication offices (Post. tele), inland or coastal cities, coastal = 1, (Indcoast) location considered with reference to the location of FDI projects, a coastal advantage is still evident.

Table 14.4 illustrates DI significant location factors by means of the same method. The results show that the DI and FDI models share some significant factors, including population density, average number and wages of employees, employees in secondary sector industry, banking and insurance, fixed assets investment, students enrolled in higher education institutions, and the area of paved roads, on the same significance level but with less model fit. In contrast to FDI heavy reliance on DI, DI is less reliant on FDI at a 5% significance level. Meanwhile in M2, it is interesting that land area is identified as a very significant factor, but negatively. In addition, a really surprising result is that employees in primary industry, is seen as a very significant factor negatively in M5, M12, and M13. Like gross output of foreign enterprises' contribution to FDI, gross output of domestic enterprises attracts DI at a very significant level. In addition, some factors that were not identified in the FDI models are recognized as significant factors in the DI models, including loans (on a 1% significance level) and gross industrial output of HK enterprises (on a 5% significance level). In addition, electricity consumption is identified as a more significant factor in M12 and M13 when the model fits are 11.6 and 11.7% respectively, compared to its significance in the FDI models.

With respect to lower model fits, the significant factors for DI are more intricate and easily affected by non-economic conditions. Generally speaking, it is concluded that labour force, market size, industrial base and capital accumulation, and institutional context, are significant to agglomerate DI. Significant banking and loans factors not only demonstrate the critical role of financial services in agglomerating DI but also indicate the importance of institutional context due to the regulatory control over banking and the financial system of governments. In addition, it is shown that industrial structure is more significant for DI than for FDI, because apart from the significance of secondary sector industry, agriculture plays a very significant negative role in DI. Combining significant land area may indicate that the development of China is still affected by a shortage of urban land supply or urban expansion, and that the dominance of traditional agriculture is a drag on the urbanization of China that is needed to facilitate a transformation to modern agriculture and liberate an increased labour supply to cities. Another interesting finding is that Hong Kong's closer relationship with DI instead of FDI, suggests that Hong Kong's capital has a greater agglomeration effect on DI.

14.5 Conclusions and Recommendations

During economic transition, China is confronted with the danger of a hard landing due to its shrinking FDI and present global economic malaise. China has slowed down its astonishing growth and begun to take steps to liberalize interest rates and reduce its dependency on exports. Since cities are equipped with abundant human

Table 14.4 DI model results

Model	(M1)	(M2)	(M3)	(M4)	(M5)	(M6)	(M7)	(M8)	(M9)	(M10)	(M11)	(M12)	(M13)	(M14)
Dependent variable	DI	DI	DI	DI	DI	DI	DI	DI	DI	DI	DI	DI	DI	DI
FDI	0.0669*													
	(2.21)													
Land area		−0.138***												
		(−4.46)												
Developed land area		0.0000818												
		(0.24)												
Population growth rate			−0.0459											
			(−1.75)											
Population density			0.00221***									0.0000126	0.0000864	
			(5.70)									(0.07)	(0.45)	
Av. Employees				0.0129***										
				(4.08)										
Average wage staff workers				0.0000819***								0.0000231	0.0000249	
				(5.84)								(1.53)	(1.66)	
Employ. Prim					−0.157***							−0.123***	−0.121***	−0.431
					(−7.03)							(−4.65)	(−4.60)	(−0.52)
Emply. secon					0.0393***							0.00990*	0.00970*	
					(6.02)							(2.07)	(2.13)	
Employ. tertia					0.00260									
					(0.39)									
Electric power gas water						0.0817								
						(0.44)								
Banking and insurance						0.462***						−0.0213	−0.0192	
						(3.76)						(−0.60)	(−0.51)	
Scientific research						−0.0709								
						(−0.47)								
Environmental management						0.388								

(continued)

Table 14.4 (continued)

Model	(M1)	(M2)	(M3)	(M4)	(M5)	(M6)	(M7)	(M8)	(M9)	(M10)	(M11)	(M12)	(M13)	(M14)
						(1.43)								
Fixed assets investment							0.000691***							
							(4.04)							
Loans							0.000272**							
							(2.87)							
GIO. HK								0.000271*						
								(2.45)						
GIO. domestic								0.000557***				0.000168**	0.000203**	
								(9.58)				(3.25)	(2.96)	
Student. HE									0.0617***			0.0306***	0.0290***	3.162***
									(7.07)			(4.34)	(4.09)	(3.38)
Student. SE									0.00352					
									(0.55)					
Area paved roads										0.000470***		−0.00000407	−0.0000219	
										(7.90)		(−0.04)	(−0.23)	
Elec. consump										0.00117*		0.000792***	0.000875**	0.208
										(2.35)		(3.48)	(3.13)	(1.86)
Post. tele										−0.0000104				
										(−0.05)				
Indcoast (dummy)											1.121***		−0.213	
											(4.02)		(−1.31)	
Model Specification	Negative Binomial	Negative Binomial	Negative Binomial	Negative Binomial	Negative Binomial	Negative Binomial	Negative Binomial	Negative Binomial	Negative Binomial	Negative Binomial	Negative Binomial	Negative Binomial	Negative Binomial	Province Fixed
McFadden R2	0.45	0.033	0.043	0.081	0.096	0.074	0.094	0.078	0.057	0.094	0.015	0.116	0.117	
R2														0.889
Constant	3.610***	4.510***	3.122***	1.149***	2.853***	2.665***	2.851***	2.850***	3.198***	2.509***	3.680***	2.113***	2.077***	−32.28
	(25.48)	(17.22)	(11.55)	(3.65)	(25.77)	(17.27)	(25.71)	(25.78)	(18.97)	(16.26)	(27.32)	(5.88)	(5.85)	(−1.06)
lnalpha constant	0.397***	0.760***	0.414***	0.0893	−0.0482	0.151	−0.0590	0.105	0.284	−0.0309	0.633***	−0.271**	−0.280**	
	(4.16)	(6.47)	(5.17)	(1.10)	(−0.54)	(1.73)	(−0.61)	(1.30)	(1.91)	(−0.33)	(7.75)	(−2.79)	(−2.84)	
N	234	185	234	234	233	234	224	230	230	231	234	227	227	229

Encode gross industrial output of domestic funded firms (GIO. domestic)

capital, financial capital, instructional capital and social capital, they are the main areas where the nation's industrial base is upgraded and where the circulation of resources is happening. Both in FDI and DI networks, outperforming cities display an agglomerated pattern in a geographical sense, just as top foreign cities show coastal metropolitan agglomeration in the US, North Western Europe, and the West Pacific, China has been experiencing high domestic agglomeration in coastal areas.

1. **Upgrade the Value Chain and Keep Eyes on Significant Location Factors**

According to FDI sector composition, FDI projects are highly clustered in tertiary APS sectors although secondary sector industries still have an important role. However, APS and other sectors look to highly skilled labour and market size as key investment factors. In DI sectors, manufacturing and heavy and light industries that are traditionally dependent on natural resources, cheap labour and market size, remain dominant. In terms of the relationship between cities and sectors, FDI-large cities are more centralized and balanced while DI-large cities have more preferences in investment profile. In short, low valued-added activities and labour intensive sectors are still mainstream in agglomerating Chinese investment. Evidence from FDI Markets suggests that nowadays, some international investors are retreating from China's markets since its low-cost labour advantage is weakening. In consequence, if China wishes to maintain its global position in attracting FDI, it has to expand and develop its knowledge-based sectors such as APS and high end activities that create major added value and stimulate industrial innovation. Hence, local social knowledge management and the development of a regional mindset that encourages knowledge sharing and collaborative learning are likely to be of key importance in stimulating regional and national development (see Asheim and Isaksen 2002; Gertler and Wolfe 2004).

In addition to the role of APS and high end activities in upgrading value chains, several other significant factors should be considered in FDI and DI agglomeration. Regarding the model results, industrial base and infrastructure, capital accumulation, market size, and financial support are identified generally as significant location factors agglomerating FDI and DI. Therefore, cities are encouraged to improve their reproduction capacity and to cooperate with scientific institutions, for example by establishing industrial parks and research centres. Given the effect of capital accumulation, local governments also need to put forward incentivization policies for foreign investors such as the promotion of enhanced business atmosphere, land policy, tax policy and infrastructure. Thirdly, local governments should reform the Household Registration System (HRS) and offer fair social services to city outsiders to improve their sense of belonging and so facilitate labour mobility and expand the market size. Meanwhile, the education system should be diversified. For instance, local governments can encourage the building of private schools, higher education and training establishments that would promote a qualified labour force. Lastly, financial services are more and more important in driving the local economy, so China should loosen the control of the financial system and improve its openness in order to promote specialized services, especially for medium and small enterprises. In addition, agricultural modernization that could be facilitated by the agglomeration of advanced services to keep the Chinese economy healthy and sustainable cannot be ignored.

2. **A Need to Recognize City Positions and Make Networking Strategies**

Recognition of Chinese city positions and the identification of sub-groups in networks are critical to efficient actions to improve opportunities and overcome constraints. In terms of similarities of investment profile, city administrations need to pay attention to other cities which share a similar investment profile because they are striving for investment from the same sources. In order to improve China's social and economic sustainability, cities can establish alliances with complementary partners that can integrate resources and circulate information efficiently. The cultivation of trust and creativity are essential preconditions for successful city alliances. Regarding the centrality analysis, city nodes play different roles in the network such as sinker, outsider, communicator, and broker. There are no absolute advantages or disadvantages implicit in these diverse roles. Nevertheless, the nodes with high degrees are more inter-linked with other highly inter-linked cities. Meanwhile, brokerage is regarded as one kind of social capital because the broker role establishes relationships between two groups that have heterogeneity and opportunity and it provides access to valuable information and translation fees by bridging isolated nodes (Burt 2009). Therefore, cities that are extremely outbalanced and poor in bridging others tend to fall apart and lose network connectivity. They should build more effective ties with significant nodes and cultivate a capacity to build bridges for others. Some scholars criticize the overemphasis on structural holes. For instance, in technical collaboration networks, increasing structural holes are contended to reduce innovation output (Ahuja 2000). The optimal structure of networks is contingent on the objectives and content of relationships which still need further empirical research. But if core cities are to maintain their core roles in the long run, they must retain their attractiveness to elites and promote cooperation with other core cities so as to consolidate their network position. Meanwhile, they also need to develop their periphery branches and consolidate their role in ego networks. It is argued that shared information is happening indigenously whilst membership and association fees are applied to keep privilege in the local network (Carroll 2007). The spill-over effect is not obvious in high-end industries whilst information circulation happens indigenously and spontaneously (Nicolini 2003). Hence, in terms of cities in the periphery, they should build more linkages with cities in the core to get involved in the highly connected group of cities. In addition, they should cooperate with each other so as to form a new cohesive city network group. Focusing on city network functional complementarities at a city region level would stimulate Taylor and Pain's Jacobsean economic expansion Process A whereby smaller towns and cities surrounding significant networked nodes for inward investment are enveloped and upgraded in highly internally and externally interconnected global mega-city regions.

References

Agosin, M.R., and R. Machado. 2007. Openness and the international allocation of foreign direct investment. *The Journal of Development Studies* 43 (7): 1234–1247.

Ahuja, G. 2000. Collaboration networks, structural holes, and innovation: A longitudinal study. *Administrative Science Quarterly* 45 (3): 425–455.

Alfaro, L., A. Chandab, and S. Kalemli-Ozcan. 2004. FDI and economic growth: The role of local financial markets. *Journal of International Economics* 64 (1): 89–112.

Anderson, D. 1990. Investment and economic growth. *World Development* 18 (8): 1057–1079.

Asheim, B.T., and A. Isaksen. 2002. Regional innovation systems: the integration of local 'sticky' and global 'ubiquitous' knowledge. *The Journal of Technology Transfer* 27 (1): 77–86.

Barrell, R., and N. Pain. 1997. Foreign direct investment, technological change, and economic growth within Europe. *The Economic Journal* 107 (445): 1770–1786.

Barro, R.J. 1989. Economic growth in a cross section of countries. *National Bureau of Economic Research* 3120.

Berry, B.J. 1964. Cities as systems within systems of cities. *Papers in Regional Science* 13 (1): 147–163.

Blomstrom, M., Globerman, S. and A. Kokko. 1999. The determinants of host country spillovers from foreign direct investment: Review and synthesis of the literature. No. 502 SSE/EFI Working Paper Series in Economics and Finance, Stockholm School of Economics.

Blomström, M., and F. Sjöholm. 1999. Technology transfer and spillovers: Does local participation with multinationals matter? *European Economic Review* 43 (4): 915–923.

Borensztein, E., J. De Gregorio, and J.W. Lee. 1998. How does foreign direct investment affect economic growth? *Journal of International Economics* 45 (1): 115–135.

Borgatti, S.P., and P.C. Foster. 2003. The network paradigm in organizational research: A review and typology. *Journal of Management* 29 (6): 991–1013.

Boschma, R. 2004. Competitiveness of regions from an evolutionary perspective. *Regional Studies* 38 (9): 1001–1014.

Burt, R.S. 2009. *Structural holes: The social structure of competition*. Cambridge: Harvard University Press.

Cairncross, F. 2001. *The death of distance: How the communications revolution is changing our lives*. Boston: Harvard Business Press.

Capello, R. 2000. The city network paradigm: Measuring urban network externalities. *Urban Studies* 37 (11): 1925–1945.

Carroll, W.K. 2007. Global cities in the global corporate network. *Environment and Planning A* 39 (10): 2297.

Castells, M. 1996. *The rise of the network society: The information age: Economy, society and culture*, vol. I. Malden: Blackwell.

Caves, R.E. 1971. International corporations: The industrial economics of foreign investment. *Economica* 38: 1–27.

De Mello, L.R. 1999. Foreign direct investment-led growth: Evidence from time series and panel data. *Oxford Economic Papers* 51 (1): 133–151.

Deok-Ki Kim, D., and J.-S. Seo. 2003. Does FDI inflow crowd out domestic investment in Korea? *Journal of Economic Studies* 30 (6): 605–622.

Domar, E.D. 1946. Capital expansion, rate of growth, and employment. *Econometrica, Journal of the Econometric Society*: 137–147.

Dunning, J.H. 1981. Explaining the international direct investment position of countries: Towards a dynamic or developmental approach. *Weltwirtschaftliches Archiv* 117 (1): 30–64.

Ellison, G., and E.L. Glaeser. 1999. The geographic concentration of industry: Does natural advantage explain agglomeration? *American Economic Review*: 311–316.

Fingleton, B. 1999. Estimates of time to economic convergence: An analysis of regions of the European Union. *International Regional Science Review* 22 (1): 5–34.

Florida, R. 2002. The economic geography of talent. *Annals of the Association of American Geographers* 92 (4): 743–755.

Glaeser, E.L. 2010. *Agglomeration economics*. Chicago: University of Chicago Press.

Glass, A.J., and K. Saggi. 1998. International technology transfer and the technology gap. *Journal of Development Economics* 55 (2): 369–398.

Gottman, J. 1961. *Megalopolis: The urbanization of the Northeastern Seaboard of the United States*. Cambridge: The MIT Press.

Håkansson, H., and I. Snehota. 1989. No business is an island: The network concept of business strategy. *Scandinavian Journal of Management* 5 (3): 187–200.

Hall, P., and K. Pain (eds.). 2006. *The polycentric metropolis: Learning from mega-city regions in Europe*. London: Earthscan.

Helsley, R.W., and W.C. Strange. 1990. Matching and agglomeration economies in a system of cities. *Regional Science and Urban Economics* 20 (2): 189–212.

Henderson, J.V. 1991. *Urban development: Theory, fact, and illusion*. Oxford: Oxford University Press. https://ideas.repec.org/b/oxp/obooks/9780195069020.html.

Henderson, J.V. 2003. Marshall's scale economies. *Journal of Urban Economics* 53 (1): 1–28.

Isard, W. 1956. *Location and space-economy: A general theory relating to industrial location, market areas, land use, trade, and urban structure*. The Technology Press of Massachusetts Institute of Technology and Wiley.http://trid.trb.org/view.aspx?id=131509.

Jacobs, J. 1969. *The economy of cities*. New York: Random House.

Jacobs, J. 1984. *Cities and the wealth of nations*. New York: Random House.

Jacobs, W., H. Koster, and P. Hall. 2011. The location and global network structure of maritime advanced producer services. *Urban Studies* 48 (13): 2749–2769.

Johansson, B. and J.M. Quigley. 2004. Agglomeration and networks in spatial economies. In *Fifty years of regional science*, ed. Florax, R. and Plane, D.A., 165–176. Berlin: Springer.

Kim, S. 1995. Expansion of markets and the geographic distribution of economic activities: The trends in US regional manufacturing structure, 1860–1987. *The Quarterly Journal of Economics*: 881–908.

Krugman, P.R. 1997. *Development, geography, and economic theory*. Cambridge: The MIT Press.

Liu, Z. 2008. Foreign direct investment and technology spillovers: Theory and evidence. *Journal of Development Economics* 85 (1): 176–193.

Mahroum, S., R. Huggins, N. Clayton, K. Pain, and P.J. Taylor. 2008. *Innovation by adoption: Measuring and mapping absorptive capacity in UK nations and regions*. National Endowment for Science, Technology and the Arts (NESTA). http://www.nesta.org.uk/assets/Uploads/pdf/ResearchReport/innovation_by_adoption_report_NESTA.pdf.

Marshall, A. 1920. *Principles of economics: An introductory volume*. Macmillan and Co. Ltd. http://www.econlib.org/library/Marshall/marP.html.

Nicolini, D., S. Gherardi, and D. Yanow. 2003. *Knowing in organizations: A practice-based approach*. Armonk: ME Sharpe.

Noorzoy, M. 1979. Flows of direct investment and their effects on investment in Canada. *Economics Letters* 2 (3): 257–261.

O'Brien, R. 1992. *Global financial integration: The end of geography*. London: Royal Institute of International Affairs.

Ouyang, P., and S. Fu. 2012. Economic growth, local industrial development and inter-regional spillovers from foreign direct investment: Evidence from China. *China Economic Review* 23 (2): 445–460.

Pain, K. 2008a. Examining core-periphery relationships in a global mega-city region—The case of London and South East England. *Regional Studies* 42 (8): 1161–1172.

Pain, K. 2008b. Spaces of practice in advanced business services: Rethinking London-Frankfurt relations. *Environment and Planning D Society and Space* 26 (2): 264.

Pain, K., and G. Van Hamme (eds.). 2014. *Changing urban and regional relations in a globalizing world: Europe as a global macro-region*. Cheltenham: Edward Elgar.

Porter, M.E. 1990. The competitive advantage of nations. *Harvard Business Review* 68 (2): 73–93.

Powell, W.W., K.W. Koput, and L. Smith-Doerr. 1996. Interorganizational collaboration and the locus of innovation: Networks of learning in biotechnology. *Administrative Science Quarterly*: 116–145.

Romer, P.M. 1986. Increasing returns and long-run growth. *The Journal of Political Economy*: 1002–1037.

Scott, A. (ed.). 2001. *Global city regions*. Oxford: Oxford University Press.

Tang, S., E.A. Selvanathan, and S. Selvanathan. 2008. Foreign direct investment, domestic investment and economic growth in China: A time series analysis. *The World Economy* 31 (10): 1292–1309.

Taylor, P.J. 2012. Extraordinary cities: Early 'city-ness' and the origins of agriculture and states. *International Journal of Urban and Regional Research* 36 (3): 415–447.

Taylor, P.J., and K. Pain. 2007. Polycentric mega-city regions: Exploratory research from Western Europe. In *The Healdsburg research seminar on megaregions*, ed. Todorovich, P., 59–67. Lincoln Institute of Land Policy and Regional Plan Association. http://library.rpa.org/pdf/2050-The-Healdsburg-Research-Seminar-on-Megaregions-2007.pdf.

Turok, I. 2004. Cities, regions and competitiveness. *Regional Studies* 38 (9): 1069–1083.

United Nations. 2013. *World population prospects: The 2012 revision.* Population Division New York, Department of Economic and Social Affairs, United Nations.

Van Oort, F.G. 2007. Spatial and sectoral composition effects of agglomeration economies in the Netherlands. *Papers in Regional Science* 86 (1): 5–30.

Wall, R.S., and G. Van der Knaap. 2011. Sectoral differentiation and network structure within contemporary worldwide corporate networks. *Economic Geography* 87 (3): 267–308.

Wolfe, D.A., and M.S. Gertler. 2004. Clusters from the inside and out: Local dynamics and global linkages. *Urban Studies* 41 (5–6): 1071–1093.

Chapter 15
Competitiveness of the Metropolis in the Global North and South: Economics, Planning, Financing and Governance

15.1 Intro: Economics and Political Economy

Metropolises today are the predominant connection between cities in the global economy. Supply chains, economic hubs, and production platforms are linked globally through cities. Metropolises are also a major axis that connects cities, countries, and rural areas. They influence major national decisions concerning infrastructure deployment and economic development, and play a fundamental political and economic role in the governance of cities and nations. The world's metropolises are also a base for multinational corporations and providers of finance, business environments, and the infrastructure that connects them.

As early as 1995, Kenichi Ohmae (1995) a McKinsey and Corp. partner, predicted the end of nation states and the emergence of mega-economies, or regional economies. More recently, Parag Khana (2016) described a world in which connectivity led by supply chains was the rule rather than the exception, configuring an almost "stateless" world.

The realities and politics of the so-called "metro-optimists," however, are more complex. Very early, Saskia Sassen defined the emergence of the metropolis, focusing on three global cities in her classic study published in 1995. *The Global City* (Sassen 1995) analyzed Tokyo, New York, and London as the ultimate metropolises where finance and production hubs integrated. More recently, Pedro Ortiz (2013) described the need to plan for the metropolis and its limits within nation-states marked by the tension between productivity and equity. Today, academic output on the metropolis and mega cities is deeper and more analytical in a moment in which metropolises are the norm rather than the exception.

The world is clearly moving toward metropolitan economies, but nation-states are still in control and will be the predominant force for the next few decades in a world that requires planning, trade, urban-rural policies, social mandates, and nation-wide planning. This chapter focuses on the major axes that define the political economy of the metropolis—connections, finance and economics—and the

© China Social Sciences Press and Springer Nature Singapore Pte Ltd. 2017

P. Ni et al., *Cities Network Along the Silk Road*,
DOI 10.1007/978-981-10-4834-0_15

new rules that govern them, in order to ensure the sustainable competitiveness of the metropolis in the global economy.

The Global Urban Competitiveness Report of 2013 and subsequent editions highlight a paradigm shift from competition for wealth to sustainable competitiveness as cities strive to ensure the creation and provision of complex and advanced social well-being for its inhabitants. The report shows that the hallmark of a sustainably competitive city lies in its ability to synthesize its economic development, innovation, social cohesion, environmental protection, cultural diversity, open and interrelated global networks and good governance.

Economics is the science that analyzes the components of a productive process. In metropolitan terms, economic policies attempt to maximize the output given a limited amount of resources. When applied to metropolises, economic policies develop a set of technical mechanisms to (1) calculate the return on a combination of resources, and (2) improve productivity.

Political Economy, instead, is the art of achieving the most desirable objective through an analytical approach situated within a specific sociopolitical context that could allow, or endanger, the efficiency of the result. Political economy tries to make the output as efficient as possible given a set of social (political) circumstances. Political economy's objective is efficacy rather than efficiency.

Economics aims to be a science, but political economics is not. A well-known quote from Bismarck says, "Politics is the art of the possible." Effectively, political economy tries to address the dichotomy between economic and social objectives to make them as compatible as possible and avoid the breaking down of the system. Disruptions could result from the failure to coordinate efficiency and equity. Metropolitan management must therefore steer between unacceptable social inequity and unsustainable economic inefficiency.

Economies of scale apply directly to metropolises. That is why metropolis are more efficient than simple cities and why they are becoming increasingly powerful. Metropolises are now reaching competitive capacities beyond those of many nation-states. We could define the current era, starting in late 20th C, as the Age of the Metropolis.

In achieving efficiency, we use numerous techniques to quantify the output of a specific set of productive inputs. Techniques are used to time and scale the inputs to maximize the output. On the social side, we have many indicators that provide for the calculation and sharing of equitable access to social facilities; such indicators help us reach a progressive distribution of consumption. We have none, however, to locate the equilibrium between efficiency and equity, despite the many efforts to develop taxation formulas to frame this dichotomy.

Above all, we must understand that there can be no equity without growth, and no growth without equity. The political programs that prioritize growth as the forerunner of equity generally do not understand that if sharing is postponed for a long time, the whole system breaks and growth is disrupted, if not halted altogether.

15.2 Features of an Efficient and Competitive Metropolis

15.2.1 *Physical Characteristics*

A key component is at play in this dichotomy: the physical substrata. It is a substantial component when we are dealing, as it is the case of metropolises, with territorial structures. This component includes both the natural environment and the urban construct and layout (UN-HABITAT 2015).

As the metropolis is an aggregate of cities and neighborhoods, the territorial build-up of a metropolis therefore depends on an efficient layout of the connections among them. This point was described by Jane Jacobs in her classic book, *The Death and Life of Great American Cities* (Jacobs, Jane 1961) in which she described the conditions for vibrant and productive cities as available public space, mixed communities, a number of intersections, and so on. Recently, these have been quantified in Italy by De Nadai (2016) using cellphone data (Fig. 15.1).

Well managed, the physical realm can mitigate socio-economic frictions through direct interventions such as breaking the center-periphery antagonism to address the marginalization of peripheral social groups, and, adopting a polycentric approach to metropolises which allows demand to control the land market and provides a plurality of locations for social access to public facilities.

Zooming out, the efficiency of the metropolis is based on two components, relative location and infrastructure investments. *Relative location* concerns territorial components; the functions and uses of land must be efficiently located to minimize costs and provide fluid mobility and accessibility throughout the metropolis. *Infrastructure investments* must be of an appropriate level and adequacy. As we know, urban and metropolitan space is created by the infrastructure that provides potential for its use[1].

A good location is the one that is related to this infrastructure. It is reflected in the value of the land and the added value generated by the impact of the infrastructure on the potential uses of that land. Added value is mostly a condensation of the positive externalities of the public (or private) investment in infrastructure upon the potential (economic) use of that land. The infrastructure provides the location's effectiveness. Time also is relevant. If the availability of the infrastructure is not timed well (typically due to financial concerns), a good location is useless. Politics therefore enters the timing game.

The metropolitan physical structure, location, and infrastructure—in other words, land-use and transport—are the plate for the course. This is what a metropolitan government must provide. The interests of land and inherited inefficient locations, historically based in shortsighted land-policy approaches, often make the pursuit of this objective very difficult, if not impossible. Political economy balances those conflicting private interests and tries to come out with a feasible proposal for land allocation decisions and provision of infrastructure.

---

[1]Lefebvre said "space does not exist; it is created". Lefebvre (1974) La production de l'espace, Paris: Anthropos.

GDP, GDP per Capita and Total Population
2014
Country and Metro Areas Comparison

Rank	Country or Metro Area	GDP (PPP, US$, Billions)	Total Population	GDP per Capita (PPP, US$)
51	Sweden	$439,2	9.696.110	$45.297,0
52	Sao Paulo (Brazil)	$430,5	20.847.500	$20.650,4
53	Kazakhstan	$418,9	17.289.224	$24.227,7
54	Hong Kong (China)	$416,0	7.267.900	$57.244,5
55	Dallas (USA)	$412,7	6.937.652	$59.483,2
56	Austria	$407,5	8.545.908	$47.682,3
57	Romania	$405,0	19.904.360	$20.348,1
58	Mexico City (Mexico)	$403,6	20.976.700	$19.238,5
59	Chile	$392,0	17.762.647	$22.071,1
60	Guangzhou (China)	$380,3	13.106.300	$29.013,8
61	Tianjin (China)	$372,0	15.355.400	$24.224,2
62	Peru	$371,3	30.973.148	$11.988,9
63	Ukraine	$370,5	45.362.900	$8.168,2
64	Singapore	$365,9	5.469.724	$66.900,6
65	Nagoya (Japan)	$363,8	9.061.100	$40.144,2
66	Shenzhen (China)	$363,2	10.768.400	$33.730,9
67	Boston (USA)	$360,1	4.725.601	$76.204,1
68	Istanbul (Turkey)	$348,7	14.023.500	$24.866,9
69	Philadelphia (USA)	$346,5	6.060.560	$57.165,5
70	Suzhou (China)	$339,0	6.517.300	$52.019,7
71	Norway	$337,1	5.136.886	$65.614,5
72	San Francisco (USA)	$331,0	4.572.807	$72.389,7
73	Czech Republic	$328,2	10.525.347	$31.185,9
74	Taipei (Taiwan)	$327,3	7.099.300	$46.102,4
75	Jakarta (Indonesia)	$321,3	32.183.300	$9.983,9
76	Rotterdam-Amsterdam (Netherlands)	$320,6	7.082.700	$45.265,2
77	Buenos Aires (Argentina)	$315,9	13.381.800	$23.605,6
78	Chongqing (China)	$315,6	30.009.800	$10.515,9
79	Milan (Italy)	$312,1	7.585.200	$41.147,0
80	Bangkok (Thailand)	$306,8	15.567.700	$19.705,2
81	Qatar	$305,5	2.172.065	$140.649,2
82	Portugal	$299,1	10.401.062	$28.760,0
83	Busan-Ulsan (South Korea)	$296,5	7.681.200	$38.602,0
84	Atlanta (USA)	$294,4	5.596.349	$52.609,3
85	Delhi (India)	$293,6	23.036.600	$12.746,5
86	Greece	$291,9	10.869.637	$26.850,9
87	Israel	$276,9	8.215.700	$33.703,4
88	Toronto (Canada)	$276,3	6.036.800	$45.771,4
89	Kuwait	$274,9	3.753.121	$73.245,7
90	Seattle (USA)	$267,5	3.663.399	$73.012,2
91	Miami (USA)	$262,7	5.905.918	$44.480,3
92	Madrid (Spain)	$262,3	6.677.300	$39.287,6
93	Morocco	$258,3	33.921.203	$7.614,6
94	Denmark	$256,8	5.638.530	$45.536,5
95	Brussels (Belgium)	$254,3	5.493.300	$46.297,7
96	Hungary	$247,3	9.863.183	$25.068,9
97	Chengdu (China)	$233,5	1.364.270.000	$171,2
98	Wuhan (China)	$231,6	1.364.270.000	$169,7
99	Sri Lanka	$230,8	20.771.000	$11.110,2

Fig. 15.1 Metropolises and Nations GDP. *Source* Prepared with data from Brookings (Cities) and World Bank (GDP) http://www.brookings.edu/research/reports2/2015/01/22-global-metro-monitor, and World Bank http://data.worldbank.org/data-catalog/world-development-indicators

The economy of the metropolis, the course, is an essential component. The forces that shape the efficiency of a metropolitan economy (labor, capital, entrepreneurship, productivity, etc.) are now global, not local. They must be dealt with in a way quite similar to a national economic policy rather than a localized urban economic policy.

15.2.2 Governance Mechanisms

Metropolises have developed as complex supra-urban systems composed of multiple cities or urban units. They have the complexity of management of modern nation-states. They have the productive capacity and the socio-economic complexity of nation-states. Their management requirements have less to do with simple urban structures than with the typical concerns of nation-states. As an example of metropolitan efficiency, the ones that are in fact nation-states, such as Singapore, perform so well that they are often benchmarked as examples of the way to go forward.

The need for a new urban dimension, the metropolitan one, has been felt since the second half of the 20th C. There have been many attempts to build up some metropolitan coordination among cities involved in various forms of metropolitan phenomena.

In a globalized world, in a competitive environment where metropolises are more competitive and economically productive than nations, and where the wealth of nations depends on the efficiency of their metropolises, there is little room for suboptimal solutions. Metropolises must be provided with the most effective system of governance to be able to maximize their economy. If not, the nation is doomed. It will not be able to compete in a globalized world.

15.2.3 Metropolitan Governance

The economic power and the social complexity of metropolises align themselves rather more with the management of nation-states than that of cities. Metropolises follow this rule even in the absence of an established government.

In all cultures, city government is a (formal or informal) unitary system. This has been true in Europe since Roman times. In either complex hierarchical systems such as the Roman Empire, or the tribal systems of the indigenous Germanic and Anglo–Saxons, the basic unit of territorial coexistence was the village, the town, and the city. A single institution deals with the issues that require joint or cooperative management.

A metropolitan governance system is much more complex. It involves many municipalities, tiers, ministries, and departments of the national government (transport, housing, finance, public administration, health, education, etc.). It also typically involves multiple utility agencies, either public, private, both, or mixed. Each of these organizations has their own framework of purposes and competences provided by the law, and none of the involved in metropolitan management can impose on any other beyond the limits established by the law.

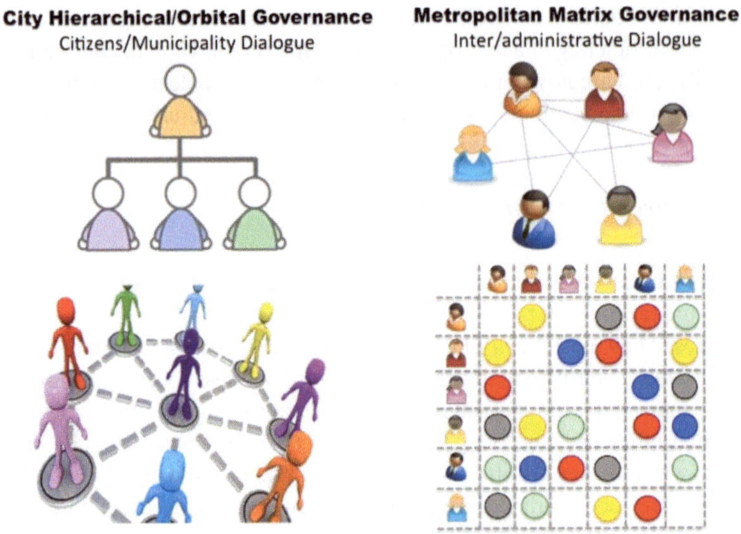

Fig. 15.2 Metropolitan Governance: matrix of dialogues. *Source* www.pedrobortiz.com

The management of a metropolis is not based on orders provided from the upper tier of a unitary system; it is based on a peer dialogue among all the institutions and organizations within the limits established. The law establishes the distribution of responsibilities and competences among them. A metropolitan management structure is not based on a unitary hierarchical pyramid (the top-down Aristotelian *potestas**) nor on a centripetal (center v. periphery) model of imposed decisions. Metropolitan management structure is based on a *matrix of dialogues* (Fig. 15.2) among the actors and stakeholders involved.

15.2.4 National Governments Taxonomy

National governments, in contrast to single municipalities, have developed from more diverse alternatives. Models range the centralized unitary system of a military conquest to the cooperative coordination of city leagues, such as the Greek Delian, Achaean, or Hellenic leagues, to the Germanic Hanseatic league. With time, the complexity of organization has evolved into such solutions as federations.

15.2.4.1 Confederate Governance System

In a confederate system, sovereignty stands at the level of member states or cities. The German Hanse and the Greek Hellenic systems are examples of it. The

Confederate States of America (government of the South during the U.S. Civil War) and the European Union closer examples.

We experience within this confederate approach an incremental process that may be simplified in four stages.

i. *Round Table*: The first stage of coordination involves meeting and revealing to the group what each member is doing. Sharing information allows learning from each other, facilitating good results by benchmarking, and most important, detecting where conflicts or inconsistencies might appear. This could lead to alternative methods to address the conflicts or inconsistencies by either negotiation of confrontation.
ii. *Parallel Projects*: Out of those round tables and their attendant cross insemination of ideas and experiences, some of the administrations involved eventually often replicate each other and develop similar projects. Such parallel projects are not integrated into a single management.
(iii) *Common Projects*: Once confidence has developed after many years of stages i and ii, some of the administrations decide to undertake common projects. Planning is done together but implementation is still run independently. Some economy-of-scale benefits could be achieved by such common initiatives.
(iv) *Management Agency*: When the complexity of a project requires strong technical skills and continuous maintenance management, a common project might be provided with a management agency. Cross-boundary transport projects common examples of this case[2]

These stages of confederation building take time: five to ten years each at least. Some arrangements never go beyond a certain stage when confidence has not been built to allow for further development. Most important, it must be understood that the process of confederation has a limit. None of the administrations involved, or of the politicians in charge of these administrations, is willing to transfer sovereignty from their administration to "the agency."

Confederation has a limit. Confederations do not willingly develop into federations or unitary systems. The Hanseatic League imploded when confronted from the outside. The Hellenic league was taken over by the Athenian Empire and the Confederate States of America terminated with the end of the U.S. Civil War. Europe, as it is, is a confederation. A unitary monetary system requires a federal fiscal and economic policy. The absence of such has created many of the troubles Europe is experiencing. A constitutional attempt was made a few years ago, but it failed. Europe in 2016 is struggling with centrifugal forces such as England and Greece.

[2]This is the case of management agencies in Washington DC.

15.2.4.2 Unitary Governance System

At the other extreme of governmental mechanisms, we have the unitary system. With the exception of Singapore, and some other cities (e.g. Monaco, the Vatican, etc.) often presented as metropolitan successes, the unitary system is mainly used at national level.

There are many ways to achieve national unity. Usually, some sort of violence is involved. The unitary system at some moment in history was imposed by either war or revolution. It is therefore to some extent an imposed system. Even when legitimized by a democratic constitution, it nevertheless has a top-down approach and is sometimes contested when it fails to respond to bottom-up community concerns.

In a unitary system, power before decentralization is instituted in a single central power. Sovereignty stands at the center. Most countries work this way; France would be a good example. The head of a department is the prefect, who is appointed by the national president and is accountable to him or her.

15.2.4.3 Federation Governance System

In a federal system, sovereignty is at the center but management is not just decentralized, it is also devolved. The various tiers of government have their own independent designation systems and are accountable to their population, not to the central unitary power that has appointed them. Germany and the United States would be actual examples.

15.2.5 Decentralization and Devolution in a National Unitary System

15.2.5.1 Decentralization

On some occasions, metropolises benefit from a decentralization framework as national unitary systems could be deaf to metropolitan needs. They tend to focus on national issues and take limited interest on metropolitan ones. These issues are difficult, conflictive, and expensive to solve (e.g. Bogota transport). This is so even when the capital metropolis might produce more than 60% of the National GDP (such as Manila, Cairo, Buenos Aires, and others do) and the whole country is at stake if the capital metropolis does not work.

An example of decentralized governance is whereby a local agency is instituted and a CEO appointed by the central government (e.g. Madrid in the 1970s). Decentralization is as democratic as the central government is. Even a legitimately democratic government does not necessarily represent the specific inhabitants of the metropolis. It represents the inhabitants of the unitary state (e.g. Kampala Minister).

Eventually the metropolitan population will require accountability of these appointees. They will be summoned to be accountable to the metropolitan population, not to the national president. Devolution would then be the next step in the establishment of sustainable metropolitan governance.

15.2.5.2 Devolution

Decentralization must not be mistaken with devolution. In a metropolitan devolution process, the accountability of the metropolitan appointees is transferred from the central government to the citizens of the metropolis. The head of the metropolitan agency is accountable to the electorate. Once their offices have devolved, metropolitan executives become elected governmental officials. The central government cannot remove them without the convergence of exceptional and specific circumstances, to be stated by law at the constitutional level.

A process of metropolitan devolution can be established in unitary states. There are, however, two difficulties. Firstly, politicians might not want to lose areas of power and control as much as national governments might not want to lose part of their capacity to manage the metropolis, which represents much of national population and possibly even a larger share of national GDP. Secondly, if the president of the metropolitan government represents an opposition party, presiding over more than 50% of the national GDP might encourage him or her to imagine the national presidency as the next rung to climb. This person would become the political enemy of the national president (e.g. Buenos Aires). No politician wants to breed enemies out of power resignation; quite the contrary.

All this is unfortunate enough. On one hand, it is impossible to build up a metropolitan government level out of a confederate approach. Such adverse circumstances are a pity, as it would be possible to build that level from unitary decentralization and devolution. Some would argue that metropolitan governments are not necessary, and that a confederation or decentralization framework would be quite enough. Political economy, however, would point otherwise, arguing that many challenges and problems of metropolises are neither municipal nor national. If they are specifically metropolitan problems, they must be addressed at the metropolitan level, and for such they need the instrument of a metropolitan institution to address them, achieved through either decentralization or devolution.

15.3 Economics and Political Economy

Metropolises must also be able to provide adequate frameworks to develop the *political economy* necessary for governance's equity objective. That is why the governmental system is an essential piece of the metropolitan political economy.

15.3.1 Metropolitan Urban Economy

Urban economy emphasizes city layout to improve productivity. Components are rooted into supply chains, activities, and procedures that facilitate the integration of production with time and efficiency. Several factors contribute to this, including fixed capital and spatial layout.

15.3.1.1 Fixed capital

Fixed capital is essential, since metropolises must accumulate fixed capital as a multiplier of labor productivity. There are three components to metropolitan fixed capital:

(i) *Location*: It must be integrated into a territorial model that allows resilience, sustainability, and flexibility.
(ii) *Typology*: It must respond to the potential needs of the metropolitan economy's strategic development.
(iii) *Timing*: No one wants to finance infrastructure that is not yet necessary. Prioritization and timing are essential ingredients of political economy and metropolitan success.

Fixed capital is not enough, and it could even be too much. Some metropolises have already achieved their actual limits of capital accumulation and therefore need to tame the complexity of their accumulated capital. Only a few metropolises have reached this level: Paris, London, New York, and Tokyo are the clearest examples.

Some of the effects of fixed capital can be achieved less expensively by running capital and management. For example, traffic management may be a less cost prohibitive alternative to building expensive and environmentally degrading infrastructure. The analysis of intermodal and overall efficiency can be approached with multiple econometric techniques.

This capacity for management governance is what we could call *intangible fixed capital.* Investment in human and social resources, resources related to entrepreneurial capacity, is necessary. Metropolises with more social and human capital can recuperate quicker and better after disasters than those with less.[3] Not that any need to be tested by disaster to compare results, these metropolises perform better in any circumstance.

We should distinguish between the *social* and *productive facilities* of tangible fixed capital. The labor force cannot be improved without health or education facilities. Even cultural and leisure facilities are essential to keep a labor force balanced and competitive. The share and prioritization, however, is impossible to approach by standardized quantitative means. No comparative standard analysis is available among well-performing metropolises. Each metropolis has its own DNA.

[3]Haiti and Chile earthquakes for example.

Cultural and spatial differences require different optimal equilibriums. Transfer of internationally trendy templates should be restrained. The share should be established by the priorities and appreciation of local consumers and the electorate. We are head on in the realm of political economy.

15.3.1.2 Spatial layout

Congestion is the nightmare monster of the metropolis. Congestion can bring a metropolis to gridlock. Often, size is seen as the cause. In this framework, the subsequent stand is that metropolitan growth should be contained. This is a moral approach, not technical, as an ethic of "small is beautiful" can be discerned. Technically, however, a congestion threshold is reached when the marginal return on the accumulation curve becomes negative. In traffic terms, that would be when the cost of one additional car on the road reducing the general speed (a negative externality) becomes greater than the benefit of accessibility provided for by that additional car. Congestion, and not only in terms of vehicular traffic, can diminish a metropolis's competitiveness. Non-congested competitors then take advantage of this weakness in global markets.

Nevertheless, *economies of scale* show that the larger the metropolis is, the more efficient it is likely to be. Better mobility should increase productivity. According to Prud'homme and Lee (1999), the elasticity of commuting speeds and labor productivity is around +0.30; this means that increasing speed by 10% increases productivity by 3%. The larger the metropolis, however, the more specialized the labor force typically becomes. Such specialization requires adequate education and immigration appeal. Larger metropolises typically enjoy larger marginal returns on fixed capital. The congestion limit must not be reached. That means we must be able to push back the congestion threshold. As Alain Bertaud said, "Mobility explains the link between city size and productivity (Bertaud 2016)".

Size and congestion are related. They are part of the same equation. That is why, instead of taking size as the factor to be limited, we should rather target congestion. *The limit on a metropolis's size is the capacity its collective intelligence to manage congestion.* The components of collective intelligence are not only the capacity of the governance system to respond. That is social capital, accumulated social and human resources integrated into institutional frameworks. It is as well the economic capacity to enable and facilitate the necessary investments.

The essential economic question is: Would the investment (fixed capital or management) necessary to raise the congestion threshold compensate the benefits of increased capacity? If not, the investment should not be undertaken. This is as simple and as complex as a cost-benefit analysis. If the project is intelligent enough and has understood the metropolis's DNA, the outcome will be positive. The issue will then be how to accommodate the discrepancy between those who pay for the investment and those who benefits from it. Should the investment be public, private, both, or neither?

15.4 Planning and Budgeting Mechanisms

15.4.1 Strategic Structural and Master Planning

15.4.1.1 Strategic Planning

Integrating economic, social, and physical approaches in the metropolis can be done through strategic planning. The physical environment is the tray for the menu items of economic and social planning. You first need know what you have on the menu to know what tray you need, for fish or meat. Strategic planning is the instrument that establishes the socio-economic priorities for the future of a specific metropolis. It does so based on the metropolis's problems, risks, weaknesses, and potentials. The transversal approach on all components that metropolitan strategic planning brings about could result in priority projects. Transversal projects that require physical dimension and promote a strategic vision for the Metropolis beyond the tactical ones.

15.4.1.2 Structural Planning

The socio-economic strategic plan then feeds a physical structural plan. Note that a structural plan, which addresses the overall general physical strategies of the metropolis, should not be confused with a detailed municipal regulatory plan. The structural plan must be designed at the metropolitan scale. The metropolitan scale requires instruments different from those used at the municipal scale. Misunderstanding this is the most common mistake made by professionals that deal with metropolitan planning, who tend to create so-called metropolitan plans that are impossible to implement because they misunderstand the biology of the metropolis. Such plans eventually become decorative elements of administrative offices.

The structural plan deals with the main projects that have a transversal metropolitan implication. Such projects are meant to affect the overall structure of the metropolis to increase both efficiency and equity of the metropolitan system. Sustainability is obviously the substrata of the physical policies that must integrate the five previously mentioned metropolitan components: green and gray infrastructure (i.e. environment and transport), housing, productive activities, and social facilities.

15.4.1.3 Master Planning

In developing metropolises, master plans should be drafted and approved. We must contextualize these master plans. This requires understanding the governance capacity of the public sector, involving multiple stakeholders to incorporate the actors, and integrating infrastructure—the core of master plans—with regional and local development. All of this must represent sound population projections, realistic financial capacity, and adequate business plans.

One potential instrument to guide master plans and integrate the different tiers of metropolitan government is a national urban policy. Such a policy must be rooted in clear aims and synergies among national, regional, metropolitan, and local infrastructure. A national urban policy also must be consider its effects on productivity, and therefore understand the existing value chains (productive sectors) in terms of the constraints on those value chains by supply chains (the logistics needed to produce). Both value chain and supply chain are essential for the integration of urban planning with urban economy. Note that, in terms of productivity and urbanization, Southeast Asian countries have been very successful often despite the lack of a formal national urban policy. This indicates that this is not a legalistic process, but rather a practical application of planning and economic principles.[4]

National urban policies and regional and national plans must also be integrated to increase their efficiency. When national urban policies achieve sufficient sophistication, in which urban form and layout is shown with direct effects on productivity and economic growth, then central governments and development banks will pay more attention.

15.4.2 Institutional Arrangements

The productive system of a metropolis is a system where all parts are interrelated, even though some of its components might be spatially discontinuous. Many metropolises do not act on this productive system in a consistent and comprehensive way. As a result, economies of metropolises are often dealt with in a disjointed way, assuming they are dealt with at all. Metropolitan economies are often as important and powerful as national economies and they must be dealt with at a similar level of concern and with similar policy management capacities.

The projects approached for common development by cities in metropolises are mainly green or gray infrastructure projects. This is because, among the five components of metropolitan structures (environment, transport, housing, productive activities, and social facilities), environment and transport are *continuous* systems. The other three are *discontinuous.*

There is a tendency to focus on the coordination of continuous systems than discontinuous systems. That is why municipalities often have a consistent metropolitan policies that deal with green and gray infrastructure, and very little policies that deal with housing, productive, or social systems. The need for coordination is more difficult to perceive for the discontinuous components and comes

[4]On National Urban Policies see UN-HABITAT http://unhabitat.org/urban-initiatives/initiatives-programmes/national-urban-policies/national-urban-policies/, and UN-HABITAT, Cities Alliance (2015) "The Evolution of National Urban Policies". http://www.citiesalliance.org/sites/citiesalliance.org/files/National%20Urban%20Policies.pdf.

about only in more complex stages of metropolitan evolution, most frequently in decentralized or devolved systems.

Beyond technical capacity, the major problem for coordination is isolation between professionals who deal with the economic policies of metropolises and those who deal with physical policies. If there is no metropolitan institution to foster collaboration, coordination, and dialogue on cross-cutting issues, therefore, isolation becomes chronic and takes place only, if ever, at the academic level. For instance:

(a) *Physical planners* would approach location in terms of separation of conflicting land use functions (e.g. polluting industry and residential areas) and as driven by traffic patterns of accessibility or congestion. Very little attention is typically given to economic needs. They lack such skills and information, and the system, ether academic or administrative, rarely provides for it.
(b) *Urban economists* would, on the other hand, bypass physical management and address their arguments to top politicians and decision-makers. They will encourage policies and projects unrelated to the physical context that is difficult to grasp and appreciate.
(c) *Governance specialists,* would focus on institutional settings. They will rarely understand the physical needs of the metropolis and so will produce proposals based on benchmarking approaches that replicate well-functioning institutions. This approach, providing a tool unrelated to the task, might leave you with the institutional dilemma of a screw in one hand and a hammer in the other.

Unfortunately, institutions from places that have problems in socio-economic contexts unrelated to the metropolis in question are hardly going to perform as they did in the native city. If officials from Kampala are urged to adopt a governance mechanism during a field trip to see the transport system of Stockholm, that mechanism must be contextualized or else this would be an exercise of science fiction. Governance is the tool to implement a proposal or a project. If the project was not selected and developed by the city leader, the tool chosen will probably be inefficient or redundant for the purpose.

15.4.3 Planning Tools for the Emerging Metropolis

The planning tools and management mechanisms of emerging metropolises must be completely different from the ones of the developed metropolises. They must be designed out of local circumstances, which is where the mechanisms of 99% of the formal developed metropolises were devised. In developing metropolises with large informal sectors, master plans are drafted and approved as in formal metropolises, but they are never implemented. Once failed, they are revised, redrafted, and approved again, and fail again.

In terms of policy, in a context of weak governance and broad informality, the capacity for economic management is severely limited. This is not yet an appropriate context for the federalized metropolis. It seems that even cultural agreement on this necessity has not yet been reached.

15.5 Finance Mechanisms

15.5.1 Metropolitan Finance Arrangements

Metropolitan financing in the context of devolution and fiscal arrangements often involves various levels of government and is of two classes: (i) revenues, expenditures, and services, and (ii) provision of infrastructure.

15.5.1.1 Revenues, Expenditures and Services

Concerning revenues, expenditures, and services, the funding responsibilities and the inter-governmental fiscal arrangements should be coordinated, clear, and efficient. Three levels are generally involved. The *state/province* level typically provides major health and education facilities, inter-urban trains, and roads. The *cross-local* level (boards, authorities, and so on) typically provide large health and education facilities, metro public transport, water supply/waste water, solid waste disposal, and metro ring roads/freeways). The *local* level typically provides local health and education facilities, solid waste collection, and local roads. Table 15.1 shows a general metropolitan finance arrangement among different layers of government (Fig. 15.3).

15.5.1.2 Provision of Infrastructure

Provision of infrastructure also involves layers of government with different objectives and interests. In general, national and regional highways, water supply, major networks, drainage, and energy are provided by the central government, whereas a local government needs the highways but may also have an urgent need for rural roads to provide access to local wholesale markets.

The point is that investment serves everybody and becomes a public good, benefiting the general population and economy, not just the individuals who are directly affected. Their personal improvement has a bouncing effect on the rest of the metropolis. Benefits are thus indivisible. The public sector pays, but there are three tiers to the metropolis: (i) the local (confederate) does not have the resources to pay, (ii) the national (unitary) does not have the will and resists as much as possible until metropolitan congestion becomes a national issue with negative

Table 15.1 General metropolitan finance arrangements

Gov't. level	Sectors	Revenue sources for		Collection yield[a]	Systems[b]	Systems to maximise net revenue[c]
		Capex	Opex			
State/province/regions	Health, Inter-urban trains, bulk electricity generation, water management, etc.	General taxes e.g. income & VAT, bonds, project loans	User fees, taxes	Rarely fully cost recoverable, but relatively easy to police payment	Health cards, smart grid, water auctions	Transparent bidding for concessions/suppliers/use rights
Metro-level cross lg (city regions, boards, etc.)	Education, metro rail, water supply/sanitation, etc.	Shares of general taxes, property tax levies, bonds, project loans	User charges, CSO transfer revenue	With the exception of water supply, rarely cost recoverable, but more difficult to police access	Integrated ticketing, smart metering,	GIS-based property tax monitoring and automated billing and other IT systems to maximise yield. Crowd sourcing of service issues and responses.
Development area/corridor authorities	Area/corridor transport and urban renewal	Property taxes, project loans	As above	Commercial basis – corporation should be in surplus	Eminent domain, area-based tax surcharges	Land banking/performance-based bids
LG	Solid waste local roads, parks, etc.	As above, plus limited bonds, transfers	As above	As for metro level	Cost recovery pricing	As for metro & development area levels

[a]Collection yield refers to how much of the tax/fee due do they actually collect
[b]Systems refers to best practice and technology supports available to maximise efficiency of use and yield
[c]System upgrades to minimise "leakage" in collection and maximise transparency/accountability
Source Linfield, Kamiya, Eguino (2016)

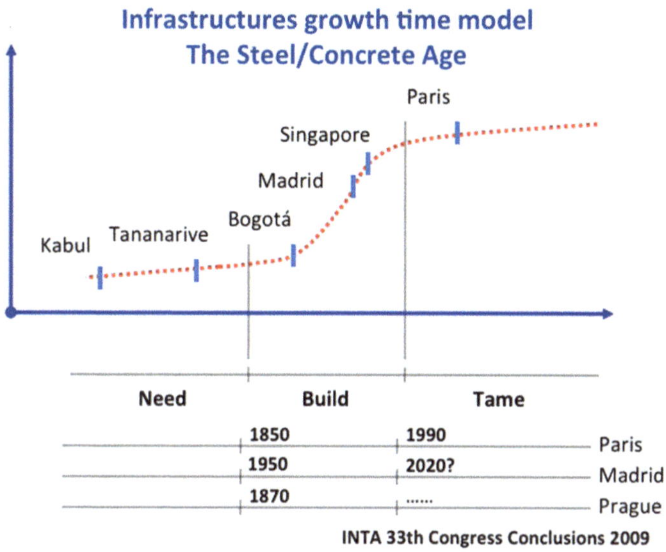

Fig. 15.3 Infrastructure growth model. *Source* INTA Congress 39th, 1999

political impacts, (iii) the metropolitan (federal) either does not exist or doesn't have the financial capacity (not devolved yet) to address these needs.

As a result, the necessary investments are not implemented and the metropolis reaches a point of inefficiency as saturation and congestion limit its output. *Diseconomies of scale* are reached due to management inefficiency. If the benefits of the investment are *divisible* (e.g. toll bridge) the private sector can take care of it. The requirement is that demand must be capable of responding to the supply cost. If an equilibrium point between supply and demand can be reached, there is no problem for private involvement. This assumes that the public sector has the skills and the will to set up the main lines for the projects (complex terms of reference) and the concessionary rights in the right way. It is not, however, always the case. Spurious interests in the political economy may be playing in the shadows.

15.5.2 Sources of Metropolitan Finance

15.5.2.1 Taxation

In terms of investment, and in the theoretical framework of a liberal free-market environment, if an investment produces benefits, it does not need to be undertaken by the public sector. The public sector should concentrate on investments that have a general interest (social or economic) and that must be made at a loss, an indivisible loss. The way to finance an indivisible good that must be financed by the public sector is through taxation.

There is a major difference between the metropolises of developed and developing countries. Developed metropolises do all right. They reside in 99% formal economies that developed mostly in the 19th sC. They have reached a level of infrastructure provision and finance capacity where the challenge is taming the system rather than furthering hardware development.

Developing metropolises have a different problem. They are the ones that suffer from the Peter Pan syndrome, the immature adult. In these emerging metropolises, most of the economy is informal (as much as 80%), and these shadow economies affect urban development (uncontrolled and slums), social provision (informal networks and families), and even governance (mafias).

There are four uncontrolled shadow sectors—economic, urban, social, and governance—and they are like Peter Pan's shadow. Peter Pan's problem was that, as he could not control his shadow, he could not develop an adult personality. These metropolises cannot grow to their full potential, as they cannot make good use of all their assets, controlled and uncontrolled, harnessing them to the development struggle.

The problem with taxation is that you cannot tax uncontrolled activities. The controlled sector in many of these developing metropolises is as little as 20%. It is difficult to pay for infrastructure by taxing just that 20% of all those who would benefit from it. The informal sector must be taxed to produce full-fledged development. This can be implemented only through indirect taxation, but that would jeopardize fiscal equity policies. The equilibrium must be balanced with expenditure policies, targeting insolvent demand, and social collective consumption—social alternatives to unleash market mechanisms.

Informal metropolitan economies must develop indirect taxation systems on public goods to accumulate their required fixed capital; such taxation does not necessarily relate to the direct usage of the required good. In such cases, the private sector could undertake the investment. In other cases, the taxation should involve divisible private goods and provide for the financing of indivisible public goods (e.g. taxing petrol to build and service a public transport line).

15.5.2.2 Land Value Capture

Another source of financing is *land value capture*, which has the effect of public investments on the value of land. Value capture allows for further public investments and starts a spin-off effect, providing additional revenue for further investment. There are two possible approaches to land value capture: *ex-post* and *ex-ante*. Either we recuperate the added value after (post) it has been produced, or we recuperate it before (ante) it is produced: Ex-post retrieval works through taxation, direct or indirect. Such is the case in consolidated urban areas (e.g. a new underground station). The owners already have development rights; only the increased value of development rights can be taxed, and only after the development occurs. It could be 30 before until the owner decides to redevelop; ex-post is therefore long and has limited potential. Ex-ante retrieval requires negotiation capacities and alternative projects. It can be monetized as soon as the agreement is reached.

In developed metropolises, land value capture is easier because of existing registration and cadastral systems, legal frameworks (adequate planning and land management laws), and management instruments (land management agencies). With this approach, you could retrieve up to 80% of the generated value.[5] In developing metropolises, registered and unregistered areas coexist. Inefficient or inexistent land management systems and unclear property rights, landowners, and assets prevent this possibility.

In the political economy of metropolises, if there is not a finalist approach to special taxation, income will be diverted by politicians to more intentionally political interests. Income will not be used for the general interest, but for all those legitimate and illegitimate interests that conform to the political decisions. We are talking about prioritizing electoral, clientele, lobbyist, party, and personal interests. Infrastructure allocation and services are also subject to such interests. This is the shadow side of political economy. It is difficult to deal with, but must be dealt with to strengthen the collective intelligence of the metropolis.

15.5.3 Other Financial Management Considerations

Discussions still wander around the different forms of prudent management arrangements, discussing alternatives with a combination of multiple components. If there are five sectors, five administrative tiers, five stakeholder groups, five management systems, and five financing alternatives, there are already a million alternative governance possibilities. To choose among a million possibilities is not the way to approach the construction of a rigorous metropolitan management system. The decision-making process must be framed down to essential decisions. There will always be time afterwards for calibration.

Metropolitan managers have two types of tools: carrots and sticks.

The stick is limited to a context of inadequate governance. To develop the stick, much more is required than just legislative paperwork. A legal framework, approving laws and regulations, is relatively cheap and easy; the hard part is implementation. The stick requires civil servants in numbers and with skills sufficient to match the challenge. Then it requires *autoritas* to implement. *Potestas* is not enough. Credibility and spotless behavior grants the legitimacy for implementation. This set of requirements is not easy to achieve, and administrators can be overrun by circumstances and overruled by judiciary decisions.

The carrot has two types of incentives: exemptions and subsidies. *Administrative exemptions* and *direct subsidies*, when managed in an informal framework and inefficient administration, can become an invitation to inconsistent implementation,

[5]Madrid, Arpegio is a reference.

favoritism, and corruption. *Indirect subsidies* are the remaining solution. There are many ways to influence the economy through complementary targeted services, facilities, and infrastructure (e.g. free infrastructure provision, accessibility and public transport, provision of serviced land, productive facilities as logistic centers, outsourced services and advisory services, export facilities, and commercial support). The options are unlimited, but they require money.

To produce any kind of indirect subsidy, finance is required, for fixed capital investment and running costs alike. Finance comes via indirect taxation or national transfers. Land value capture can play an important role. Ex-ante catchment value initiatives can be developed to grow capital. Up to 67% of added value generated can be recuperated. Ex-post options can reach only 40% at most. Returns can be reinvested in social and economic projects. Since this is using metropolitan wealth and endogenous sources of revenues, land value capture can create a virtuous circle for the political economy.

To spur finance, more governance instruments are required. These include an adequate legal framework to enforce planning decisions, a legal economic framework for a private/public collaboration setting, skills to implement it all, accountability to avoid opaque deviations, and the ethics. When this capacity is in place in developing economies, the size of the metropolis can drive the development of more complex financial instruments, such as bonds and loans from commercial banks and international markets. Development banks are also working on lending and financial instruments for metropolises and subnational governments in developing contexts.

15.5.3.1 A Look Ahead: The Next Years

Metropolitan economies will expand and multiply. Global connectivity will progressively link mega-cities to the global economy. This process requires appropriate governance and sufficient technical capacity of governments and citizens. Metropolitan leaders will face stronger demand in a world where more is required from metropolitan and global cities. But as the world marches towards a new urban agenda with global sustainable development goals, with Goal 9 on infrastructure and Goal 11 on urbanization, the entry points for finance, planning, governance are open.

Metropolises are at square one. Governance, social and human resources, and collective intelligence are imperatives. Most of all, what is unavoidable is the strategic capacity to generate the metropolitan project with enough leadership to achieve the convergence of all these forces, which are dispersed in the actual scenario of the metropolitan political economy. Two models are possible, the federalist nation-state oriented as a financial and productive hub, and the national champions supported by the central states, in which relative autonomy is traded for more investment.

References

Bertaud, Alain. 2016. *Mobility: Transport is a real estate issue—The Design of Urban Roads and Transport Systems*. Marron Institute: New York University.

CASS (2016 and previous editions) "Global Urban Competitiveness Report" Chinese Academy of Social Sciences. Beijing, China.

De Nadai, M. et al. 2016. "The Death and Life of Great Italian Cities: A Mobile Phone Data Perspective" http://arxiv.org/abs/1603.04012.

INTA. 1999. Documents for 39th conference.

Jacobs, Jane. 1961. "The Death and Life of Great American Cities " Vintage, US.

Lefebvre, Henri. 1974. "La production de l'espace" Paris: Anthropos.

Lindfield, Kamiya, Eguino; forthcoming (2016) UN-HABITAT and IADB. "Sustainable Metropolitan Finance for Development: Global Policies and Experiences for the New Urban Agenda and Local Finance" Washington DC and Nairobi.

Khana, Parag. 2016. *Connectography: Mapping the Future of Global Civilization*. US: Random House.

Ohmae, Kenichi. 1995. *The End of Nation State: The Rise of Regional Economies*. US: Free Press.

Prud'Homme, Remy; and Lee, Chang-Woon. 1999. Sprawl, speed and the efficiency of cities, Urban Studies, 36, pp. 1849–1858.

Sassen, Saskia. 1995 "The Global City: New York, London, Tokyo" Princeton University Press.

Ortiz, Pedro. 2013. *The Art of Shaping the Metropolis*. US: McGraw-Hill.

UN-HABITAT. 2015. "Planned City Extensions: Analysis of Historical Examples".

UN-HABITAT, Cities Alliance. 2015. "The Evolution of National Urban Policies". http://unhabitat.org/books/planned-city-extensions-analysis-of-historical-examples/.

References

[illegible]

Appendix

The state of urban competitiveness of 505 cities

City	Company strength		Local elements		Local demand		Software environment		Hardware environment		Global connection	
	Index	Rank	Index	Rank	Index	Rank	Index	Rank	Index	Rank	Index	Rank
London	1.000	1	1.000	1	0.842	4	1.000	1	0.845	11	1.000	1
New York	0.990	2	0.889	3	0.923	3	0.948	13	0.726	91	0.949	3
Tokyo	0.947	3	0.870	4	1.000	1	0.691	154	0.697	142	0.813	7
Paris	0.773	8	0.556	86	0.984	2	0.653	178	0.726	91	0.959	2
Singapore	0.840	4	0.735	12	0.622	11	0.953	4	0.717	111	0.727	11
Hong Kong	0.776	7	0.670	30	0.628	10	0.951	5	0.694	150	0.795	8
Shanghai	0.816	5	0.816	7	0.604	13	0.758	109	0.619	259	0.852	6
Beijing	0.813	6	0.956	2	0.560	19	0.565	242	0.472	416	0.872	4
Sydney	0.511	16	0.684	27	0.649	7	0.972	3	0.708	125	0.584	30
Frankfurt	0.406	32	0.581	61	0.399	108	0.826	66	1.000	1	0.754	10
Seoul	0.635	9	0.857	5	0.619	12	0.613	208	0.687	163	0.627	23
Moscow	0.577	10	0.706	19	0.764	5	0.555	256	0.538	358	0.861	5
Chicago	0.369	49	0.617	46	0.585	15	0.948	13	0.748	65	0.700	14
Toronto	0.457	21	0.726	15	0.553	20	0.907	30	0.714	116	0.555	40
Amsterdam	0.388	42	0.737	11	0.448	57	0.837	60	0.757	57	0.713	12
Los Angeles	0.434	26	0.781	9	0.709	6	0.916	24	0.487	403	0.630	22
Houston	0.364	53	0.685	25	0.572	16	0.948	13	0.646	222	0.637	20
Milan	0.520	15	0.542	98	0.417	81	0.670	161	0.889	5	0.694	15
Dublin	0.483	18	0.669	31	0.426	72	0.865	46	0.717	111	0.605	26
Seattle	0.318	69	0.723	16	0.421	75	0.949	11	0.803	28	0.524	54
Madrid	0.566	11	0.642	39	0.482	38	0.662	167	0.647	218	0.708	13
Oslo	0.326	64	0.718	17	0.592	14	0.832	63	0.742	69	0.487	63
San Francisco	0.409	30	0.654	34	0.445	59	0.919	19	0.684	168	0.567	36
Vienna	0.395	37	0.555	87	0.518	24	0.828	64	0.776	47	0.554	41
Taipei	0.529	14	0.786	8	0.385	137	0.746	113	0.693	153	0.529	50
Melbourne	0.393	38	0.566	77	0.629	9	0.908	28	0.654	211	0.457	75
Zurich	0.305	79	0.838	6	0.512	27	0.565	242	0.793	30	0.562	38
Philadelphia	0.271	103	0.607	49	0.502	28	0.947	17	0.710	119	0.528	51
San Jose	0.331	63	0.732	14	0.471	42	0.885	37	0.816	21	0.326	162
Osaka	0.454	23	0.562	79	0.643	8	0.659	171	0.718	107	0.485	66
Stockholm	0.403	34	0.630	42	0.466	44	0.727	121	0.736	76	0.566	37

(continued)

© China Social Sciences Press and Springer Nature Singapore Pte Ltd. 2017

P. Ni et al., *Cities Network Along the Silk Road*,
DOI 10.1007/978-981-10-4834-0

(continued)

City	Company strength		Local elements		Local demand		Software environment		Hardware environment		Global connection	
	Index	Rank	Index	Rank	Index	Rank	Index	Rank	Index	Rank	Index	Rank
Phoenix City	0.317	70	0.642	39	0.499	29	0.916	24	0.644	224	0.544	44
Dallas	0.381	44	0.479	143	0.489	34	0.917	22	0.637	233	0.635	21
Boston	0.367	50	0.715	18	0.415	83	0.885	37	0.636	238	0.551	42
Dubai	0.400	35	0.420	203	0.420	76	0.614	206	0.878	7	0.688	16
San Diego	0.294	88	0.698	21	0.489	34	0.951	5	0.691	155	0.408	102
Barcelona	0.392	40	0.585	58	0.405	99	0.694	145	0.721	102	0.678	17
Munich	0.334	62	0.567	75	0.464	46	0.762	108	0.760	54	0.561	39
Copenhagen	0.407	31	0.524	112	0.452	54	0.806	88	0.814	22	0.436	87
Oakland (US)	0.254	118	0.686	24	0.385	137	0.949	11	0.787	36	0.416	98
Washington D.C.	0.389	41	0.652	35	0.417	81	0.948	13	0.504	395	0.615	25
Atlanta	0.435	25	0.569	71	0.392	123	0.853	55	0.565	325	0.665	19
Berlin	0.393	38	0.475	146	0.561	18	0.697	141	0.661	203	0.622	24
Hamburg	0.371	46	0.522	115	0.491	33	0.729	117	0.740	71	0.527	52
Austin	0.355	57	0.734	13	0.436	65	0.887	32	0.605	280	0.445	81
Vancouver	0.290	92	0.775	10	0.386	133	0.874	44	0.637	233	0.485	66
Charlotte	0.219	158	0.597	52	0.424	73	0.854	51	0.729	86	0.551	42
Montreal	0.277	100	0.534	104	0.495	30	0.875	43	0.673	189	0.505	57
Helsinki	0.312	74	0.624	43	0.408	96	0.716	135	0.803	28	0.441	83
Rome	0.396	36	0.524	112	0.493	31	0.670	161	0.565	325	0.678	17
Bangkok	0.412	29	0.650	36	0.386	133	0.791	93	0.551	343	0.578	32
Jacksonville	0.239	133	0.610	47	0.429	69	0.915	26	0.768	50	0.332	156
Yokohama	0.204	177	0.489	140	0.566	17	0.788	96	0.781	43	0.419	96
Edinburgh	0.268	106	0.664	33	0.346	216	0.833	61	0.736	76	0.446	80
Miami	0.365	52	0.561	81	0.372	171	0.885	37	0.540	355	0.589	29
Brussels	0.404	33	0.582	60	0.276	304	0.810	83	0.616	264	0.605	26
Milwaukee	0.225	151	0.554	90	0.410	92	0.853	55	0.828	17	0.365	129
Cincinnati	0.274	101	0.502	131	0.365	191	0.950	7	0.752	63	0.389	113
Manchester	0.374	45	0.416	208	0.478	40	0.704	139	0.668	193	0.568	35
Bergen	0.148	263	0.591	56	0.522	23	0.833	61	0.779	44	0.340	151
Portland	0.305	79	0.554	90	0.396	115	0.791	93	0.790	33	0.363	131
Baltimore	0.239	133	0.579	65	0.414	87	0.885	37	0.671	192	0.441	83
Columbus	0.326	64	0.573	68	0.434	67	0.886	34	0.696	145	0.310	178
Arlington	0.240	131	0.465	154	0.374	164	0.918	20	0.814	22	0.363	131
Wellington	0.296	87	0.551	92	0.226	389	0.864	47	0.843	12	0.382	117
Shenzhen	0.317	70	0.599	51	0.466	44	0.726	124	0.612	268	0.465	74
Utrecht	0.168	226	0.561	81	0.367	187	0.839	58	0.732	83	0.486	65
Kuala Lumpur	0.530	13	0.667	32	0.262	327	0.635	190	0.599	287	0.497	58
Minneapolis	0.292	89	0.692	22	0.372	171	0.821	76	0.523	375	0.495	59
Brisbane	0.247	121	0.512	120	0.518	24	0.811	80	0.649	214	0.393	109
Kyoto	0.138	291	0.687	23	0.460	50	0.659	171	0.831	15	0.324	166
Cleveland	0.317	70	0.385	228	0.378	155	0.950	7	0.718	107	0.368	127
Stuttgart	0.209	168	0.506	125	0.388	130	0.826	66	0.694	150	0.484	68
Guangzhou	0.313	73	0.699	20	0.492	32	0.533	268	0.557	336	0.542	45
Auckland (NZ)	0.233	142	0.393	222	0.369	182	0.864	47	0.843	12	0.357	137
Glasgow	0.311	75	0.580	64	0.358	197	0.675	160	0.685	165	0.492	60
Hague	0.148	263	0.575	67	0.409	94	0.807	84	0.728	88	0.430	90

(continued)

(continued)

City	Company strength		Local elements		Local demand		Software environment		Hardware environment		Global connection	
	Index	Rank	Index	Rank	Index	Rank	Index	Rank	Index	Rank	Index	Rank
Denver	0.261	114	0.559	85	0.419	77	0.823	72	0.505	392	0.579	31
Istanbul	0.419	28	0.385	228	0.472	41	0.563	252	0.478	412	0.770	9
Geneva	0.340	60	0.503	128	0.458	52	0.564	251	0.736	76	0.448	78
Macao	0.184	199	0.435	186	0.428	71	0.728	118	0.904	3	0.322	170
Nashville	0.301	84	0.533	106	0.403	101	0.821	76	0.631	243	0.401	106
Birmingham	0.359	55	0.427	197	0.401	104	0.774	103	0.665	196	0.434	89
Leeds	0.343	59	0.461	160	0.396	115	0.895	31	0.569	319	0.429	91
Liverpool	0.346	58	0.436	183	0.327	245	0.735	115	0.729	86	0.448	78
Sacramento	0.221	156	0.463	157	0.385	137	0.886	34	0.793	30	0.276	213
Tel Aviv	0.266	109	0.564	78	0.352	205	0.819	79	0.656	210	0.408	102
Bristol	0.309	77	0.447	170	0.333	235	0.801	91	0.705	131	0.425	95
Nottingham	0.206	172	0.585	58	0.302	273	0.807	84	0.720	105	0.415	99
Tampa	0.247	121	0.454	165	0.359	195	0.950	7	0.683	172	0.324	166
Raleigh	0.167	227	0.601	50	0.372	171	0.887	32	0.679	180	0.324	166
Fukuoka	0.279	98	0.621	44	0.448	57	0.659	171	0.746	67	0.246	247
Essen	0.187	192	0.349	273	0.381	148	0.826	66	0.707	127	0.520	56
Budapest	0.458	20	0.569	71	0.299	278	0.689	156	0.584	305	0.437	85
Anaheim	0.158	245	0.303	317	0.356	199	0.885	37	0.817	19	0.417	97
Las Vegas	0.188	191	0.420	203	0.401	104	0.724	129	0.689	160	0.541	46
Sheffield	0.224	152	0.456	164	0.346	216	0.710	136	0.738	73	0.473	71
Detroit	0.234	140	0.503	128	0.452	54	0.915	26	0.681	177	0.209	290
Adelaide	0.166	231	0.412	211	0.458	52	0.811	80	0.753	60	0.314	177
Plymouth	0.213	162	0.511	123	0.288	295	0.839	58	0.740	71	0.343	148
Hanover	0.219	158	0.383	234	0.371	175	0.794	92	0.760	54	0.372	123
Palo Alto	0.131	315	0.561	81	0.248	350	0.982	2	0.766	51	0.260	229
Ottawa	0.303	82	0.495	135	0.414	87	0.843	57	0.532	367	0.387	114
Nagoya	0.149	261	0.592	54	0.527	21	0.659	171	0.760	54	0.226	270
Pittsburgh	0.253	119	0.621	44	0.356	199	0.756	111	0.584	305	0.398	107
Rotterdam	0.279	98	0.442	176	0.415	83	0.807	84	0.684	168	0.295	196
Bonn	0.241	129	0.422	199	0.332	236	0.826	66	0.690	157	0.390	112
Wilmington	0.147	267	0.595	53	0.272	314	0.724	129	0.850	9	0.287	199
Canberra	0.186	195	0.519	116	0.368	184	0.917	22	0.717	111	0.209	290
Lima	0.268	106	0.315	304	0.356	199	0.626	197	0.784	38	0.481	69
Prague	0.357	56	0.576	66	0.303	270	0.646	179	0.598	288	0.427	93
Doha	0.219	158	0.432	191	0.488	36	0.778	101	0.606	278	0.361	135
Sao Paulo	0.481	19	0.572	69	0.449	56	0.555	256	0.486	407	0.381	118
Calgary	0.212	164	0.671	29	0.438	63	0.908	28	0.582	309	0.132	373
St. Louis	0.292	89	0.542	98	0.364	193	0.692	151	0.657	209	0.325	163
Valencia	0.206	172	0.447	170	0.337	232	0.694	145	0.722	99	0.427	93
Virginia	0.244	125	0.365	263	0.379	154	0.727	121	0.783	40	0.309	180
El Paso	0.213	162	0.304	315	0.408	96	0.694	145	0.925	2	0.217	278
San Antonio	0.227	147	0.379	242	0.470	43	0.822	75	0.650	213	0.299	189
Kuwait	0.133	309	0.338	285	0.462	47	0.727	121	0.715	114	0.428	92
Memphis	0.241	129	0.310	311	0.410	92	0.788	96	0.692	154	0.373	121
Indianapolis	0.208	169	0.631	41	0.439	62	0.725	125	0.596	294	0.280	209
Buffalo	0.181	204	0.413	210	0.339	230	0.886	34	0.778	45	0.224	271

(continued)

(continued)

City	Company strength		Local elements		Local demand		Software environment		Hardware environment		Global connection	
	Index	Rank	Index	Rank	Index	Rank	Index	Rank	Index	Rank	Index	Rank
Santa Ana	0.115	353	0.493	137	0.359	195	0.920	18	0.632	241	0.340	151
Mumbai	0.543	12	0.609	48	0.403	101	0.384	385	0.376	464	0.574	34
Cardiff	0.248	120	0.421	202	0.312	256	0.807	84	0.757	57	0.261	227
Aurora	0.265	110	0.359	266	0.356	199	0.823	72	0.547	349	0.491	61
Buenos Aires	0.511	16	0.378	243	0.319	252	0.430	372	0.569	319	0.595	28
Newcastle	0.190	187	0.567	75	0.296	282	0.646	179	0.721	102	0.386	115
Fort Worth	0.164	234	0.441	178	0.419	77	0.725	125	0.593	298	0.472	72
Mesa	0.235	137	0.422	199	0.389	128	0.885	37	0.595	297	0.310	178
Kawasaki	0.139	288	0.465	154	0.444	60	0.723	133	0.722	99	0.296	194
Long Beach	0.153	253	0.339	284	0.384	143	0.918	20	0.647	218	0.360	136
New Orleans	0.244	125	0.285	348	0.350	209	0.950	7	0.694	150	0.267	222
Kansas	0.271	103	0.372	251	0.387	132	0.854	51	0.590	300	0.329	159
Mexico City	0.371	46	0.532	107	0.527	21	0.382	389	0.464	423	0.526	53
Dortmund	0.215	161	0.373	248	0.381	148	0.730	116	0.697	142	0.363	131
Tianjin	0.291	91	0.540	102	0.479	39	0.629	195	0.521	379	0.348	143
Hangzhou	0.119	345	0.685	25	0.414	87	0.597	220	0.665	196	0.309	180
Athens	0.385	43	0.541	100	0.429	69	0.250	473	0.610	272	0.523	55
Cologne	0.237	136	0.294	331	0.431	68	0.697	141	0.685	165	0.380	120
Christchurch	0.144	272	0.468	151	0.266	321	0.864	47	0.849	10	0.147	357
Honolulu	0.208	169	0.445	172	0.369	182	0.791	93	0.698	140	0.243	252
San Diego	0.257	117	0.409	214	0.400	106	0.783	98	0.555	338	0.368	127
Lyon	0.303	82	0.430	194	0.355	203	0.592	234	0.623	256	0.437	85
Nice	0.186	195	0.280	357	0.329	240	0.654	177	0.755	59	0.481	69
Dusseldorf	0.310	76	0.251	391	0.385	137	0.826	66	0.460	426	0.538	47
Goteborg	0.223	154	0.411	212	0.412	90	0.663	165	0.835	14	0.146	358
Hamilton (CA)	0.210	167	0.548	94	0.375	161	0.780	100	0.635	239	0.216	279
Hiroshima	0.142	278	0.592	54	0.438	63	0.626	197	0.720	105	0.199	296
Bologna	0.105	374	0.534	104	0.306	264	0.670	161	0.722	99	0.371	125
Marseille	0.176	214	0.281	355	0.398	111	0.623	203	0.732	83	0.443	82
Dresden	0.197	181	0.395	219	0.371	175	0.698	140	0.688	162	0.327	161
Dongguan	0.085	423	0.482	142	0.391	124	0.565	242	0.805	27	0.297	193
Oklahoma	0.085	423	0.422	199	0.404	100	0.821	76	0.626	250	0.321	173
Johannesburg	0.337	61	0.282	352	0.328	243	0.770	105	0.514	387	0.453	76
Tulsa	0.226	148	0.312	309	0.370	179	0.854	51	0.710	119	0.179	322
Leipzig	0.141	281	0.350	272	0.374	164	0.633	192	0.784	38	0.325	163
Edmonton	0.165	232	0.568	73	0.407	98	0.870	45	0.551	343	0.162	341
Riyadh	0.189	189	0.285	348	0.460	50	0.636	188	0.751	64	0.272	216
Xi'an	0.234	140	0.512	120	0.382	147	0.533	268	0.602	284	0.385	116
Hobart	0.122	338	0.337	286	0.328	243	0.692	151	0.891	4	0.189	312
Belfast	0.182	202	0.394	220	0.292	292	0.742	114	0.680	179	0.330	158
Lisbon	0.263	112	0.333	291	0.247	351	0.598	219	0.627	249	0.531	49
Tucson	0.229	145	0.382	235	0.397	113	0.823	72	0.487	403	0.344	147
Shizuoka	0.235	137	0.561	81	0.393	122	0.594	222	0.709	122	0.129	380
Warsaw	0.452	24	0.428	196	0.294	286	0.507	310	0.551	343	0.392	110
Kaohsiung	0.195	183	0.472	147	0.322	250	0.811	80	0.663	202	0.163	338
Kobe	0.134	307	0.508	124	0.461	49	0.594	222	0.623	256	0.285	201

(continued)

(continued)

City	Company strength		Local elements		Local demand		Software environment		Hardware environment		Global connection	
	Index	Rank	Index	Rank	Index	Rank	Index	Rank	Index	Rank	Index	Rank
St. Petersburg	0.235	137	0.470	148	0.354	204	0.550	260	0.521	379	0.488	62
Bremen	0.130	316	0.297	327	0.378	155	0.665	164	0.705	131	0.381	118
Bucharest	0.362	54	0.370	254	0.278	300	0.728	118	0.561	329	0.315	176
Sakai	0.114	355	0.465	154	0.409	94	0.626	197	0.731	85	0.216	279
Chiba	0.156	247	0.492	138	0.415	83	0.626	197	0.724	96	0.157	349
Dalian	0.226	148	0.524	112	0.388	130	0.630	193	0.619	259	0.213	285
Mannheim	0.137	295	0.419	206	0.330	237	0.827	65	0.624	255	0.260	229
Himeji-shi	0.151	256	0.468	151	0.366	189	0.659	171	0.726	91	0.190	311
Incheon	0.175	216	0.466	153	0.391	124	0.645	181	0.639	229	0.254	238
Southampton	0.157	246	0.497	134	0.284	296	0.614	206	0.672	190	0.331	157
Busan	0.205	176	0.518	117	0.415	83	0.644	183	0.620	258	0.174	327
Omaha	0.098	390	0.486	141	0.385	137	0.854	51	0.490	402	0.301	186
Winnipeg	0.083	428	0.462	158	0.395	118	0.803	89	0.527	372	0.322	170
Quebec	0.121	341	0.532	107	0.371	175	0.748	112	0.726	91	0.061	456
Suzhou	0.108	368	0.436	183	0.462	47	0.565	242	0.737	74	0.199	296
Sendai	0.153	253	0.568	73	0.424	73	0.594	222	0.679	180	0.125	385
Hsinchu city	0.128	321	0.526	111	0.225	391	0.680	158	0.786	37	0.177	324
Nanjing	0.206	172	0.675	28	0.400	106	0.630	193	0.442	432	0.257	233
Saitama	0.109	366	0.307	312	0.436	65	0.691	154	0.747	66	0.188	315
Toledo	0.095	396	0.268	365	0.345	221	0.692	151	0.808	25	0.250	244
Jakarta	0.455	22	0.254	387	0.367	187	0.419	377	0.480	410	0.532	48
Riverside	0.195	183	0.500	133	0.344	222	0.855	50	0.403	447	0.299	189
Toulouse	0.268	106	0.314	305	0.346	216	0.591	235	0.638	231	0.328	160
Reykjavik	0.090	409	0.476	145	0.222	394	0.708	138	0.766	51	0.228	267
Bordeaux	0.211	166	0.267	367	0.298	281	0.588	237	0.742	69	0.339	154
Ljubljana	0.297	86	0.340	282	0.222	394	0.693	150	0.682	174	0.250	244
Aarhus	0.137	295	0.293	334	0.389	128	0.710	136	0.793	30	0.122	389
Bangalore	0.428	27	0.562	79	0.314	254	0.381	392	0.396	454	0.466	73
Xiamen	0.190	187	0.647	38	0.311	258	0.565	242	0.532	367	0.296	194
Corpus Christi	0.127	324	0.229	401	0.348	215	0.725	125	0.736	76	0.271	218
Porto	0.180	207	0.370	254	0.204	432	0.467	328	0.753	60	0.449	77
Kanazawa	0.180	207	0.555	87	0.350	209	0.594	222	0.710	119	0.093	420
Zhongshan	0.129	317	0.503	128	0.299	278	0.611	213	0.691	155	0.238	254
Kiev	0.226	148	0.539	103	0.268	320	0.374	413	0.674	188	0.372	123
Sofia	0.243	127	0.490	139	0.228	384	0.636	188	0.518	383	0.395	108
Chennai	0.229	145	0.479	143	0.326	247	0.382	389	0.639	229	0.392	110
Niigata	0.159	243	0.531	109	0.395	118	0.659	171	0.618	262	0.131	375
Okayama	0.088	412	0.516	118	0.385	137	0.594	222	0.773	49	0.088	428
Windsor	0.121	341	0.358	268	0.303	270	0.802	90	0.608	275	0.284	204
Venice	0.148	263	0.337	286	0.279	298	0.573	240	0.734	82	0.346	145
Sapporo	0.128	321	0.459	163	0.483	37	0.594	222	0.608	275	0.195	302
Fresno	0.245	124	0.201	424	0.380	152	0.724	129	0.706	128	0.163	338
Stockton	0.078	431	0.218	414	0.346	216	0.723	133	0.788	35	0.234	259
Ho Chi Minh City	0.289	93	0.256	385	0.344	222	0.481	321	0.660	206	0.371	125
Kagoshima	0.133	309	0.470	148	0.377	158	0.627	196	0.735	80	0.092	421

(continued)

(continued)

City	Company strength		Local elements		Local demand		Software environment		Hardware environment		Global connection	
	Index	Rank	Index	Rank	Index	Rank	Index	Rank	Index	Rank	Index	Rank
Wuhan	0.170	224	0.546	96	0.419	77	0.565	242	0.526	373	0.253	241
Zagreb	0.223	154	0.259	381	0.241	368	0.676	159	0.721	102	0.282	205
Ningbo	0.059	459	0.424	198	0.396	115	0.533	268	0.700	136	0.287	199
Aberdeen	0.042	474	0.372	251	0.277	303	0.775	102	0.718	107	0.229	265
Wichita	0.147	267	0.325	298	0.366	189	0.724	129	0.617	263	0.244	250
Hamamatsu	0.132	313	0.512	120	0.399	108	0.594	222	0.709	122	0.077	436
Changsha	0.108	368	0.547	95	0.384	143	0.520	282	0.582	309	0.300	188
Ansan	0.180	207	0.451	167	0.273	311	0.644	183	0.682	174	0.194	306
Bogota	0.299	85	0.237	397	0.373	168	0.624	202	0.465	421	0.436	87
Albuquerque	0.171	222	0.442	176	0.394	120	0.725	125	0.540	355	0.189	312
Nicosia	0.172	220	0.435	186	0.242	362	0.606	215	0.889	5	0.031	483
Qingdao	0.139	288	0.470	148	0.411	91	0.694	145	0.475	414	0.282	205
Chengdu	0.259	116	0.590	57	0.442	61	0.565	242	0.338	480	0.304	183
Strasbourg	0.173	218	0.287	345	0.311	258	0.623	203	0.683	172	0.285	201
Sagamihara City	0.163	236	0.325	298	0.391	124	0.594	222	0.695	148	0.194	306
San Juan	0.137	295	0.259	381	0.341	228	0.491	315	0.699	138	0.403	105
Panama	0.322	67	0.204	416	0.242	362	0.499	312	0.661	203	0.411	101
Zhuhai	0.212	164	0.505	126	0.245	357	0.520	282	0.703	134	0.195	302
Daejeon	0.143	275	0.648	37	0.330	237	0.613	208	0.637	233	0.052	464
Penang	0.150	259	0.460	161	0.273	311	0.607	214	0.690	157	0.192	309
Vilnius	0.321	68	0.385	228	0.214	416	0.588	237	0.612	268	0.261	227
Daegu	0.104	379	0.581	61	0.373	168	0.645	181	0.629	245	0.075	439
Huizhou	0.106	371	0.571	70	0.320	251	0.579	239	0.708	125	0.092	421
Bratislava	0.284	95	0.314	305	0.245	357	0.783	98	0.632	241	0.117	398
Halifax	0.086	420	0.419	206	0.352	205	0.773	104	0.696	145	0.042	474
Kumamoto	0.182	202	0.432	191	0.386	133	0.594	222	0.690	157	0.065	450
Quanzhou	0.105	374	0.433	190	0.384	143	0.520	282	0.700	136	0.186	317
Rio de Janeiro	0.370	48	0.392	224	0.377	158	0.496	313	0.445	431	0.299	189
Jeonju	0.167	227	0.502	131	0.313	255	0.612	212	0.724	96	0.024	490
Palermo	0.126	327	0.261	378	0.344	222	0.509	308	0.713	117	0.323	169
Cape Town	0.246	123	0.250	392	0.310	261	0.542	264	0.603	283	0.357	137
Yantai	0.179	211	0.373	248	0.381	148	0.552	259	0.658	207	0.170	331
Taichung	0.149	261	0.505	126	0.292	292	0.662	167	0.616	264	0.131	375
Lille	0.135	304	0.252	389	0.296	282	0.688	157	0.625	251	0.304	183
Higashiosaka-shi	0.135	304	0.303	317	0.365	191	0.626	197	0.728	88	0.117	398
Belgrade	0.284	95	0.181	428	0.228	384	0.728	118	0.559	332	0.325	163
Jerusalem	0.204	177	0.222	408	0.323	248	0.824	71	0.614	266	0.120	393
Tallinn	0.273	102	0.290	340	0.199	447	0.478	326	0.776	47	0.228	267
Ulsan	0.092	403	0.529	110	0.329	240	0.644	183	0.666	195	0.059	459
Bakersfield	0.058	461	0.221	411	0.349	213	0.757	110	0.676	186	0.207	293
Alexander	0.138	291	0.276	359	0.303	270	0.533	268	0.753	60	0.230	262
Kunming	0.180	207	0.386	227	0.351	207	0.513	305	0.625	251	0.215	283
Wenzhou	0.065	452	0.393	222	0.384	143	0.533	268	0.706	128	0.168	335
Zhengzhou	0.025	487	0.440	179	0.394	120	0.520	282	0.596	294	0.298	192
Medellin	0.095	396	0.178	431	0.301	274	0.600	218	0.783	40	0.244	250
Changchun	0.087	416	0.546	96	0.376	160	0.560	255	0.612	268	0.115	401

(continued)

(continued)

City	Company strength		Local elements		Local demand		Software environment		Hardware environment		Global connection	
	Index	Rank	Index	Rank	Index	Rank	Index	Rank	Index	Rank	Index	Rank
Changzhou	0.070	446	0.325	298	0.339	230	0.521	281	0.637	233	0.351	140
Nantong	0.068	449	0.369	257	0.374	164	0.520	282	0.586	303	0.340	151
Santo Domingo	0.138	291	0.193	425	0.290	294	0.389	383	0.808	25	0.351	140
Shaoxing	0.141	281	0.374	246	0.340	229	0.520	282	0.646	222	0.229	265
Jiaxing	0.085	423	0.345	275	0.329	240	0.520	282	0.605	280	0.362	134
Kurashiki-shi	0.164	234	0.385	228	0.350	209	0.594	222	0.725	95	0.026	488
Guadalajara	0.125	330	0.416	208	0.342	225	0.362	434	0.649	214	0.337	155
Seongnam	0.094	399	0.555	87	0.301	274	0.613	208	0.695	148	0.019	496
Turin	0.139	288	0.380	239	0.374	164	0.605	216	0.583	307	0.188	315
Nanning	0.123	337	0.394	220	0.351	207	0.546	261	0.684	168	0.136	368
Shenyang	0.154	251	0.453	166	0.399	108	0.694	145	0.421	438	0.198	298
Ankara	0.204	177	0.328	295	0.349	213	0.535	267	0.501	398	0.345	146
Suwon	0.138	291	0.581	61	0.305	266	0.613	208	0.601	286	0.055	461
Harbin	0.145	271	0.438	182	0.402	103	0.561	254	0.534	363	0.180	320
Trieste	0.144	272	0.311	310	0.261	329	0.542	264	0.727	90	0.211	286
Jinan	0.080	430	0.541	100	0.375	161	0.520	282	0.483	408	0.272	216
Fuzhou	0.113	359	0.444	173	0.370	179	0.565	242	0.561	329	0.195	302
Durban	0.187	192	0.191	426	0.311	258	0.695	144	0.604	282	0.223	272
Wuxi	0.191	186	0.429	195	0.391	124	0.520	282	0.505	392	0.210	287
Saskatoon	0.088	412	0.409	214	0.299	278	0.766	107	0.544	352	0.150	353
Hyderabad	0.240	131	0.551	92	0.312	256	0.383	387	0.413	443	0.365	129
Manila	0.306	78	0.202	420	0.241	368	0.446	349	0.507	391	0.487	63
Kitakyushu	0.135	304	0.290	340	0.419	77	0.594	222	0.715	114	0.017	497
Keelung	0.117	347	0.385	228	0.202	438	0.662	167	0.672	190	0.159	344
Chongqing	0.142	278	0.444	173	0.518	24	0.597	220	0.254	498	0.322	170
Monterrey	0.242	128	0.380	239	0.346	216	0.334	445	0.536	361	0.343	148
Nuremberg	0.140	285	0.252	389	0.371	175	0.697	141	0.521	379	0.216	279
Weifang	0.137	295	0.411	212	0.386	133	0.520	282	0.592	299	0.139	364
Delhi	0.367	50	0.460	161	0.378	155	0.381	392	0.118	504	0.577	33
Weihai	0.136	301	0.439	181	0.293	289	0.520	282	0.648	217	0.135	370
Malmo	0.184	199	0.343	279	0.375	161	0.663	165	0.397	453	0.260	229
Matsuyama	0.059	459	0.360	265	0.362	194	0.594	222	0.735	80	0.027	484
Tainan	0.005	501	0.514	119	0.257	337	0.662	167	0.664	199	0.082	431
Taizhou	0.099	387	0.390	225	0.350	209	0.520	282	0.665	196	0.123	387
Pretoria	0.113	359	0.236	399	0.278	300	0.770	105	0.563	327	0.210	287
Zibo	0.117	347	0.434	188	0.336	233	0.520	282	0.580	312	0.183	318
Riga	0.232	143	0.283	351	0.238	373	0.563	252	0.664	199	0.149	354
Shijiazhuang	0.172	220	0.434	188	0.397	113	0.528	277	0.468	419	0.170	331
Krakow	0.178	213	0.294	331	0.228	384	0.635	190	0.606	278	0.191	310
Naples	0.133	309	0.285	348	0.372	171	0.638	187	0.342	479	0.408	102
Foshan	0.105	374	0.449	168	0.398	111	0.546	261	0.520	382	0.143	359
Gyeongju	0.136	301	0.420	203	0.199	447	0.644	183	0.698	140	0.024	490
Montevideo	0.231	144	0.204	416	0.258	335	0.553	258	0.578	313	0.270	220
El Salvador	0.187	192	0.305	313	0.305	266	0.321	450	0.790	33	0.118	395
Cairo	0.326	64	0.275	360	0.358	197	0.533	268	0.287	492	0.373	121
Yangzhou	0.092	403	0.358	268	0.327	245	0.565	242	0.658	207	0.077	436

(continued)

(continued)

City	Company strength		Local elements		Local demand		Software environment		Hardware environment		Global connection	
	Index	Rank	Index	Rank	Index	Rank	Index	Rank	Index	Rank	Index	Rank
Leon	0.010	498	0.440	179	0.256	338	0.384	385	0.678	182	0.273	215
Hanoi	0.283	97	0.286	346	0.275	307	0.481	321	0.477	413	0.278	212
Amman	0.289	93	0.238	396	0.224	393	0.428	374	0.574	316	0.289	198
Thane	0.128	321	0.269	364	0.221	398	0.381	392	0.718	107	0.280	209
Hefei	0.126	327	0.345	275	0.368	184	0.533	268	0.534	363	0.158	347
Haikou	0.101	384	0.305	313	0.258	335	0.514	298	0.723	98	0.112	405
Curitiba	0.114	355	0.358	268	0.275	307	0.480	323	0.685	165	0.109	406
Quito	0.160	242	0.133	452	0.226	389	0.439	367	0.711	118	0.301	186
La Paz	0.075	435	0.250	392	0.259	334	0.279	463	0.746	67	0.348	143
Kazan	0.173	218	0.345	275	0.241	368	0.483	319	0.536	361	0.249	246
Nanchang	0.224	152	0.373	248	0.336	233	0.533	268	0.450	429	0.131	375
Jaipur	0.146	270	0.367	260	0.261	329	0.381	392	0.558	333	0.282	205
Xuzhou	0.075	435	0.335	289	0.380	152	0.529	276	0.590	300	0.081	432
Taiyuan	0.093	402	0.399	217	0.319	252	0.528	277	0.541	354	0.130	378
Guayaquil	0.106	371	0.109	467	0.266	321	0.302	455	0.817	19	0.271	218
Genoa	0.134	307	0.267	367	0.342	225	0.573	240	0.479	411	0.210	287
Minsk	0.095	396	0.444	173	0.251	344	0.374	413	0.590	300	0.228	267
Hohhot	0.165	232	0.304	315	0.294	286	0.528	277	0.598	288	0.088	428
Kaliningrad	0.072	444	0.376	244	0.180	470	0.516	297	0.709	122	0.104	410
Beirut	0.305	79	0.163	441	0.242	362	0.310	453	0.635	239	0.263	224
Caracas	0.238	135	0.174	434	0.300	276	0.052	500	0.689	160	0.414	100
Damascus	0.189	189	0.212	415	0.261	329	0.320	451	0.697	142	0.221	275
Merida	0.105	374	0.313	308	0.222	394	0.374	413	0.664	199	0.245	249
Wuhu	0.111	362	0.289	342	0.300	276	0.488	317	0.582	309	0.179	322
Kingston	0.176	214	0.462	158	0.149	496	0.338	444	0.609	273	0.222	274
Brasilia	0.263	112	0.179	430	0.323	248	0.435	369	0.549	348	0.176	325
Nassau	0.163	236	0.259	381	0.193	451	0.378	403	0.649	214	0.255	236
Rizhao	0.148	263	0.258	384	0.283	297	0.520	282	0.607	277	0.107	408
Guiyang	0.114	355	0.374	246	0.261	329	0.514	298	0.578	313	0.098	416
Karachi	0.261	114	0.166	439	0.370	179	0.415	379	0.374	466	0.353	139
Liuzhou	0.161	241	0.222	408	0.306	264	0.514	298	0.619	259	0.069	445
Tunisia	0.137	295	0.128	456	0.173	476	0.478	326	0.810	24	0.100	415
Havana	0.075	435	0.328	295	0.273	311	0.278	464	0.644	224	0.263	224
Tangshan	0.102	381	0.260	380	0.279	298	0.513	305	0.667	194	0.046	470
Kalyan	0.110	363	0.221	411	0.217	405	0.377	405	0.647	218	0.262	226
Veracruz	0.116	351	0.347	274	0.219	402	0.353	442	0.555	338	0.282	205
Islamabad	0.221	156	0.156	446	0.181	469	0.546	261	0.523	375	0.246	247
Pune	0.264	111	0.371	253	0.278	300	0.377	405	0.299	490	0.350	142
Ahmedabad	0.137	295	0.494	136	0.304	268	0.383	387	0.353	474	0.267	222
Campinas	0.051	467	0.356	271	0.235	379	0.379	402	0.678	182	0.127	383
Tijuana	0.032	480	0.381	237	0.253	342	0.310	453	0.598	288	0.257	233
Perm	0.143	275	0.396	218	0.236	377	0.436	368	0.465	421	0.197	299
Medan	0.151	256	0.148	447	0.251	344	0.258	466	0.706	128	0.238	254
Aguascalientes	0.066	451	0.291	338	0.213	418	0.357	440	0.612	268	0.259	232
Casablanca	0.270	105	0.172	435	0.269	317	0.363	433	0.558	333	0.161	342
Mysore	0.155	249	0.324	301	0.160	484	0.376	411	0.625	251	0.159	344

(continued)

(continued)

City	Company strength		Local elements		Local demand		Software environment		Hardware environment		Global connection	
	Index	Rank	Index	Rank	Index	Rank	Index	Rank	Index	Rank	Index	Rank
Lanzhou	0.141	281	0.381	237	0.293	289	0.514	298	0.434	434	0.098	416
Cuernavaca	0.122	338	0.370	254	0.215	414	0.149	492	0.678	182	0.223	272
Baroda	0.181	204	0.314	305	0.192	452	0.369	424	0.575	315	0.163	338
Georgetown	0.107	370	0.268	365	0.102	503	0.354	441	0.829	16	0.064	452
Tripoli	0.133	309	0.108	468	0.294	286	0.374	413	0.777	46	0.026	488
Puebla	0.018	490	0.382	235	0.271	315	0.360	438	0.501	398	0.270	220
Sana'a	0.102	381	0.017	500	0.242	362	0.616	205	0.737	74	0.009	501
Accra	0.127	324	0.124	457	0.236	377	0.457	331	0.572	317	0.233	260
Surat	0.055	466	0.431	193	0.264	323	0.367	428	0.414	442	0.291	197
Visakhapatnam	0.121	341	0.272	362	0.203	435	0.382	389	0.652	212	0.118	395
Cordoba	0.167	227	0.172	435	0.221	398	0.493	314	0.550	346	0.161	342
Nasik	0.074	438	0.302	319	0.213	418	0.381	392	0.630	244	0.136	368
Lagos	0.186	195	0.181	428	0.342	225	0.136	493	0.539	357	0.320	174
Morella	0.092	403	0.297	327	0.216	409	0.322	449	0.644	224	0.151	351
Nagpur	0.132	313	0.302	319	0.246	354	0.362	434	0.508	390	0.204	295
Asuncion	0.196	182	0.112	464	0.238	373	0.489	316	0.458	427	0.254	238
Novosibirsk	0.094	399	0.449	168	0.263	325	0.508	309	0.301	489	0.216	279
Yinchuan	0.050	469	0.323	303	0.264	323	0.514	298	0.533	365	0.070	443
Pondicherry	0.069	448	0.267	367	0.159	486	0.377	405	0.705	131	0.113	404
Samara	0.105	374	0.334	290	0.249	347	0.449	344	0.384	460	0.255	236
Lusaka	0.121	341	0.028	496	0.213	418	0.518	296	0.684	168	0.103	412
Bandung	0.179	211	0.130	454	0.260	333	0.258	466	0.558	333	0.285	201
Bhopal	0.208	169	0.244	394	0.217	405	0.365	431	0.511	388	0.170	331
Lucknow	0.102	381	0.389	226	0.237	376	0.380	399	0.423	437	0.221	275
Rajkot	0.015	494	0.229	401	0.186	465	0.380	399	0.687	163	0.164	337
Coimbatore	0.098	390	0.299	324	0.214	416	0.369	424	0.515	386	0.215	283
Belo Horizonte	0.113	359	0.380	239	0.304	268	0.332	446	0.483	408	0.114	402
Porto Alegre	0.153	253	0.261	378	0.256	338	0.371	420	0.530	369	0.129	380
San Luis Potosi	0.000	505	0.324	301	0.220	400	0.290	461	0.677	185	0.140	363
São Bernardo do Campo	0.162	239	0.225	407	0.219	402	0.459	330	0.491	400	0.139	364
Calcutta	0.163	236	0.175	432	0.381	148	0.385	384	0.357	472	0.239	253
Douala	0.115	353	0.097	476	0.229	383	0.189	483	0.782	42	0.158	347
Baotou	0.023	488	0.226	406	0.295	285	0.528	277	0.550	346	0.055	461
Ordos	0.018	490	0.237	397	0.368	184	0.514	298	0.502	397	0.043	473
Vladivostok	0.092	403	0.367	260	0.201	443	0.466	329	0.450	429	0.137	367
Managua	0.129	317	0.241	395	0.171	479	0.408	380	0.530	369	0.181	319
Tampico	0.010	498	0.359	266	0.217	405	0.324	448	0.628	248	0.104	410
Alma-Ata	0.064	453	0.296	330	0.253	342	0.540	266	0.473	415	0.061	456
Lahore	0.184	199	0.103	471	0.330	237	0.416	378	0.384	460	0.235	258
Tehran	0.155	249	0.166	439	0.373	168	0.220	479	0.435	433	0.275	214
Chihuahua	0.028	483	0.340	282	0.216	409	0.189	483	0.562	328	0.279	211
Recife	0.096	393	0.228	404	0.269	317	0.299	457	0.609	273	0.101	414
Yerevan	0.061	458	0.291	338	0.209	425	0.440	363	0.569	319	0.066	447
Queretaro	0.014	495	0.286	346	0.222	394	0.362	434	0.555	338	0.180	320
Toluca	0.086	420	0.288	344	0.262	327	0.339	443	0.470	418	0.195	302

(continued)

(continued)

City	Company strength		Local elements		Local demand		Software environment		Hardware environment		Global connection	
	Index	Rank	Index	Rank	Index	Rank	Index	Rank	Index	Rank	Index	Rank
Rabat	0.110	363	0.119	460	0.157	489	0.395	381	0.762	53	0.010	499
Dacre	0.140	285	0.191	426	0.246	354	0.174	489	0.560	331	0.257	233
Guatemala City	0.200	180	0.292	336	0.213	418	0.294	459	0.420	439	0.205	294
Varanasi	0.056	463	0.367	260	0.188	460	0.366	429	0.516	385	0.125	385
Krasnoyarsk	0.087	416	0.369	257	0.232	381	0.440	363	0.398	450	0.127	383
Tver	0.127	324	0.384	233	0.174	475	0.442	356	0.452	428	0.065	450
Betim	0.186	195	0.123	458	0.191	454	0.280	462	0.696	145	0.051	465
Colombo	0.074	438	0.145	448	0.159	486	0.299	457	0.569	319	0.303	185
Xining	0.099	387	0.262	376	0.296	282	0.514	298	0.398	450	0.066	447
Guarulhos	0.020	489	0.110	465	0.250	346	0.434	370	0.597	292	0.134	371
Duque de Caxias	0.087	416	0.113	463	0.225	391	0.421	376	0.625	251	0.062	454
São Jose dos Campo	0.088	412	0.132	453	0.200	445	0.390	382	0.703	134	0.000	505
Sarajevo	0.116	351	0.082	481	0.128	502	0.243	474	0.699	138	0.219	277
Surabaya	0.077	432	0.160	444	0.275	307	0.258	466	0.467	420	0.308	182
Ufa	0.156	247	0.368	259	0.233	380	0.447	347	0.274	495	0.171	329
Tyumen	0.171	222	0.343	279	0.195	449	0.442	356	0.376	464	0.090	427
Shiraz	0.136	301	0.104	470	0.227	388	0.251	471	0.638	231	0.130	378
Tula	0.056	463	0.407	216	0.184	466	0.483	319	0.360	470	0.129	380
Kursk	0.084	427	0.273	361	0.173	476	0.452	339	0.533	365	0.041	475
Trivandrum	0.206	172	0.119	460	0.173	476	0.381	392	0.504	395	0.143	359
Yekaterinburg	0.051	467	0.293	334	0.256	338	0.507	310	0.332	482	0.159	344
Madurai	0.096	393	0.267	367	0.178	472	0.366	429	0.472	416	0.170	331
Yaounde	0.011	496	0.035	493	0.212	422	0.158	491	0.860	8	0.122	389
Gaborone	0.048	470	0.024	497	0.089	504	0.603	217	0.643	227	0.091	426
Yaroslavl	0.143	275	0.332	292	0.204	432	0.484	318	0.380	463	0.054	463
Faridabad	0.070	446	0.282	352	0.219	402	0.378	403	0.385	459	0.233	260
Kaluga	0.062	457	0.332	292	0.150	494	0.446	349	0.537	359	0.027	484
Khabarovsk	0.008	500	0.263	373	0.183	468	0.434	370	0.567	323	0.073	442
Agra	0.083	428	0.298	326	0.209	425	0.373	418	0.415	441	0.176	325
Dhaka	0.129	317	0.160	444	0.310	261	0.424	375	0.284	493	0.251	243
Acapulco	0.073	441	0.301	321	0.201	443	0.251	471	0.509	389	0.171	329
Manaus	0.181	204	0.145	448	0.276	304	0.302	455	0.505	392	0.084	430
Harare	0.154	251	0.048	488	0.211	424	0.080	497	0.661	203	0.254	238
Krasnodar	0.074	438	0.266	371	0.205	430	0.440	363	0.430	435	0.120	393
Amritsar	0.124	336	0.299	324	0.187	464	0.381	392	0.402	449	0.148	355
Baku	0.151	256	0.376	244	0.249	347	0.371	420	0.306	487	0.121	392
Chinchwad	0.110	363	0.093	477	0.230	382	0.377	405	0.596	294	0.051	465
Ivanovo	0.090	409	0.202	420	0.175	474	0.451	342	0.537	359	0.041	475
Cebu	0.167	227	0.100	473	0.179	471	0.255	469	0.546	351	0.208	292
Meerut	0.109	366	0.143	450	0.205	430	0.371	420	0.464	423	0.196	301
Lipetsk	0.077	432	0.256	385	0.188	460	0.446	349	0.526	373	0.010	499
Chelyabinsk	0.077	432	0.436	183	0.243	361	0.441	360	0.283	494	0.103	412
Djibouti	0.125	330	0.001	504	0.142	498	0.116	494	0.681	177	0.317	175
Tashkent	0.063	455	0.110	465	0.239	372	0.261	465	0.583	307	0.173	328
Yangon	0.174	217	0.116	462	0.276	304	0.000	505	0.682	174	0.134	371

(continued)

(continued)

City	Company strength		Local elements		Local demand		Software environment		Hardware environment		Global connection	
	Index	Rank	Index	Rank	Index	Rank	Index	Rank	Index	Rank	Index	Rank
Vladimir	0.031	481	0.202	420	0.165	481	0.446	349	0.403	447	0.252	242
Voronezh	0.126	327	0.106	469	0.220	400	0.454	334	0.544	352	0.009	501
Volgograd	0.088	412	0.344	278	0.238	373	0.479	324	0.303	488	0.092	421
Nairobi	0.193	185	0.121	459	0.256	338	0.184	485	0.365	469	0.341	150
Port-au-Prince	0.106	371	0.023	498	0.184	466	0.203	480	0.637	233	0.230	262
Srinagar	0.092	403	0.092	478	0.203	435	0.369	424	0.566	324	0.107	408
Maputo	0.045	472	0.015	501	0.217	405	0.176	488	0.825	18	0.057	460
Dar Es Salam	0.091	408	0.065	483	0.249	347	0.173	490	0.585	304	0.230	262
Arkhangelsk	0.096	393	0.292	336	0.159	486	0.441	360	0.487	403	0.014	498
Murmansk	0.036	478	0.227	405	0.156	491	0.453	335	0.522	377	0.068	446
Kanpur	0.118	346	0.281	355	0.247	351	0.360	438	0.348	477	0.143	359
Dushanbe	0.011	496	0.294	331	0.150	494	0.316	452	0.629	245	0.027	484
Indore	0.103	380	0.175	432	0.216	409	0.361	437	0.404	445	0.197	299
Penza	0.125	330	0.342	281	0.188	460	0.457	331	0.344	478	0.050	467
Ryazan	0.085	423	0.362	264	0.188	460	0.453	335	0.388	455	0.021	493
Belgorod	0.159	243	0.301	321	0.164	482	0.441	360	0.350	475	0.066	447
Luanda	0.064	453	0.039	491	0.293	289	0.191	482	0.530	369	0.237	256
Torreon	0.026	484	0.235	400	0.240	371	0.328	447	0.491	400	0.092	421
Kinshasa	0.094	399	0.049	487	0.308	263	0.072	499	0.642	228	0.151	351
Urumqi	0.117	347	0.280	357	0.263	325	0.513	305	0.204	502	0.123	387
Izhevsk	0.141	281	0.301	321	0.204	432	0.446	349	0.336	481	0.040	478
Howrah	0.056	463	0.099	474	0.209	425	0.377	405	0.557	336	0.060	458
Blantyre	0.017	492	0.055	485	0.154	493	0.371	420	0.675	187	0.049	468
Barnaul	0.003	504	0.263	373	0.200	445	0.442	356	0.427	436	0.078	435
Addis Ababa	0.162	239	0.020	499	0.247	351	0.002	504	0.647	218	0.194	306
Ulan Bator	0.043	473	0.219	413	0.202	438	0.591	235	0.354	473	0.022	492
Orenburg	0.004	502	0.337	286	0.189	458	0.442	356	0.388	455	0.063	453
Ulyanovsk	0.100	385	0.264	372	0.202	438	0.447	347	0.371	468	0.034	482
Abidjan	0.004	502	0.130	454	0.269	317	0.083	496	0.597	292	0.189	312
Stavropol	0.034	479	0.297	327	0.160	484	0.455	333	0.398	450	0.046	470
Saltillo	0.150	259	0.202	420	0.216	409	0.293	460	0.383	462	0.118	395
Cochin	0.169	225	0.069	482	0.146	497	0.380	399	0.518	383	0.037	479
Allahabad	0.026	484	0.222	408	0.191	454	0.377	405	0.420	439	0.117	398
Petrozavodsk	0.029	482	0.262	376	0.140	499	0.440	363	0.462	425	0.027	484
Tegucigalpa	0.125	330	0.010	503	0.190	457	0.221	477	0.553	342	0.168	335
Omsk	0.099	387	0.253	388	0.242	362	0.449	344	0.229	500	0.122	389
Bryansk	0.042	474	0.289	342	0.171	479	0.448	346	0.387	458	0.020	494
Freetown	0.087	416	0.052	486	0.161	483	0.192	481	0.598	288	0.139	364
Smolensk	0.068	449	0.204	416	0.156	491	0.450	343	0.412	444	0.036	480
Tambov	0.125	330	0.263	373	0.140	499	0.452	339	0.350	475	0.020	494
Isfahan	0.147	267	0.056	484	0.242	362	0.255	469	0.487	403	0.074	441
Phnom Penh	0.122	338	0.099	474	0.208	428	0.046	502	0.522	377	0.236	257
Jabalpur	0.071	445	0.204	416	0.202	438	0.374	413	0.388	455	0.075	439
Lome	0.142	278	0.032	495	0.203	435	0.109	495	0.614	266	0.098	416
Saratov	0.140	285	0.326	297	0.216	409	0.453	335	0.159	503	0.094	419
Ludhiana	0.073	441	0.168	438	0.191	454	0.364	432	0.358	471	0.141	362

(continued)

(continued)

City	Company strength		Local elements		Local demand		Software environment		Hardware environment		Global connection	
	Index	Rank	Index	Rank	Index	Rank	Index	Rank	Index	Rank	Index	Rank
Rostov	0.038	477	0.329	294	0.244	359	0.453	335	0.214	501	0.062	454
Patna	0.125	330	0.142	451	0.244	359	0.373	418	0.255	497	0.153	350
Ciudad Juarez	0.026	484	0.272	362	0.246	354	0.013	503	0.555	338	0.080	433
Orel	0.097	392	0.163	441	0.157	489	0.479	324	0.374	466	0.002	504
Algiers	0.144	272	0.085	480	0.274	310	0.179	487	0.404	445	0.108	407
Kampala	0.048	470	0.038	492	0.215	414	0.184	485	0.547	349	0.114	402
Kemerovo	0.058	461	0.229	401	0.192	452	0.429	373	0.292	491	0.041	475
Ranchi	0.129	317	0.170	437	0.195	449	0.369	424	0.268	496	0.092	421
Conakry	0.114	355	0.035	493	0.206	429	0.052	500	0.602	284	0.077	436
Brazzaville	0.063	455	0.000	505	0.212	422	0.074	498	0.570	318	0.132	373
Kish	0.090	409	0.042	490	0.000	505	0.225	475	0.629	245	0.048	469
Astrakhan	0.017	492	0.163	441	0.189	458	0.445	354	0.315	483	0.008	503
Mashhad	0.117	347	0.101	472	0.271	315	0.221	477	0.311	486	0.070	443
Makhachkala	0.073	441	0.012	502	0.178	472	0.445	354	0.314	484	0.080	433
Grozny	0.086	420	0.047	489	0.137	501	0.452	339	0.314	484	0.035	481
Ghazi Abad	0.042	474	0.282	352	0.202	438	0.375	412	0.000	505	0.148	355
Tabriz	0.100	385	0.086	479	0.228	384	0.222	476	0.233	499	0.046	470

MIX
Papier aus verantwortungsvollen Quellen
Paper from responsible sources
FSC® C105338

If you have any concerns about our products,
you can contact us on
ProductSafety@springernature.com

In case Publisher is established outside the EU,
the EU authorized representative is:
Springer Nature Customer Service Center GmbH
Europaplatz 3, 69115 Heidelberg, Germany

Printed by Libri Plureos GmbH
in Hamburg, Germany